OXFORD DATA PROTECTION AND PRIVACY LAW

Series Editors

CHRISTOPHER KUNER

Affiliated Professor of Law, University of Copenhagen

GRAHAM GREENLEAF

Professor of Law and Information Systems, University of New South Wales

Coherence between Data Protection and Competition Law in Digital Markets

OXFORD DATA PROTECTION AND PRIVACY LAW

Series Editors

Christopher Kuner, Affiliated Professor of Law, University of Copenhagen
Graham Greenleaf, Professor of Law and Information Systems, University of New South Wales

The aim of this series is to publish important and original books on legal issues of data protection and privacy. This includes many different areas of law, including comparative law, EU law, human rights law, international law, privacy on the Internet, and others.

Prospective authors are welcome to submit proposals for the series, as outlined on the series website: global.oup.com/academic/content/series/o/oxford-data-protection-and-privacy-law-odppl/

Coherence between Data Protection and Competition Law in Digital Markets

KLAUDIA MAJCHER
Vienna University of Economics and Business

OXFORD
UNIVERSITY PRESS

OXFORD
UNIVERSITY PRESS

Great Clarendon Street, Oxford, OX2 6DP,
United Kingdom

Oxford University Press is a department of the University of Oxford.
It furthers the University's objective of excellence in research, scholarship,
and education by publishing worldwide. Oxford is a registered trade mark of
Oxford University Press in the UK and in certain other countries

First Edition published in 2023

Published in the United States of America by Oxford University Press
198 Madison Avenue, New York, NY 10016, United States of America

British Library Cataloguing in Publication Data

Data available

Library of Congress Control Number: 2023942733

ISBN 978–0–19–888561–0

DOI: 10.1093/oso/9780198885610.001.0001

Printed and bound by
CPI Group (UK) Ltd, Croydon, CR0 4YY

Foreword

Digital markets are spaces shaped by economic forces of supply and demand. However, digital markets can also be characterized as societal spaces where individuals interact, co-create content, and develop and share their ideas, implicating human rights and democratic values. The digitization of societal activities, reflected in the emergence of digital markets, makes it more challenging to disentangle the economic from the civic and political. The data generated and diffused in digital markets has economic value, subsidising the provision of digital content and services, but also more inherent dignitary value, allowing those who utilize this data to gain insights into individuals and groups and to influence and mould their behaviour and opportunities. To what extent then should the application of the law, in particular data protection and competition law, reflect this interdependence of economic and broader societal factors in digital markets?

Attention to this question has intensified from policy-makers and scholars across the world since it was raised in the EU by the European Data Protection Supervisor in 2014. While dissenting voices remain, there is a now vast academic and policy literature documenting the potential touchpoints between data protection and competition law, in particular merger control and constraints on monopoly power. Majcher encapsulates this work by highlighting the common objectives pursued by these legal regimes as well as by mapping the ways in which they currently interact. The interaction remains stubbornly limited, with the theoretical connections between data protection and competition law largely failing to translate into more integrated practical outcomes. This suggests that more needs to be done to convince regulators and legislatures of the need for such coherence between legal fields. It is here that Majcher's work breaks from previous research in an important and original move.

Building on the work of legal philosophers on global coherence (coherence within an entire legal system) and local coherence (coherence with a field of law), Majcher introduces a new paradigm of sectional coherence (coherence between two or more branches of law in the same legal system). By developing the normative value of sectional coherence, first theoretically and then through a series of concrete examples, this work continues to push the dial on this discussion forward offering a clear and compelling blueprint for future interactions between these two fields of law. Majcher's monograph therefore offers an accessible and complete introduction to this ongoing debate for those new to the discussion as well as significant new theoretical insights for those who are keen to move beyond a siloed approach to the governance of the digital sphere.

Dr Orla Lynskey
LSE Law School and College of Europe, Bruges

Preface

Competition law is a fascinating and complex area of law, so is data protection law. The idea of merging these two together and exploring their entanglements was bound to become a journey filled with new discoveries, challenging questions, and thrilling encounters. I first became interested in this subject in 2014, when I was preparing my PhD applications. Back then, the topic of interactions between competition law and data protection was only slowly gaining in prominence. While the EU Court's *Asnef-Equifax* decision and the Google's acquisition of DoubleClick had triggered some reflections about the privacy-competition nexus already few years earlier, the 2014 Opinion by the European Data Protection Supervisor on privacy and competitiveness in the age of big data was a watershed moment for the discourse in the EU and beyond. It also inspired me to embark on a long-term project of reflecting on this subject-matter, resulting in my PhD dissertation on coherence between competition and data protection law in digital markets, which I defended in September 2020 at the Vrije Universiteit Brussel (VUB). Whereas this book is underpinned by the same core research question as my PhD, the ideas it presents, its focus areas, and its structure differ to a significant extent.

In writing my thesis and this book, I have been grateful to many that I would like to sincerely thank. First, I would like to express my gratitude to those directly involved in my PhD project. Special thanks to my promotors Harri Kalimo and Ben Smulders, and my co-promotors Christopher Kuner and Caroline Buts, for helping me develop as an academic, for their intellectual support, and their always encouraging and friendly attitude. I would also like to thank Orla Lynskey and Peggy Valcke for being members of my PhD committee and providing excellent feedback, the Institute for European Studies for the opportunity to pursue my PhD project, and my former colleagues for creating an inspiring and fun working environment.

Throughout the years of conducting my research on the interface of competition and data protection law, I have met numerous inspiring colleagues and friends who helped me shape ideas and develop both professionally and personally. I am thankful to my colleagues from the European Political Strategy Center—and particularly to Mario Mariniello—for helping me better understand the practical relevance of my theoretical arguments. I also learned immensely from the colleagues I met at the Fordham University, the NYU, the Commission's Digital Single Market Task Force, and at numerous professional events and conferences.

I wrote this book while working as an Assistant Professor at the Vienna University of Economics and Business. I would very much like to thank Vicky

Robertson for her continuous intellectual support and for giving me the time and space to finalize my manuscript. I sincerely appreciate it.

Last but certainly not least, I am grateful to my family for their love and support. My heartfelt thanks go to my mother for her care and for nurturing my passions and ambitions, and to my brother for always being there for me. Many thanks to all my wonderful friends for their kindness, support, fun, talks, laughter, dinners, concerts, trips, adventures, and for helping me put things in perspective. And finally, many thanks to Joseph for being my life companion and filling my days with love and brightness.

16 June 2023
Hochreit, Austria

Contents

Table of Cases

A. INTERNATIONAL

Court of Justice of the European Union

JUDGMENTS

Opinions of Advocates General

European Commission

European Court of Human Rights

B. NATIONAL

France

Germany

Greece

Ireland

US

Table of Legislation

EUROPEAN UNION

Primary Law

SECONDARY LAW

NATIONAL

Germany

US

List of Abbreviations

A29WP	Article 29 Working Party
ACCC	Australian Competition and Consumer Commission
AG	Advocate General
AI	artificial intelligence
API	application programming interface
AR	augmented reality
BEUC	European Consumer Organisation
BRICS	Brazil, Russia, India, China, South Africa
CCI	Competition Commission of India
Charter	Charter of Fundamental Rights of the European Union
CJEU	Court of Justice of the European Union
CMA	Competition and Markets Authority (UK)
CoE	Council of Europe
CWS	consumer welfare standard
DMA	Digital Markets Act
DMU	Digital Markets Unit (UK)
DOJ	Department of Justice (US)
DPA	Data Protection Authority
DPC	Data Protection Commission (Ireland)
DPD	Data Protection Directive
DPIA	Data Protection Impact Assessment
DSA	Digital Services Act
DPO	Data Protection Officer
ECHR	European Convention on Human Rights
ECtHR	European Court of Human Rights
EDPB	European Data Protection Board
EDPS	European Data Protection Supervisor
EUMR	European Union Merger Regulation
FIPs	fair information principles
FTC	Federal Trade Commission (US)
GDPR	General Data Protection Regulation
GWB	Gesetz gegen Wettbewerbsbeschränkungen (German Competition Act)
ICO	Information Commissioner's Office (UK)
IoT	Internet of Things
IP	intellectual property
JFTC	Japan Fair Trade Commission
ML	machine learning
NCA	national competition authority
OBA	online behavioural advertising

OECD	Organisation for Economic Co-operation and Development
SIEC	significant impediment to effective competition
SME	small and medium-sized enterprise
SSNIP	small but significant and non-transitory increase in price
TEU	Treaty on European Union
TFEU	Treaty on the Functioning of the European Union
UPSCAM	undertakings with paramount significance for competition across markets
VR	virtual reality

Introduction

A. Entanglements between data protection and competition law in digital markets

For better or worse, societies transform over time. Naturally, change always comes along with opportunities for some and risks for others. In the current age of digital transformation, two interconnected phenomena stand out: unprecedented commercial exploitation of personal data and remarkable consolidation of private power within the hands of a few technology companies. How deeply these empirical facts affect our fundamental rights and freedoms, competitive dynamism, and even political participation and democratic processes, is becoming widely recognized. In our roles as consumers and data subjects, we strive to navigate this digital reality in ways that we believe are beneficial to us. Acting as policy-makers, enforcers, judges, and commentators, we try to make sense of the empirical shifts and offer courses of action with the hope and intention of creating market conditions where individuals' rights and freedoms are protected, innovation can thrive, and fairness is preserved.

This book adopts a perspective of contemporary law on modern digital markets. The two areas of law that prove particularly relevant in the face of current challenges posed by personal data exploitation and power consolidation are data protection and competition law. Not only do they transform the markets, but also fundamentally shape the landscape of individual rights and freedoms. Important as data protection and competition law are individually, they also display plenty of intriguing points of interface in the context of the digital economy. The fact that the regulation of data protection affects markets, and that the regulation of market power and competitive conduct has a bearing on data processing and on fundamental rights and freedoms of individuals more broadly, is beyond doubt. The objective of this book is to bring to the fore the entanglements between data protection and competition law and offer a blueprint for their future interactions.

Over a decade ago, the active existence of data protection and competition law, their mutual influences, encounters, conflicts, and synergies ushered in a period of intense global debate about how their individual paths could be reconciled. Thus far, the debate's perspective has centred primarily on competition law: whether and how competition law should adapt to complement data protection law's mission to protect individuals. The first institution to weigh in with a compelling call for rethinking competition law was the European Data Protection Supervisor (EDPS).

Coherence between Data Protection and Competition Law in Digital Markets. Klaudia Majcher, Oxford University Press.
 DOI: 10.1093/oso/9780198885610.003.0001

In the opinions published in 2014 and 2016, it advocated adopting a 'holistic approach' to enforcement,[1] the crux of which should lie in creating positive synergies between the rules of data protection and competition law by interpreting and enforcing them in a coordinated manner, ultimately ensuring 'privacy friendly, fundamental-rights-enhancing products and services'.[2] Such coordination of enforcement efforts is necessary because these two legal fields are underpinned by 'compatible and complementary' objectives, as the EDPS claimed, for example transparency, fairness, effective choice, and absence of market foreclosure for privacy-friendly alternatives.[3] Crémer, de Montjoye, and Schweitzer, who in 2018 were appointed by the European Commission to provide expert advice on the direction of change for competition policy in the digital era, also pointed to the need to approach the law holistically. In their 2019 report (Special Advisers' Report), they observed that there is 'a notable interdependency between competition law and data protection law as the latter affects competition and as market power affects both the choices that data subjects realistically have and the privacy risks they are exposed to'.[4] Thus, Europe's ambition must be 'to provide a *coherent* overall framework that promotes the overarching goals of protecting individual rights, fostering innovation, and fostering competitive markets'.[5] It is of essence, as the authors added, 'to bring the different policy perspectives together'.[6] Several national competition authorities (NCAs) of the EU Member States have also contributed to this debate. For example, a joint study by the French NCA and the German Federal Cartel Office (Bundeskartellamt) argued that the requirements from other bodies of law could be considered, at least as a context, when conducting competition law assessments.[7] Support for EU competition law that is not agnostic to the value of data protection has also been expressed by a number of scholars.[8]

Jurisdictions outside the EU have in the past years equally invested considerable intellectual and policy efforts to shape antitrust law's response to growing digital power. For example, US scholars and commentators gathered around the neo-Brandeisian school of thought, also known as 'hipster antitrust', are becoming a powerful force in reinvigorating antitrust law that is concerned with much more

[1] EDPS, 'Privacy and Competitiveness in the Age of Big Data' (2016) 37.

[2] EDPS, 'Opinion 8/2016 on Coherent Enforcement of Fundamental Rights in the Age of Big Data' (2016) 16.

[3] ibid.

[4] Jacques Crémer, Yves-Alexandre de Montjoye, and Heike Schweitzer, 'Competition Policy for the Digital Era', Report for the European Commission (2019) 72.

[5] ibid 76 (emphasis added).

[6] ibid 77.

[7] Autorité de la concurrence and Bundeskartellamt, 'Competition Law and Data' (2016) 23.

[8] See eg Francisco Costa-Cabral and Orla Lynskey, 'Family Ties: The Intersection between Data Protection and Competition in EU Law' (2017) 54 Common Market Law Review 11; Harri Kalimo and Klaudia Majcher, 'The Concept of Fairness: Linking EU Competition and Data Protection Law in the Digital Marketplace' (2017) 42 European Law Review 210.

than merely the economic well-being of consumers.[9] The 'whole-of-government' approach announced in the Executive Order issued by US President Biden in 2021 called for more robust scrutiny of issues on the interface of antitrust and data privacy, marking an important policy shift.[10] As the book will show, other jurisdictions such as Canada, Australia, Japan, the BRICS countries (Brazil, Russia, India, China, and South Africa), Mexico, and Brazil, to name but a few, have been actively engaged in the discourse on how competition law might need to adjust to face new challenges.

While there is an overall consensus that some competition law's tools and analytical methods need to be redesigned in the wake of the digital transformation, not everyone concurs with the suggestion that data protection should play a prominent role in competition analysis. The sceptics' view is that competition law is an economic field of law established to protect consumers' economic interests rather than fundamental rights and freedoms. Ohlhausen and Okuliar, for example, have argued that combining the two could lead to 'confusion and doctrinal issues'[11] within competition law. Such endeavours would also undermine the recent consensus that has emerged in antitrust enforcement. As the argument goes, integrating data protection concerns might create the risk of the decision-making practice drifting away from the thorough methodological approaches of the last decades back towards the inclusion of subjective 'non-competition' elements.[12] These authors consider competition law to offer 'at best a convoluted and indirect approach to protecting people's expectations of privacy online'.[13] Others have noted that competition law does not serve the purpose of protecting 'all citizens' interests against every possible violation of those interests'.[14] According to others, as the empirical case for regulating data as a competition concern is weak, and the theories on how to do it uncertain, antitrust agencies should proceed with caution.[15]

[9] See eg Tim Wu, *The Curse of Bigness: Antitrust in the New Gilded Age* (Columbia Global Reports 2018); Lina M Khan, 'The New Brandeis Movement: America's Antimonopoly Debate' (2018) 9 Journal of European Competition Law & Practice 131; Lina M Khan, 'Amazon's Antitrust Paradox' (2017) 126 Yale Law Journal 710; Lina M Khan and Sandeep Vaheesan, 'Market Power and Inequality: The Antitrust Counterrevolution and its Discontent' (2017) 11 Harvard Law and Policy Review 234. For a criticism of the movement, see eg Elyse Dorsey, Jan Rybnicek, and Joshua D Wright, 'Hipster Antitrust Meets Public Choice Economics: The Consumer Welfare Standard, Rule of Law, and Rent-Seeking' [2018] CPI Antitrust Chronicle; Thomas W Hazlett, 'The Nirvana Fallacy in "Hipster Antitrust"' (2021) 28 George Mason Law Review 1253.

[10] Joseph R Biden Jr, 'Executive Order on Promoting Competition in the American Economy' (2021) <https://www.whitehouse.gov/briefing-room/presidential-actions/2021/07/09/executive-order-on-promoting-competition-in-the-american-economy/> accessed 13 September 2022.

[11] Maureen K Ohlhausen and Alexander Okuliar, 'Competition, Consumer Protection and The Right (Approach) to Privacy' (2015) 80 Antitrust Law Journal 121, 138.

[12] ibid 156.

[13] ibid.

[14] Kevin Coates, *Competition Law and Regulation of Technology Markets* (OUP 2011) 394.

[15] Daniel Sokol and Roisin Comerford, 'Antitrust and Regulating Big Data' (2016) 23 George Mason Law Review 1129, 1161. See also James C Cooper, 'Privacy and Antitrust: Underpants Gnomes, the First Amendment, and Subjectivity' (2013) 4 George Mason Law Review 1129; Geoffrey Manne and Ben Sperry, 'The Problems and Perils of Bootstrapping Privacy and Data into an Antitrust Framework' [2015] CPI Antitrust Chronicle.

The enforcement practice in the EU and beyond also reflects the hesitance to integrate data protection considerations into antitrust and merger cases. The cases adopting an integrated approach are scarce and contested. This is rather curious as there has also recently been a stark realization that the unprecedented consolidation of power requires a more thorough overview and a regulatory response. This is illustrated by the EU Digital Markets Act (DMA)[16] that came into force in November 2022 with the aim of governing powerful digital 'gatekeepers', and is a breakthrough regulation with a number of prohibitions merging competition-style theories of harm with data protection issues.

While a crucial one, competition law is not the only perspective that can be adopted to consider the interactions between data protection and competition in digital markets. The second perspective is data protection law. Yet, the question how data protection law affects market competitiveness and what adjustments might bring it in line with the values commonly promoted under competition law has attracted much less attention. Criticizing this asymmetrical focus, Gal and Aviv invoked the concept of a legal 'anamorphosis', which refers to an optical illusion whereby an image can only be seen when looked at from a certain angle.[17] This anamorphosis is not justified, as data protection law has enormous potential to positively support market competitiveness. Responding to the criticism voiced prior to the establishment of the EU General Data Protection Regulation (GDPR)[18] that the new law might limit competitiveness,[19] Viviane Reding, former Vice-President of the European Commission, insisted:

> Privacy and competitiveness should not be presented as antagonistic objectives. On the contrary, modernised data protection rules are a crucial market opener in our digital economy. We are encouraging innovation by introducing tools, such as 'privacy by design' or data portability, which will give companies the right incentives to gain a competitive edge in digital marketplaces where privacy does increasingly matter for consumers.[20]

While theoretically sound, data protection law's potential to be a powerful force in incentivizing more fierce competition on data protection is yet to be realized.

[16] Regulation (EU) 2022/1925 of the European Parliament and of the Council of 14 September 2022 on contestable and fair markets in the digital sector and amending Directives (EU) 2019/1937 and (EU) 2020/1828 (Digital Markets Act) [2022] OJ L265/1.

[17] Michal S Gal and Oshrit Aviv, 'The Competitive Effects of the GDPR' (2020) 16 Journal of Competition Law & Economics 349, 350.

[18] Regulation (EU) 2016/679 of the European Parliament and of the Council of 27 April 2016 on the protection of natural persons with regard to the processing of personal data and on the free movement of such data, and repealing Directive 95/46/EC (General Data Protection Regulation) [2016] OJ L119/1.

[19] Letter from Chris Grayling, UK's Lord Chancellor, to Viviane Reding, European Commission Vice-President in charge of Justice, Fundamental Rights and Citizenship (4 June 2013).

[20] Letter from Viviane Reding, European Commission Vice-President in charge of Justice, Fundamental Rights and Citizenship, to Chris Grayling, UK's Lord Chancellor (6 June 2013).

B. A blueprint for a coherent future

Data protection and competition law differ in many significant respects. The most conspicuous one is that data protection law is underpinned by the fundamental rights rationale, whereas competition law is an economic field of law. As Lianos framed it, their underlying logics represent distinct 'orders of worth': 'it is clear that competition law employs different rules and criteria in judging the value and appropriateness of a specific social arrangement, in comparison, for instance, to data protection law'.[21] Whereas there are multiple other divergences between the fields of data protection and competition, including their different evolutionary paths, fundamental goals, and key features and concepts, their touchpoints are numerous and varied too. Above all, as the book will demonstrate, they share a number of broader values such as individual well-being, fairness, and individual sovereignty. Given that on a normative level data protection and competition law display more synergies than is commonly assumed, the question central to this book is how to bring these areas closer together and ensure their coherent future.

The debate on creating synergies between data protection and competition law can be seen as a part of the more general discussion about interactions between various legal rules and defining the objectives of law in pluralistic societies, where numerous societal values are promoted in parallel. Should the objectives of each field of law be limited to the protection of those values that are specific to the field in question in a narrow sense, or should the objectives be defined more broadly? Are there values that may be common to different fields of law? Are some objectives or values a tool or proxy to protect other, more fundamental values? And how should the law's openness to 'external' values translate into practical enforcement?

With this in mind, the book's argument proceeds as follows. Chapter 1 offers an introductory overview of data protection and competition law. Adopting an EU perspective, it provides insights into the evolutionary paths of these two legal fields, their fundamental rationale, and their key features and concepts. The analysis of data protection law centres on the GDPR, whereas the book's exposition of competition law is focused on Article 102 TFEU that addresses abuse of a dominant position, and the EU Merger Regulation (EUMR).[22] Article 101 TFEU, which regulates anti-competitive agreements and constitutes the third key area of competition law, is not discussed in this book given its more limited potential to be a bridge between competition and data protection law. The introductory accounts in this chapter will be particularly useful for competition law experts who might not be well acquainted with data protection law, and vice versa. The chapter concludes with a number of comparative reflections that illustrate how the evidently

[21] Ioannis Lianos, 'Polycentric Competition Law' (2018) 71 Current Legal Problems 161.

[22] Council Regulation (EC) No 139/2004 of 20 January 2004 on the control of concentrations between undertakings (EC Merger Regulation) [2014] OJ L24/1.

distinctive features of the two areas of law are matched with an equally prominent number of similarities which might not at first be apparent.

Chapter 2 provides a taxonomy of objectives and empirical challenges common to data protection and competition law. As regards the objectives, it explores the thesis that while the different orders of worth embraced by these two fields of law cannot be disputed, they share several remarkably similar normative considerations. Protecting the welfare of individuals, strengthening individual sovereignty, ensuring fairness, mitigating power asymmetries, as well as improving transparency and mitigating information asymmetries are the points of convergence that can be leveraged to formulate the presumption of a normative proximity of data protection and competition law. The book also explores the triple empirical challenge that affects these two legal areas to a similarly significant degree. The three-pronged challenge consists in the 'datafication' of the economy and society, the lack of competitive dynamism, as well as the emergence of new technologies and new ways of interacting with technologies.

In Chapter 3, the book tests the hypothesis that the multitude of ways in which data protection and competition law cohere on a broader normative and conceptual level, as well as on the level of specific challenges posed by the empirical reality of digital markets, is barely mirrored in the regulatory, enforcement, policy, and institutional approaches in the EU and beyond. To verify this thesis, the chapter first sheds light on competition law by scrutinizing the extensive policy discourse related to digital competition law, exploring how competition law's boundaries in this respect are tested through enforcement, and investigating the contribution of new policy and regulatory initiatives (eg the DMA) in fostering a synergetic approach towards data protection and competition. Turning subsequently to data protection law's repercussions for competition, the chapter advances the claim that it is an effectively enforced rather that a weakened data protection regime that has the potential to positively complement competition law. The enforcement of data protection law and a fragmented legal landscape for data protection in Europe therefore also raise concerns for market competitiveness. The chapter additionally explores how agnostic or supportive data protection law's substantive provisions actually are vis-à-vis market competitiveness. Reflecting on the institutional dimension, the chapter shows that enormous progress still needs to be made before both an effective dialogue and enforcement collaborations between data protection and competition authorities take a desired shape.

Chapter 4 introduces the notion of 'sectional coherence', which breaks fresh theoretical ground and is used in this book as a conceptual framework for the discussion of a more synergetic future for data protection and competition law. With this aim, it first relies on the legal theory, and specifically on the theory of coherence, to define sectional coherence, to discuss its scope, and to present its normative strength. As will be shown, sectional coherence is a demanding principle that would require data protection and competition law to be interpreted and enforced in a mutually cognizant and reinforcing manner. The chapter then turns to EU constitutional law to investigate how it approaches and qualifies coherence as a legal principle. Putting in the spotlight Article 7 TFEU, it argues that this provision can provide a legal foundations for sectional coherence in the EU.

In Chapter 5, the analysis is devoted to one of the book's central inquiries, namely how competition law could and should adapt to better integrate the value of data protection into its analysis. Starting with the notion of 'data power', it first explores how the economic strength of technology companies should be better reflected in competition law assessments of market power. It then turns to the area of abuse of a dominant position to discuss a number of exploitative and exclusionary theories of harm that could better capture new data protection harms in digital markets. This is complemented with an overview of the role of data protection in antitrust justifications and remedies. Next to abuse of dominance, merger control constitutes another major focal point of the chapter. It explores how merger theories of harm, justifications, and remedies should be rethought to better respond to the demands of sectional coherence.

Chapter 6 complements this inquiry by shedding light on how data protection can contribute to coherence, representing the other side of the coin. With this aim, it first revisits a risk-based approach to data protection and various balancing mechanisms in order to evaluate how data protection assessments could consider the unprecedented power of technology firms. The chapter also explores how data protection law, which currently places great emphasis on the idea of individual empowerment, should focus instead on a collective dimension to better stimulate competition on data protection. In addition, the chapter emphasizes that data protection law might inadvertently contribute to a further consolidation of the power of large technology companies, and calls for closer scrutiny of such unintended repercussions of competition.

In the spirit of offering preliminary conclusions, Chapter 7 steps back to present a bigger picture. The conceptual, practical, constitutional, and institutional implications of the transition towards sectional coherence, and well as its implications for other jurisdictions, provide an overarching perspective on the multifactored repercussions of introducing sectional coherence. The book concludes with a chapter on final reflections.

1

An Overview of EU Data Protection and Competition Law

A. Introduction

Introducing data protection and competition law is a necessary and first step in an analysis of how these two fields can be rendered more coherent, in particular as it cannot be assumed that experts specialized in one of these legal fields are well acquainted with the other. The introduction to data protection and competition law provided in this chapter is divided into three broader themes. Section B provides a glimpse into the evolution of these two areas of law: their histories and the landmark transformations that they have undergone over time. Section C contains an overview of the fundamental rationale and goals embraced by data protection and competition law. The key features and concepts of the two legal fields are outlined in Section D. Those three parts provide a basis for and enable a comparative summary presented in Section E, which distils a number of key similarities and divergences between data protection and competition law.

B. A glimpse into the evolution of data protection and competition law

1. The gradual emergence of data protection law in Europe

In the EU, the main legislative framework governing the collection and use of personal data is the GDPR, which entered into force in 2016 and is applicable as of 2018. The history of data protection in Europe is, however, much longer: its origins can be traced back to the 1970s, when few European countries enacted data protection laws applicable both vertically (government-to-citizen) and horizontally (business-to-citizen).[1] While the first data protection law was established in the German state of Hesse (1970), the early data protection legislation introduced in Sweden (1973), the Federal Republic of Germany (1977), and France (1978), for

[1] Chris Jay Hoofnagle, Bart van der Sloot, and Frederik Zuiderveen Borgesius, 'The European Union General Data Protection Regulation: What It Is and What It Means' (2019) 28 Information & Communications Technology Law 65, 70.

Coherence between Data Protection and Competition Law in Digital Markets. Klaudia Majcher, Oxford University Press.
 DOI: 10.1093/oso/9780198885610.003.0002

example, embraced, built on, and deepened the Fair Information Principles (FIPs) developed in the US.[2] Subsequently articulated in the 1980 OECD's *Guidelines on the Protection of Privacy and Transborder Flows of Personal Data*,[3] the set of eight FIPs included principles such as data collection limitation, data quality, purpose specification, and use limitation. By 1980, many other countries in Europe, including Austria, Denmark, Luxembourg, and Norway, had data protection frameworks in place, and some other had incorporated data protection as a fundamental right in their constitutions (ie Portugal, Spain, and Austria). Following these national legal developments, and recognizing the need for international rules regulating the processing and free flow of personal data across borders, in 1980 the Council of Europe (CoE) adopted a Convention for the Protection of Individuals with Regard to Automatic Processing of Personal Data (Convention 108).[4] Ratified by fifty-five countries, Convention 108 lays down a set of obligations (eg legitimacy of data processing, data security, transparency of processing) and rights (eg right to information, right to rectification and erasure), and is the first and only binding international legal instrument for data protection.

At the European level, the legal developments relating to data protection reflect the continent's long-standing commitment to the protection of privacy as a fundamental right in the context of family life, home, and communications, and, with the advancement of the information markets, also its commitment to the protection of personal data.[5] In the wake of new technological developments in data processing, in 1975 the European Parliament enacted a resolution calling for data protection legislation in order to harmonize and create a safe data protection landscape in Europe.[6] While Convention 108 was a milestone in data protection history, the Member States were initially reluctant to sign and ratify the Convention, which was another reason for the EU to take action.[7]

Enacted in the midst of the Third Industrial Revolution, and in the early days of the ubiquitous use of information, the 1995 Data Protection Directive[8] (DPD) was a breakthrough piece of legislation. The goal of the new comprehensive European

[2] Robert Gellman, 'Fair Information Practices: A Basic History—Version 2.21' (2021) 9 <https://papers.ssrn.com/abstract=2415020> accessed 25 January 2022. See also Hoofnagle, van der Sloot, and Borgesius (n 1) 70.

[3] OECD, 'Guidelines on the Protection of Privacy and Transborder Flows of Personal Data' (1980).

[4] Council of Europe, Convention for the Protection of Individuals with Regard to Automatic Processing of Personal Data (ETS No 108).

[5] Hoofnagle, van der Sloot, and Borgesius (n 1) 70. For an extensive discussion on the emergence of the right to data protection in Europe, see Gloria González Fuster, *The Emergence of Personal Data Protection as a Fundamental Right* (Springer 2014).

[6] European Parliament, 'Resolution on the Protection of the Rights of the Individual in the Face of Developing Technical Progress in the Field of Automatic Data Processing' [1975] OJ C60/48.

[7] Eleni Kosta, 'The Future of Data Protection: Collapse or Revival?' (2014) 28 International Review of Law, Computers & Technology 115, 115.

[8] Directive 95/46/EC of the European Parliament and of the Council of 24 October 1995 on the protection of individuals with regard to the processing of personal data and on the free movement of such data [1995] OJ L281/31.

regime was not to prevent or limit the use of information technology, but rather to provide a set of obligations and safeguards aimed at protecting information relating to an individual, and to ensure the safe free flow of personal data within the internal market.[9] In 2009, the Treaty of Lisbon further contributed to the shaping of the constitutional data protection landscape in Europe. The fundamental change brought about by the Lisbon Treaty was the introduction of the right to data protection and the establishment of an explicit legal basis for the enactment of data protection legislation in Article 16 TFEU. In addition, the Lisbon Treaty gave the EU Charter of Fundamental Rights (EU Charter),[10] which includes both the right to privacy (art 7) and the right to data protection (art 8), the same legal status as the EU constitutional treaties, as well as introduced a provision requiring the EU to accede to the European Convention on Human Rights (ECHR)[11]—a further noteworthy development in the data protection landscape.

At around that time, as industry was becoming more digitalized and globalized, the consensus was growing that the 1995 DPD needed to be revisited to more effectively address the risks associated with online activity, as well as to prevent legal fragmentation and boost legal certainty. A failure to harmonize national data protection laws and the DPD's weak enforcement were among the shortfalls to be addressed through data protection reform. In 2012, the Commission proposed a comprehensive reform of EU data protection law and published a package that included the proposal for a GDPR[12] and the Directive on Data Processing for Law Enforcement Purposes.[13] While acknowledging that the existing data protection framework remained sound as regards its objectives and principles, the GDPR proposal made it explicit that in order to build trust and facilitate the development of innovative uses of new technologies, a legal update was essential.[14] The arrival of the GDPR was applauded as a watershed moment in the history of fundamental rights in the EU.

[9] Peter Hustinx, 'EU Data Protection Law: The Review of Directive 95/46/EC and the Proposed General Data Protection Regulation', *Collected Courses of the European University Institute's Academy of European Law*, 1–12 July 2013.

[10] Charter of Fundamental Rights of the European Union [2012] OJ C326/391.

[11] In the ECHR, the right to respect for private and family life is enshrined in art 8. On the interpretation of art 8 by the ECtHR, see eg *Malone v United Kingdom* (1985) 7 EHRR; *Niemietz v Germany* (1992) 16 EHRR 97; *Perry v United Kingdom* (2004) 39 EHRR 3; *S and Marper v United Kingdom* (2009) 48 EHRR 50; *Satakunnan Markkinapörssi Oy and Satamedia Oy v Finland* (2017) 66 EHRR 8.

[12] European Commission, 'Proposal for a Regulation of the European Parliament and of the Council on the protection of individuals with regard to the processing of personal data and on the free movement of such data (General Data Protection Regulation)', COM (2012) 11 final (hereafter: Proposal for a GDPR).

[13] European Commission, 'Proposal for a Directive of the European Parliament and of the Council on the protection of individuals with regard to the processing of personal data by competent authorities for the purposes of prevention, investigation, detection or prosecution of criminal offences or the execution of criminal penalties and the free movement of such data', COM (2012) 10 final.

[14] Proposal for a GDPR, Explanatory Memorandum.

The legal developments in the area of data protection law in Europe have served—and continue to serve—as an inspiration for other jurisdictions across the globe. Today, over 145 jurisdictions have data protection laws, and the laws enacted in recent years (eg in Brazil, Israel, Turkey, Jamaica, Egypt, Uzbekistan, Tajikistan, Uganda, Kenya, and Barbados) are significantly influenced by the GDPR.[15] Commenting on this path to convergence with the GDPR, Schwartz and Peifer noted that 'EU data protection has been stunningly influential: most of the rest of the world follows it'.[16]

2. Competition law as a central pillar of European integration

Together with the fundamental market freedoms, competition law—in contrast to data protection law as we know it—has been a central pillar of European integration since the beginning of its legal history. As one of the building blocks of the common market project, competition law had already been introduced in the 1951 Founding Treaty establishing the European Coal and Steel Community (ECSC), and the competition rules were among the first to have direct effect at a national level.[17] The fundamental rationale behind enacting pan-European competition rules was straightforward: as Wahl framed it, '[w]hat was the point of removing state-made obstacles to trade if companies could basically re-create them by dividing the market?'[18]

Given the prevailing integrationist motivation underpinning the European project, creating a seamless internal market in the EU was, and still remains, one of the main objectives of competition law.[19] Developing from a different history and concern, EU competition law distinguishes itself in this respect from other jurisdictions, where integrating the economies of various states was not a driving force.[20] For example, the main motivation for introducing the Sherman Act in 1890, the foundational antitrust legislation in the US, was to control the power of the big corporations.[21] As Meagher put it, the aim was to 'break up industry consolidations

[15] Graham Greenleaf, 'Global Data Privacy Laws 2021: Despite COVID Delays, 145 Laws Show GDPR Dominance' (2021) 169 Privacy Laws & Business International Report 3.

[16] Paul M Schwartz and Karl Nikolaus Peifer, 'Transatlantic Data Privacy Law' (2017) 106 Georgetown Law Journal 115, 122.

[17] Kiran Klaus Patel and Heike Schweitzer, 'Introduction' in Kiran Klaus Patel and Heike Schweitzer (eds), *The Historical Foundations of EU Competition Law* (OUP 2013) 1.

[18] Nils Wahl, 'Recent Trends at the Court of Justice of the European Union' [2018] Concurrences No 4-2018, art no 88071, 1.

[19] See eg Pablo Ibáñez Colomo, 'Article 101 TFEU and Market Integration' (2016) 12 Journal of Competition Law & Economics 749; Claus-Dieter Ehlermann, 'The Contribution of EC Competition Policy to the Single Market' (1992) 29 Common Market Law Review 257.

[20] Eleanor M Fox, 'US and EU Competition Law: A Comparison' in Edward M Graham and David J Richardson (eds), *Global Competition Policy* (Institute for International Economics 1997) 339–40.

[21] For a discussion on the history of the US Sherman Act, see eg George J Stigler, 'The Origin of the Sherman Act' (1985) 14 Journal of Legal Studies 1.

that had used the legal "trust" structure to ward off regulation'.[22] Addressing a threat to democracy resulting from economic concentration and exclusionary practices was another goal that motivated the enactment of both the US Clayton Antitrust Act of 1914, which clarified and strengthened the Sherman Act, and its amendment in 1950 that extended the reach of the law.[23]

Although in Europe market integration was the key impetus for the enactment of competition law, the rules on competition also had another rationale. To ensure convergence with other jurisdictions, in particular with the US, EU competition law was supposed to provide a clear set of rules of conduct for undertakings and a legal framework for the operation of a free market economy, as well as to safeguard consumers' welfare and prosperity.[24] Scholars who conducted a reflective historical analysis of the origins of competition law pointed out that 'some of the emerging goals of competition law were rooted in economics: competition as a game of supply and demand servicing consumers and their freedom of choice'.[25]

To reach these goals, enforcement was entrusted to the European Commission, which since the outset has been the central agency shaping the competition landscape. Enacted in 1962, Regulation 17 on procedural rules governing the implementation and public enforcement of competition law endowed the Commission with sweeping enforcement powers and competence.[26] A particular feature of Regulation 17 was a centralized notification and authorization system for individual exemptions laid down in Article 81(3) of the EC Treaty (now art 101(3) TFEU), which implied that only the Commission could exempt an otherwise anti-competitive agreement.

This substantive and procedural status quo of the 1960s underwent a significant transformation in subsequent years. The process of fundamentally rethinking competition policy started in the 1990s, leading to two major developments: a radical overhaul of the substantive assessment standards by introducing a 'more economic approach',[27] and a procedural modernization, which culminated in the decentralization of competition enforcement. The remainder of this section briefly discusses these two far-reaching transformations.

The main reconsideration of substantive competition law started in the mid-1990s, with the Commission deciding to integrate mainstream economic

[22] Michelle Meagher, *Competition Is Killing Us: How Big Business Is Harming Our Society and Planet - and What to Do About It?* (Penguin Business 2020) 74.

[23] Eleanor M Fox, 'Platforms, Power, and the Antitrust Challenge: A Modest Proposal to Narrow the U.S.–Europe Divide' (2019) 98 Nebraska Law Review 23, 300.

[24] Patel and Schweitzer (n 17) 1.

[25] Anca D Chiriță, 'A Legal-Historical Review of the EU Competition Rules' (2014) 63 International and Comparative Law Quarterly 281, 288.

[26] For an overview of the regulation's drafting process, see Lorenzo Federico Pace and Katja Seidel, 'The Drafting and the Role of Regulation 17: A Hard-Fought Compromise' in Patel and Schweitzer (n 17).

[27] For an extensive discussion on the more economic approach, see Anne C Witt, *The More Economic Approach to EU Antitrust Law* (Hart Publishing 2016).

principles into competition law assessments: this was captured by the Commission's Guidance on Article 102 TFEU enforcement priorities (Guidance Paper).[28] Besides rethinking the area of abuse of dominance, the reform included a review of anti-competitive agreements and the introduction of the EU merger regime in 2004.[29] The decision to revisit the style of competition law enforcement came after the initial formalistic phase, during which the Commission aggressively applied the competition provisions to abusive conduct and relied heavily on presumptions of legality and illegality. The substantive transformation was supposed to elevate competition law from its earlier legalistic approach to one that squared with economic reality.[30] The Commission embarked on this challenging reform even though there had been little fundamental criticism of competition law enforcement in the years preceding the reform.[31] While there had been proposals to increase the predictability of the assessment methods used and to refocus competition rules,[32] the basic objectives and rationale of competition law had not been challenged, and there had been a general satisfaction with how the Court of Justice of the European Union (CJEU) and the Commission had enforced competition law.[33] As some have argued, the reform was thus partially inspired by calls for 'a more American-style' enforcement method.[34] The suggestion to more closely integrate competition law and economics—an idea propagated by the Chicago School and which revolutionized US antitrust law in 1980s—sparked enthusiasm among its European counterparts.

The key change brought about by the substantive reform was the reorientation of the EU competition framework towards the objective of consumer welfare. Prioritizing welfare over multiple economic and non-economic values (including fairness, efficiency, employment, democracy, economic freedom, consumer interests, and the interest of society at large), which, as Witt argued, had guided enforcement in Europe prior to the reform,[35] aimed to put competition law on a more

[28] European Commission, 'Guidance on the Commission's enforcement priorities in applying Article 82 of the EC Treaty to abusive exclusionary conduct by dominant undertakings' [2009] OJ C45/7 (hereafter: Commission's Guidance Paper).

[29] On a more economic approach in merger control, see Jorgen Basedow, 'The Modernization of European Competition Law: A Story of Unfinished Concepts' (2007) 42 Texas International Law Journal 13.

[30] Anne C Witt, 'The European Court of Justice and the More Economic Approach to EU Competition Law—Is the Tide Turning?' (2019) 64 Antitrust Bulletin 172, 174.

[31] David J Gerber, 'Two Forms of Modernisation in European Competition Law' (2007) 31 Fordham International Law Journal 1235, 1246.

[32] See eg Mario Siragusa, 'The Millenium Approaches: Rethinking Article 85 and the Problems and Challenges in the Design and Enforcement of the EC Competition Rules' (1997) 21 Fordham International Law Journal 650; Alberto Pera and Mario Todino, 'Enforcement of EC Competition Rules: Need for a Reform?' in Barry E Hawk (ed), *Annual Proceedings of the Fordham Corporate Law Institute* (Fordham Corporate Law Institute 1997); Barry E Hawk, 'System Failure: Vertical Restraints and EC Competition Law' (1995) 32 Common Market Law Review 973.

[33] Gerber (n 31) 1246.

[34] ibid 1248.

[35] Witt (n 30) 177.

economic path. Also the concept of competitive harm, as well as an understanding of what justified otherwise anti-competitive conduct, evolved to reflect the new objective of consumer welfare.[36] There were two main practical repercussions of this shift towards a 'more economic' analysis: focusing on the effects of a specific practice rather than on its form to determine its legality, and embracing the premise that the only relevant effects were the economic effects.[37] To conduct economic assessments of harm and the countervailing effects, the toolbox also had to be updated to include a variety of econometric and quantitative tools.[38]

The second prong of the transformation of competition law in Europe was procedural, focused on decentralizing and dispersing enforcement powers and authority to the Member States.[39] This phase, referred to as a 'modernization' project, covered roughly the same time period as the substantive overhaul that led to a 'more economic' approach.

As mentioned earlier, the enforcement regime created by Regulation 17, which dated back to 1962, was characterized by the centralization of enforcement powers (in particular related to art 101 TFEU) within the Commission's hands. In the light of the substantive developments in competition law, and the planned accession of ten more Member States, in 1997 the Commission set up a Modernisation Group to discuss the need to update competition law procedures.[40] This led to the enactment of Regulation 1/2003,[41] which strengthened and decentralized enforcement by transferring more responsibility from the Commission to the national courts and competition authorities.[42] The new regulation allowed the NCAs to apply Article 101(3) TFEU (exemptions to anti-competitive agreements), required them to apply Articles 101 and 102 TFEU to practices that could affect trade between Member States, reinforced the Commission's investigative powers, and strengthened cooperation between the NCAs and the Commission.

While the above-mentioned transformations are the important milestones in the history of competition law in Europe, a normative soul-searching, in particular as concerns the objectives of antitrust rules, continues to the present. Section D, which discusses the main goals of data protection and competition law, will

[36] Niamh Dunne, 'Public Interest and EU Competition Law' (2020) 65 Antitrust Bulletin 256, 266.

[37] Jan Blockx, 'The Limits of the "More Economic" Approach to Antitrust' (2019) 42 World Competition 475, 477.

[38] Witt (n 30) 186.

[39] Gerber (n 31) 1243.

[40] WPJ Wils, 'Ten Years of Regulation 1/2003—A Retrospective' (2013) 4 Journal of European Competition Law & Practice 293, 293–94.

[41] Council Regulation (EC) No 1/2003 of 16 December 2002 on the implementation of the rules on competition laid down in Articles 81 and 82 of the Treaty [2003] OJ L1/1.

[42] For a discussion of the impact of Regulation 1/2003, see Or Brook, 'Struggling with Article 101(3): Diverging Approaches of the Commission, EU Courts, and Five Competition Authorities' (2019) 50 Common Market Law Review 121; Wils (n 40); Kati Cseres, 'The Impact of Regulation 1/2003 in the New Member States' (2010) 5 Competition Law Review 145.

demonstrate how the scope of competition law in particular remains a moot point, shaping both law and policy.

C. The fundamental rationale and goals

1. The bifurcated objective in data protection law

The subject matter and the key goals of the GDPR are laid down in Article 1. While the first paragraph clarifies that the regulation establishes 'rules relating to the protection of natural persons with regard to the processing of personal data and rules relating to the free movement of personal data', the second and the third paragraph point to the regulation's two underlying rationales. The first is the protection of the fundamental rights of individuals, and in particular the right to data protection. This broad formulation implies that the rules on data protection also aim to reinforce the protection of other fundamental rights, such as the freedom of expression and information (art 11 of the EU Charter) and the right to non-discrimination (art 21 of the EU Charter).[43] The second goal, ensuring the free flow of data within the internal market, is an expression of the GDPR's economic dimension. Unleashing the potential of the Digital Single Market, as well as fostering economic growth, innovation, and job-creation are tasks that the Commission specifically assigned to the GDPR in the Communication accompanying the proposal for a GDPR.[44] This bifurcated objective of the GDPR mirrors the approach already adopted in the DPD, which had an internal market legal basis (art 114 TFEU). The internal market goal that coexists with the aim of protecting fundamental rights and freedoms found expression in the GDPR even though the new regulation's legal basis is Article 16 TFEU, which refers directly to the right to data protection.

The coexistence of these two objectives, which have distinct rationales and may find themselves in tension, has been reflected upon by the CJEU in several judgments. In the early cases relating to the DPD, market integration was considered an overriding goal of data protection law.[45] Despite its initial commitment to the internal market objective, the Court has stressed in other decisions that the supervisory authorities of the Member States need to establish a fair balance between market integration and the right to private life in case the two aims cannot be reconciled.[46] Lynskey noted that in its decisions on how to balance the right to privacy

[43] Hielke Hijmans, 'Article 1. Subject-Matter and Objectives' in Christopher Kuner, Lee A Bygrave, and Christopher Docksey (eds), *The EU General Data Protection Regulation (GDPR). A Commentary* (OUP 2020) 50–51.

[44] European Commission, 'Safeguarding Privacy in a Connected World: A European Data Protection Framework for the 21st Century' (Communication), COM (2012) 9 final, 8.

[45] eg Case C-139/01 *Österreichischer Rundfunk and Others* [2003] ECLI:EU:C:2003:294, para 39; Case C-101/01 *Bodil Lindqvist* [2003] ECLI:EU:C:2003:596, para 41.

[46] eg Case C-518/07 *Commission v Germany* [2010] ECLI:EU:C:2010:125, para 30; Case C-582/14 *Patrick Breyer v Bundesrepublik Deutschland* [2016] ECLI:EU:C:2016:339, para 58; Hijmans (n 43) 53.

and data protection with the other rights enshrined in EU law, the Court jeopardized the internal market rationale, which it was so eager to promote in its earlier judgments.[47] In *Satamedia*,[48] which triggered the question about how to reconcile data protection with freedom of expression, the Court provided Member States with significant discretion when balancing different fundamental rights, directly endangering the DPD's harmonization objective. A likely explanation for this, as Lynskey observed, were the constrains related to the EU's lack of fundamental rights competence, and specifically the DPD's internal market legal basis as well as the EU Charter's lack of binding force.[49]

After the entry into force of the Lisbon Treaty, which, as already mentioned, reshaped the data protection landscape in a way that demonstrated the EU's commitment to the right to data protection, the Court continued to promote the DPD's goal of market integration.[50] In *ASNEF*, it noted that Member States cannot add new principles relating to the lawfulness of data processing under Article 7 DPD or amend the scope of the provision by imposing additional requirements,[51] as that would endanger the harmonization of data protection laws across EU jurisdictions. Yet, as Lynskey noted, after the Treaty of Lisbon, the CJEU accompanied the emphasis on the goal of market integration with an equal emphasis on the rights to data protection and privacy.[52] In cases such as *Bavarian Lager*[53] or *Google Spain*,[54] the CJEU even arguably tipped 'the balance too in favour of the data protection rules',[55] and in *Digital Rights Ireland*,[56] it entirely invalidated EU secondary legislation on the grounds of its non-compliance with the EU Charter.

Under the current legal set up where data protection is elevated to a fundamental human right and the judicial assertions shift the focus from the internal market to a rights-based rationale for data protection law, two questions emerge: (1) what are the specific normative dimensions that underlie the goal of protecting fundamental rights, in particular the right to data protection and (2) what is an adequate approach to the internal market objective?

As regards the first question, there is no one definitive understanding of the exact premise underlying the legal framework for data protection. Instead, the

47 Orla Lynskey, *The Foundations of EU Data Protection Law* (OUP 2015) 58.

48 Case C-73/07 *Satakunnan Markkinapörssi and Satamedia* [2008] ECLI:EU:C:2008:727.

49 Lynskey (n 47) 58–62.

50 ibid 62.

51 Joined Cases C-468 and 469/10 *Asociación Nacional de Establecimientos Financieros de Crédito (ASNEF) and Federación de Comercio Electrónico y Marketing Directo (FECEMD) v Administración del Estado* [2011] ECLI:EU:C:2011:777, para 36.

52 Lynskey (n 47) 62.

53 Case C-28/08 P *European Commission v The Bavarian Lager Co Ltd* [2010] ECLI:EU:C:2010:378.

54 Case C-131/12 *Google Spain SL and Google Inc v Agencia Española de Protección de Datos (AEPD) and Mario Costeja González* [2014] ECLI:EU:C:2014:317.

55 Lynskey (n 47) 65.

56 Joined Cases C-293 and 594/12 *Digital Rights Ireland Ltd v Minister for Communications, Marine and Natural Resources and Others and Kärntner Landesregierung and Others* [2014] ECLI:EU:C:2014:238.

tenets advanced in this context range from a narrow concept of informational self-determination to the idea of human dignity, from a broad concept of fairness to addressing informational asymmetries and protecting other values and rights. Importantly, the GDPR is not limited to the right to data protection but has a more expansive prerogative. As stressed by Ausloos, the GDPR provides 'useful tools for individuals wishing to safeguard a variety of interests, rights, and freedoms in the face of information power asymmetries'.[57] The GDPR thus has an instrumental role in ensuring values such as human dignity, integrity, data protection, freedom of thought and expression, economic freedoms, democracy, equality, and non-discrimination.[58] Commenting on the case law on the essence of the rights to data protection and privacy, Brkan has observed that it resembles 'a muddled maze where the final destination remains concealed due to reasoning that is full of meanders and unpredictable curves'.[59] Young and Bygrave noted that despite a long-running contestation as regards the objectives of data protection law in Europe, 'the GDPR can be understood as a regulatory governance regime in that it is fundamentally *purposive* in nature, entailing an organized attempt to achieve some prespecified objective or objectives involving behavioral change or the management of risk'.[60]

The multifaceted nature of the rights to data protection and privacy, as well as the absence of their precise definitions, is subject to discussion not only in Europe; reflecting on informational privacy from the US perspective, Solove claimed that it is 'a concept in disarray' as no one is able to articulate its specific meaning.[61] What exactly is at stake when the rights to data protection or privacy are violated and what needs to be done to effectively protect these rights are a continuing subject of reflection.

In addition to the lack of clarity on the precise rationale underlying data protection, what is also undefined is the exact role of the market harmonization goal of the GDPR and the extent to which the economic dimension of data protection law should be able to influence the interpretation of its provisions. The exact relevance of market integration is intriguing when looked at from a competition perspective, in particular as a well-functioning and competitive digital economy requires a coherent approach to data flows. In the face of continued fragmentation of data protection laws in the EU (see Chapter 6 Section B), the

[57] Jeff Ausloos, *The Right to Erasure in EU Data Protection Law. From Individual Rights to Effective Protection* (OUP 2020) 71–72.

[58] ibid 73.

[59] Maja Brkan, 'The Essence of the Fundamental Rights to Privacy and Data Protection: Finding the Way Through the Maze of the CJEU's Constitutional Reasoning' (2019) 20 German Law Journal 864, 865.

[60] Karen Yeung and Lee A Bygrave, 'Demystifying the Modernized European Data Protection Regime: Cross-Disciplinary Insights from Legal and Regulatory Governance Scholarship' (2021) 16 Regulation & Governance 137, 138.

[61] Daniel J Solove, *Understanding Privacy* (Harvard UP 2008) 1.

data protection regime should not abandon its original intention of facilitating safe data flows.

2. The multiplicity of objectives in competition law

In the majority of jurisdictions with competition law systems, the consumer welfare standard (CWS) is a central, or even exclusive, normative paradigm guiding competition enforcement. In contrast to the competition standards of total welfare (gains for society as a whole) and producer welfare (producers' profits), CWS assumes that competitive markets should yield a twofold benefit for consumers, namely low prices and high output levels. Consumer welfare can be further broken down to include factors such as quality, choice, and innovation.

The centrality of the CWS in competition law regularly sparks discussions about the dimensions of individual well-being that this notion embraces, as well as its interactions with other values. As regards the contours of the CWS, although competition law is traditionally price-focused, the surfacing of competition on parameters other than price continues to challenge the understanding of the CWS. As already mentioned, there is a wide consensus that choice, quality, and innovation are, next to prices and output, the relevant dimensions of consumer welfare in competition law. The prominent question that arose more recently is whether—and, if so, when and how—values such as data protection can be designated as welfare dimensions that competition law should account for more directly. Chapter 2 Section B will discuss how in the modern online environment data protection is inextricably intertwined with certain traditional dimensions of the CWS, for example quality and choice.

Besides the precise dimensions of the CWS, its interactions with other goals are subject to vigorous debate. New market developments and ensuing socio-political and economic concerns frequently reignite the discussion about the proper scope of competition law and the goals other than the CWS that it should aim to embrace. Nowadays in particular, the burning question is whether and how to integrate non-economic values into competition law assessments. While social policy values and employment, industrial policy, cultural diversity and identity are examples of non-economic considerations that have already been invoked in European competition law decisions, the exact extent of the role of socio-political concerns in the overall philosophy of competition enforcement is not commonly agreed.

At one extreme, one could present a vision of competition law pursuing a set of very narrow policy goals, such as consumer welfare and economic efficiencies. That vision portrays competition law as an inherently economic instrument that should rely on (seemingly) objective economic evaluation criteria. This 'purity argument', as Ezrachi calls it, was inspired by the US Chicago school of thought and continues to find a receptive ear in Europe and beyond. Such a narrow conceptualization of competition law corresponds to what Makris referred to as 'autonomous law'.[62] In an autonomous legal ordering, as he noted following Nonet and Selznick, upholding the rule of law is central, and law as such 'is perceived as a normatively fixed set of rules which enforcers have some discretion to apply and adjudicators need to elaborate, without transgressing their role as "mouthpieces of the law"'.[63] Framing competition law as autonomous law would therefore imply that its interpretation and implementation can be insulated from normative value judgements and can to a large extent rely on economic technocracy. Those who claim that competition law pursues total or consumer welfare goals, and does not encompass other values, regard competition law as a normatively closed and monocentric legal field and advocate in Makris's view an autonomous law approach to competition law. This is definitely far from ideal: as Ezrachi pointed out, when 'government officials argue for purity, one would expect raised eyebrows. But few question competition officials who, in speeches in foreign lands, praise 'purity' of competition.'[64]

At the other extreme, one could envision competition law as an elastic set of rules, which are constantly in flux, adaptable to the external empirical context, and serving as a 'catch all', applied wherever other legal instruments are unable to reach. Just like the first extreme, this is not the ideal for which one should strive— for many sound reasons, including the lack of legal certainty and the inability to effectively enforce the law if its mandate were to be significantly expanded.

As each of the two visions has significant downsides, many voices in the competition law discipline are located somewhere in between, speaking for preserving economic soundness while remaining cognizant of fluctuating socio-political and economic realities that competition law should also reflect. As opposed to the concept of autonomous law described earlier, competition law can in this sense be conceptualized as 'responsive law': 'a relatively open normative system and a purposive interpretive practice facing constant conflicts between openness and integrity'.[65] In addition to its conceptually elastic language, an indicator of competition law's openness is its 'fuzzy mandate', that is the indeterminacy of competition law's goals.[66] Although disagreements also exist with regard to the extent to which competition law should be approached more holistically, there is a rather broad consensus that multiple considerations—such as consumer welfare and efficiencies, economic freedom and market structure, fairness, the protection of internal market, as well as non-economic public policy goals—can influence the contours of competition law and policy. This vision seems to be supported in the

[62] Stavros Makris, 'EU Competition Law as Responsive Law' (2021) 23 Cambridge Yearbook of European Legal Studies 228.

[63] ibid 235. See also Philippe Nonet and Philip Selznick, *Law and Society in Transition: Toward Responsive Law* (Harper and Row 1978).

[64] Ariel Ezrachi, 'Sponge' (2016) 5 Journal of Antitrust Enforcement 49, 49.

[65] Makris (n 62) 238.

[66] ibid 246.

most recent policy initiatives of the European Commission. On 27 March 2023, the Commission announced an intention to adopt new Guidelines on exclusionary abuses of dominance—an initiative marking the first major policy revision of the abuse of dominance rules since 2009, when the Guidance Paper on enforcement priorities in the area of abuse of dominance came into force.[67] Announcing the initiative, the Commission published a Communication and Annex amending the 2009 Guidance Paper: in the Communication, the Commission used rather new language to discuss the goals of competition law. Notably, it asserted that the enforcement of Articles 101 and 102 TFEU contributes to 'a level playing field where markets serve consumers', and 'can moreover contribute to achieving objectives that go beyond consumer welfare, such as plurality in a democratic society'.[68] The latter part of the Commission's statement, which is particularly noteworthy as it explicitly flags a traditionally 'non-competition' goal as relevant, is supported by reference to the General Court's ruling in *Google Android*.[69] It is curious that the Commission decided to give such prominence to the Court's pronouncement in *Google Android*, not least because in another recent case, *Enel*, the CJEU stressed that 'the well-being of both intermediary and final consumers must be regarded as the ultimate objective warranting the intervention of competition law'.[70]

In another recent Commission's initiative, namely the draft revised Market Definition Notice, the Commission highlighted that parameters of competition may, besides the product's price, include aspects such as the security and privacy protection afforded by the product in question.[71]

All of this points to the role that ideology plays in shaping the competition law field, which is often the case for the social sciences, as Lianos noted.[72] These continuous ideological debates on how competition law enforcement can contribute to creating an efficient, resilient, and fairer economy reflect the fact that competition is 'a tool of economic and social regulation'.[73] The implications of economic power

[67] European Commission, 'Antitrust: Commission announces Guidelines on exclusionary abuses and amends Guidance on enforcement priorities' (27 March 2023)IP/23/1911 <https://ec.europa.eu/commission/presscorner/detail/eN/ip_23_1911> accessed 28 March 2023. For an academic discussion on the need to update the 2009 Guidance Paper in order to better respond to the challenges of the digital economy, see eg Germain Gaudin and Despoina Mantzari, '*Google Shopping* and the As-Efficient-Competitor Test: Taking Stock and Looking Ahead' (2022) 13 Journal of European Competition Law & Practice 125.

[68] European Commission, 'Amendments to the Communication from the Commission Guidance on the Commission's enforcement priorities in applying Article 82 of the EC Treaty to abusive exclusionary conduct by dominant undertakings' (Communication), COM (2023) 1923 final, para 1 (emphasis added).

[69] Case T-604/18 *Google and Alphabet v Commission (Google Android)* [2022] ECLI:EU:T:2022:541, para 1028.

[70] Case C-377/20 *Servizio Elettrico Nazionale SpA and Others v Autorità Garante della Concorrenza e del Mercato and Others* [2022] ECLI:EU:C:2022:379, para 46 (emphasis added).

[71] European Commission, 'Commission Notice on the definition of the relevant market for the purposes of Union competition law', Draft (2022).

[72] Ioannis Lianos, 'Reorienting Competition Law' (2022) 10 Journal of Antitrust Enforcement 1, 3.

[73] ibid 4.

are not only felt in economic structures and dynamics, as power also has a great potential to shape other spheres, from political to social to cultural.[74] Competition law is thus not an insulated area but rather a social construct, and part and parcel of a broader set of instruments created and enforced to serve higher level aims of fostering the well-being of societies. Such high-level considerations, in turn, stem from foundations and values inherent in individual jurisdictions and the particularities of social realities and experiences.[75] According to Margrethe Vestager, Executive Vice-President of the European Commission, competition law is 'a political endeavour' that helps in reaching overall goals.[76]

D. The key features and concepts

1. Data protection law

1.1 Selected new features of the GDPR

The GDPR mimics to a large extent the provisions enshrined in the DPD enacted in 1995.[77] Preserving the principles-based approach, the legal revolution brought about by the GDPR lies not in a major overhaul of the substantive data protection rules, but rather in the choice of legal instrument—a regulation replacing a directive—and in procedural reforms aimed at creating a more effective protection regime. The core principle behind the latter was to ensure a shift from compliance by a 'box-ticking exercise' towards the idea of 'accountability'.[78] The accountability-oriented approach resulted in 'a number of important newcomers'[79] introduced in the GDPR, including the principles of data protection by design and by default,[80] the obligation to conduct data protection impact assessments,[81] and the requirement to appoint a data protection officer.[82] Furthermore, as Article 24(1) GDPR stipulates, data controllers should take appropriate technical and organizational measures to implement the law, taking into account 'the nature, scope, context and purposes of processing as well as the risks of varying likelihood and severity for the

74 ibid.

75 Ezrachi (n 64) 51.

76 Margrethe Vestager, 'The Values of Competition Policy' (CEPS Corporate Breakfast, Brussels, 13 October 2015).

77 Orla Lynskey, 'Aligning Data Protection Rights with Competition Law Remedies? The GDPR Right to Data Portability' (2017) 42 European Law Review 793, 794.

78 On the need for a more accountability-based approach, see A29WP, 'Statement of the Working Party on Current Discussions Regarding the Data Protection Reform Package' (2013); A29WP, 'Statement on the Role of a Risk-Based Approach in Data Protection Legal Frameworks' (2014).

79 Claudia Quelle, 'Enhancing Compliance under the General Data Protection Regulation: The Risky Upshot of the Accountability- and Risk-Based Approach' (2018) 9 European Journal of Risk Regulation 502, 503.

80 GDPR, art 25.

81 ibid art 35.

82 ibid art 37.

rights and freedoms of natural persons'. The new 'risk-based approach' introduced in the GDPR, which applies to all compliance measures, was aimed at ensuring that controllers implement the abstract data protection provisions appropriately and effectively.[83] Kuner compared the data protection reform brought by the GDPR to a 'Copernican revolution' initiated in philosophy by Kant in the eighteenth century, arguing that the new regulation gives rise to a revolutionary framework 'by seeking to shift its focus away from paper-based, bureaucratic requirements and towards compliance in practice, harmonization of the law, and individual empowerment'.[84]

1.2 GDPR's material and territorial scope

Article 2(1) GDPR stipulates that the regulation applies to the processing of personal data, whereas Article 2(2) GDPR lists four different exceptions (eg data processing by natural persons in the context of a purely personal or household activity,[85] processing by competent authorities for the purpose of prevention or investigation of criminal activities[86]). Interesting for the discussion about the material scope of the GDPR is its conceptualization of 'personal data'. To ensure that a wide range of data practices fall within its scope, the GDPR defines personal data in an all-encompassing way, as 'any information relating to an identified or identifiable natural person'.[87] There are, however, disagreements as to whether the expansion of the notion of personal data is a positive development. For example, the debate is still unsettled as to whether profiles of individuals should constitute personal data.[88] Some argue that profiles do not amount to personal data, unless such profiles are created using additional information that can help to identify an individual.[89] Others suggest the opposite: as noted by Gellert, the CoE's recommendation on profiling considers final intentions rather than the type of data used for profiling, and rests on the premise that profiling 'results in application of the outcome to identified or identifiable individuals',[90] and hence needs to be considered

[83] Quelle (n 79) 503. For an extensive analysis of the risk-based approach in data protection law, see Raphaël Gellert, *The Risk-Based Approach to Data Protection* (OUP 2020).

[84] Christopher Kuner, 'The European Commission's Proposed Data Protection Regulation: A Copernican Revolution in European Data Protection Law' (2012) Bloomberg BNA Privacy and Security Law Report 1, 1.

[85] GDPR, art 2(2)(c).

[86] ibid art 2(2)(d).

[87] eg, in the US, personal data is conceptualized in a narrower way, as 'personally identifiable information'.

[88] Raphaël Gellert, 'Personal Data's Ever-Expanding Scope in Smart Environments and Possible Path(s) for Regulating Emerging Digital Technologies' (2021) 11 International Data Privacy Law 196, 197.

[89] Wim Schreurs and others, '*Cogitas, Ergo Sum*. The Role of Data Protection Law and Non-Discrimination Law in Group Profiling in the Private Sector' in Mireille Hildebrandt and Serge Gutwirth (eds), *Profiling of the European Citizen: Cross-Disciplinary Perspectives* (Springer 2008) 246–47.

[90] Council of Europe, 'The Protection of Individuals with Regard to Automatic Processing of Personal Data in the Context of Profiling' (2010) Recommendation CM/Rec(2010)13 and Explanatory Memorandum, para 57.

as part of personal data processing. More generally, Purtova has cautioned that the expansion of the notion of personal data risks transforming data protection into 'the law of everything'.[91] Divergent viewpoints on such a central concept that determines the material scope of data protection law resembles to a certain extent the discourse on widening the scope of competition law to encompass certain non-economic values, which might exceedingly broaden its reach.

As regards the GDPR's territorial scope, the regulation applies to data processing activities that have a link to the EU's territory or market. Article 3 GDPR sets out two main criteria that define the territorial scope: the 'establishment' criterion in Article 3(1) and the 'targeting' criterion in Article 3(2), one of which needs to be satisfied for the GDPR to apply.[92] The first criterion stipulates that the data protection provisions apply to the data processing activities conducted by controllers or processors established in the EU, even if the data processing takes place outside the Union. Responding to the concern that the DPD did not sufficiently protect personal data processed or stored outside the Union,[93] the GDPR introduced a 'targeting' criterion, officially widening the law's territorial reach. Accordingly, even if a controller or a processor is established outside the EU, the GDPR applies where its data processing activities relate to: (1) the offering of goods or services to data subjects located in the EU, or (2) the monitoring of their behaviour if that behaviour takes place in the Union. By virtue of the 'targeting' criterion, the GDPR also created obligations for parties that process data in third countries, resulting 'in the extraterritorial reach or territorial extension of EU data protection law', as noted by Kuner.[94] In addition, Article 3(3) confirms that the GDPR applies to processing by controllers not established in the EU but in a place where Member State law applies by virtue of public international law.

1.3 The obligations of data controllers and the rights of data subjects

Recital 11 of the GDPR stipulates that an effective data protection framework requires 'the strengthening and setting out in detail of the rights of data subjects and the obligations of those who process and determine the processing of personal data'. There are thus two main categories of substantive data protection rules: (1) obligations of data controllers and (2) data subjects' rights. These two categories partially correspond to the dichotomy proposed by Ausloos, who distinguished between 'protective' and 'empowerment' measures.[95] Whereas the first category embraces measures aimed at offering protection without requiring a proactive attitude by

[91] Nadezhda Purtova, 'The Law of Everything. Broad Concept of Personal Data and Future of EU Data Protection Law' (2018) 10 Law, Innovation and Technology 40.

[92] EDPB, 'Guidelines 3/2018 on the Territorial Scope of the GDPR (Article 3)' (2018) 4.

[93] Christopher Kuner, 'Territorial Scope and Data Transfer Rules in the GDPR: Realising the EU's Ambition of Borderless Data Protection' (2021) Cambridge Legal Studies Research Series, Paper No 20/2021, 11.

[94] ibid 12.

[95] Ausloos (n 57) 87.

an individual (passive role of data subjects), the empowerment measures provide individuals with tools to strengthen control over their data and protect themselves (active role of data subjects). As regards data controllers' duties, the types of obligations they need to comply with depend on whether a data user qualifies as a data controller[96] or a data processor.[97] Although it is not in the scope of this section to discuss the exact differences in obligations imposed on these two sets of users, it is important to note that the demarcation line between controllers and processors is relatively thin and confusion about who falls into which category is unavoidable.[98]

In addition to the division between protective and empowering measures, the GDPR's provisions can be divided according to whether they are activated before or after the data processing starts: they can thus be categorized as 'ex ante' (a lawful basis for data processing) or 'ex post' (right to object) measures, though some measures fall in both categories.[99]

The main principles that determine how data users should handle personal data are listed in Article 5 GDPR.[100] These include, for example, lawfulness, fairness, transparency, purpose limitation, data minimization, and accuracy. Among other obligations imposed on data users is the implementation of appropriate technical and organizational measures (eg pseudonymization) to comply with data protection principles, such as data minimization, and to effectively protect individuals ('data protection by design and by default', art 25 GDPR). While some of the GDPR's provisions are detailed and concrete, the regulation also contains vague language and 'speaks at the level of aspirational principles—hence the GDPR can be characterised as a partially "principles-based regulation"'.[101]

The second set of the GDPR's constitutive provisions that aim at protecting and empowering individuals are the rights that can be exercised by data subjects. In line with the GDPR, a data subject is 'an identified or identifiable natural person', one 'who can be identified, directly or indirectly' by reference to identifiers such as a name, an identification number, location data, or to factors related to the physical, psychological, genetic, economic, of social identity of that natural person.[102] The catalogue of eight subjective rights of data subjects, which can be referred to as 'micro rights', 'subjective rights', or 'control rights', are clustered in the GDPR around the following themes: (1) information and access to personal data;[103]

[96] GDPR, art 4(7).
[97] ibid art 4(8).
[98] Helena U Vrabec, *Data Subject Rights under the GDPR* (OUP 2021)32.
[99] Ausloos (n 57) 86–89.
[100] For a discussion of how some of these principles protect individuals, see eg Bart van der Sloot, 'Do Data Protection Rules Protect the Individual and Should They? An Assessment of the Proposed General Data Protection Regulation' (2014) 4 International Data Privacy Law 307.
[101] Hoofnagle, van der Sloot, and Borgesius (n 1) 67.
[102] GDPR, art 4(1).
[103] ibid arts 13–15.

(2) rectification, erasure, and data portability;[104] and (3) right to object and not to be subject to automated individual decision making.[105]

By setting out a detailed framework for how data users should handle data collection and processing, and which rights of individuals they should respect, the GDPR created not only the most comprehensive data governance framework, but also triggered a shift in data protection culture across organizations. As McDermott noted, it is difficult to 'think of another human right that product designers must take into account when developing new products, as required under the GDPR'.[106] The EU data protection framework assumes that data and its protection are so important that every aspect of interacting with them requires careful planning.[107] For all these reasons, scholars have referred to the GDPR as 'the most consequential regulatory development in information policy in a generation'.[108]

1.4 Institutions and enforcement

The supervision and monitoring of data protection law in the EU is entrusted to Data Protection Authorities (DPAs): as the GDPR maintains a decentralized enforcement system, each Member State shall, according to Article 51 GDPR, provide for one or more independent public authorities. The GDPR gives DPAs a range of tasks, including enforcing the regulation and promoting public awareness related to data processing, as well as provides them with a number of investigative, corrective, and advisory powers.[109] In line with the one-stop-shop mechanism, in the case of cross-border data processing, enforcement leadership is assigned to the DPA of the data user's main establishment.[110] The GDPR also established the European Data Protection Board (EDPB), which replaced the Article 29 Data Protection Working Party (A29WP) as a body of the Union composed of the heads of all national DPAs and the EDPS. Its tasks are defined in Article 70 GDPR.

As regards administrative fines, these are laid down in Article 83 GDPR: depending on the type of violation, DPAs may impose fines ranging from €10 million to €20 million or 2–4 per cent of the company's total worldwide annual turnover in the preceding financial year, whichever is higher.

[104] ibid arts 16–20.
[105] ibid arts 21 and 22.
[106] Yvonne McDermott, 'Conceptualising the Right to Data Protection in an Era of Big Data' (2017) 4 Big Data & Society 1, 2.
[107] Hoofnagle, van der Sloot, and Borgesius (n 1) 66.
[108] ibid.
[109] GDPR, arts 57 and 58.
[110] ibid art 56.

2. Competition law

EU competition law consists of three main areas: anti-competitive agreements and abuse of a dominant position, which are enshrined respectively in Articles 101 and 102 TFEU, and merger rules that are laid down in the EU Merger Regulation. A similar legal design also characterizes competition laws in many other jurisdictions. Given this book's focus on the area of abuse of a dominant position and on merger control, the subsequent paragraphs briefly introduce them and present their key ideas.

2.1 Abuse of a dominant position

Formulated as a general, sector-neutral, and abstract prohibition, Article 102 TFEU stipulates that any abuse by one or more undertakings of a dominant position within the internal market or a substantial part thereof violates competition law.[111] The Treaty does not further specify the core concepts underlying this provision (eg dominant position, abuse), nor does it exhaustively list concrete anti-competitive practices.[112]

Dominant position. While no definition of the core concepts is provided in the TFEU, the CJEU's case law and the Commission's decisions provide some clarification. As regards the notion of dominance, the CJEU defined it in *United Brands* in the following way:

> The dominant position ... relates to a position of economic strength enjoyed by an undertaking which enables it to prevent effective competition being maintained on the relevant market by affording it the power to behave to an appreciable extent independently of its competitors, its customers and ultimately of the consumers.[113]

In practice, competition authorities in the EU refer to a number of factors to establish dominance. While the primary indicator is market share (presumption of dominance where market share is above 50 per cent over time[114]), other factors such as the market position of competitors, the economic strength of buyers, and barriers to market expansion and entry are also considered. Other jurisdictions rely on similar factors, although differences exist as regards market shares indicative of dominance (eg approximately 20 per cent in Brazil, 50 per cent in Japan

[111] Pablo Ibáñez Colomo and Andriani Kalintiri, 'The Evolution of EU Antitrust Policy: 1966–2017' (2020) 83 Modern Law Review 321, 321.

[112] ibid 321–22.

[113] Case 27/76 *United Brands Co and United Brands Continental BV v Commission of the European Communities* [1978] ECLI:EU:C:1978:22, para 65.

[114] Case 62/86 *AKZO Chemie BV v Commission of the European Communities* [1991] ECLI:EU:C:1991:286, para 60.

and the US, and 40 per cent in the UK[115]), and the relevance of specific factors (eg Australia and New Zealand focus more on barriers to entry than on market share[116]). As this book will illustrate, the questions that many jurisdictions grapple with in the context of law enforcement in the digital economy are whether, when, and to what extent access to personal data confers power upon undertakings.

Abuse of a dominant position. In the EU and in the majority of other jurisdictions, competition law does not prohibit market power. Rather, what falls under the scope of a competition law prohibition is an abuse of a dominant position. This is an important point of divergence between the EU and the US: in the latter, Section 2 of the Sherman Act prohibits monopolization or attempts at monopolizing any aspect of interstate trade or commerce.

As mentioned earlier, the concept of abuse does not have a concrete legal definition. Although there have been a few attempts to delineate the boundaries of illegal conduct in various cases and decisions, the existing conceptualizations are comprised of vague benchmarks. The CJEU's definition in *Hoffmann-La Roche* stipulates the following:

> The concept of an abuse is an objective concept relating to the behaviour of an undertaking in a dominant position which is such as to influence the structure of a market where, as a result of the very presence of the undertaking in question, the degree of competition is weakened and which, through recourse to *methods different from those which condition normal competition* in products or services . . ., has the effect of hindering the maintenance of the degree of competition still existing in the market or the growth of that competition.[117]

In *Michelin*, the CJEU established that a dominant undertaking has '*a special responsibility* not to allow its conduct to impair genuine undistorted competition in the common market'.[118] Another term used by competition enforcers in various jurisdictions to delineate a conduct's legality and to justify their decisions is 'competition on the merits'[119]—a term that due to its vagueness does not in fact provide any effective guidance.[120]

As regards examples of abuse of dominance, Article 102 TFEU includes in its clauses (a)–(d) a list of potentially problematic conduct: (a) unfair prices and

115 OECD, 'Abuse of Dominance in Digital Markets' (2020) Background Note by the Secretariat, DAF/COMP/GF(2020)4, 18–19.

116 Deborah Healey, 'Abuse of Dominance' in *Dictionary of Competition Law*, Concurrences, art no 20101.

117 Case 85/76 *Hoffmann-La Roche & Co AG v Commission of the European Communities* [1979] ECLI:EU:C:1979:36, para 91 (emphasis added).

118 Case 322/81 *NV Nederlandsche Banden Industrie Michelin v Commission of the European Communities* [1983] ECLI:EU:C:1983:313, para 70 (emphasis added).

119 See also OECD, 'Policy Roundtable: Competition on the Merits' (2005) DAF/COMP(2005)27.

120 Barry E Hawk, 'About "Competition on the Merits" A Comparative View of Article 82 EC and s. 2 Sherman Act' (2005) Concurrences No 3-2005, art no 232, 33.

trading conditions; (b) limiting market or technical development to the prejudice of consumers; (c) discriminatory conditions for trading partners; and (d) supplementary obligations that have no connection to the subject of contracts. This list is non-exhaustive[121] and the examples are framed in very general terms. Ibáñez Colomo and Kalintiri observed that these provisions 'can be conceived and applied as modest tools aimed at fighting the most blatant and socially harmful violations', or 'they can be construed as a form of meta-regulation addressing a wide range of market and/or government failures'.[122] The abstract nature of the core competition rules characterizes not only the EU legal system but can also be observed in other jurisdictions.

More broadly, prohibited conduct may fall into one of the two main categories of infringements: 'exploitative' and 'exclusionary'. Exploitation, which is a theory of harm rarely pursued by competition authorities, encompasses 'unfair prices' and 'unfair trading conditions' that a dominant firm may impose on customers or consumers. The second main category of competition offences—namely exclusion—is typically the preferred option as it allows target practices that impede effective competition. The fundamental problem behind exclusionary practices is that they have an indirect detrimental impact on consumers by restricting rivals' ability to profitably enter or remain active in a given market.[123] Commenting on its Guidance Paper on the enforcement of Article 102 TFEU, the Commission explained its prioritization of exclusionary over exploitative abuses in the following way: 'because it is better to prevent than to cure—i.e. if markets are not functioning properly, it makes more sense to prioritize the tackling of unilateral conduct which undermines the structure and functioning of the market itself than to address the symptoms'.[124]

Among the prominent examples of exclusionary practices both in the EU and beyond are tying and bundling,[125] refusals to deal,[126] predatory pricing,[127] exclusive dealing (eg exclusivity and loyalty rebates[128]), and margin

[121] Case 6/72 *Europemballage Corp and Continental Can Co v Commission* [1973] ECLI:EU:C:1973:22, para 26.

[122] Ibáñez Colomo and Kalintiri (n 111) 322.

[123] Case C-52/09 *Konkurrensverket v TeliaSonera Sverige AB* [2011] ECLI:EU:C:2010:484, para 24.

[124] European Commission, 'Antitrust: Guidance on Commission Enforcement Priorities in Applying Article 82 to Exclusionary Conduct by Dominant Firms—Frequently Asked Questions' (3 December 2008) MEMO/08/761 <https://ec.europa.eu/commission/presscorner/detail/en/MEMO_08_761> accessed 21 November 2021.

[125] Supplying one product (the 'tying product') conditional upon obtaining another one from the supplier (the 'tied product'). See eg *Microsoft* (Case COMP/37.792) Commission Decision of 24 March 2004; Case T-201/04 *Microsoft Corp v Commission of the European Communities* [2007] ECLI:EU:T:2007:289.

[126] These can take the form of refusals to supply new or existing customers, refusals to license, or the essential facilities doctrine. See eg Case C-7/97 *Oscar Bronner GmbH & Co KG v Mediaprint* [1998] ECLI:EU:C:1998:569; Cases C-241–42/91 P *Radio Telefis Eireann (RTE) and Independent Television Publications Ltd (ITP) v Commission of the European Communities* [1995] ECLI:EU:C:1995:98.

[127] Below-cost pricing designed to drive competitors from the market. See eg *AKZO Chemie* (n 114).

[128] eg Case C-23/14 *Post Danmark A/S v Konkurrencerådet* [2015] ECLI:EU:C:2015:651.

squeezing.[129] While these are some of the most common types of abuse, enforcement authorities have a broad discretion to sanction other, novel exclusionary strategies. Enforcers also create new 'labels' for established violations occurring in new market settings, arguably to demonstrate shifts in their enforcement focus.[130] For example, in *Google Shopping*, the Commission formulated a theory of harm based on the notion of 'self-preferencing', which describes conduct whereby an integrated firm (Google, in this case) leverages its power from the market where it is dominant (general internet search) to favour its affiliates to the detriment of its competitors on another market (comparison shopping services).[131] While the term 'self-preferencing' is new, the concern it represents, namely power leveraging, has been present in competition law since the discipline's inception.[132]

While exploitation and exclusion are the main types of abuse, 'discriminatory abuses' and 'reprisal abuses' are two additional categories. Discrimination is addressed in Article 102(c) TFEU, which states that an abuse might consist in 'applying dissimilar conditions to equivalent transactions with other trading parties, thereby placing them at a competitive disadvantage'. Given that such discriminatory conduct might have an exploitative or exclusionary character or end effect[133]—or exploitation or exclusion might involve an element of discrimination[134]—clearly, distinguishing between these three categories is not always straightforward. The fourth category, namely reprisal abuses, encompasses scenarios where a dominant firm punishes another undertaking, for example for dealing with or promoting the product of a rival firm.[135] As the common logic underlying reprisals is to exclude competitors, they can also be classified as a sub-category of exclusionary abuse.[136]

Justifications. Although the text of Article 102 TFEU does not explicitly envisage any justifications, the EU case law as well as the Commission's guidance on enforcing Article 102 TFEU[137] both stipulate that a dominant undertaking can justify its conduct provided that it satisfies a number of requirements. The way in

[129] Unfair pricing by a vertically integrated firm dominant on the upstream market, eg setting a high price for the input. See eg Case C-280/08 P *Deutsche Telekom AG v European Commission* [2010] ECLI:EU:C:2010:603.

[130] See Pablo Ibáñez Colomo, 'Self-Preferencing: Yet Another Epithet in Need of Limiting Principles' (2020) 43 World Competition 417, 418.

[131] *Google Search (Shopping)* (Case AT.39740) Commission Decision of 27 June 2017. On appeal, the CJEU dismissed for the most part the action brought by Google: Case T-612/17 *Google LLC, formerly Google Inc and Alphabet, Inc v European Commission* [2021] ECLI:EU:T:2021:763, paras 71 and 180 (on appeal).

[132] Ibáñez Colomo (n 130) 418.

[133] John Temple Lang, 'Monopolisation and the Definition of "Abuse" of a Dominant Position under Article 86 EEC Treaty' (1979) 16 Common Market Law Review 345, 358–60.

[134] Robert O'Donoghue and Jorge Padilla, *The Law and Economics of Article 102 TFEU* (3rd edn, Hart Publishing 2020) 302.

[135] Temple Lang (n 133) 358.

[136] Alison Jones and Brenda Sufrin, *EU Competition Law* (4th edn, OUP 2011) 364.

[137] Commission's Guidance Paper (n 28) para 30.

which a competition law concept of justification can encompass data protection claims will be extensively addressed in this book.

Institutions and enforcement. The previous section has already explained that both the EU and the national enforcement authorities have competence to enforce Article 102 TFEU in the context of practices that affect trade between Member States. The fines that may be imposed for a violation of Article 102 TFEU depend of the gravity and duration of the infringement, the maximum level of fines being capped at 10 per cent of the overall turnover of the company[138]—competition law fines are thus significantly higher compared to fines for a violation of the GDPR. Alternatively, the enforcer can also adopt a commitment decision[139] or impose interim measures.[140]

2.2 Merger control

The rules on merger control are laid down in the EU Merger Regulation. As opposed to Articles 101 and 102 TFEU, this regulation is an ex ante regime that contains a set of substantive and procedural provisions on how mergers with an EU dimension are to be assessed. While the EUMR is the principal merger control instrument discussed in this book, many insights relating to merges will be transposable to other jurisdictions that also have rules on merger control in place. As reported by the OECD, as of 2019, 135 jurisdictions have either a full merger control regime or sector-specific laws that require examination of certain types of transaction.[141]

The substantive test. Despite the more prescriptive nature of the merger rules as compared to Article 102 TFEU, the core test to substantively evaluate whether a notifiable merger adversely impacts competition is framed broadly and leaves room for interpretation. The substantive assessment of mergers in the EU concentrates on the concept of 'significant impediment to effective competition' (SIEC). In line with Article 2(3) EUMR, a concentration is incompatible with competition law if it significantly impedes effective competition in the internal market or in a part thereof, 'in particular as a result of the creation or strengthening of a dominant position'.

Specific SIEC-based theories of harm depend on the type of a merger, which can be categorized as horizontal, vertical, or conglomerate.[142] Horizontal mergers, which are mergers between actual or potential competitors, might affect competition in two main ways: by eliminating important competitive constraints on one

[138] European Commission 'Guidelines on the method of setting fines imposed pursuant to Article 23(2)(a) of Regulation No 1/2003' [2006] OJ C210/2.

[139] Reg 1/2003, art 9.

[140] ibid art 8.

[141] OECD, 'OECD Competition Trends 2021: Global Merger Control (Volume II)' (2021) 9.

[142] On a blurry distinction between these categories, see eg Lina M Khan, 'Remarks of Chair Lina M. Khan' (CRA Conference, Brussels, 31 March 2022).

of more firms, leading to increased market power ('non-coordinated effects'), or by changing the nature of competition in a way that facilitates the coordination of firms' behaviour, which may lead to consumer harm ('coordinated effects').[143] Besides horizontal mergers, there are also non-horizontal mergers that include vertical and conglomerate mergers. Vertical mergers are transactions between companies operating at different stages of the supply chain (eg between a producer and a retailer). A vertical merger may be incompatible with competition law, for example if it raises the costs for a downstream competitor by restricting its access to an important input ('input foreclosure'), or where it leads to foreclosing an upstream competitor by restricting its access to a relevant customer base ('customer foreclosure').[144] The third category of mergers are conglomerate mergers, which describe transactions between firms that are neither in a purely horizontal nor in a purely vertical relationship, but are rather active in separate, albeit frequently related, markets.[145] While conglomerate mergers are generally presumed to be compatible with competition law, the ability of such transactions to foreclose rivals is assessed on a case-by-case basis.

Institutions and enforcement. On the EU level, the authority exclusively responsible for reviewing mergers with a European dimension is the European Commission ('one-stop-shop' system). Mergers that do not satisfy the jurisdictional benchmarks stipulated in the EUMR may fall under the remit of the NCAs. There also exists a referral mechanism enshrined in Article 22 EUMR that under specific circumstances allows Member States to refer a smaller merger to the Commission for review.

As the EUMR stipulates, following investigation, the competition authority may take a clearance decision, a prohibition decision, a commitment decision, or an infringement decision.[146]

E. A comparative summary

At first glance, data protection and competition law and their underlying logics differ to a rather considerable extent. To name just some obvious differences: while data protection law is human rights-focused, competition law is an economic field of law; while the GDPR is an ex ante system of rules, the central competition provisions have an ex post logic; and while data protection's nature is prescriptive,

[143] European Commission, 'Guidelines on the Assessment of Horizontal Mergers under the Council Regulation on the Control of Concentrations between Undertakings' [2004] OJ C31/03, para 22.

[144] European Commission, 'Guidelines on the Assessment of Non-Horizontal Mergers under the Council Regulation on the Control of Concentrations between Undertakings' [2008] OJ C265/07, paras 29–79.

[145] ibid 91.

[146] EUMR, art 8.

competition law is prohibitive. Closer scrutiny reveals, however, a more nuanced picture, one where the evident divergences are matched by a number of equally prominent similarities. This section brings to the fore the most notable examples of the dimensions in which data protection and competition law diverge and converge.

As is evident from the discussion of the evolution of data protection and competition law, their legal trajectories are markedly different. Whereas competition law has since the outset been one of the central pillars of European integration, data protection legislation as we know it, and the fundamental right to data protection as such, arrived much later. Yet, the evolution of the data protection landscape in the EU—the introduction of the right to data protection in Article 16 TFEU as well as the elevation of the constitutional importance of the EU Charter—implies that, at present, the constitutional standing of data protection law matches, if not surpasses, the constitutional importance of competition law in the EU.

Normatively, both sets of laws were born out of the same aspiration to integrate the common European market. While still prominent, the objective of market harmonization in data protection law is currently overshadowed by the law's fundamental rights dimension—a logical development given the evolution of the fundamental rights landscape in Europe. In competition law, the common market rationale remains one of the central values in which the law is anchored.

As regards a wider set of objectives pursued, both data protection and competition law display a similarity: they are both characterized in this respect by a certain level of indeterminacy. Although data protection presents itself as a regime with a clear bifurcated objective (ie the protection of fundamental rights and the promotion of the free flow of data), it is, in fact, not at all obvious how its underlying value system is conceptualized. Human dignity, sovereignty, autonomy, fairness, and the protection of a range of fundamental rights are all examples of the normative premises that underpin the data protection framework, although disagreements exist as to the appropriate weight that should be assigned to these individual premises. Comparable—if not sharper—disagreements also characterize competition law and the discourse on its aims. From consumer welfare to economic efficiencies, from the protection of the competitive processes to promoting fairness and economic freedom and pursuing public policy and other non-economic aims, EU competition law has since its inception been influenced by different sets of ideologies and theories.

Scrutiny on a more granular level of provisions also reveals a number of important similarities and differences between these two legal areas. While data protection law includes a set of ex ante regulatory provisions, competition law is traditionally devised as an ex post control instrument. Despite competition law's strong ex post focus, the prominence of mechanisms such as sector inquiries demonstrates competition enforcers' ability to also monitor the market in an ex ante way. Furthermore, the new regulatory tools to ensure competitive and fair markets—the DMA being the prime example—introduce a new competition regulatory model that embraces an ex ante logic.

Competition law, in particular its provisions enshrined in the TFEU, is broad and abstract, leaving it to the enforcers and ultimately the CJEU to expound the law. Also the contours of the SIEC test laid down in the EUMR are not entirely inflexible. Thus, competition rules leave—at least in theory—significant room for interpretation. Also, the broad wording allows competition law as a discipline to change and evolve in seamless ways and without legislative amendments.[147] In data protection law, the provisions are formulated in a more detailed manner: the GDPR is an extensive legal text that includes comprehensive explanations of the various obligations, rights, and other provisions. The discipline is thus more constrained through the existence of specific rules put in place to realize the vision of the effective protection of the fundamental rights and freedoms of individuals.[148] This notwithstanding, the key principles enshrined in Article 5 GDPR are characterized by a certain level of vagueness. There are also data protection concepts—for example, 'fairness'—that span several data protection provisions and which can, as will be shown in this book, embrace several meanings.

At the same time, there remain important divergences between the two legal fields. While the GDPR and other data protection regulations are outcome-oriented, this is not the case with competition law, as its rules do not mandate firms' decisions. As Evans has noted, 'the rules for the game of competition say little about how the game should be played, only how the game should not be played'.[149] Competition law's nature is thus prohibitory and, contrary to data protection law, does not explicitly prescribe the outcomes.

Another important respect in which competition law diverges from data protection law is the former's necessary consideration of the appropriate level of enforcement: competition law needs to strike a delicate balance between over- and under-enforcement. As scholars have noted, such a 'balance between market freedom and government control of market failings is a difficult act of compromise that will be with us forever'.[150] On the contrary, data protection law, once legislation is put in place, does not need to reflect on the amount of enforcement that is optimal from a market and consumer perspective: the goal is simply to ensure as vigorous enforcement of the extant law as possible.

From an institutional angle, the lack of a centralized enforcement system for data protection law in Europe constitutes a major difference as compared to

[147] Ibáñez Colomo, and Kalintiri (n 110) 322.

[148] Kati Cseres, 'Integrate or Separate Institutional Design for the Enforcement of Competition Law and Consumer Law' (2013) Amsterdam Law School Legal Studies Research Paper No 2013-03, 30.

[149] David S Evans, 'Why Different Jurisdictions Do Not (and Should Not) Adopt the Same Antitrust Rules' (2009) 10 Chicago Journal of International Law 161, 164.

[150] Abbott B Lipsky Jr, 'The Global Antitrust Explosion: Safeguarding Trade and Commerce or Runaway Regulation' (2002) 26 Fletcher Forum of World Affairs 59, 66.

competition law. Furthermore, there is a notable discrepancy in relation to the levels of fines: the significantly higher administrative fines available in competition law might provide a better incentive for compliance.

The analysis throughout the book will demonstrate how some of the mentioned similarities might facilitate a coherent approach towards these two legal fields moving forward, and how their divergences might provide opportunities for them to complement one another if a synergetic approach were to be adopted.

2
Common Objectives and the Triple Challenge

A. Introduction

In his article published in 2019, Giovanni Buttarelli, former European Data Protection Supervisor, noted that 'data protection, privacy, and competition have for a long time acted as if they did not originate from the same creative energy'.[1] Convinced of their common normative underpinnings, Buttarelli invoked the figure of Louis Brandeis, a US Supreme Court Justice, who already in 1980 had not only identified privacy protection as a foundation underlying individual freedom, but had also sparked antitrust activism aimed at curbing the power of large firms and ensuring the conditions for democracy.[2] 'As much as in privacy and data protection, there will hardly be any meaningful exercise of freedoms and rights if private actors grow so big as to control information, decisions, knowledge, change, and to ultimately determine the course of disinformation, ignorance, stagnation'[3]—Buttarelli noted.

In the spirit of the border-transcending idea that data protection and competition share a unique set of objectives, and that similar empirical factors challenge the values they strive to protect, the aim of this section is to unpack and present these objectives and challenges to illustrate the closeness of the two legal fields. To this end, Section B on common objectives sheds light on how data protection and competition law converge in their endeavour to protect the welfare of individuals, strengthen their autonomy, ensure fairness, mitigate power asymmetries, improve transparency, and address information asymmetries. Focused on the empirical dimension, Section C outlines the triple challenge faced by data protection and competition law in the modern digital economy: the 'datafication' of the economy and society, the lack of competitive dynamism, and technological innovations and new ways of interacting with technologies. Section D presents key takeaway points.

[1] Giovanni Buttarelli, 'This Is Not an Article on Data Protection and Competition Law' [2019] CPI Antitrust Chronicle, 1.
[2] ibid 2.
[3] ibid.

Coherence between Data Protection and Competition Law in Digital Markets. Klaudia Majcher, Oxford University Press.
 DOI: 10.1093/oso/9780198885610.003.0003

B. Common objectives

1. Protecting individual welfare

A broad objective shared by both data protection and competition law is the welfare of individuals.[4] Although the direct beneficiaries of data protection law are individuals in their role as data subjects, whereas competition law is concerned with the well-being of people when they act as consumers, these two roles converge when individuals' personal data is processed in the market context.[5] For competition law, this convergence raises important questions about the extent to which the goal of protecting data can and should be incorporated into legal assessments. From a data protection standpoint, one consideration is how to ensure that personal data is protected while the economy based on responsible use of personal data is allowed to thrive. As the claim that data protection is a dimension of consumer welfare in a competition sense continues to spur controversies—at the same time it is logical that welfare, when looked at from a data protection standpoint, embraces the right to data protection—the remaining of this section will be devoted to the competition perspective of this issue.

In the past few years, the question whether and how to capture data protection harms in competition assessments has preoccupied policy-makers, enforcement authorities, academics, and commentators around the world. As the discourse and enforcement practices related to the intersecting data protection and competition concerns are discussed thoroughly in Chapter 4, suffice it to say here that there is a gradual realization that as long as 'competition on data protection'[6] exists in the market, data protection concerns might fall under the scope of the mandate of competition enforcers. A growing recognition that competition law has—at least in theory—a role to play when businesses compete on data protection is reassuring. At the same time, a twin assertion is often made that competition on this dimension is limited, which is reflective of individuals' low valuation of data protection. The basis for this claim is the theory of 'revealed preferences': this assumes that the market choices made by consumers demonstrate their preferences, and that if

[4] Orla Lynskey, 'Aligning Data Protection Rights with Competition Law Remedies? The GDPR Right to Data Portability' (2017) 42 European Law Review 793, 794.

[5] Francisco Costa-Cabral and Orla Lynskey, 'Family Ties: The Intersection between Data Protection and Competition in EU Law' (2017) 54 Common Market Law Review 11, 21.

[6] Costa-Cabral and Lynskey argued that the expression 'competition on data protection' is preferred in the context of EU law given important differences between the notions of data protection and privacy. Eg the privacy concept does not capture certain aspects of EU data protection law, such as rights of access to data, data security standards, and the right to data portability: ibid 20. On the distinction between data protection and privacy, see also eg Orla Lynskey, 'Deconstructing Data Protection: The "Added-Value" of a Right to Data Protection in the EU Legal Order' (2014) 63 International and Comparative Law Quarterly 569; Juliane Kokott and Christoph Sobotta, 'The Distinction between Privacy and Data Protection in the Jurisprudence of the CJEU and the ECtHR' (2013) 3 International Data Privacy Law 222.

there were more demand for privacy-friendly services, businesses would compete more intensely to offer them.

The theory of revealed preferences was developed by Samuelson in his seminal article published in 1938.[7] It posits that the actual choices of consumers are the most accurate indicator of their preferences. Thus, when consumers choose to purchase product *A* when products *B* and *C* are also available, consumers are ascribed a preference for product *A*. Market actions of consumers are thus assumed to be linked to actual choices, choices as to preferences, and preferences as to welfare. In this sense, revealed preferences are supposed to represent the normative preferences of consumers. Moving away from the idea of utility, which was deemed impossible to accurately evaluate from an economic standpoint, the purpose of the revealed preferences theory was to formulate a choice theory based only on observable and measurable factors. The aim was therefore practical, and the questions why people make certain choices and whether those choices genuinely improve their welfare were irrelevant.

Although competition theory and practice are strongly grounded in the revealed preferences theory, preferences that individuals manifest through their market behaviour might not always be a reliable yardstick in digital data-driven markets. The choice paradigm and the related concept of revealed preferences are not flawless. The main criticism of conflating choices and preferences is based on the argument that individuals' choices are not always determined solely by the considerations of their own welfare,[8] and that choices might be distorted. Solove, for example, calls attention to the 'behaviour distortion argument', pointing to a number of distorting influences on individuals' conduct.[9] It has been suggested that people have 'bounded rationality' that makes it challenging for them to make decisions when it requires a complex balancing of costs, benefits, and risks[10]—something that data protection choices undeniably entail. There are also other biases and heuristics, one example being a cognitive condition called 'hyperbolic discounting', which means that people tend to choose short-term gains (ie exchanging data for immediate access to a service) and disregard long-term costs.[11] In addition, the very framing of available choices is a tool that can influence decisions in the market. As Oremus observed, 'people's valuations of data privacy are driven less by rational assessments of the risks they face than by factors like the wording of the questions

[7] Paul A Samuelson, 'A Note on the Pure Theory of Consumer's Behaviour' (1938) 5 Economica 61.

[8] See the critique expressed in eg Amartya Sen, 'Behaviour and the Concept of Preference' (1973) 40 Economica 241; Amartya Sen, 'Rational Fools: A Critique of the Behavioural Foundations of Economic Theory' (1977) 6 Philosophy & Public Affairs 317; Amartya Sen, 'Internal Consistency and Choice' (1993) 61 Econometrica 495.

[9] Daniel J Solove, *Understanding Privacy* (Harvard UP 2008)11.

[10] See Alessandro Acquisti and Jens Grossklags, 'Privacy Attitudes and Privacy Behavior' in Jean L Camp and Stephen Lewis (eds), *Economics of Information Security* (Springer 2004) 172–73.

[11] ibid 174. See also Daniel J Solove, 'The Myth of the Privacy Paradox' (2021) 89 George Washington Law Review 1, 16.

they're asked, the information they're given beforehand, and the range of choices they're presented'.[12] Other factors include behavioural manipulation by companies, skewed technological designs, or lack of transparency and knowledge.[13] Thus, the behaviour distortion argument questions the very premise that market behaviour is a reliable metric of individuals' genuine data protection preferences.

If a consensus is reached that data protection preferences revealed in the market context might be considerably distorted through factors exogenous (eg choice design) and endogenous (eg biases) to an individual, hence cannot serve as reliable indicators of their normative preferences, the approach to considering individuals' preferences in competition assessments needs to be revisited. The relationship between preferences and the well-being of individuals should be treated as evidential rather than constitutive, and, as some have suggested, welfare economists should also accept additional evidence of individuals' well-being in case such evidence exists.[14] One way forward is to rely on other methods of measuring preferences, for example surveys. Another approach—one that is certainly more groundbreaking—is to endorse a presumption that the right to data protection is a value in and of itself, and the lack of competition on this parameter is a market failure. Competition already presumes that consumers value low prices, higher output, more choices, and innovation. It is not preposterous to assume that, if alternatives existed, and consumers' market decisions were not skewed, consumer preferences as expressed through market choices would reveal preferences for data protection-friendly products and services.

To conclude, the view that data protection is not a dimension of welfare as understood in competition law, or that it is only a relevant value when competition on data protection exists and when consumers clearly express their preference for privacy-friendly options, thoroughly disregards the behaviour distortion argument outlined earlier. As the insights from behavioural economics are as such not foreign to competition law, it is, hopefully, simply a matter of time and the will to do so before they are finally properly applied to competition cases dealing with personal data.

2. Strengthening individual sovereignty

Creating an effective choice architecture and providing individuals with control over their data are the objectives of data protection law, as well as the key preconditions for well-functioning competition. Central to both legal fields is the idea

[12] Will Oremus, 'How Much Is Your Privacy Really Worth?' *OneZero* (19 September 2019) <https://onezero.medium.com/how-much-is-your-privacy-really-worth-421796dd9220> accessed 28 February 2022.

[13] Solove (n 9) 18.

[14] Daniel M Hausman, *Preference, Value, Choice, and Welfare* (CUP 2012) 98.

that individuals should be entrusted with enhanced powers and agency, and have at their disposal adequate tools to express their preferences. Given the normative proximity of the notions of control and choice, both of which represent the idea of individual sovereignty—whether in individuals' roles of data subjects or consumers—this section considers both concepts to demonstrate the closeness of data protection and competition law.

In data protection law, directly related to the idea of control is the right to informational self-determination, which was first articulated by the German Federal Constitutional Court in its judgment on the constitutionality of the Federal Census Act of 1983.[15] The Act included provisions requiring the collection of detailed data concerning the demographic and social structure of the Federal Republic (eg name, gender, religious affiliation). Referring to Articles 1 and 2 of the Constitution, which address human dignity and the personality right respectively, the court ruled that they warrant 'the capacity of the individual to determine in principle the disclosure and use of his/her personal data'.[16] As the court explained, at stake is 'the authority of the individual to decide himself, on the basis of the idea of self-determination, when and within what limits information about his private life should be communicated to others'.[17] Even before this groundbreaking judicial recognition of the right to self-determination, in 1967, Alan Westin conceptualized privacy as 'the claim of individuals, groups or institutions to determine for themselves when, how and to what extent information about them is communicated to others'.[18]

Today, informational self-determination, control over personal data, and autonomy are among the core premises of data protection law. Lynskey argued that the right to self-determination, which aims to contribute directly to the promotion of self-development and the right to personality, 'remains a central tenet of the right to data protection'.[19] The centrality of these notions can also be framed as fitting with the 'will theory' of rights, which assumes that the function of rights is to provide individuals with increased control.[20] Similarly, Rouvroy and Poullet argued for an interpretation of the rights to privacy and data protection as instruments for 'fostering the specific yet changing *autonomic capabilities* of individuals that are, in a given society at a given time, necessary for sustaining a vivid democracy'.[21] The

[15] BVerfG, Urteil vom 15.12.1983, 1 BvR 209/83. See also Edward J Eberle, 'Observations on the Development of Human Dignity and Personality in German Constitutional Law: An Overview' (2012) 33 Liverpool Law Review 201.

[16] BVerfG (n 15), quoted in Antoinette Rouvroy and Yves Poullet, 'The Right to Informational Self-Determination and the Value of Self-Development: Reassessing the Importance of Privacy for Democracy' in Serge Gutwirth and others (eds), *Reinventing Data Protection?* (Springer 2009) 45.

[17] Rouvroy and Poullet, ibid 45.

[18] Alan F Westin, *Privacy and Freedom* (Athenum 1967) 7.

[19] Lynskey, 'Deconstructing Data Protection: The "Added-Value" of a Right to Data Protection in the EU Legal Order' (n 6) 591.

[20] Yvonne McDermott, 'Conceptualising the Right to Data Protection in an Era of Big Data' (2017) 4 Big Data & Society 1, 3.

[21] Rouvroy and Poullet (n 16) 46.

focus on control is grounded in the faith in individuals as the ultimate decision-makers able to make the best choices as to how their data should be handled.[22] The fact that privacy has historically and theoretically been focused on the individual self was also stressed by Kaminski, who made a distinction between privacy's two main tenets: 'the autonomy version of privacy' that implies freedom, choice, and control, and 'the dignitary version of privacy', which aims to prevent objectification and preserve personhood.[23]

In EU case law, the right to informational self-determination was mentioned explicitly only on one occasion. In *Digital Rights Ireland*, a case focusing on the question whether the EU legislature had violated the principle of proportionality by adopting the Data Retention Directive, Advocate General Cruz Villalón stated that data protected by the EU data protection legal framework 'is subject to the express authorization of each individual, in respect of which he has a "right to informational self-determination"'.[24] The control paradigm finds its explicit reflection in recital 7 of the GDPR, which states that '[n]atural persons should have control of their personal data'. The aim of ensuring control underlies several of the GDPR's provisions: consent as a legal basis and a set of individual rights are its primary expressions. In its opinion on the definition of consent, for example, the A29WP said that control and consent are traditionally linked concepts, as the former can be exercised through the latter.[25] In other jurisdictions, data protection laws are also partially conceptualized through the notion of control. California's Consumer Privacy Act of 2018, for example, indicates that: '[f]undamental to this right of privacy is the ability of individuals to control the use, including the sale, of their personal information'.[26]

Choice conceptualized as an individual's right and ability to freely select products and services that most accurately correspond to their needs and preferences, as well as companies they want to deal with,[27] is also one of the premises of competition law.[28] This idea of vesting powers in consumers can also be captured by the

[22] Elettra Bietti, 'The Discourse of Control and Consent over Data in EU Data Protection Law and Beyond' (2020) Stanford University Aegis Paper Series No 2001, 5 <https://www.hoover.org/research/discourse-control-and-consent-over-data-eu-data-protection-law-and-beyond> accessed 6 July 2022.

[23] Margot E Kaminski, 'The Case for Data Privacy Rights (Or "Please, a Little Optimism")' (2022) 97 Notre Dame Law Review Reflection 385, 390.

[24] Case C-293/12 *Digital Rights Ireland Ltd v Minister for Communications, Marine and Natural Resources and Others* and Case C-594/12 *Kärntner Landesregierung and Others* [2013] ECLI:EU:C:2013:845, Opinion of AG Cruz Villalón, para 57.

[25] A29WP, 'Opinion 15/2011 on the Definition of Consent' (2011) 8.

[26] California Consumer Privacy Act of 2019 (AB375), Section 2(a).

[27] Paul Nihoul, '"Freedom of Choice": The Emergence of a Powerful Concept in European Competition Law' in Paul Nihoul, Nicolas Charbit, and Elisa Ramundo (eds), *Choice—A New Standard for Competition Law Analysis?* (Concurrences 2016) 55.

[28] On the history of the choice paradigm in EU competition law, see Peter Behrens, 'The Consumer Choice Paradigm in German Ordoliberalism and Its Impact on EU Competition Law' in Nihoul, Charbit, and Elisa, ibid.

notion of 'consumer sovereignty' that should exist in a free market economy.[29] It can be defined as 'the set of societal arrangements that causes the economy to act primarily in response to the aggregate signals of consumer demand, rather than in response to government directives or the preferences of individual businesses'.[30] In short, in well-functioning markets, sovereignty of consumers is 'the stimulus to which productive effort is a response'.[31]

Protecting unrestricted consumer choice, which is a precondition for competitive forces to deliver desired market outcomes, is part of the mandate of competition enforcers. In Europe, the concept of choice has on numerous occasions either implicitly determined the outcome of specific cases or was explicitly referred to by the CJEU to justify prohibitions.[32] For example, in *Hoffmann-La Roche*, the first case enforcing Article 102 TFEU, both the Commission and the CJEU conceptualized the notion of abuse as embracing freedom of choice.[33] Choice is also an important consideration in the enforcement of provisions on anti-competitive agreements and mergers.[34] Although competition law does not as such mandate the maximization of choice or the creation of new options, it can prohibit business conduct 'that harmfully and significantly limits the range of choice that the free market, absent the restraints being challenged, would have provided'.[35]

Although choice is a relevant, and sometimes a decisive consideration in competition law, Nihoul noted that it is in many cases 'joined by other considerations', and no clarity exists as to how they are prioritized.[36] In *Microsoft*, for example, the Commission invoked negative impacts on choice alongside those on innovation to explain why Microsoft's refusal to provide rivals with access to interoperability information was anti-competitive.[37] In *Deutsche Telekom*, squeezing competitors out of the market by the German telecommunications operator was assessed through the lens of choice,[38] although the CJEU noted in the same decision that low prices are an integral goal of competition law, leaving some perplexed as to how these goals of choice and low prices are to be balanced.[39]

[29] Neil W Averitt and Robert H Lande, 'Consumer Sovereignty: A Unified Theory of Antitrust and Consumer Protection Law' (1997) 65 Antitrust Law Journal 713, 715.

[30] ibid.

[31] William H Hutt, *Economists and the Public: A Study of Competition and Opinion* (Alden Press 1936) 260.

[32] See eg *Chiquita* (Case IV/26.699) Commission Decision of 17 December 1975; Case 322/81 *NV Nederlandse Banden-Industrie Michelin v Commission* [1983] ECLI:EU:C:1983:313; Case C-202/07 P *France Télécom v Commission* [2009] ECLI:EU:C:2009:214; *Microsoft* (Case COMP/37.792) Commission Decision of 24 March 2004.

[33] Case 85/76 *Hoffmann-La Roche & Co AG v Commission of the European Communities* [1979] ECLI:EU:C:1979:36, para 90.

[34] Nihoul (n 27) 24–26.

[35] Neil W Averitt and Robert H Lande, 'Using the "Consumer Choice" Approach to Antitrust Law' in Nihoul, Charbit, and Ramundo (n 27) 49.

[36] Nihoul (n 27) 33.

[37] *Microsoft* (n 32) para 782.

[38] Case C-280/08 P *Deutsche Telekom v Commission* [2010] ECLI:EU:C:2010:603.

[39] Nihoul (n 27) 66.

The value of choice also implies a challenge to determine what amount of choice can be expected to be beneficial for individuals. As Stucke observed, the complexity for enforcers lies in being confronted with two heuristics 'less is more, and more is better'.[40] Even though the general assumption is that more choice is preferred, choice overload combined with increased product complexity going beyond the optimal level might be detrimental to individuals and society.[41] Enforcers guided by the choice benchmark therefore need to be aware of the careful balancing that might be necessary in individual cases.

That said, there are arguments in favour of ranking choice among the key goals of competition law. One of them is choice's pervasiveness in competition assessment: 'in addition to being "always" there, *choice* [is] also "everywhere" '.[42] It is inherent, at least in an analysis of an abuse of dominance, at the stage of defining the market, determining market power, and establishing infringements. Prioritizing choice as a benchmark to guide competition enforcement might also prove more effective where more traditional notions, such as price, are not able to encompass consumer harm, as in the context of digital markets. As noted by Averitt and Lande, '[t]he consumer choice approach is fundamentally superior to the price and efficiency paradigms because it asks the right question', namely it 'recognizes that consumers do not just want competitive prices—they want options'.[43] Others claimed that choice is in fact a more encompassing paradigm, which includes a price or an efficiency approach, but also goes beyond that, capturing other dimensions of competitive harm,[44] including data protection.

Despite the fact that the values of informational self-determination and consumer sovereignty—the control and choice mechanisms—share important commonalities, there are also divergences in how data protection and competition law approach them on a more granular level. An important divergence concerns the quality of the choice of alternatives. In data protection law, the normative assumption behind the mechanism of control is that it allows data subjects to choose options that best correspond to their wishes about how their data are collected and processed. The fact that the mechanism of control is embedded in the data protection law framework where a set of rights and obligations guarantees a high level of data protection implies, however, that the choice left for individuals is between legally and morally sound alternatives. Competition law, on the other hand, protects the freedom of choice in general, irrespective of what that choice turns out to deliver. In other words, competition law ensures that there is market choice, but does

40 Maurice E Stucke, 'When More Is Better and When Less Is More: Behavioural Antitrust and Choice' in Nihoul, Charbit and Ramundo (n 27) 302.

41 ibid.

42 Nihoul (n 27) 68.

43 Averitt and Lande (n 35) 44.

44 Robert H Lande, 'Consumer Choice as the Best Way to Re-Center the Mission of Competition Law' in Nihoul, Charbit, and Ramundo (n 27) 155.

not prescribe how beneficial or attractive the available alternatives should be: what plays a key role is that available options are perceived as welfare-enhancing by individuals. Overall, despite this divergence, the same twin logic behind the notions of control and choice is individual sovereignty of data subjects and consumers. Hence, if one field of law succeeds in strengthening it, the other one will unavoidably benefit.

3. Ensuring fairness

Fairness is another concept that continues to shape the discourse about conceptual underpinnings of data protection and competition law in the EU, and is mentioned explicitly in the provisions of both legal fields. Given its vagueness and open-endedness, however, a conceptual analysis of fairness in both areas of the law is crucial before reaching a conclusion on how unifying the concept of fairness actually is.

In data protection law, fairness can be discussed together with the idea of control: both are framed as alternative goals of data protection. Hijmans stressed, however, a lack of clarity in this area, inquiring whether the right to data protection is 'a claim based on fairness, providing safeguards when personal data are processed' or whether it serves the objective of enhancing control.[45] Relying on a similar bifurcation, Kranenborg challenged the narrow goal of promoting informational self-determination and advocated a more comprehensive view, construed in terms of fairness.[46] Fairness frames a vision of EU data protection rules constituting an 'elaborated and conclusive system of checks and balances which ensures lawful processing of personal data'.[47] Similarly, others have claimed that although informational self-determination can be described as a value underpinning data protection as a distinct right, the GDPR's prerogative as a secondary legal framework is more expansive.[48] Fairness is, in fact, a notion that pervades the entire data protection framework: according to Clifford and Ausloos, it is 'easier to distinguish where the notion of fairness in the GDPR is not specifically engaged as opposed to highlighting its more specific appearances'.[49] When defined so broadly, fairness also supports and reflects other objectives of data protection law, such as preventing power asymmetries and striking the right balance between the rights and interests of data subjects and data controllers, which the checks and balances

[45] Hielke Hijmans, *The European Union as Guardian of Internet Privacy: The Story of Art 16 TFEU* (Springer 2018) 54–55.

[46] Herke Kranenborg, 'Commentary on Article 8' in Steve Peers and others (eds), *The EU Charter of Fundamental Rights: A Commentary* (Hart Publishing 2014) 229.

[47] ibid.

[48] Damian Clifford and Jeff Ausloos, 'Data Protection and the Role of Fairness' (2018) 37 Yearbook of European Law 130, 152.

[49] ibid 159.

also promote. The same view was adopted by Hustinx, who also referred to the system of checks and balances and noted that the right to data protection is intended to guarantee a broader structural protection of individuals.[50] While fairness can thus be considered a principle with a more expansive reach as compared to control, there are considerations that in data protection law coexist with fairness and constitute values in their own right, for example human dignity.[51]

Apart from featuring in the general discussions on data protection's underlying premises, fairness figures explicitly in other legal instruments of the Union. Fairness is enshrined in Article 8 of the EU Charter, which states that personal data 'must be processed *fairly* for specified purposes and on the basis of the consent of the person concerned or some other legitimate basis laid down by law, as well as in the secondary legislation'.[52] The GDPR features fairness of data processing as one of its basic principles referred to in Article 5(1)(a), stating, similar to the EU Charter, that data shall be 'processed lawfully, *fairly* and in a transparent manner in relation to the data subject'.[53] The analysis of these specific legal provisions reveals that the two primary expressions of fairness relate to the requirement of transparency and fair balancing of competing rights, freedoms, and interests:[54] while fairness has an 'explicit' expression in the requirement of fair and transparent processing, it is 'implicit' in the need to achieve a fair balance.[55] This narrowing of fairness to concrete and tangible points of expression—transparency and the balancing of interests—helps to mitigate the concept's ambiguity. It needs to be stressed, however, that other definitions such as good administrative procedures (ie burden of care and timeliness)[56] can also be ascribed to the value of fairness.

Fairness has recently also re-emerged as a notion inherent in competition law.[57] While the idea of fairness has always existed in competition law, albeit in a less

[50] Peter Hustinx, 'EU Data Protection Law: The Review of Directive 95/46/EC and the Proposed General Data Protection Regulation' (2014) <https://edps.europa.eu/data-protection/our-work/publications/speeches-articles/eu-data-protection-law-review-directive_en> accessed 25 October 2021.

[51] The inviolable right to human dignity is explicitly enshrined in both the EU Charter as well as in the 1948 Universal Declaration of Human Rights. Floridi noted that 'human dignity is the fundamental concept that provides the framework within which one needs to interpret what the GDPR—and more generally European culture and jurisdiction—understand by informational privacy'. To operationalize it, however, one would need to explain 'what human dignity may mean in the twenty-first century': Luciano Floridi, 'On Human Dignity as a Foundation for the Right to Privacy' (2016) 29 Philosophy & Technology 307, 307–08. On various dimensions of dignity in the context of data processing, see eg Anne de Hingh, 'Some Reflections on Dignity as an Alternative Legal Concept in Data Protection Regulation' (2018) 19 German Law Journal 1269.

[52] Emphasis added.

[53] Emphasis added.

[54] Inge Graef, Damian Clifford, and Peggy Valcke, 'Fairness and Enforcement: Bridging Competition, Data Protection, and Consumer Law' (2018) 8 International Data Privacy Law 200, 203–04.

[55] Clifford and Ausloos (n 48) 138–41.

[56] ibid 163. This account of procedural fairness is an indirect manifestation of the right to good administration enshrined in art 41 of the EU Charter.

[57] See eg Damien Gerard, Assimakis Komninos, and Denis Waelbroeck (eds), *Fairness in EU Competition Policy: Significance and Implications. An Inquiry Into the Soul and Spirit of Competition Enforcement in Europe* (Bruylant 2020).

explicit form, it is only in the past few years that fairness has started visibly to underpin the competition enforcement discourse and guide cases in the EU and its Member States.[58] Largely credited for reinvigorating fairness and spurring a renewed interest in the idea of fair markets is Vice-President Vestager,[59] whose discourse is characterized by '[t]he steady crescendo of references to "fairness" '.[60] In one of her speeches, she maintained that the role of fairness in competition law represents 'one of the most fundamental questions in our work', namely '[w]hat, exactly, is competition policy for?'[61]

In competition law, fairness can be discussed from a substantive and a procedural viewpoint.[62] From a substantive perspective, which is more relevant for the present discussion, fairness figures as an objective of competition law. It is, however, rarely in a stand-alone role and its contents are not well defined. Fairness can in fact be found in varying legal occurrences, with potentially 'different meanings in different contexts'.[63] For example, Ahlborn and Padilla claimed that 'fairness goals' include 'fairness, the protection of economic freedom, the protection of rivalry and the competitive process and the protection of small and medium-size firms'.[64] Behrans noted that fairness may encompass values as different as equality of opportunities and a fair distribution of outputs or of capabilities.[65] Fairness can also be linked to welfare economics as a factor in the concerns of distributive justice, forming a consideration within the Social Welfare Function.[66] According to Nazzini, fairness in competition law should be understood as having a formal function.[67] In this sense, fairness relates to the process in which all market participants are given 'equal opportunities to benefit from the market'.[68] Yet, he also concluded that a free-standing concept of fairness cannot entirely define anti-competitive behaviour and that further criteria need to be identified.[69]

[58] Damien Gerard, 'Fairness in EU Competition Policy: Significance and Implications' (2018) 9 Journal of European Competition Law & Practice 211, 211.

[59] ibid.

[60] Lewis Crofts, 'Vestager's "Fairness" Mantra Rattles through EU Competition Law' *Mlex* (15 November 2016) <https://mlexmarketinsight.com/news-hub/editors-picks/area-of-expertise/antitrust/vestagers-fairness-mantra-rattles-through-eu-competition-law> accessed 4 November 2021.

[61] Margrethe Vestager, 'Fairness and Competition' (GCLC Annual Conference, Brussels, 25 January 2018).

[62] Laura Parret, 'The Multiple Personalities of EU Competition Law: Time for a Comprehensive Debate on Its Objectives' in Daniel Zimmer (ed), *The Goals of Competition Law* (Edward Elgar 2012) 74.

[63] Roberto Nazzini, *Normative Theory of Competition Law* (OUP 2011) 21.

[64] Christian Ahlborn and Jorge Padilla, 'From Fairness to Welfare: Implications for the Assessment of Unilateral Conduct under EC Competition Law' in Claus-Dieter Ehlermann and Mel Marquis (eds), *European Competition Law Annual 2007: A Reformed Approach to Article 82 EC* (Hart Publishing 2008) 61–62.

[65] Ioannis Lianos, 'Some Reflections on the Question of the Goals of EU Competition Law' (2013) CLES Working Paper Series No 3/2013, 31.

[66] See Matthew D Adler and Chris William Sanchirico, 'Inequality and Uncertainty: Theory and Legal Applications' (2006) 155 University of Pennsylvania Law Review 279; Matthew D Adler, 'Future Generations: A Prioritarian View' (2009) 77 George Washington Law Review 1478.

[67] Nazzini (n 63) 22.

[68] ibid 24.

[69] ibid. See also Massimo Motta, *Competition Policy: Theory and Practice* (CUP 2004) 26.

Besides referring to the process of competition, the second dimension of the fairness concept—and one that is more relevant in the context of data-related harms—is fairness towards consumers.[70] Along these lines, Gerber conceptualized fairness as a two-dimensional notion that encompasses horizontal and vertical aspects,[71] the latter implying fairness towards trading partners or final consumers.[72] Parret made a similar observation: '[f]airness can come in when competition law protects competitors, the customers or the consumers'.[73] The expression of the vertical dimension of fairness is encapsulated in Article 102(a) TFEU,[74] which expressly refers to fairness. As outlined in the previous chapter, exploitative behaviour entails causing direct harm to consumers, as distinct from exclusionary conduct through which companies intend to exclude rivals.

Despite the explicit reference to fairness towards consumers in Article 102(a) TFEU, its conceptualization and the debate on the factors that need to be evaluated to determine behaviour as fair or unfair is underdeveloped, or at least unsystematic.[75] Abuses that harm consumers directly have until very recently received limited attention in EU competition law, as is apparent from the scarcity of cases. The previously mentioned speech on exploitative abuses given by Vice-President Vestager in November 2016, as well as her frequent references to the notion of fairness, constitute an important evolution in this respect. While competition authorities protect consumers indirectly by keeping market structures competitive, the Commissioner highlighted that they are also 'bound to come across cases ... where dominant businesses are exploiting their customers, by charging excessive prices or imposing unfair terms'.[76]

In past years, the prohibition of unfair conduct towards consumers has surfaced in particular in discussions on the application of competition law to unilateral conduct involving personal data. As a granular analysis of the notion of fairness in the data-related context is presented in Chapter 4 Section C, it suffices to say here that the notion of fairness in competition law can embrace a variety of data protection concerns and harms ranging from non-transparent, misleading, or deceptive data practices to the lack of proportionality and necessity as applied to data processing. Fair data processing and the competition law notion of fairness might therefore converge in multiple various ways and instances.

[70] Motta, ibid 24.

[71] David J Gerber, 'Fairness in Competition Law: European and U.S. Experience' (Conference on Fairness and Asian Competition Laws, Kyoto, March 2004) 2.

[72] Pinar Akman, *The Concept of Abuse in EU Competition Law* (Hart Publishing 2012) 149.

[73] Parret (n 62) 74.

[74] For a similar focus on art 102 in the context of discussing the objectives of EU competition law, see eg Lianos (n 65).

[75] Akman (n 72) 146.

[76] Margrethe Vestager, 'Protecting Consumers from Exploitation' (Chillin' Competition Law Conference, Brussels, 21 November 2016).

4. Mitigating power asymmetries

Both data protection and competition law have a role to play in preventing and mitigating possible exploitation of vulnerabilities—or simply the weaker status of the individual in market transactions—by those who enjoy and take advantage of asymmetrical powers. As Cole noted, there has recently been a 'dawning realisation that privacy is ultimately about power—in myriad forms and ways'.[77] The same concern preoccupies competition law, whose task is to oversee how concentrations of private power impact competitive processes and, ultimately, individuals.

From a data protection perspective, power asymmetries may have tangible impacts on users' ability to control their information. Asymmetries might also give rise to a sense of powerlessness vis-à-vis data users, causing an intangible harm of feeling helpless and uneasy.[78] The GDPR stipulates a number of mechanisms to shift the balance of power. For example, by requiring data controllers to obtain a legal basis for data processing and to respect other data protection safeguards, including the provision of information about the processing activity, data protection law regulates data power by requiring its holders to comply with specific legal obligations. Power imbalances play an explicit role is individuals' consent, for example, which, as the GDPR explains, is not freely given and therefore not valid where 'there is a clear imbalance between the data subject and the data controller'.[79] As Lynskey observed, power asymmetries are reduced through an opt-in as a default mechanism.[80] Indeed, the GDPR clarifies that consent is legally valid if data subjects express their wishes 'by a statement or by a clear affirmative action'.[81]

Individual rights can also be a tool to mitigate power asymmetries. For example, the right of access (art 15 GDPR) enables individuals to obtain a range of information about the processing of their data. The rights to the rectification of inaccurate data (art 16) and the erasure of data (art 17) serve the purpose of enhancing an individual's control vis-à-vis powerful actors. The same aim underlies other rights, such the right to data portability (art 20) and the right to object to data processing (art 21), including profiling. Collectively, this set of rights, if exercised effectively, has the potential to tilt the balance of power towards individuals.

Data protection laws in various jurisdictions also provide more explicit protections of vulnerable categories of individuals, in particular children who have a lower awareness of risks, safeguards, as well as their rights in the context of data processing.[82] Article 8 GDPR, for example, requires that where the provision of a digital service to a child is based on consent, parental consent in required when the

[77] Ryan Cole, 'Privacy, Vulnerability, and Affordance' (2017) 66 DePaul Law Review 591, 601.
[78] Orla Lynskey, *The Foundations of EU Data Protection Law* (OUP 2015) 211.
[79] GDPR, recital 43.
[80] Lynskey (n 78) 214.
[81] GDPR, art 4(11).
[82] ibid recital 38.

child is below the age of 16 years. In addition to specifically singling out vulnerable categories, data protection law also regulates the processing of sensitive data and data processing in contexts that might expose individuals to power imbalances. Indeed, not only specific categories of individuals might be more vulnerable as compared to others, but there might also be situations that can expose vulnerabilities. In this sense, vulnerability is not a fixed status, but rather a position in which individuals might find themselves.[83] The GDPR captures this idea by regulating the processing of 'special categories of personal data'.[84] According to Article 9(1) GDPR, processing of data that reveal, for example, racial or ethnic origins, political opinions, and religious beliefs, as well as the processing of genetic, biometric, and health data, or data related to a person's sex life or sexual orientation, is prohibited, unless one of the conditions stipulated in Article 9(2) GDPR applies (eg data subject has given explicit consent). As the GDPR's recital 51 explains, such data are 'by their nature, particularly sensitive in relation to fundamental rights and freedoms' and 'merit specific protection as the context of their processing could create significant risks to the fundamental rights and freedoms'.[85] Besides substantively regulating the processing of specific categories of data, the GDPR also requires in such contexts the designation of a data protection officer[86] and conducting a data protection impact assessment.[87]

Acknowledging the risks related to certain technologies, in particular algorithms, and the power imbalances they might help to instigate, the GDPR also aims to mitigate vulnerabilities by protecting data that are processed through specific means. With some exceptions, individuals should, according to Article 22 GDPR, 'have the right not to be subject to a decision based solely on automated processing, including profiling, which produces legal effects concerning him or her or similarly affects him or her'. Risks resulting from algorithm-enabled power asymmetries, which without protection might leave individuals defenceless, include discrimination in recruitment contexts (e-recruiting practices) or an automatic refusal of an online credit application.[88]

Power over markets, and indirectly over individuals who participate in market transactions, is also central to competition law. Although in the majority of jurisdictions competition law does not prohibit the possession of power per se, powerful undertakings have a 'special responsibility' not to abuse it to the detriment of competition and consumers.[89]

[83] See eg Gianclaudio Malgieri and Jędrzej Niklas, 'Vulnerable Data Subjects' (2020) 37 Computer Law & Security Review 1, 7.

[84] For a detailed discussion of sensitive data in EU data protection law, see eg Paul Quinn and Gianclaudio Malgieri, 'The Difficulty of Defining Sensitive Data—The Concept of Sensitive Data in the EU Data Protection Framework' (2022) 22 German Law Journal 1538.

[85] GDPR, recital 51.

[86] ibid art 37(1)(c).

[87] ibid art 35(3)(b).

[88] ibid recital 71.

[89] *Michelin* (n 32) para 57.

In the wake of the emergence of powerful technology firms, few jurisdictions have introduced new concepts to more accurately handle the economic power of some of these businesses, and effectively address the harm resulting from power asymmetries. In December 2020, the Commission proposed a new regulatory instrument, the DMA, to regulate the conduct of powerful digital 'gatekeepers'. As it explained in the proposal for a DMA, '[a] few large platforms increasingly act as gateways or gatekeepers between business users and end users and enjoy an entrenched and durable position'.[90] The need for intensified legal oversight of powerful companies also underlies the new Section 19a of the German Competition Act (GWB).[91] It was introduced in January 2021 as part of a major overhaul of German competition law (the tenth amendment) and includes a new set of rules targeting abusive conduct by 'undertakings with paramount significance for competition across markets' (UPSCAM). A company might be qualified as an UPSCAM if it has a dominant position on one or several markets, financial strength or access to important resources or data relevant for competition, is vertically integrated and active on related markets, or its activities are relevant for third parties. Although the new rules do not explicitly target digital companies, Amazon, Apple, Google, and Meta are the companies that the German competition authority has thus far qualified as UPSCAM. Once a company is qualified as an UPSCAM, it needs to comply with substantive obligations indicated in Section 19a(2) GWB. For example, an UPSCAM cannot make the use of its services conditional on individuals agreeing to the processing of data from other services of the provider or a third-party provider without giving users sufficient choice regarding whether, how, and for what purpose such data are processed.

In competition law, power is also a factor in conducting a substantive analysis of merger transactions. Under the EUMR, the Commission needs to assess whether a concentration poses a significant impediment to effective competition. Recital 26 of the EUMR explicitly states that an impediment can be caused by the creation or strengthening of a dominant position, which results from acquiring power over a certain market.

Data protection and competition law thus converge in their endeavour to minimize asymmetries in power relations between power holders and non-holders. As Costa-Cabral and Lynskey rightly put it, 'when undertakings maintain or reinforce their position *vis-à-vis* individuals in one field of law, this may have consequences for the other: less control over personal data may result in (more) market power, and market power may allow undertakings to impose unfair data processing conditions on individuals'.[92]

[90] European Commission, 'Proposal for a Regulation of the European Parliament and of the Council on contestable and fair markets in the digital sector (Digital Markets Act)', COM (2020)842 final, 1 (hereafter: Proposal for a DMA).

[91] Gesetz gegen Wettbewerbsbeschränkungen.

[92] Costa-Cabral and Lynskey (n 5) 22.

5. Improving transparency and mitigating information asymmetries

Besides interacting in their common effort to rebalance power relationships between individuals and businesses, data protection and competition law also share a concern for lack of transparency and resulting information asymmetries. Although information asymmetries and power asymmetries do not represent the same challenge, they are in a close relationship as the former might contribute to the latter.

Following the A29WP, transparency can be understood in terms of 'engendering trust in the processes which affect the citizen by enabling them to understand, and if necessary, challenge those processes'.[93] In the context of personal data, insufficient information about data collection and processing disadvantages individuals, impinges on their right to data protection, and tilts the balance of power towards online businesses.[94] As opposed to power asymmetries, which data protection law only 'governs', information asymmetries are expected to be fully 'addressed' through transparency and information provision requirements.[95] Transparency of data processing is, next to lawfulness and fairness, one of the core overarching principles embraced in Article 5(1)(a) GDPR. Recital 39 of the GDPR notes that 'it should be transparent to natural persons that personal data concerning them are collected, used, consulted or otherwise processed' as this—at least in theory—empowers individuals to exercise control and hold those who collect and process their data accountable.[96]

On a more granular level, data protection law features several provisions that prescribe the quality and content of information obligations: as the AWP29 observed, they aim to realize the concept of transparency that as such is user-centric rather than legalistic.[97] To this end, Articles 13 and 14 GDPR, for example, contain a detailed list of information to be provided by controllers where they collect personal data from individuals directly, and where data is collected from third parties (eg the identity and the contact details of the controller, the purposes of the processing, the legitimate interests of the controller, the recipients of data). As well as the type of information to be communicated, the GDPR also stipulates the quality of information and communication: in line with Article 12 GDPR, they have to be concise and transparent, intelligible, as well as easily accessible.

Providing individuals with market-related information also benefits competition.[98] The theory of perfect competition is premised on the need to ensure

[93] A29WP, 'Guidelines on Transparency under Regulation 2016/679' (2017) 4.

[94] ibid.

[95] Angela Daly, 'Private Power, Online Information Flows and EU Law: Mind the Gap' (Hart Publishing 2016).

[96] A29WP (n 93) 5.

[97] ibid.

[98] Philippe Gugler, 'Transparency and Competition Policy in an Imperfectly Competitive World' in Jens Forssbæck and Lars Oxelheim (eds), *The Oxford Handbook of Economic and Institutional Transparency* (OUP 2015) 144.

market transparency, which entails that buyers and sellers have sufficient information about market conditions, such as changes in demand, product attributes and price. Lack of transparency may, from a competition point of view, even be considered as a market failure.[99] Given that information asymmetries, in particular when combined with economic concentration, might make it impossible for users to express their genuine preferences,[100] competition processes might be impaired in non-transparent market contexts. As Stiglitz noted, '[i]mperfect information concerning quality can result in important barriers to competition'.[101]

Ensuring that individuals are equipped with sufficient information to meaningfully express their preferences is thus equally relevant in the context of data protection and competition. Although uniting on a broader level, data protection and competition law diverge as regards what they are able to do to address information asymmetries. While a lack of transparency or insufficient information can amount to a legal offence under the GDPR, it is less likely that competition law can be invoked to address this market failure. Instead, the preference from a competition viewpoint is to rely on other laws and regulations—including data protection law—to create the market conditions necessary for individuals to exercise informed choices. Thus, competition law can be expected to be only passively concerned with possible instances of non-transparent data processing and information asymmetries.

C. The triple challenge

Complementing the previous analysis of the values and objectives shared by data protection and competition law, this section aims to demonstrate how these premises are challenged by the novel features of digital markets and the dynamics prevailing therein. It thus explores the other side of the coin, one that zeros in on the empirical reality. The welfare of individuals, choice, control, fairness, and power and information asymmetries related to power are all affected by how firms interact with personal data, use their economic power, and implement new technologies. The subsequent sections are thus clustered around the following themes to present the triple challenge: (1) 'datafication' of the economy and society; (2) lack of competitive dynamism; and (3) technological innovations and new ways of interacting with technologies.

[99] ibid.

[100] Filippo Lancieri, 'Narrowing Data Protection's Enforcement Gap' (2022) 74 Maine Law Review 15, 28.

[101] Joseph E Stiglitz, 'Towards a Broader View of Competition Policy' in Tembinkosi Bonakele, Eleanor M Fox, and Liberty Mncube (eds), *Competition Policy for the New Era. Insights from the BRICS Countries* (OUP 2017) 11.

1. 'Datafication' of the economy and society

Data is of central importance for undertakings operating in digital markets, including search engines, social networks, and other technology companies that rely on data to finance or improve their services. 'Datafication',[102] 'surveillance capitalism',[103] and 'data power'[104] are among the concepts that have been coined in the past years to better grasp the modern data-driven economic and social reality. While the phenomenon of datafication has multiple noteworthy facets, this section highlights its most salient expressions and repercussions, namely the race for a data advantage, the ubiquity of data-based and data-supported business models, as well as opacity and lack of transparency.

1.1 The race for a data advantage

There are multiple ways in which firms collect personal data: the methods used depend on factors such as the business model, the type of services provided, internal structure, and market power.[105] The subsequent two sections expand on two noteworthy and related methods of data collection, namely data tracking and inference analytics. While the former captures a common fixture of the contemporary online world, the latter refers to a technique popularized recently thanks to the advancement of machine learning (ML).

1.1.1 Data tracking

On a modern web, a commonplace method for gathering detailed insights into individuals' behaviour is online tracking. The World Wide Web Consortium defined tracking as 'the collection of data regarding a particular user's activity across multiple distinct contexts and the retention, use, or sharing of data derived from that activity outside the context in which occurred'.[106] Online tracking originated in the 1990s, when a key tracking technology—the HTTP cookie (a text file with

[102] Kenneth Cukier and Viktor Mayer-Schönberger, 'The Rise of Big Data: How It's Changing the Way We Think About the World' (2013) 92 Foreign Affairs 28. 'Datafication' can be defined as 'the process by which subjects, objects, and practices are transformed into digital data': Clare Southerton, 'Datafication' in Laurie A Schintler and Connie L McNeely (eds), *Encyclopedia of Big Data* (Springer 2020).

[103] Shoshana Zuboff, *The Age of Surveillance Capitalism: The Fight for a Human Future at the New Frontier of Power* (PublicAffairs 2019). Zuboff defined surveillance capitalism 'as the unilateral claiming of private human experience as free raw material for translation into behavioural data': John Laidler, 'High Tech Is Watching You' *The Harvard Gazette* (4 March 2019) <https://news.harvard.edu/gazette/story/2019/03/harvard-professor-says-surveillance-capitalism-is-undermining-democracy/> accessed 15 February 2022.

[104] Orla Lynskey, 'Grappling with "Data Power": Normative Nudges from Data Protection and Privacy' (2019) 20 Theoretical Inquiries in Law 189.

[105] The basic taxonomy that categorizes data according to the manner in which they originate distinguishes between four categories: provided, observed, derived, and inferred. See eg OECD, 'Protecting Privacy in a Data-Driven Economy: Taking Stock of Current Thinking' (2014) Summary of the OECD Privacy Roundtable DSTI/ICCP/REG(2014)3.

[106] W3C Working Group, 'Tracking Preference Expression (DNT)' (2019) < https://www.w3.org/TR/tracking-dnt/> accessed 15 February 2022.

small pieces of information such as a username or password)—was invented.[107] While a cookie was envisioned as a simple technology stored by a domain (a website) to remember basic information, the arrival of online advertising affected the way cookie technology developed, resulting in the emergence of 'third-party tracking'.[108] Introduced in the early 2000, programmatic advertising (see Section 1.2.1) marked yet another development in the evolution of tracking, namely the 'flourishing of new intermediaries for tracking, to meet the demand of advertisers to know more about the users whose attention they were paying to reach'.[109] Thus, creating ever-more detailed profiles of individuals became the principal aim of many intermediaries in the advertising sector.

As opposed to first-party tracking enabled by cookies stored directly by the visited website ('first-party cookies'), third-party tracking is performed by an entity other than the visited website (eg trackers such as ad networks embedded in the majority of web pages), and consists in following users across the web through placing third-party cookies.[110] Tracking across websites, also described as 'web-wide tracking',[111] enables the creation of detailed profiles of individuals that might include various information, for example ethnicity, socio-economic class, or political opinions. The common reasons for data tracking invoked by platforms such as Meta or Google is to offer personalized experiences.[112] Dubious purposes for which data tracking is exploited—personalized political advertising exposed in the Cambridge Analytica scandal being one example—show a darker side of the data tracking economy. A host of other ethical repercussions of data tracking that relate to bias, raced and gender discrimination, socio-economic inequality, or identity articulation are increasingly documented phenomena that occur across the contemporary web.

Third-party tracking has over the past years garnered much attention, primarily for reasons of its prevalence and harmful effects for individuals. According to the 2018 study of almost one million free apps in the mobile ecosystem, over 90 per cent of all apps included at least one tracker, and almost 18 per cent more than twenty.[113] To capture the power dynamics in this complex environment, scholars

[107] 'What are Cookies?' *Kaspersky* <https://www.kaspersky.com/resource-center/definitions/cookies> accessed 4 May 2022.

[108] Reuben Binns, 'Tracking on the Web, Mobile and the Internet-of-Things' (2022) 8 Foundations and Trends in Web Science 1, 6–7.

[109] ibid 8.

[110] W3C Working Group, 'Tracking Compliance and Scope' (2019) <https://www.w3.org/TR/tracking-compliance/> accessed 15 February 2022. A distinction between explicit tracking and inferred tracking is described in eg Michael Veale and Frederik J Zuiderveen Borgesius, 'Adtech and Real-Time Bidding under European Data Protection Law' (2022) 23 German Law Journal 226, 227–31.

[111] Frederik J Zuiderveen Borgesius and others, 'Tracking Walls, Take-It-Or-Leave-It Choices, the GDPR, and the EPrivacy Regulation' (2018) 3 European Data Protection Law Review 353, 354.

[112] Tanya Kant, 'A History of the Data-Tracked User' (*The MIT Press Reader*, 8 October 2021) <https://thereader.mitpress.mit.edu/a-history-of-the-data-tracked-user/> accessed 16 February 2022.

[113] Reuben Binns and others, 'Third Party Tracking in the Mobile Ecosystem' (10th ACM Conference on Web Science, Amsterdam, May 2018) 3.

compared trackers to tree branches that reach distinct corners of the online landscape.[114] However, when one follows the trackers from their branches to their roots, it turns out that only a few companies own these trackers and dominate the market.[115] In their 2016 study, Englehardt and Narayanan conducted an analysis of online tracking on the top one million websites, concluding that the top five third parties present on the top one million sites are Google-owned domains (ie google-analytics.com, gstatic.com, doubleclick.net).[116] In addition, 'Google, Facebook, Twitter, and AdNexus are the only third-party entities present on more than 10% of sites'.[117] For companies with the highest third-party presence, Google has the top position, followed by Facebook, Twitter, and Amazon.[118] The power dynamics are similar in the apps ecosystem, where Alphabet is the most prevalent root parent tracking company with trackers present on 88.44 per cent of nearly one million analysed apps, followed by Meta (42.55 per cent), Twitter (33.88 per cent), and Verizon (26.27 per cent).[119]

The pervasiveness of online tracking, dubious data collection and processing practices, as well as asymmetrical power structures in the tracking ecosystem, challenge both data protection and competition in numerous ways. From a data protection perspective, concerning strategies include take-it-or-leave-it choices, also known as 'tracking walls' or 'cookie walls', which imply that users cannot visit a certain website if they do not consent to web-wide tracking, thus impairing their autonomy. The omnipresence of data tracking, the lack of transparency regarding the amount and type of data collected, as well as the questionable purposes for which data are collected are among salient concerns. From a competition standpoint, the fact that the market is dominated by a couple of large market players with entrenched power risks reinforcing the current status quo of pervasive and opaque data tracking and limits market contestability, with potentially detrimental impacts on web users.

1.1.2 Inference analytics

In addition to observed data and data provided directly by individuals, inferences and predictions about users' unknown attributes or future behaviour are another source of information that data analytics can draw from available data points. Wachter and Mittelstadt noted that inferential analytics methods are employed to infer user preferences, their sensitive attributes such as race, gender, or sexual

[114] Ariel Ezrachi and Viktoria HSE Robertson, 'Competition, Market Power and Third-Party Tracking' (2019) 42 World Competition 5, 7.

[115] ibid.

[116] Steven Englehardt and Arvind Narayanan, 'Online Tracking: A 1-Million-Site Measurement and Analysis' (23rd ACM Conference on Computer and Communications Security, Vienna, October 2016) 8.

[117] ibid.

[118] ibid.

[119] Binns and others (n 113) 5.

orientation, and to predict their behaviour.[120] Inference analytics is already a method available to many businesses, including the most popular services. In 2018, a *Guardian* newspaper investigation conducted with the Danish Broadcasting Corporation found that Meta infers information such as homosexuality, Islamism, or liberalism, and allows advertisers to target users based on such inferred data without their consent.[121] Since 2017, Meta has in many countries been using machine learning to infer suicidal thoughts as part of its suicide prevention project,[122] allegedly without providing an option to opt out.[123]

Besides the invasive nature of inferring practices that often take place without data subjects' knowledge, consent, or understanding, what is also disturbing is the lack of certainty that those inferences are in fact accurate. In 2013, Tene and Polonetsky had already noted that in the Big Data world, 'what calls for scrutiny is often not the accuracy of the *raw data* but rather the accuracy of the *inferences* drawn from the data', as perfectly innocuous and accurate data may form the basis for inaccurate, manipulative, or discriminatory inferences.[124] Direct profiling of individuals,[125] which can be fully or partially based on inferences, might lead to misclassifying, misidentifying, or misjudging people, seriously and disproportionately affecting certain groups of individuals.[126] The precise mechanisms that make algorithmic inferences unjust or unfair are often a source of confusion.[127] As Hildebrandt has observed, 'inferences will be contingent on the input (the so-called training set) and on the computational techniques employed to detect the output (patterns, correlations, association rules or clusters in the data set), neither of which can be taken for granted'.[128]

[120] Sandra Wachter and Brent Daniel Mittelstadt, 'A Right to Reasonable Inferences: Re-Thinking Data Protection in the Age of Big Data and AI' (2019) 2019 Columbia Business Law Review 494, 497.

[121] Alex Hern, 'Facebook Lets Advertisers Target Users Based on Sensitive Interests' *The Guardian* (16 May 2018) <https://www.theguardian.com/technology/2018/may/16/facebook-lets-advertisers-target-users-based-on-sensitive-interests> accessed 16 February 2022.

[122] 'Suicide Prevention' *Facebook* <https://www.facebook.com/safety/wellbeing/suicideprevention> accessed 16 February 2022.

[123] Josh Constine, 'Facebook Rolls out AI to Detect Suicidal Posts before They're Reported' *Techcrunch* (27 November 2017) <https://techcrunch.com/2017/11/27/facebook-ai-suicide-prevention/?guccounter=1> accessed 13 February 2022.

[124] Omar Tene and Jules Polonetsky, 'Big Data for All: Privacy and User Control in the Age of Analytics' (2013) 11 Northwestern Journal of Technology and Intellectual Property 239, 270–71.

[125] While 'direct profiling' implies that the information derived from the data collected from a person or a group will be applied to the same person or the same group, 'indirect profiling' relies on data from a larger population to profile individual users. See eg David-Olivier Jaquet-Chiffelle, 'Direct and Indirect Profiling in the Light of Virtual Persons' in Mireille Hildebrandt and Serge Gutwirth (eds), *Profiling the European Citizen: Cross-Disciplinary Perspective* (Springer 2008).

[126] Frederike Kaltheuner and Elettra Bietti, 'Data Is Power: Towards Additional Guidance on Profiling and Automated Decision-Making in the GDPR' (2018) 2 Journal of Information Rights, Policy and Practice 1, 9.

[127] Solon Barocas and Andrew D Selbst, 'Big Data's Disparate Impact' (2016) 104 California Law Review 671, 677.

[128] Mireille Hildebrandt, 'Law as Information in the Era of Data-Driven Agency' (2016) 79 Modern Law Review 1, 24.

From a data protection perspective, challenges posed by inference analytics are manifold, ranging from bringing inferred data within the scope of data protection law to establishing a legal basis for data processing, from addressing opacity of such practices to empowering individuals and acting against (unreasonable) inferences.[129] Access to analytics technology and the ability to draw inferences can also entrench market power and raise barriers to entry for undertakings that are not able to conduct a similarly sophisticated analysis. Furthermore, if inferences are used by dominant firms to discriminate or otherwise harm individuals, consumer welfare in a competition sense can be at stake.

1.2 The ubiquity of data-based and data-supported business models

The race for a data advantage does not happen without a reason. The scale and scope of available data, combined with the rise of advanced data analytics, has moved data to the centre of many business models. Following Nguen and Paczos, a distinction can be made between 'data-enabled' and 'data-enhanced' models.[130] Search engines, social networks, online stores, and news media publishers are a few prominent examples of online undertakings whose existence is solely or to a very considerable extent supported by data. It is not within the scope of this section to discuss all data-enabled and data-enhanced business models. Instead, the section provides an insight into the business model that rests on the profiling of individuals and personalizing products and services: what ad to show, what content to recommend, what online experience to propose.[131] To offer a glimpse into data-based personalization, the two subsequent sections discuss personalized advertising and personalized online content and experiences.

1.2.1 Personalized advertising

In economic terms, the data-enabled business model employed by many online businesses from large companies such as Meta or Alphabet to small online news publishers can be defined as two- or multi-sided. The theory of two-sided markets was formulated in the seminal article by Rochet and Tirole.[132] Their definition

[129] For a discussion proposing a new right to reasonable inferences, see Wachter and Mittelstadt (n 120).

[130] David Nguyen and Marta Paczos, 'Measuring the Economic Value of Data and Cross-Border Data Flows: A Business Perspective' (2020) OECD Digital Economy Papers No 297, 10–12.

[131] For a definition of profiling, see art 4(4) GDPR. See also A29WP, 'Advice paper on essential elements of a definition and a provision on profiling within the EU General Data Protection Regulation' (2013) 2–3; Council of Europe, 'The Protection of Individuals with Regard to Automatic Processing of Personal Data in the Context of Profiling' (2010) Recommendation CM/Rec(2010)13 and Explanatory Memorandum, 9; Mireille Hildebrandt, 'Defining Profiling: A New Type of Knowledge?' in Hildebrandt and Gutwirth (n 125) 19.

[132] Jean-Charles Rochet and Jean Tirole, 'Platform Competition in Two-Sided Markets' (2003) 1 Journal of the European Economic Association 990. Other important contributions include Bernard Caillaud and Bruno Jullien, 'Chicken and Egg: Competition among Intermediation Service Providers' (2003) 34 RAND Journal of Economics 309; David S Evans, 'The Antitrust Economics of Multi-Sided Platform Markets' (2003) 20 Yale Journal on Regulation 325; Mark Armstrong, 'Competition in Two-Sided Markets' (2006) 37 RAND Journal of Economics 668.

provides that a 'market with network externalities is a two-sided market if platforms can effectively cross-subsidize between different categories of end users that are parties to a transaction',[133] for example between social media users and advertisers. The creation of benefits and the market structure is therefore based on positive indirect network effects, which emerge when 'the value obtained by one group of customers increases with the number of customers (or, generally, the demand) of the other group'.[134] From the viewpoint of companies, the price strategies in such two-sided settings can be characterized as being of a 'divide-and-conquer' nature, 'subsidizing the participation on one side (divide) and recovering the loss on the other side (conquer)'.[135]

As Koops noted, business models that generate revenue from data-based profiling and advertising are the most prominent two-sided strategies in the online context.[136] Born in 1993, online advertising has grown tremendously since that time, with ad spending amounting to $332 billion globally in 2020 and expected to reach $526.17 in 2024.[137] Display advertising and search advertising are the two main categories of online advertising.[138] The social media advertising segment, which accounts for the largest share of display advertising revenues, is dominated by Meta, which has around a 75–80 per cent market share in the US and Europe, while the leading service in the video advertising segment is Alphabet's YouTube.[139] Next to display advertising, search advertising (ie ads on a search engine results page), is the second main segment of online advertising worldwide, and Alphabet is a leading player both in Europe and in the US.[140]

Over the past years, the economic structures behind the advertising model have changed considerably, shifting from pre-negotiated contracts between publishers and advertisers to the rapid growth of personalized online advertising. While display advertisements were initially contextual, as of the late 2000s they have been increasingly paired with targeted audiences rather than content, marking a shift from contextual to behavioural advertising.[141] The latter, 'online behavioural

[133] Rochet and Tirole (n 132) 1018.

[134] Lapo Filistrucchi, Damien Geradin, and Eric van Damme, 'Identifying Two-Sided Markets' (2013) 36 World Competition 33, 37–38.

[135] Caillaud and Jullien (n 132) 310.

[136] Bert-Jaap Koops, 'The Trouble with European Data Protection Law' (2014) 4 International Data Privacy Law 250, 252.

[137] Ethan Cramer-Flood, 'Global Digital Ad Spending Update Q2 2020' *eMarketer* (6 July 2020) <https://www.emarketer.com/content/global-digital-ad-spending-update-q2-2020> accessed 17 February 2022.

[138] Another category is 'classified advertising': advertisers directly purchase an advertising space on a publisher's website. Niklas Fourberg and others, 'Online Advertising: The Impact of Targeted Advertising on Advertisers, Market Access and Consumer Choice', Study requested by the European Parliament Committee on the Internal Market and Consumer Protection (2021) 18.

[139] ibid 17.

[140] ibid 16.

[141] Damien Geradin, Dimitrios Katsifis, and Theano Karanikioti, 'Google as a de Facto Privacy Regulator: Analysing the Privacy Sandbox from an Antitrust Perspective' (2021) 17 European Competition Journal 617, 623.

advertising' (OBA), consists in 'monitoring people's online behaviour and using the collected information to show them targeted advertisements'.[142] As observed by Tambini, the shift towards the OBA model 'is not something that is happening at the margins: it is a massive structural change transforming media systems everywhere'.[143] The rationale behind moving to the OBA model is straightforward: to generate more ad-clicks by showing an ad to the right person at the right time. While some believe that behavioural is a more effective and profitable way of advertising as compared to contextual, this claim is increasingly contested.[144]

Besides transforming the ways of handling individuals' data, the transition towards OBA has also influenced the power structures in the online advertising market. Large incumbents with access to data benefited enormously from this transition: the online advertising market has turned into an Alphabet–Meta digital advertising duopoly, which captures a dominant share of the global online advertising spend.[145] As the French NCA observed in its 2018 opinion on data processing in online advertising, one of the 'clearest findings is the considerable economic weight of two stakeholders, both in absolute volume and growth share: Google and Facebook, which currently generate most of their revenue through the sale of advertising services (90%)'.[146] This is owed both to the fact that these two platforms provide the world's most popular services and, relatedly, to their superior position for harvesting data from both their proprietary services and third-party websites and applications.[147] The data collected by these two platforms offers a variety of targeting options, such as location, interest, and geolinguistic targeting.[148]

In addition to the shifts from traditional to online advertising, as well as from contextual to behavioural targeting, the mechanism of placing ads has also undergone a major transformation. The past years have witnessed a rise of 'programmatic advertising', which refers to the automatic, as opposed to more traditional, placement of targeted ads. The currently employed model of programmatic advertising is a complex and opaque system powered largely by auction-based methods such as real-time bidding, an online auction that allows real-time buying and selling of online ad impressions. Personal data is the bedrock of this model.

Online advertising made free online services possible and is the core enabler of the internet as we know it. Yet, the benefit of free services has not been

[142] Sophie Boerman, Sanne Kruikemeier, and Frederik J Zuiderveen Borgesius, 'Online Behavioural Advertising: A Literature Review and Research Agenda' (2017) 46 Journal of Advertising 363, 364.

[143] Damian Tambini, 'How advertising fuels fake news' (*LSE Media Policy Project* blog, 24 February 2017) <https://blogs.lse.ac.uk/medialse/2017/02/24/how-advertising-fuels-fake-news/> accessed 17 February 2022.

[144] See eg Zuiderveen Borgesius and others (n 111) 354.

[145] See e.g. Geradin, Katsifis, and Karanikioti (n 141) 627..

[146] Autorité de la concurrence, 'Opinion No. 18-A-03 of 6 March 2018 on Data Processing in the Online Advertising Sector' (2018) 7.

[147] ibid. See also Jianqing Chen and Jan Stallaert, 'An Economic Analysis of Online Advertising Using Behavioral Targeting' (2014) 38 Management Information Systems Quarterly 429.

[148] Autorité de la concurrence (n 146) 7.

without peril. As the ability of platforms to create detailed profiles of individuals has increased, so have the risks related to data protection, which are manifold and evident. In addition, the consolidation of power in the advertising sector and restricted competition renders it resistant to change.

1.2.2 Personalized online content and experience

As well as the transformative impact of data and new technologies on the advertising sector, data provides a unique opportunity to personalize online content with the aim of strengthening engagement and generating faster rates of revenue growth. Whether individuals go online to scroll through their social news feeds, buy a new pair of shoes, or look for news, their experience is inescapably shaped by personalization algorithms—a practice that has recently achieved a new level of granularity and scale. For example, Meta uses a sophisticated personalization software to curate the News Feed and determine for each individual, based on their interests and traits, the posts they see and in which order.[149] In the e-commerce context, a study of sixteen e-commerce websites in the US found that they all contain differences in the products shown to customers, which were based on their data such as a history of clicks or purchases.[150] Amazon was in another study reported to integrate recommendations into almost every phase of the purchasing process, from discovery of the product to finalization of the purchase.[151] Recommended and personalized content across Alphabet's services, such as Google Search or YouTube, is equally commonplace.

Personalization generates benefits for consumers, for example reduced transaction and information costs. On the other hand, as Vice-President Vestager noted, 'the risk is that we only see what these algorithms—and the companies using them—choose to show us' and 'the things that they hide might well not exist'.[152] While this alone is not proof that individuals exposed to personalized content are worse off, there is mounting evidence that such content and data-based nudging of users towards specific choices might have serious impacts on their autonomy, and on the economic and political spheres more broadly. In 2019, the final report on disinformation and 'fake news' published by the UK House of Commons presented evidence that personalized political messages that contained false information and were spread on the Meta platform influenced the Brexit referendum.[153] A study

[149] Will Oremus, 'Why Facebook Won't Let You Control Your Own News Feed' *The Washington Post* (15 November 2021) <https://www.washingtonpost.com/technology/2021/11/13/facebook-news-feed-algorithm-how-to-turn-it-off/> accessed 17 February 2022.

[150] Aniko Hannak and others, 'Measuring Price Discrimination and Steering on E-Commerce Web Sites' (ACM Internet Measurement Conference, Vancouver, November 2014).

[151] JP Mangalindan, 'Amazon's Recommendation Secret' *Fortune* (30 July 2012) <http://fortune.com/2012/07/30/amazons-recommendation-secret/> accessed 17 March 2022.

[152] Margrethe Vestager, 'When Technology Serves People' (Brain Bar event, Budapest, 1 June 2018).

[153] UK House of Commons, Digital, Culture, Media and Sport Committee, 'Disinformation and "Fake News": Final Report' (2019).

conducted in 2017 showed that personalization technology led to increased clicks on and time spent reading pro-attitudinal political content, and decreased the number of clicks on counter-attitudinal articles, providing empirical support for the claim that echo chambers and filter bubbles are noteworthy phenomena,[154] though there also exist studies that present evidence that challenges that claim.[155] As regards individuals' attitudes towards algorithmic personalization and the use of personal data online, the findings of a 2021 study focused on the US, Germany, and the UK showed that while people were willing to accept certain personalized services (eg relating to shopping or entertainment), they largely opposed the idea of being targeted in political campaigning and, in Germany and the UK, of having their news personalized.[156]

Looking through the lens of the market and consumers, an important repercussion of personalization is how it transforms the traditional mechanism of choice. The employment of personalization technologies often influences—if not indirectly imposes—market choices as to what news to read, what products to choose, or what content to engage with. Personalized recommendations often act as 'hidden persuaders'[157] that influence consumer behaviour and replace real choice with an illusion of choice. Scholars have compared them to a trap, having the purpose of 'hooking users', which is enabled by the fact that people have 'tendencies and compulsions that make them susceptible to persuasion and targets for capture'.[158]

What all this implies is a gradual move from 'revealed preferences' and 'consumer sovereignty'—the tenets of competition that assume the existence of market options and the ability to choose freely[159]—to 'inferred preferences' and 'consumer subordination'. At times, the only choice left might be to reject the imposed product or service all together. More broadly, this amounts to a steady transformation of social organization, a macro-level problem that according to Posner and Weyl has bizarrely received little attention in the artificial intelligence (AI) discourse, for example.[160] At some point, as they argued, '"market" may no longer seem to

[154] Ivan Dylko and others, 'The Dark Side of Technology: An Experimental Investigation of the Influence of Customizability Technology on Online Political Selective Exposure' (2017) 73 Computers in Human Behavior 181.

[155] See e.g. Tobias D Krafft, Michael Gamer, and Katharina A Zweig, 'What Did You See? A Study to Measure Personalization in Google's Search Engine' (2019) 8 EPJ Data Science 38; Vittoria Cozza and others, 'Experimental Measures of News Personalization in Google News' in Sven Casteleyn, Peter Dolog, and Cesare Pautasso (eds), *Current Trends in Web Engineering: ICWE 2016 International Workshops* (Springer 2016).

[156] Anastasia Kozyreva and others, 'Public Attitudes towards Algorithmic Personalization and Use of Personal Data Online: Evidence from Germany, Great Britain, and the United States' (2021) 8 Humanities and Social Sciences Communications 3.

[157] Sören Köcher and others, 'New Hidden Persuaders: An Investigation of Attribute-Level Anchoring Effects of Product Recommendations' (2019) 95 Journal of Retailing 24.

[158] Nick Seaver, 'Captivating Algorithms: Recommender Systems as Traps' (2018) 24 Journal of Material Culture 421, 425.

[159] Averitt and Lande (n 29) 716.

[160] Eric Posner and Glen E Weyl, *Radical Markets: Uprooting Capitalism and Democracy for a Just Society* (Princeton UP 2018) 287.

be the right word for economic organization, though central planning might not, either'.[161] In their view, 'vast corporations—islands of centralized planning in the ocean of the market economy—produce a significant amount of economic value by exploiting computational power'.[162]

Implications that the shift towards the type of organization with restricted market choice may have on competitive dynamics are profound. One is the exclusion of firms that produce desirable or new products, but which do not fit squarely with past consumer behaviour. Predictions, even if accurate, may also not always correspond to how an individual would behave in the market. In line with empirical studies of choice behaviour, individuals tend to be stochastic in their decision-making:[163] their preference orderings fluctuate randomly and are not constant over time.[164] Designing a technology that would reflect stochastic consumer nature and factor in alternating preferences seems like an impossible endeavour. The practice of substituting consumer market choices with imposed goods or services based on data-derived preferences may lead to growing 'an economic pie' for which there is simply insufficient appetite, negatively affecting consumer welfare.

A restricted ability to choose resulting from personalization can also be considered problematic for data protection if it involves automated decision-making. As the A29WP noted, to be prohibited under Article 22(1) GDPR, automatically generated decisions must have the potential to 'significantly affect the circumstances, behaviour or *choices* of individuals concerned'.[165] At the same time, it put forward other factors that should be scrutinized while assessing the significance of effects under Article 22(1). In relation to targeted advertising, for example, it mentioned factors such as 'the intrusiveness of the profiling process, including the tracking of individuals across different websites, devices and services; the expectations and wishes of the individual concerned; the way the advert is delivered; using knowledge of the vulnerabilities of the data subject targeted'.[166] Thus, merely offering customized products, services, and experiences is not expressly prohibited. Instead, this assessment must be context-dependent, and in case the business strategy significantly limits choice and involves disturbing or invasive techniques, as is often the case, it may prove problematic for data protection law.

In addition to limiting individuals' freedom to choose, personalization might also feature bias and lead to unfairness. It is by now well documented that

[161] ibid 293.

[162] ibid 287–88.

[163] See eg Daniel L McFadden, 'Revealed Stochastic Preference: A Synthesis' (2005) 26 Economic Theory 245.

[164] Bert Smeulders, Yves Crama, and Frits CR Spieksma, 'Revealed Preference Theory: An Algorithmic Outlook' (2019) 272 European Journal of Operational Research 803, 813.

[165] A29WP, 'Advice Paper on Essential Elements of a Definition and a Provision on Profiling within the EU General Data Protection Regulation' (2013) 21 (emphasis added).

[166] ibid 22.

algorithms are inescapably value-laden,[167] and their employment is likely to result in biased decisions and stereotyping.[168] Whereas the role of competition law in addressing these types of harms is yet to be explored, data protection law certainly belongs in the toolbox of legal instruments that can create a fairer algorithmic environment.

1.3 Opacity and lack of transparency

Digital markets often resemble a game of hide and seek: companies hide the information about what personal data they collect and how they process it, while online users and enforcers seeking this information have to put considerable effort into finding it. While sometimes the seekers' efforts are futile as the information is nowhere to be found, in other instances they have to search for it with the vision blurred by confusing legalese and vague formulations.

The benefits of pervasive data collection and intrusive processing seem to have triggered a realization among many undertakings that the lack of full transparency about their activities or opaque and vague ways of communicating them might be the way forward. It seems evident that fitness trackers would be less appealing to consumers if they knew that their biometric data might be used to raise their health insurance rates, or they might hesitate to search online for psychological help if they were aware that they would be profiled based on their mental illness.[169] Notice and choice—a commonly used transparency mechanism—is a transparency illusion rather than an effective tool to inform individuals. To a large extent, the ineffectiveness of privacy policies can be attributed to their design. Among the commonly acknowledged design failures are their complexity and intentional vagueness. Notices are also too long for individuals to read and understand. As recently reported, an average person in the US would need to spend almost 250 hours to properly read all the privacy notices of the online services she uses.[170] Commenting on the results of a special Eurobarometer survey on data protection published in 2019, Věra Jourová, EU Commissioner for Values and Transparency, noted that 'of 60% of Europeans who read their privacy statements, only 13% read them fully', adding that the reason for that is their length and complexity.[171] There

[167] Brent Daniel Mittelstadt and others, 'The Ethics of Algorithms: Mapping the Debate' (2016) 3 Big Data & Society 1, 1; Frank Pasquale, *The Black Box Society: The Secret Algorithms That Control Money and Information* (Harvard UP 2016) 38.

[168] Bart Schermer, 'Risks of Profiling and the Limits of Data Protection Law' in Bart Custers and others (eds), *Discrimination and Privacy in the Information Society. Data Mining and Profiling in Large Databases* (Springer 2013) 138–39.

[169] Katharine Kemp, 'Concealed Data Practices and Competition Law: Why Privacy Matters' (2020) 16 European Competition Journal 628, 637.

[170] Nicolas LePan, 'Visualizing the Length of the Fine Print, for 14 Popular Apps' *Visual Capitalist* (18 April 2020) <https://www.visualcapitalist.com/terms-of-service-visualizing-the-length-of-internet-agreements/> accessed 18 February 2022.

[171] European Commission, 'Data Protection Regulation One Year on: 73% of Europeans Have Heard of at Least One of Their Rights' (13 June 2019) IP/19/2956 <https://ec.europa.eu/commission/presscorner/detail/en/IP_19_2956> accessed 1 February 2022.

is an overall 'notice fatigue', making privacy policies largely meaningless to individuals.[172] In Australia, a Consumer Policy Research Centre reported that in 2020, 94 per cent of consumers said they do not read privacy policies or terms and conditions and, of those who do, 69 per cent accept the terms even though they do not feel comfortable with them.[173] This problem is further exacerbated by constrained interfaces on mobile devices, wearables and fitness trackers, and other Internet of Things (IoT) devices.[174]

As regards the apps environment, A29WP identified 'the lack of transparency and awareness of the types of processing an app may undertake combined with a lack of meaningful consent from end users' as a key data protection risk.[175] A recent study of data security and privacy policies of mobile apps for depression in the US revealed that the majority of 116 analysed apps retrieved from iTunes and Google Play did not provide sufficient information about how they handle data.[176] In fact, only 4 per cent of reviewed apps received a transparency score for their privacy policies that the study's authors deemed as acceptable, and 51 per cent of apps did not have a privacy policy at all.[177] Another study pointed to misconceptions of users of gaming apps as regards data collection and sharing, as well as their preferences to be better informed about data sharing.[178]

Problematic transparency practices have already given rise to a number of data protection decisions. In the first major decision following the entry into force of the GDPR, the French DPA found that Google's architecture for providing information to users, which included spreading such information across several documents, failed to meet the accessibility requirement laid down in Article 12 GDPR.[179] The clarity and intelligibility of information were equally impaired, in particular as Google implemented 'particularly extensive and intrusive' data processing that was not easy for individuals to grasp.[180] In addition, Google did not provide all information required by Article 13 GDPR, notably information about

[172] Florian Schaub and others, 'A Design Space for Effective Privacy Notices' (11th Symposium on Usable Privacy and Security, Ottawa, July 2015) 3.

[173] Consumer Policy Research Centre, 'Data and Technology Consumer Survey' (2020).

[174] Schaub and others (n 172) 1.

[175] A29WP, 'Opinion 02/2013 on Apps on Smart Devices' (2013) 6. A similar conclusion was reached by the US FCT: see Federal Trade Commission, 'Mobile Privacy Disclosures: Building Trust Through Transparency' (2013) Staff Report.

[176] Kristen O'Loughlin and others, 'Reviewing the Data Security and Privacy Policies of Mobile Apps for Depression' (2019) 15 Internet Interventions 110.

[177] Not all the analysed apps were collecting identifiable information. As the authors indicated, mobile apps collecting identifiable information were more likely to have a privacy policy (79 per cent) as compared to the apps collecting non-identifiable data (34 per cent).

[178] Rebecca Balebako and others, '"Little Brothers Watching You": Raising Awareness of Data Leaks on Smartphones' (9th Symposium on Usable Privacy and Security, Newcastle, July 2013).

[179] Commission Nationale de l'informatique et des Libertés, Délibération de la formation restreinte no SAN-2019-001 du 21 janvier 2019 concernant la société Google LLC, paras 96–103.

[180] ibid paras 104–28.

data retention periods.[181] The French Administrative Court dismissed Google's appeal and upheld the fine of €50 million.[182]

Similarly, in August 2021, the Irish Data Protection Commission (DPC) imposed a fine of €225 million on WhatsApp for failing to provide clear and sufficient information about its processing activities. In particular, the DPC found that WhatsApp's privacy policy was 'an abundant of text that, ultimately, communicated very little', and no information required by Article 13 GDPR had been provided.[183] The ambiguous and high-level language as well as the piecemeal fashion in which the information was presented were examples of concerning practices noted in the decision. Furthermore, the way in which WhatsApp provided the information—in multiple linked documents—failed to comply with the requirement of Article 12(1) GDPR to ensure an easily accessible format.[184]

Opacity and lack of transparency are also some of the concerning features of algorithmic decision-making. To illustrate this, Pasquale relied on a 'black box' metaphor: a black box represents both the secrecy of the system and the data monitoring and tracking experienced daily by consumers.[185] The strategies that enable companies to keep algorithms secret result in 'opacity', which Pasquale used as a blanket term for 'remedial incomprehensibility'.[186] Referring to the problem of opacity, Burrell also claimed that this is a feature at the heart of the currently emerging concerns about algorithms.[187] Opacity signals a lack of understanding by those subjected to algorithmic decision-making of how or why a specific decision is arrived at, but also the absence or incompleteness of information concerning the inputs used to generate that decision.[188] Algorithmic opacity is also likely to obstruct the rule of law and the adjudication of disputes relating to unjust decisions rendered by algorithms.[189] Such opacity could additionally frustrate the detection of harm caused by algorithms, identifying the cause of that harm, or tracing responsibility for the harm.[190] The problem, as Hildebrandt claimed, 'is not in the bias, but in hidden bias and in our inability to test the assumptions and the operations that nourish data-driven agency'.[191] In the EU, the Digital Services

[181] ibid paras 119–20.

[182] Conseil d'État 430810, lecture du 19 juin 2020, ECLI:FR:CECHR:2020:430810.20200619, Decision no 430810.

[183] Data Protection Commission, Decision of the Data Protection Commission Made Pursuant to Section 111 of the Data Protection Act, 2018 and Articles 60 and 65 of the General Data Protection Regulation in the matter of WhatsApp Ireland Ltd, Case IN-18-12-2 (20 August 2021) para 620.

[184] ibid para 337.

[185] Pasquale (n 167) 5.

[186] ibid 7.

[187] Jenna Burrell, 'How the Machine "Thinks": Understanding Opacity in Machine Learning Algorithms' (2016) 3 Big Data & Society 1, 1.

[188] ibid.

[189] Pasquale (n 167) 40.

[190] For a more general discussion on the ethics of algorithms, see e.g. Mittelstadt and others (n 167).

[191] Hildebrandt (n 131) 25.

Act (DSA)[192] that entered into force in November 2022 aims to offer a solution to the lack of algorithmic transparency by introducing rules on algorithmic audits. To support the enforcement of the new rules, in 2023 the Commission set up a European Centre for Algorithmic Transparency (ECAT).

Left unaddressed, the opacity surrounding data-related practices and algorithmic decision-making has negative repercussions for both data protection and competition. Processing personal data in ways that individuals do not comprehend and over which they have no control is an obvious concern for data protection.[193] Opaque and non-transparent market practices are also problematic for competition, as already discussed. The main reason is that consumers might not be able to express their genuine preferences and respond to unfair treatment by companies due to systematic information gaps[194] and the prevalence of secrecy which challenge the premise that individuals are 'far from defenceless' in digital markets.[195] Whereas traditionally buyers had the information advantage enabling them to compare products, data- and technology-related opacity deepens information asymmetries to the advantage of the sellers.[196] In relation to personalized pricing, for example, the report issued by the UK's Office of Fair Trading (OFT) acknowledged that the likelihood of pricing strategies to be opaque is substantial in the online retailing, in particular due to consumers' inability to observe what price is offered to other consumers.[197] As noted by Patterson, 'an individual buyer's price comparisons are not comparisons of prices in the market, but only of prices designed for that particular buyer'.[198] This observation holds true not only in relation to personalized pricing, but also in the broader context of personalized content and experience. Information asymmetries challenge our fundamental understanding of competition.[199] In addition to harming consumers directly, deliberately clouding the judgement of consumers when it comes to their market choices can also have exclusionary effects. For example, a customer who wishes to find a cloud computing service that offers a high level of data storage security might end

[192] Regulation (EU) 2022/2065 of the European Parliament and of the Council of 19 October 2022 on a Single Market For Digital Services and amending Directive 2000/31/EC (Digital Services Act) [2022] L 277/1 (hereafter: DSA).

[193] Sylvia Lu, 'Data Privacy, Human Rights, and Algorithmic Opacity' (2022) 110 California Law Review 101, 118.

[194] Frank Pasquale and Oren Bracha, 'Federal Search Commission? Access, Fairness, and Accountability in the Law of Search' (2008) 93 Cornell Law Review 1150, 1183.

[195] Alessandro Acquisti and Hal R Varian, 'Conditioning Prices on Purchase History' (2004) 24 Marketing Science 367, 367.

[196] Mark R Patterson, *Antitrust Law in the New Economy: Google, Yelp, LIBOR, and the Control of Information* (Harvard UP 2017) 13.

[197] Office of Fair Trading, 'The Economics of Online Personalised Pricing' (2013). See also Ariel Ezrachi and Maurice E Stucke, *Virtual Competition: The Promise and Perils of the Algorithm-Driven Economy* (Harvard UP 2016); 115; Autoritat Catalana de la Competència, 'The Data-Driven Economy. Challenges for Competition' (2016) 29.

[198] Patterson (n 196) 14.

[199] ibid.

up not choosing the most secure option if cloud service providers, in particular those with poor security standards, are not transparent about that dimension of their service. Opacity might thus be a strategy desirable from the viewpoint of profit maximization.

2. The lack of competitive dynamism

The pervasive 'datafication' of the economy and society is a phenomenon that in digital markets is coupled with a lack of competitive dynamism, which aggravates the resulting risks. This section discusses competition dynamics in digital markets by shedding light on the concentration of power and wealth in the digital sector, as well the features and factors driving concentration.

2.1 Concentration of power and wealth

For the vast majority of users, the experience of navigating the modern internet is inescapably shaped by the well-known technology giants. The value provided by their services and products is beyond doubt, as is increasingly the fact that their economic strength needs to be more clearly on the radar of policy-makers and enforcers across jurisdictions.

In the EU, the Special Advisers' Report commissioned by the European Commission drew attention to 'the stickiness of market power' in the digital sector, which needs to be acknowledged to mitigate the risk of under-enforcement of competition law.[200] Similarly, the proposal for a DMA explained that in the digital sector '[a] few large platforms increasingly act as gateways or gatekeepers between business users and end users and enjoy an entrenched and durable position'.[201] The same concern motivated the German legislator to introduce the tenth amendment of the GWB, as discussed earlier. The key reasons for the expansion of the scope of competition law in Germany were the features of the digital economy, in which 'tendencies towards concentration can be strong and set in quickly', and which 'make it very difficult to challenge a business's strong market position once it has been attained'.[202]

The lack of a sufficient competitive dynamism in digital markets is also perceived as problematic outside Europe. In July 2021, US President Biden in an executive order highlighted the information technology sector as one in which competition

[200] Jacques Crémer, Yves-Alexandre de Montjoye, and Heike Schweitzer, 'Competition Policy for the Digital Era' (2019) Report for the European Commission 3.

[201] Proposal for a DMA (n 90) 1.

[202] Bundeskartellamt, 'Control of Abusive Practices' <https://www.bundeskartellamt.de/EN/Abusecontrol/abusecontrol_node.html> accessed 11 June 2022.

has weakened over the past years.[203] Particularly disturbing is the existence of only a few dominant platforms that 'use their power to exclude market entrants, to extract monopoly profits, and to gather personal information that they can exploit for their own advantage'.[204]

There are several indicators that one can rely on to evidence (insufficient) competitiveness in digital markets. Among the most prominent are market concentration, mark-ups, and profitability.[205] As regards market concentration, there is a substantial body of evidence showing the tendency of rising levels of concentration in the US and Europe, though to a lesser extent in the latter.[206] Increased concentration does not seem to be an idiosyncratic characteristic of digital markets, but rather a trend that can be observed across different sectors and industries—though not across the board. For example, the Commission showed that in the five largest European economies (France, Germany, Italy, Spain, and the UK), the industries particularly affected by tendencies of concentration are communications, finance, transportation, and digitally-intensive industries.[207]

Market concentration as measured by market shares or the Herfindahl–Hirschman Index (HHI)[208] is an indicator of competitive intensity, albeit an imperfect one as the relationship between market structure and the intensity of competition is ambiguous.[209] To obtain more reliable data, a tool that can be relied on to evaluate the competitive dynamics are mark-ups, which measure the value added to the cost of a product (ie the ratio of price to marginal cost). Scholars presented evidence of average global mark-ups increasing in the past couple of decades, in particular in the US and Europe.[210] The results of another study suggested that mark-ups tends to be higher in digitally-intensive sectors as compared to less digitally-intensive ones,[211] indicating larger market power in the digital economy.

[203] Joseph R Biden Jr, 'Executive Order on Promoting Competition in the American Economy' (2021) <https://www.whitehouse.gov/briefing-room/presidential-actions/2021/07/09/executive-order-on-promoting-competition-in-the-american-economy/> accessed 13 September 2022.

[204] ibid.

[205] OECD, 'Market Concentration' (2018) Issues Paper by the Secretariat, DAF/COMP/WD(2018)46. According to the OECD, other useful indicators include rate of market entry and exit, corporate investment, and the labour share of income.

[206] See eg ibid 10; David Autor and others, 'Concentrating on the Fall of the Labor Share' (2017) 107 American Economic Review 180; Maria Chiara Cavalleri and others, 'Concentration, Market Power and Dynamism in the Euro Area' (2019) European Central Bank, Working Paper Series No 2253.

[207] European Commission, 'Industry Concentration and Competition Policy' (2021) Competition Policy Brief, Issue 2021-02.

[208] The HHI index is calculated by squaring the market share of each firm in the market and adding the resulting numbers. The score can range from almost zero to 10,000.

[209] OECD (n 205) 4–5.

[210] Jan De Locker and Jan Eeckhout, 'Global Market Power' (2018) NBER Working Paper Series, Working Paper No 24768; Federico Díez and others, 'The Rise of Corporate Market Power and Its Macroeconomic Effects' (2019) IMF World Economic Outlook.

[211] Sara Calligaris, Chiara Criscuolo, and Luca Marcolin, 'Mark-Ups in the Digital Era' (2018) OECD Science, Technology and Industry Working Papers No 2018/10.

Besides increasing mark-ups, there is also evidence pointing to the trend of growing levels of the aggregate profitability of companies, which is yet another factor to consider in the overall assessment of competitive dynamist. For example, the *Economist* magazine reported that what are called 'abnormal profits' are in the US found to be predominantly in the technology sector.[212]

Taken together, the available data and evidence of concentrated power and accumulated wealth provide support for the claim that policy-makers and enforcers should remain vigilant. To formulate an informed and balanced solution to the challenge of concentration, it is key to understand the forces and factors that have driven and contributed to the suboptimal status quo, a few examples of which are outlined in the subsequent sections. While certain features of online markets, such as economies of scale or network effects, are already well recognized and are commonly associated with concentration tendencies, some unprecedented behavioural and structural trends (eg the creation of digital ecosystems) need to be more thoroughly investigated and potentially integrated into competition assessments.

2.2 Features and factors driving concentration

Among the key features of digital markets that facilitate the emergence of large online companies are significant economies of scale and scope and strong network effects.[213] As regards economies of scale, digital markets typically feature a cost structure with high fixed set-up and maintenance costs, but no or relatively low variable costs.[214] Thus, companies such as Alphabet or Meta, with extreme economies of scale on the demand side, have the ability to quickly scale up their businesses by gaining new users at negligible extra cost, making it challenging for others to enter the market. Relatedly, what enables concentration are economies of scope: technology companies offering one service become efficient at providing other, often distinct, services. In digital markets, among the main sources of economies of scope are data, the ability to leverage existing user bases, and technology redeployment.[215] Data, for example, creates strong user and monetization feedback loops: data improves the quality of market offerings, drawing more users and creating a virtuous circle; likewise, the revenues generated thanks to data can be reinvested to improve products and services and attract more users.[216] This fuels

[212] 'Too Much of a Good Thing' *The Economist* (26 March 2016) <https://www.economist.com/briefing/2016/03/26/too-much-of-a-good-thing> accessed 1 March 2022.

[213] Marc Bourreau and Anne Perrot, 'Digital Platforms: Regulate before It's Too Late' (2020) 60 Conseil d'analyse économique 1, 2.

[214] Justus Haucap, 'Competition and Competition Policy in a Data-Driven Economy' (2019) 54 Intereconomics 201, 204. See also Hal R Varian, Joseph Farrell, and Carl Shapiro, *The Economics of Information Technology: An Introduction* (CUP 2014); Geoffrey Parker, Georgios Petropoulos, and Marshall Van Alstyne, 'Digital Platforms and Antitrust' (2020) Bruegel Working Paper No 06/2020.

[215] Crémer, de Montjoye, and Schweitzer (n 200) 33.

[216] Jason Furman, 'Unlocking Digital Competition. Report of the Digital Competition Expert Panel' (2019) 33 (the Furman Report).

market incontestability, as it might be impossible for rivals to challenge the incumbent who enjoys strong economies of scope.

Network effects—already mentioned in the context of data-based business models—are another defining feature that supports concentration tendencies. Direct network effects that occur on one side of the market (eg the value of a social network increases with more users) are particularly relevant, as they can 'strengthen the position of incumbents, lock in consumers, and make it difficult for new entrants to gain a foothold in a market'.[217] High switching costs caused by direct network effects, particularly in markets where multi-homing is not likely, can be problematic. In combination with other factors, network effects give rise to a 'winner-takes-all' phenomenon, which means that competition becomes stifled once there is a clear market leader.[218] As some have expressed, dominant technology firms can be 'eclipsed' but not 'displaced'.[219] On the demand market side, a range of consumer biases (eg default bias), for example, contribute to the lack of competitive dynamism.

In addition to these recognized features on both the supply and demand market sides, the concerning level of competition in digital markets can be attributed to the new ways in which firms organize themselves, for example 'the resurgence of conglomerism'.[220]As Borreau and de Streel pointed out, large technology companies 'have achieved high degrees of diversification, entering weakly related—or even sometimes entirely unrelated—new markets'.[221] This diversification strategy can be exemplified by Meta expanding from a social network into messaging (WhatsApp), retail (Facebook Marketplace), gaming (Facebook Gameroom), and virtual reality (Oculus VR), or Alphabet diversifying its activity into payment services (Google Checkout), mobile phone operating systems (Android), maps (Google Maps), or productivity software (Google Docs).

The emergence of 'digital ecosystems' is a closely related phenomenon that merges conglomerate and multi-sided platform issues.[222] The management literature defines an ecosystem as 'a network of interconnected organizations that are

[217] OECD, 'Abuse of Dominance in Digital Markets' (2020) Background Note by the Secretariat, DAF/COMP/GF(2020)4, 2.

[218] Wil van der Aalst, Oliver Hinz, and Christof Weinhardt, 'Big Digital Platforms' (2019) 61 Business & Information Systems Engineering 645, 645.

[219] Patrick Barwise, 'Nine Reasons Why Tech Markets Are Winner-Take-All' (*London Business School Review*, 10 July 2018) <https://www.london.edu/think/nine-reasons-why-tech-markets-are-winner-take-all> accessed 4 March 2022.

[220] Marc Bourreau and Alexandre de Streel, 'Digital Conglomerates and EU Competition Policy' (2019) CERRE Report 2. See also Nicolas Petit, 'Technology Giants, the "Moligopoly" Hypothesis and Holistic Competition: A Primer' (2016) <https://papers.ssrn.com/sol3/papers.cfm?abstract_id=2856502> accessed 4 March 2022.

[221] Bourreau and de Streel (n 220) 4.

[222] Amelia Fletcher, 'Digital Competition Policy: Are Ecosystems Different?' (2020) Background Paper, 134th Meeting of the OECD Competition Committee, 2.

linked to or operate around an organization or a technology platform'.[223] Following Jacobides, two types of ecosystems can be distinguished: 'multi-product ecosystems' and 'multi-actor ecosystems'. Multi-product ecosystems 'deliver new forms of integrated or bundled products or services that offer solutions for customers',[224] and are 'born out of the ability to digitally stitch together services about broader customer needs'.[225] Examples include Facebook Messenger and WhatsApp, or Apple devices and the iCloud.[226] Multi-actor ecosystems, on the other hand, represent a community of independent organizations that provide complementary products and services, hence require 'a different organizational form'.[227] For example, Apple's multi-actor ecosystem relies on independent app developers. As Jacobides has stressed, large technology companies orchestrate both of these ecosystems at the same time, and there is a causal relationship between them: when a company offers multi-product ecosystems, it might be difficult for that company to deliver all the products and services itself.[228] Thus, it might need to engage with complementors, creating a multi-actor ecosystems.

Narrowing down the concept of digital ecosystems, van de Waerdt referred to the notion of 'data ecosystems' that in his view better captures the power that companies orchestrating ecosystems derive from access to data. He defined data ecosystems as business structures 'characterized by the collection, aggregation, analysis and monetization of personal data; achieved through offering many different (online) products on various markets, which interact with each other through shared data'.[229]

Digital ecosystems can certainly deliver efficiencies and bring benefits to consumers. For example, demand-side synergies between various services offered by a digital ecosystem might make it easier for individuals to access and use them.[230] At the same time, they can prove problematic from the perspective of competitive dynamism and contestability, particularly when companies that consolidate into ecosystems are incumbents with entrenched market positions. In addition to consolidating their power even further, ecosystems enable their orchestrators to gain

[223] Tomás Dias Sant'ana and others, 'The Structure of an Innovation Ecosystem: Foundations for Future Research' (2020) 58 Management Decision 2725, quoted in Ariel Ezrachi and Maurice E Stucke, *How Big-Tech Barons Smash Innovation—And How To Strike Back* (HarperCollins 2022) 10.

[224] Michael G Jacobides, 'How to Compete When Industries Digitize and Collide: An Ecosystem Development Framework' (2022) 64 California Management Review 99, 103.

[225] ibid 100.

[226] Fletcher (n 222) 2.

[227] Jacobides (n 224) 103.

[228] ibid.

[229] Peter J van de Waerdt, '"Everything the Data Touches Is Our Kingdom": Market Power of "Data Ecosystems"' (2023) 46 World Competition 65, 68.

[230] Harry Hong, 'What Are Digital Ecosystems and What Are Their Characteristics?' (*OECD On the Level*, 9 January 2021) <https://oecdonthelevel.com/2021/01/09/digital-ecosystems-a-new-economic-paradigm/> accessed 4 March 2022.

access to a variety of data, which might help them to improve the other services they offer, but is also likely to pose data protection risks.

There are various strategies employed by firms to expand their power and ecosystems. One such strategy is 'platform envelopment', which Eisenmann, Parket, and Van Alstyne define as 'entry by one platform provider into another's market by bundling its own platform's functionality with that of the target's so as to leverage shared user relationships and common components'.[231] The bundling enables the enveloping platform to extend into the new market certain efficiencies resulting from network effects, data, or infrastructure-related cost savings.[232] This entry path is not based on disruptive innovation, but rather on leveraging existing market power and exploiting the features of the digital economy. Such power leveraging—envelopment being one example—may also take other forms, such as tying or 'self-preferencing', which are discussed in Chapter 5 Section C.

Companies wishing to expand their power and ecosystems also rely on acquisitions. Acquisitions of nascent but fast-growing innovative firms with a view to terminating or integrating their innovations, as well as pre-empting future competition, have attracted plenty of attention over the past years (see Chapter 3 Section B). To describe transactions that eliminate promising, but likely competing, innovators, Cunningham, Ederer, and Ma coined the term 'killer acquisitions'.[233] While the concept was introduced in reference to the pharmaceutical industry, the question emerged whether the same phenomenon could be detected in digital markets. The 2019 report from the UK's Digital Expert Panel authored by Jason Furman (Furman Report), for example, noted that Apple, Meta, Google, Amazon, and Microsoft had in the five years preceding the publication of the report made close to 250 acquisitions, none of which had been blocked.[234] Despite the sheer scale of the acquisition practice in digital markets, it is however contentious to claim that these acquisitions can be labelled as killer acquisitions. While there might be instances where a dominant online platform 'kills' an innovative target by acquiring it, that is not a typical scenario.[235] Instead, the acquired start-up is usually integrated into the larger ecosystem of the acquiring company.[236] Recognizing possible benefits and harms, Bourreau and de Streel noted that acquisitions of promising start-ups can be explained by efficiency motives, when large companies provide skills and resources complementary to the innovation developed by smaller firms, but it might well also be that they are driven by the motives to pre-empt and

[231] Thomas Eisenmann, Geoffrey Parker, and Marshall Van Alstyne, 'Platform Envelopment' (2011) 32 Strategic Management Journal 1270, 1271.

[232] Gregor Langus and Vilen Lipatov, 'Does Envelopment through Data Advantage Call for New Regulation?' (2021) CESifo Working Papers No 8932, 2.

[233] Colleen Cunningham, Florian Ederer, and Song Ma, 'Killer Acquisitions' (2021) 129 Journal of Political Economy 650.

[234] Furman (n 216) 91.

[235] Crémer, de Montjoye, and Schweitzer (n 200) 117.

[236] ibid 118.

eliminate competition.[237] As the majority of acquisitions by the large technology companies occurs in data-intensive markets, a vigilant approach is necessary not only to protect competition but also ensure that a merger practice does not dissolve privacy.

In an article in 2022, Athey and Scott Morton coined the concept of 'platform annexation' to describe another strategy where, in pursuit of market power, a company 'possesses or acquires complementary multi-homing tools and operates those tools in a way that restricts or lessens efficient multi-homing by platform users'.[238] 'Annexing' a service originally aiding multi-homing and manipulating it to impede multi-homing is in their view a practice that lessens competition and requires more attention. An example is Meta's acquisition of Giphy, which would limit Giphy's interoperability across social media (see Chapter 3 Section B). Besides acquisitions, there are other types of tactics to realize platform annexation, including bundling and tying, which Chapter 4 Section C analyses in more detail.

To sum up, power concentration is as such not an indicator of eroding the quality of a market segment. However, it warrants greater scrutiny as consolidated markets can be fertile ground from which harmful conduct could emerge. While it is by now acknowledged that harm materializing in concentrated digital markets takes new forms, increasingly involving some form of a data protection violation, neither competition nor data protection enforcement approaches seem to be entirely prepared to prevent and mitigate such new types of harm—a concern that subsequent chapters will explore in more detail.

3. Technological innovations and new ways of interacting with technologies

Digital markets are in constant flux. This is owed not only to ever-evolving methods of competing and new structural features of digital markets, but also, or rather predominantly, to technological innovations made use of—or exploited—by online companies. This section highlights examples of technological innovations and new ways of interacting with technologies that are poised to further transform digital markets and give rise to new questions and legal concerns at the interface of data protection and competition law. The IoT, cloud computing, blockchains, and the metaverse are among the relevant innovations that are either emerging or gradually establishing themselves, and that display plenty of potential for further experimentation.

[237] Bourreau and de Streel (n 220) 22.

[238] Susan Athey and Fiona Scott Morton, 'Platform Annexation' (2022) 2–3 <https://papers.ssrn.com/sol3/papers.cfm?abstract_id=3786434> accessed 5 October 2022.

3.1 Internet of Things

The IoT sector can be defined as encompassing 'various services, devices and technologies that support the interaction of consumers with connected devices ("things"), which collect and exchange data over the internet'.[239] Over the past years, the sector has witnessed an exponential growth in Europe and beyond: from smart watches and voice-control devices to smart appliances, home robots, and TV sets, smart devices are becoming an inherent part of our day-to-day activities. While IoT solutions already have numerous landmark applications in diverse areas such as Industry 4.0, smart homes, smart cities, e-health, and connected cars, the sector continues to evolve.[240] Among the new trends that are expected to transform the IoT environment in the coming years are IoT edge computing (ie bringing the processing of IoT-generated data closer to the devices, rather than relying on the cloud),[241] the expansion of the industrial adoption of IoT, the convergence of IoT with immersive reality technologies, as well as IoT's greater reliance on 5G.[242]

As the sector rapidly evolves, new risks can be expected to emerge. Besides security threats that constitute a key challenge, data protection in the IoT sector is increasingly studied and debated, which is justified considering that one of the defining characteristics of IoT is the 'pervasive, often opaque collection and seamless linkage of user data to provide personalized experiences'.[243] Limitations and risks related to data protection in IoT environments can take various forms: risks resulting from inherent tensions between the non-transparent nature of IoT and the need to inform users about how their data is processed,[244] multifaceted privacy threats resulting from profiling and inference, or the lack of meaningful options

[239] European Commission, 'Commission Staff Working Document Accompanying Report from the Commission to the Council and the European Parliament "Final Report—Sector Inquiry into Consumer Internet of Things"', COM (2022) 19 final.

[240] Fredrik Dahlqvist, Mark Patel, and Jonathan Shulman, 'Growing Opportunities in the Internet of Things' *McKinsey* (22 July 2019) <https://www.mckinsey.com/industries/private-equity-and-principal-investors/our-insights/growing-opportunities-in-the-internet-of-things> accessed 8 March 2022.

[241] Jody Medich, 'Edge Computing is about to Solve the IoT's Biggest Problems' *Wired* (25 January 2021) <https://www.wired.co.uk/article/edge-computing-iot> accessed 8 March 2022.

[242] See eg Edward Wilford, '10 IoT Technology Trends to Watch in 2022' *IoT Analytics* (26 January 2022) <https://iot-analytics.com/iot-technology-trends/> accessed 10 March 2022; Bernard Marr, 'The 5 Biggest Internet of Things (IoT) Trends in 2022' *Forbes* (13 December 2021) <https://www.forbes.com/sites/bernardmarr/2021/12/13/the-5-biggest-internet-of-things-iot-trends-in-2022/> accessed 12 April 2022.

[243] Sandra Wachter, 'The GDPR and the Internet of Things: A Three-Step Transparency Model' (2018) 10 Law, Innovation and Technology 266, 267. See also Scott R Peppet, 'Regulating the Internet of Things: First Steps Toward Managing Discrimination, Privacy, Security, and Consent' (2014) 93 Texas Law Review 85. Security and privacy were also the two main challenges identified in the IoT report published by the FTC: Federal Trade Commission, 'Internet of Things: Privacy & Security in a Connected World' (2015) Staff Report. See also eg Moussa Witti and Dimitri Konstantas, 'IoT and Security–Privacy Concerns: A Systemic Mapping Study' (2018) 10 International Journal of Network Security & Its Applications 25; Nóra Ni Loideain, 'A Port in the Data-Sharing Storm: The GDPR and the Internet of Things' (2019) 4 Journal of Cyber Policy 178.

[244] Wachter (n 243) 267.

to port data from one IoT service provider to another.[245] Furthermore, IoT typically features a significant number of stakeholders, such as device manufacturers, data aggregators, data brokers, app developers, and social platforms, creating a complicated ecosystem that may challenge data protection compliance and enforcement.[246]

The IoT sector is also on the radar of competition enforcers. In January 2022, the Commission published the results of its sector inquiry into IoT.[247] Among the identified competition concerns are data-related features and practices in this environment. For example, data portability seems to be restricted in the context of data collected via voice assistants,[248] the leading ones currently being Amazon's Alexa, Google's Google Assistant, and Apple's Siri.[249] Not only do these voice assistant providers control data flows and user relationships, but they can also use these advantages to expand to adjacent markets, providing an opportunity for incumbents to enlarge their ecosystems and limit the possibilities for smaller firms to gain a foothold in the IoT sector.[250] The report warned that data protection arguments should not be used by IoT companies to 'lock up' certain datasets for themselves.[251] Other competitive hurdles identified by the relevant IoT stakeholders arise in relation to interoperability, standardization, exclusivity (eg of voice assistants on smart devices), as well as dependencies and commercial imbalances between smaller businesses and leading IoT platform providers.[252]

3.2 Cloud computing

Cloud computing—'a service model for computing services based on a set of computing resources that can be accessed in a flexible, elastic, on-demand way with low management effort'[253]—becomes increasingly relevant for individuals (eg Apple iCloud or Google Drive to store pictures, contacts, or documents), business organizations, and the public sector. As a catalyst for the efficient and effective

[245] Sarah Turner and others, 'The Exercisability of the Right to Data Portability in the Emerging Internet of Things (IoT) Environment' (2020) 23 New Media & Society 2861.

[246] A29WP, 'Opinion 8/2014 on the on Recent Developments on the Internet of Things' (2014).

[247] European Commission, 'Final Report—Sector Inquiry into Consumer Internet of Things', COM (2020) 19 final.

[248] ibid para 31.

[249] ibid para 10.

[250] ibid para 42. For a discussion on competition law, data access, and interoperability in relation to connected cars, see Wolfgang Kerber, 'Data Sharing in IoT Ecosystems and Competition Law: The Example of Connected Cars' (2019) 15 Journal of Competition Law & Economics 381.

[251] European Commission (n 247) para 43.

[252] ibid paras 39–48. See also Bill Batchelor and Grant Murray, 'Internet of Things: Antitrust Concerns in the Pipeline?' (*Kluwer Competition Law blog*, 12 May 2016) <http://competitionlawblog.kluwercompetitionlaw.com/2016/05/12/internet-of-things-antitrust-concerns-in-the-pipeline/> accessed 10 March 2022.

[253] OECD, 'Cloud Computing: The Concept, Impacts and the Role of Government Policy' (2014) OECD Digital Economy Papers No 240, 8.

application of other technologies and innovations, including AI and IoT, the cloud computing infrastructure is currently experiencing an increasing uptake.

As cloud enables data storage, privacy and security risks are inevitable. Challenges relate to implementing data subjects' consent, data storage policies, data breaches, and data erasure.[254] Scholars have also reflected on the uncertainties around applying data protection law to certain data processing activities by cloud service providers.[255] The opinion of the EDPS on cloud computing in Europe had already in 2012 listed a range of data protection concerns, also highlighting the risk of market consolidation that could reinforce the existing imbalance between the providers of cloud services and users—a risk that now, over a decade later, certainly materialized, merging both data protection and competition concerns.[256]

A discussion is also surfacing on the competitive dynamics in the cloud sector. Until recently, there were only a few competition law commentaries and little enforcement attention devoted to the subject. There is, however, a growing realization that competition in the cloud industry should be scrutinized more carefully. In January 2022, the French NCA launched an inquiry to analyse competition conditions in the cloud computing sector, focusing in particular on 'defining markets in the cloud sector, assessing the position and competitive advantages of the various players involved and examining the commercial practices that may be put in place'.[257] The Japan Fair Trade Commission conducted a similar inquiry and published its results in June 2022. According to the summary of the report,[258] there is evidence that the degree of market concentration is increasing, and the three companies whose market shares are significantly expanding are Amazon Web Services, Microsoft, and Google. This trend is expected to continue due to certain characteristics of the cloud sector such as economies of scale and scope, indirect network effects, and preferential use of services provided by the current players. It has also been found that most users do not readily switch to new providers. The lack of transparency in the sector, insufficient data portability, and the processing of users' data by cloud service providers are other areas that require more attention.

[254] Barbara Russo and others, 'Cloud Computing and the New EU General Data Protection Regulation' (2018) 5 IEEE Cloud Computing 58.

[255] Kuan Hon, Julia Hörnle, and Christopher Millard, 'Data Protection Jurisdiction and Cloud Computing—When Are Cloud Users and Providers Subject to EU Data Protection Law? The Cloud of Unknowing' (2012) 26 International Review of Law, Computers & Technology 129. As the article's analysis focuses on the DPD, some of the concerns it highlights are not relevant in the context of the GDPR.

[256] EDPS, 'Opinion on the Commission's Communication on "Unleashing the Potential of Cloud Computing in Europe"' (2012) paras 20–21.

[257] Autorité de La Concurrence, 'The Autorité de La Concurrence Starts Proceedings Ex Officio to Analyse Competition Conditions in the Cloud Computing Sector' (27 January 2022) <https://www.autoritedelaconcurrence.fr/en/press-release/autorite-de-la-concurrence-starts-proceedings-ex-officio-analyse-competition> accessed 28 September 2022.

[258] Japan Fair Trade Commission, 'Summary of Report Regarding Cloud Services' (2022).

3.3 Blockchain

Blockchain technology, commonly associated with cryptocurrencies such as Bitcoin and Ethereum, can be defined as 'a shared ledger of transactions between parties in a network, not controlled by a single central authority'.[259] While some believe blockchain technology to be just a buzzword with little substance behind it, others recognize its potential to revolutionize areas such as trade, supply chain management, or logistics. Increased transparency, improved efficiency, enhanced security, and easier traceability are among the common promises of the blockchain application.[260] Although it is still too early to judge whether and how the revolutionary potential of blockchain will materialize, anticipating its impacts on individuals and the markets is already under way.

From a data protection perspective, Finck has highlighted tensions between data protection law and blockchains that result from their incompatibility at a conceptual level: as she observed, 'the data protection mechanisms developed for centralized data silos cannot be easily reconciled with a decentralized method of data storage and protection'.[261] On a micro-level, this fundamental incompatibility may take the shape of the violation of basic data protection provisions such as data minimization, data protection by design and by default, individuals' rights to obtain rectification of personal data as information stored on blockchains cannot be easily modified, as well as the rights of access and to be forgotten.[262] It might also be difficult to identify on a blockchain data processors and controllers, making compliance and enforcement more complicated.

The competition law discussion of the impacts of blockchain technology on competitive dynamics has thus far focused largely on data sharing in the context of anti-competitive agreements (art 101 TFEU).[263] Typically, reaching a consensus on blockchain requires a wide distribution of transaction-related information among the members of a blockchain. While such near-instant data sharing and resulting transparency are key to blockchain's effective functioning, generating

[259] OECD, 'OECD Blockchain Primer' (2018).

[260] Ilker Koksal, 'The Benefits of Applying Blockchain Technology in Any Industry' *Forbes* (23 October 2019) <https://www.forbes.com/sites/ilkerkoksal/2019/10/23/the-benefits-of-applying-blockchain-technology-in-any-industry/> accessed 10 March 2022.

[261] Michèle Finck, 'Blockchains and Data Protection in the European Union' (2018) 4 European Data Protection Law Review 17, 17.

[262] ibid. See also Michèle Finck, 'Blockchain and the General Data Protection Regulation: Can Distributed Ledgers be Squared with European Data Protection Law?' (2019) Study for the European Parliament; Florian Martin-Bariteau, 'Blockchain and the European Union General Data Protection Regulation: The CNIL's Perspective' (2018) Blckchn.ca Working Paper Series No 2018-01.

[263] See eg Marixenia Davilla, 'Unravelling the Complexity of Blockchain and EU Competition Law' (2022) 13 Journal of European Competition Law & Practice 387; Michael Ristaniemi and Klaudia Majcher, 'Blockchains in Competition Law—Friend or Foe?' (*Kluwer Competition Law blog*, 21 July 2018) <http://competitionlawblog.kluwercompetitionlaw.com/2018/07/21/blockchains-competition-law-friend-foe/> accessed 10 March 2022; OECD, 'Blockchain Technology and Competition Policy' (2018) Issues Paper by the Secretariat, DAF/COMP/WD(2018)47. For a comprehensive analysis of the interactions between blockchain technology and antitrust law, see Thibault Schrepel, *Blockchain + Antitrust. The Decentralization Formula* (Edward Elgar 2021).

efficiencies and improving contractibility, questions also emerge about its collusive potential. Particularly susceptible to competition scrutiny are thus scenarios where direct competitors use shared blockchains or collaborate in blockchain consortia, and where such collaboration enables them to exchange strategic information in order to exclude rivals, fix prices, and share customer groups or geographic markets. The type of information strategic for competition includes price-related data (eg prices, rebates), customer lists, production costs, quantities, turnover, sales, risks, technologies, and R&D programmes.[264] Concerns about the interface of competition and data protection may emerge where competitively strategic and collusion-enabling information shared between competitors includes personal data—the scenario that, although not impossible, might not be likely to often materialize.

While future closer interactions between data and competition in the context of blockchain-related activities cannot be excluded, blockchain technology does not seem, at the moment, to pose imminent interlocking concerns to be jointly monitored by data protection and competition enforcers.

3.4 Metaverse

Besides technological innovations, the way of interacting with technologies is subject to change. The most recent model of interactions that some believe will mark the next evolution of the internet is the 'metaverse'. While there is not yet an established definition of the metaverse, it can be broadly understood as 'a digital reality that combines aspects of social media, online gaming, augmented reality (AR), virtual reality (VR), and cryptocurrencies to allow users to interact virtually'.[265] It thus represents a network where users, via their avatars, can work, shop, play, or interact with others in various ways. While this sounds like a futuristic environment, metaverse-aspiring companies are already developing their versions of the metaverse. Epic Games, a video game and software developer and publisher, is a pioneer: it has already organized virtual concerts and movie showings, and recently secured significant funding from Sony to further expand its metaverse environment.[266] Meta's CEO, Mark Zuckerberg, announced in October 2021 his new vision for the next platform, which is to 'be even more immersive—an embodied internet where you're in the experience, not just looking at it'.[267] For Microsoft, the

[264] Davilla (n 263) 393.

[265] Jean Folger, 'What Does Metaverse Mean and How Does This Virtual World Work?' *Investopedia* (5 August 2022) <https://www.investopedia.com/metaverse-definition-5206578> accessed 12 March 2022.

[266] GlobalData Thematic Intelligence, 'Epic Games Is Strengthening Its Metaverse Ambition' *Verdict* (20 April 2022) <https://www.verdict.co.uk/epic-games-metaverse/> accessed 12 March 2022.

[267] Meta, 'Founder's Letter' (28 October 2021) <https://about.fb.com/news/2021/10/founders-letter/> accessed 12 March 2022.

metaverse it wants to create involves 'the ability to bridge the digital and the physical worlds'.[268]

Although the metaverse is still in its infancy, the discussion is already ongoing about the potential risks and legal issues that metaverse-aspiring firms should consider and enforcers and policy-makers should prepare for.[269] From a data protection perspective, the danger is that the metaverse will provide companies with new and improved ways of collecting data thus enhancing the risk of intrusive data practices. While it is still to be seen which monetization strategies companies offering a metaverse will employ, it can be predicted that data and ad-supporting models will also drive revenues in the metaverse context.[270] Demonstrating the gravity of potential metaverse's privacy implications, a recent study based on experiments with thirty participants playing an 'escape room' game with VR devices showed how many types of data could be collected about them: around twenty-five data attributes, including various types of biometric and demographic data.[271] This represents a scale of data collection that far exceeds what is possible in the traditional web and mobile environments. Given that the metaverse is likely to be governed by multiple business actors and feature a web of new types of relationships between them, it might also be difficult to determine who is responsible for protecting individuals' personal data (ie who is a controller and who is a processor for the purpose of applying the GDPR). Other questions that relate to the collection and use of biometric data (eg generated through the use of VR headsets that feature a wide array of biometric scanners), consent, transparency, and data sharing for the purpose of ensuring interoperability may be further complicated by the new immersive environment of connected digital spaces and actors.

The metaverse is also likely to trigger new competition-related questions. In January 2022, Vice-President Vestager signalled the need for more competition scrutiny of the future metaverse environments. In her view, the metaverse 'will present new markets and a range of different businesses', creating 'a marketplace where someone may have a dominant position'.[272] Controlling access to a

[268] Michael Muchmore, 'What Is Microsoft's Metaverse Strategy?' *PC Magazine* (25 May 2022) <https://uk.pcmag.com/business-1/140569/what-is-microsofts-metaverse-strategy> accessed 27 May 2022.

[269] See eg David Uberti, 'Come the Metaverse, Can Privacy Exist?' *The Wall Street Journal* (4 January 2022) <https://www.wsj.com/articles/come-the-metaverse-can-privacy-exist-11641292206?page=1> accessed 13 March 2022; Shelly Kramer, 'Metaverse Privacy Concerns: Are We Thinking About Our Data?' *Forbes* (1 June 2022) <https://www.forbes.com/sites/forbestechcouncil/2022/06/01/metaverse-privacy-concerns-are-we-thinking-about-our-data/> accessed 5 June 2022.

[270] Friedrich Wenzel Bulst and Sophie De Vinck, 'Understanding the Metaverse—A Competition Perspective' *European American Chamber of Commerce* (17 October 2022) <https://eaccny.com/news/chapternews/dg-comp-understanding-the-metaverse-a-competition-perspective/> accessed 5 November 2022.

[271] Vivek Nair, Gonzalo Munilla Garrido, and Dawn Song, 'Exploring the Unprecedented Privacy Risks of the Metaverse' (2022) ArXiv.

[272] Samuel Stolton, 'Vestager: Metaverse Poses New Competition Challenges' *Politico* (18 January 2022) <https://www.politico.eu/article/metaverse-new-competition-challenges-margrethe-vestager/> accessed 14 March 2022.

metaverse, for example by creating a closed ecosystem featuring non-interoperable services, may contribute to dominance or a gatekeeper status. This position of power may then be exploited to exclude rivals and harm consumers: imposing high prices for accessing the metaverse, bundling services and products, or engaging in exclusive deals with metaverse-related third-party providers are some examples of potentially anti-competitive conduct.[273] Calls for future scrutiny are justified when looking at the market strategies already employed by companies expanding into the metaverse. For example, it was recently reported that some incumbents, including Meta and Microsoft, cooperate on developing industry standards that would foster compatibility between their future metaverse ecosystems, which might as a result have exclusionary effects for companies which are not part of that collaboration.[274] Meta is at the same time expanding its operations by acquiring metaverse-related companies (eg a VR fitness company Within and a number of game developers and e-sport companies, including Downpour Interactive, Unit 2 Games, BigBox VR, Sanzaru Games, and Ready at Dawn), strengthening Meta's position and leading to potential competition issues.[275] Authors have also highlighted how other likely anti-competitive effects, for example an input foreclosure resulting from a conglomerate acquisition and impacting the entire metaverse value chain, might be difficult for enforcers to identify and needs a thorough understanding of how the metaverse functions.[276] Indirectly, these foreclosure effects can have repercussions for data protection, as the market opportunities for services offering higher data protection standards might be curbed.

D. Conclusions

This chapter's goal was twofold: to demonstrate the proximity of data protection and competition law by shedding light on the multiplicity of objectives and values that these two fields of law have in common, and to illustrate how the same empirical phenomena pose, and will continue to pose, a challenge for protecting data and market competitiveness.

As regards the first part of the inquiry, the commonalities between the objectives of the two areas of the law allow for a conclusion that, at a normative level,

[273] Bulst and De Vinck (n 270).

[274] 'Tech Giants Form Metaverse Standards, Excluding Apple' *Competition Policy International* (22 June 2022) <https://www.competitionpolicyinternational.com/tech-giants-form-metaverse-standards-excluding-apple/> accessed 18 September 2022.

[275] Constantine Cannon, 'Antitrust Enforcers Enter the Metaverse' *Lexology* (16 March 2022) <https://www.lexology.com/library/detail.aspx?g=99eb485b-0e45-451b-b2b5-4ba35a5c2971> accessed 19 March 2022.

[276] Dwayne Bach and Fabian Ziermann, 'Conglomerate Foreclosure in the Metaverse' (*D'Kart*, 22 June 2022) <https://www.d-kart.de/en/blog/2022/06/22/conglomerate-foreclosure-in-the-metaverse/> accessed 2 September 2022.

data protection and competition law display more synergies than is commonly assumed. This conclusion can underpin the hypothesis that the substantive enforcement of these two areas would lead to mutually beneficial outcomes.

The second part of the inquiry that concentrated on the empirical reality illustrates that the synergies between data protection and competition exist not only in the theoretical-normative domain, but that the market reality as such provides the external justification for the two areas of the law to be more unified and join forces. While some of the identified challenges can in the future be addressed by applying existing data protection and competition law concepts and theories of harm, others, due to their novelty, will undoubtedly expose the shortcomings of the established frameworks and call for their rethinking.

3

Mapping the Interactions: Status Quo

A. Introduction

The multitude of ways in which data protection and competition law cohere on a broader normative and conceptual level, as well as on the level of specific challenges posed by the empirical reality of digital markets, should ideally be expected to be mirrored in the legal, enforcement, policy, and institutional approaches. The aim of this chapter is to map and discuss the status quo of how competition law integrates data protection, and how data protection law reflects on competition—themes that represent two sides of the same coin.

Over the past years, a competition law perspective on the coherence between the two fields has been the principal one adopted in the policy and academic discourses. The underlying challenge, as commonly framed, is how to apply competition law in a way that integrates data protection concerns. There are many reasons that justify the attention that data protection-conscious competition law continues to attract: competition law's provisions are flexible enough to capture a wide range of market practices, the fines imposed for competition violations are substantial, and enforcement at the EU level is centralized and performed by an authority with significant resources. At the same time, placing the focus solely on the competition dimension is asymmetrical, and ignores the data protection perspective. Criticizing this asymmetrical intellectual focus, Gal and Aviv invoked the concept of a legal 'anamorphosis', which refers to an optical illusion whereby an image can only be seen when looked at from a certain angle.[1]

By discussing both perspectives, namely how competition law supports data protection and how data protection law supports competitiveness, this chapter aims to ensure that no relevant facet of the coherence debate is overlooked and the current legal anamorphosis is addressed. The chapter illustrates that while the close intertwining of these fields is increasingly acknowledged, the approach continues to be disjointed in respect of policy, law, and enforcement in the EU and beyond. The substantive insights outlined in Section A that focuses on a competition perspective, and in Section B that zooms in on data protection law, are in Section C complemented by an institutional perspective, which demonstrates the absence

[1] Michal S Gal and Oshrit Aviv, 'The Competitive Effects of the GDPR' (2020) 16 Journal of Competition Law & Economics 349, 350.

Coherence between Data Protection and Competition Law in Digital Markets. Klaudia Majcher, Oxford University Press.
 DOI: 10.1093/oso/9780198885610.003.0004

of institutional reforms to bridge data protection and competition law. Section D offers concluding reflections.

B. Data protection-agnostic competition law

The topic of optimizing competition law in a way that integrates data protection concerns has over the past few years become established in policy and academic agendas in Europe and elsewhere. The following three sections discuss policy discourse, enforcement, and new policy and regulatory initiatives. As they illustrate, although the intellectual output of how—and how not—to adjust competition law has grown exponentially, no significant development can be observed in enforcement practice, and the actual substantive reforms are limited in scope. As will be seen, the few instances where data protection and competition law have been approached in a more synergetic way represent isolated examples from which a progressive coherence-oriented attitude cannot yet be inferred.

1. Understanding the interactions: the extensive global policy discourse

Ever since the realization that competition in digital markets is not sufficiently intense, competition authorities and other institutions around the world have been putting significant efforts into mapping its weaknesses and discussing solutions. A wave of policy reports published over the last few years documents this endeavour well. Organizations and stakeholders which have offered valuable contributions include the European Commission,[2] several NCAs from the EU Member States,[3] the UK Competition and Markets Authority (CMA),[4] the UK government,[5] the US Stigler Committee on Digital Platforms,[6] the Australian Competition and Consumer Commission (ACCC),[7] the Competition Bureau of Canada,[8] the Japan

[2] Jacques Crémer, Yves-Alexandre de Montjoye, and Heike Schweitzer, 'Competition Policy for the Digital Era', Report for the European Commission (2019).

[3] eg Bundeswettbewerbsbehörde, 'Considerations on Digitalization Challenges in the Economy and Competition Law Enforcement' (2020); Autoridade da Concorrência, 'Digital Ecosystems, Big Data and Algorithms' (2019); Autorité de la concurrence and Bundeskartellamt, 'Competition Law and Data' (2016); Bundeskartellamt, 'Market Power of Platforms and Networks' (2016).

[4] eg CMA, 'Online Platforms and Digital Advertising, Market Study Final Report' (2020).

[5] Jason Furman, 'Unlocking Digital Competition', Report of the Digital Competition Expert Panel (2019).

[6] Stigler Committee on Digital Platforms, 'Final Report' (2019).

[7] ACCC, 'Digital Platforms Inquiry—Final Report' (2019).

[8] Competition Bureau of Canada, 'Big Data and Innovation: Key Themes for Competition Policy in Canada' (2018).

Fair Trade Commission (JFTC),[9] the BRICS Competition Law and Policy Centre,[10] the BRICS Competition Authorities,[11] the competition authorities of the Latin American countries,[12] and the OECD.[13] While the reports and studies they have published investigate a range of topics related to digital competition—from the characteristics of digital markets to market definition and market power and from the concept of abuse to remedies—most of them also include reflections on the role of data and data protection in a competition analysis. This section provides a synopsis of the main data- and data protection-related insights presented in the various studies and reports. Although this discussion does not do justice to all the nuanced dialogues, it will identify and discuss in a comparative fashion the key arguments and suggestions.

One of the common themes and often a starting point in the reviewed reports is how access to data may raise barriers to entry and strengthen companies' market power in digital markets. The majority of publications agreed that data contributes to increasing returns of scale and scope, and may drive concentration in the digital economy. Where data is of central importance to the market offer, but it is simultaneously inaccessible to competitors, it can constitute 'an unmatchable advantage', as the Furman Report noted.[14] Barriers to equivalent data sources are 'a side effect of not having the history, scale, or scope of the incumbent', inhibiting entry, expansion, and innovation.[15] Relatedly, creating large ecosystems by leveraging power from the core to adjacent markets was indicated in some reports as a related obstacle to market entry.[16] The EU Special Advisers' Report mentioned both 'anonymous access to a large amount of individual-level data' and access to 'non-anonymous individual-level data' as representing a competitive advantage.[17] Interestingly, in Japan, the JFTC observed that poor privacy protections may also constitute a barrier to entry: to promote 'new entry and competition of businesses utilizing data, it is desirable to ensure individuals' security and trust when businesses obtain their personal data'.[18] To lower these barriers, businesses should provide a better explanation of their data practices, obtain valid consent, or be required to comply with other 'data fiduciary duties'.[19] The report published by the US Stigler Committee

[9] JFTC, 'Report of the Study Group on Data and Competition Policy' (2021); JFTC, 'Report Regarding the Trade Practices of Digital Platforms' (2019).

[10] BRICS Competition Law and Policy Centre, 'Digital Era Competition: A BRICS View' (2019).

[11] BRICS Competition Authorities, 'BRICS in the Digital Economy: Competition Policy in Practice Report' (2019).

[12] eg Comisión Federal de Competencia Económica, 'Rethinking Competition in the Digital Economy' (2018).

[13] eg OECD, 'Rethinking Antitrust Tools for Multi-Sided Platforms' (2018); OECD, 'Considering Non-Price Effects in Merger Control' (2018) Background Note by the Secretariat, DAF/COMP(2018)2.

[14] Furman (n 5) 34.

[15] Stigler Committee on Digital Platforms (n 6) 40; BRICS Competition Authorities (n 11) 19.

[16] JFTC (n 9) 54.

[17] Crémer, de Montjoye, and Schweitzer (n 2) 30–31.

[18] JFTC (n 9) 50–51.

[19] ibid 52–53.

(Stigler Report) stressed that besides enhancing market power, data also helps to strengthen companies' 'political power'.[20]

The majority of publications acknowledged that the peculiar characteristics of digital markets challenge established competition concepts and analytical methods. The Stigler Report stressed 'fundamental difficulties in applying standard antitrust analysis', which concern, among other matters, the prevalence of various behavioural effects (ie the chosen options may not always reflect consumers' true preferences) and the nature of exchanges in the digital economy (ie individuals barter data and attention for services).[21] While few BRICS countries (ie Brazil, India, and South Africa) recognized new analytical challenges, they were of the view that their respective legal frameworks leave sufficient room to adapt existing concepts and tools.[22] The Competition Commission of India (CCI) noted that the existing antitrust tools are sufficient to address competition issues related to privacy violations,[23] which is a relevant statement as at the time of writing India has not yet adopted its Digital Personal Data Protection Bill that was put forward in 2019. Even though competition authorities have the tools and powers to detect and correct a variety of digital practices, any intervention, as stressed by Mexico's Federal Economic Competition Commission (COFECE), 'requires a more delicate analysis of the effects it may have on the market'.[24]

Some reports reflected on the consumer welfare standard, which remains a central benchmark guiding competition enforcement in many jurisdictions. According to the Competition Bureau of Canada, the consumer welfare notion is flexible enough to consider new types of concerns, such as privacy, although some specific methods of analysing their competitive effects may need to be adapted.[25]

As regards theories of harm, a common view was that privacy can be approached as a dimension of quality, and a lack of competitive pressures may enable companies to decrease privacy protection.[26] While this point was highlighted in many reports, some of them expressed uneasiness about this claim. The Furman Report noted that 'privacy is not directly within the scope of the Panel's review', but 'the misuse of consumer data and harm to privacy is arguably indicator of low quality caused by lack of competition'.[27] The Mexican competition authority was less convinced, noting that it cannot be assumed that more intense competition will result in better data protection policies.[28] Similarly, the Canadian Competition

[20] Stigler Committee on Digital Platforms (n 6) 17.
[21] ibid 66–67.
[22] BRICS Competition Authorities (n 11) 41.
[23] Competition Commission of India, 'Market Study on the Telecom Sector in India. Key Findings and Observations' (2021) para 71.
[24] Comisión Federal de Competencia Económica (n 12) 77.
[25] Competition Bureau of Canada (n 8) 6.
[26] Stigler Committee on Digital Platforms (n 6) 57, 66. The Competition Commission of India noted explicitly that privacy 'can take the form of non-price competition': Competition Commission of India (n 23) para 70.
[27] Furman (n 5) 43.
[28] Comisión Federal de Competencia Económica (n 12) 63.

Bureau wrote that while it 'is aware of no convincing evidence to rule out categorically privacy as a factor that may affect consumer perception of the quality', it is at the same time not 'aware of evidence to necessarily rule privacy in as a factor'.[29] The Canadian authority also acknowledged that data-related practices may negatively affect consumer choice, for example when data is collected through deceptive means, including false or misleading representations.[30] The concern that non-transparent data practices negatively affect choice was also expressed by other institutions.[31]

Some authorities flagged new competition-relevant types of data abuse. As explained by the Japanese competition agency, when a digital platform obtains personal data in ways that are 'unjustly disadvantageous' to individuals, this might constitute an abuse of 'a superior bargaining position' the Japanese competition law unless valid consent has been obtained.[32] The US Stigler Report expressed its concern about other data-related harms, for example exploiting consumers by manipulating their preferences, as well as making use of digital defaults, framings, and nudges[33]—without, however, explicitly asserting that these can be categorized as antitrust problems. The Mexican competition authority highlighted data-enabled price discrimination as a practice that can be pursued under competition law.[34]

One specific practice that many reports described as particularly worthy of enhanced antitrust scrutiny was online targeted advertising.[35] The Stigler Report stressed that targeted advertising is one of the key sources of the new types of harm. It suggested that 'the fastest route to more accurate measures of welfare might well be for a digital regulator to limit the business models that serve harmful content', which can be compared to limiting 'the harm from prescription drugs by requiring access through a physician'.[36] Product design decisions—for example, interfaces, mobile device screen layouts, as well as decisions about data storage and analysis—are other business strategies that the US courts should be more willing to consider.[37] In addition, almost all reports discussed data portability and interoperability as mechanisms for boosting competition and bridging it with data protection.[38] For example, Singapore's Personal Data Protection Commission in collaboration with

[29] Competition Bureau of Canada (n 8) 8–9.
[30] ibid 12.
[31] Stigler Committee on Digital Platforms (n 6) 53–54.
[32] JFTC (n 9) 51.
[33] Stigler Committee on Digital Platforms (n 6) 58–60.
[34] Comisión Federal de Competencia Económica (n 12) 63.
[35] See eg Stigler Committee on Digital Platforms (n 6) 44–45; Furman (n 5) 112–17; JFTC (n 9) 54–55.
[36] Stigler Committee on Digital Platforms (n 6) 67.
[37] ibid 98.
[38] See eg Competition Commission Singapore, 'Data: Engine for Growth—Implications for Competition Law, Personal Data Protection, and Intellectual Property Rights' (2017) 97.

Competition and Consumer Commission of Singapore jointly published a discussion paper studying the introduction of a data portability requirement.[39]

More broadly, the problem of under-enforcement of competition law—especially in the area of merger control—was a key discussion point. The fact that the authorities clear too many acquisitions by large digital firms, some of which might be problematic, was brought to the fore in the Stigler Report[40] and in the Furman Report,[41] among others. Under-enforcement was also mentioned as a concern in the area of exclusionary conduct by powerful firms: the Stigler Report stressed the lack of antitrust challenges to such conduct in the US since the 1998 case against Microsoft.[42]

To correct this, it was suggested that the balance that competition law needs to strike between the enforcement risks of false positives and false negatives should be recalibrated.[43] Striking a right balance is an urgent requirement as under-enforcement seems to be costlier than previously thought—particularly due to the enduring market power of technology firms—and over-enforcement less costly given these companies' abilities to realize efficiencies in new ways.[44] Thus, the Stigler Report suggested relaxing the burden of proof that currently applies in the US to antitrust claimants, or reversing it entirely.[45] Reversing the burden of proof in certain instances was also supported by the Austrian competition authority.[46]

As regards merger control, presumptions of illegality could be introduced where a transaction involves a dominant undertaking and a potential competitor.[47] Acknowledging the danger of under-enforcement, the Furman Report suggested that the UK's CMA should 'take more frequent and firmer action' to challenge potentially harmful mergers.[48] The strategy could be to select more digital market cases for examination, for example by requiring companies with 'a strategic market status' to inform the CMA about all of their intended concentrations.[49] This should be complemented by updating the substantive assessment frameworks for digital mergers. A consideration that should be given more weight is how an incumbent could increase its advantage and harm competition by pursuing a merger that allows it to merge data from various sources.[50] The EU Special Advisors' Report made a similar suggestion about rethinking the substantive test used in assessments of

39 Personal Data Protection Commission Singapore and Competition and Consumer Commission of Singapore, 'Data Portability' (2019).

40 Stigler Committee on Digital Platforms (n 6) 84.

41 Furman (n 5) 49.

42 Stigler Committee on Digital Platforms (n 6) 85.

43 ibid 94–95.

44 ibid; Comisión Federal de Competencia Económica (n 12) 76.

45 Stigler Committee on Digital Platforms (n 6) 98.

46 Bundeswettbewerbsbehörde (n 3) 10.

47 Stigler Committee on Digital Platforms (n 6) 98.

48 Furman (n 5) 93.

49 ibid 94–95.

50 ibid 95–97.

digital mergers. While the report posited that the currently employed SIEC test and the 'strengthening of dominance' criterion remain sound, theories of harm should be updated to more accurately assess conglomerate mergers.[51] In Australia, the ACCC recommended amending merger legislation to incorporate 'the nature and significance of assets, including data and technology'.[52] According to the Mexican competition authority, among the substantive factors that deserve more attention when dealing with digital mergers are transactions' long-term effects, access to data, and innovation potential.[53] While the Competition Commission of South Africa noted that it might modify its merger policy to be able to effectively review large firms' acquisitions of smaller companies, the Brazilian Administrative Council for Economic Defense (CADE) warned against potential risks to innovation that a restrictive merger policy might cause.[54]

The ineffectiveness of the current competition law remedies was stressed in a number of reports. Mandating the sharing of data (not only historical, but also present and future) was indicated as a new remedy for competition authorities to explore.[55] According to the EU Special Advisors' Report, data sharing may generate benefits for competition and innovation that outweigh the potential negative effects on incumbents.[56] At the same time, it was acknowledged that the data openness remedy is interventionist and should be pursued only when necessary and proportionate and does not violate the right to data protection.[57] A 'duty to deal', as the Canadian authority observed, should be imposed only in exceptional cases.[58]

While many organizations encouraged new behavioural remedies, some proposed the application of structural remedies (eg ordering a divestiture),[59] with the caveat that such remedies should be a tool of last resort.[60] In the EU Special Advisors' Report, a potential application of structural remedies was discussed only in the limited context of 'self-preferencing' (ie a market practice of favouring own products or services over those of competitors). The German Commission Competition 4.0 suggested that the European Commission should conduct a study analysing the previous policy on remedies.[61] A more sceptical view was expressed by the Australian competition regulator. In its view, it is best that the markets are shaped by competitive forces, that structural remedies might not always be effective (eg they are unlikely to address barriers to entry in the markets of search or

[51] Crémer, de Montjoye, and Schweitzer (n 2) 117.
[52] ACCC (n 7) 108.
[53] Comisión Federal de Competencia Económica (n 12) 70–71.
[54] BRICS Competition Authorities (n 11) 17.
[55] Stigler Committee on Digital Platforms (n 6) 117.
[56] Crémer, de Montjoye, and Schweitzer (n 2) 106.
[57] Furman (n 5) 74–76; Crémer, de Montjoye, and Schweitzer (n 2) 108.
[58] Competition Bureau of Canada (n 8) 9.
[59] Stigler Committee on Digital Platforms (n 6) 99–100.
[60] German Federal Ministry of Economic Affairs, 'A new competition framework for the digital economy' (2019) 74.
[61] ibid 75.

social networks), and that designing and implementing structural remedies is not straightforward.[62]

Some institutions suggested the bolder step of introducing ex ante regulatory regimes, which in conjunction with strengthening competition enforcement can help to prevent new risks. From a US perspective, it was proposed that a regulatory framework should be either broadly applicable or its scope limited only to companies with 'bottleneck power'.[63] The reason for having a single regulator overseeing digital platforms is that the concerns they spur—'all linked to the power of data'—span different fields.[64] Similarly, the UK Furman Report advocated developing a code of conduct for companies with a 'strategic market status', which should be based on a number of core principles.[65] Referring to the DMA and the regulatory plans put forward by the UK, the JFTC asserted that based on these 'overseas trends, rules for digital platform operators in Japan can be an option from the viewpoint of promoting competition in data market'.[66] Such ex ante rules should be designed with a view to promoting data distribution as well as encouraging new entry and protecting innovation. Whether a 'smart regulation' should complement competition enforcement is a question that the Competition Commission of South Africa also reflected on.[67]

As the overview of policy reports and studies illustrates, while progress in thinking about interactions between personal data and competition can be detected, the landscape of ideas is fragmented and no trans-jurisdictional consensus exists on the way forward. Complementing this policy-centred overview, the next section investigates competition law enforcement with a view to establishing how data protection is integrated into competition assessments in practice.

2. Testing competition law boundaries through enforcement

Reflecting on the trajectory of competition law enforcement in cases involving data protection concerns, the following sections describe the initial silo approach, the continued reluctance to thoroughly integrate data protection issues in merger control, and experimentation in the area of abuse of a dominant position and monopolization.

62 ACCC (n 7) 116.
63 Stigler Committee on Digital Platforms (n 6) 107–16.
64 ibid 18.
65 Furman (n 5) 59–64.
66 JFTC (n 9) 56.
67 BRICS Competition Authorities (n 11) 29.

2.1 The initial silo approach

The initial reluctance to analyse data protection repercussions in competition cases is best illustrated by the CJEU's *Asnef-Equifax* judgment,[68] as well as the decisions relating to the merger between Google and DoubleClick taken by the European Commission[69] and the Federal Trade Commission (FTC) in the US.[70]

Asnef-Equifax is so far the only instance in which the CJEU has had a chance to reflect on the interaction between data protection and competition law. The case concerned the competition repercussions of the exchange of information between competing credit organizations. It also had a link to personal data as Asnef-Equifax sought authorization of a register that included information relating to 'the identity and economic activity of debtors, as well as to special situations, such as bankruptcy or insolvency'.[71] While the credit information exchange was declared legal from a competition standpoint, the CJEU did not consider its data protection implications. The Court noted that as 'any possible issues relating to the sensitivity of personal data are not, as such, a matter for competition law, they may be resolved on the basis of the relevant provisions governing data protection'.[72]

A slightly more nuanced position was expressed by Advocate General Geelhoed. While he also admitted that '[a]ny problems concerning the sensitivity of personal data can be resolved by other instruments, such as data protection legislation', his Opinion noted that '[i]t is clear that there must be some way of informing borrowers concerned of what data are recorded and of granting them the right to check the data concerning them and to have them corrected where necessary'.[73] This pronouncement, while it supported the silo approach, also acknowledged the relevance of ensuring the lawfulness and fairness of data processing, albeit with different instruments. *Asnef-Equifax* continues to be widely referenced to justify the separation of data protection and competition law. Yet, the conclusion as to the applicability of the case's findings to the current digital reality is not evident, in particular as the judgment, rendered almost two decades ago, was underpinned by a different empirical context and the facts of the case differ notably from those that surface in more recent cases.

A couple of years after *Asnef-Equifax*, the Commission and the FTC were confronted with a merger case—Google's acquisition of DoubleClick—where data protection was a prominent concern.[74] As many feared, the transaction could have

[68] Case C-238/05 *Asnef-Equifax, Servicios de Información sobre Solvencia y Crédito, SL v Asociación de Usuarios de Servicios Bancarios (Ausbanc)* [2006] ECLI:EU:C:2006:734.

[69] *Google/DoubleClick* (Case COMP/M.4731) Commission Decision of 12 February 2001.

[70] *Google/DoubleClick*, Statement of the Federal Trade Commission, FTC File No 071-0170 (20 December 2007).

[71] *Asnef-Equifax* (n 68) para 7.

[72] ibid para 63.

[73] Case C-238/05 *Asnef-Equifax, Servicios de Información sobre Solvencia y Crédito, SL v Asociación de Usuarios de Servicios Bancarios (Ausbanc)* [2006] ECLI:EU:C:2006:440, Opinion of AG Geelhoed, para 56.

[74] Julia Brockhoff and others, '*Google/DoubleClick*: The First Test for the Commission's Nonhorizontal Merger Guidelines' (2008) Competition Policy Newsletter No 2, 59.

resulted in the combination of both companies' datasets, enabling the merged entity to track consumers and use their data for targeting purposes.[75] Commenting on the acquisition from a US perspective, Rotenberg noted that it undoubtedly 'is the single biggest privacy meltdown that the Internet is currently facing'.[76] Even though the criticism was justified, neither competition authority meaningfully engaged with the potential data protection implications of the transaction. Having approved the acquisition in 2008, the Commission stressed that its decision 'is without prejudice to the obligations imposed onto the parties' by data protection law.[77] Similarly, the FTC's approval decision, issued in 2007, noted that although issues such as privacy 'may present important policy questions for the Nation, the sole purpose of federal antitrust review of mergers and acquisitions is to identify and remedy transactions that harm competition'.[78] Interestingly, it also highlighted the dangers of regulating the privacy policies of only a single company through a merger enforcement, noting that this might cause serious detriment to competition in that sector.[79]

In the US, FTC Commissioners Leibowitz and Harbour issued opinions reflecting a different, more forward-looking, and holistic approach to the scope of antitrust law. While Commissioner Leibowitz recognized that substantial privacy issues 'clearly transcend[ed]' Google's proposed acquisition of DoubleClick,[80] and that behavioural advertising posed fundamental concerns in the area,[81] Commissioner Harbour went a step further, issuing a dissenting opinion. Privacy concerns, as Harbour said, 'represent the "other side of the coin" of the exact same merger of datasets'.[82] As a traditional competition assessment of the transaction fails to capture possible harms to individuals whose privacy might be affected, new harm theories that 'make privacy "cognizable" under the antitrust laws' are needed.[83] The opinion stressed the FTC's ability to conduct such an intersectional competition and consumer protection analysis, noting that the FTC is in fact 'uniquely situated to evaluate the implications of this kind of data merger' on both competition and privacy.[84] Recently, FTC Commissioner Bedoya said that he was carefully rereading Harbour's 'prescient' dissenting opinion, noting that Section

75 ibid.

76 Patrick Thibodeau, 'Rotenberg Fears Internet "Privacy Meltdown" from Google-DoubleClick Combo' *Computer World* (20 December 2007) <https://www.computerworld.com/article/2538270/q-a--rotenberg-fears-internet--privacy-meltdown--from-google-doubleclick-combo.html> accessed 2 April 2022.

77 *Google/DoubleClick* (European Commission) (n 69) para 368.

78 *Google/DoubleClick* (Federal Trade Commission) (n 70) 2.

79 ibid.

80 Jon Leibowitz, 'Concurring Statement of Commissioner Jon Leibowitz, Google/Double Click, FTC File No 071-0170' (20 December 2007) 1.

81 ibid 2.

82 Pamela Jones Harbour, 'Dissenting Statement of Commissioner Pamela Jones Harbour, Google/Double Click, FTC File No 071-0170' (20 December 2007) 9.

83 ibid 10.

84 ibid 4.

5 of the FTC Act enables the FTC to look into the privacy repercussions of mergers and that there are several various ways to incorporate privacy into a merger review.[85]

Although the approach to Google/DoubleClick demonstrated in both jurisdictions the realization that concerns about data protection and individual privacy might interact with competition, it also displayed the authorities' reluctance to expand their legal assessments beyond the traditional confines of competition law.

2.2 Continued reluctance in merger cases

In the aftermath of Google/DoubleClick, merger control continued to be a testing ground for competition authorities' readiness to integrate data protection into competition assessments. Among the notable transactions that attract attention due to their novel data-related impacts are acquisitions of small firms by powerful technology companies. In 2021 alone, Google announced the acquisition of 120 companies, Microsoft fifty-six, and Amazon twenty-nine.[86] As these numbers refer only to publicly announced transactions, the actual number of acquired companies is likely to be much higher. Quite paradoxically, the legal response to this phenomenon has been underwhelming. While only a small fraction of the planned acquisitions were notified to the relevant competition authorities, all the acquisitions notified in the EU (to the Commission and to the Member States) and in the US were cleared. The only quasi-prohibition decision was issued by the UK's CMA in 2023 in relation to Meta's acquisition of Giphy.[87]

This section presents and discusses the most relevant merger decision that have posed data protection-related questions. The aim is not to be exhaustive; rather, the selected merger decisions aim to be illustrative of the current sceptical—but also gradually evolving—approach to integrating data concerns into merger review.

2.2.1 Facebook/WhatsApp

In the 2014 *Facebook/WhatsApp* decision,[88] one of the theories of harm formulated by the European Commission was the possible merging of Facebook's and WhatsApp's datasets after the transaction. While the theory was developed from a competition perspective, it brought to the fore the potential data protection risk. The Commission considered two specific scenarios: (1) 'introducing advertising

[85] Flavia Fortes and Mike Swift, 'Data Protection Issues to Get Closer Look in US Merger Analyses from FTC Commissioner Bedoya' *Mlex* (9 November 2022) <https://content.mlex.com/#/content/1423773> accessed 3 April 2022.

[86] Alex Sherman and Lauren Feiner, 'Amazon, Microsoft and Alphabet Went on a Buying Spree in 2021 despite D.C.'s Vow to Take on Big Tech' *CNBC* (22 January 2022) <https://www.cnbc.com/2022/01/22/amazon-microsoft-alphabet-set-more-deals-in-2021-than-last-10-years.html> accessed 3 April 2022.

[87] CMA, 'Final Order made by the Competition and Markets Authority pursuant to section 84 of the Enterprise Act 2002, *Meta Platforms, Inc./Giphy, Inc.*' (6 January 2023).

[88] *Facebook/WhatsApp* (Case COMP/M.7217) Commission Decision of 3 October 2014.

on WhatsApp' and/or (2) 'using WhatsApp as a potential source of user data for the purpose of improving the targeting of Facebook's advertising activities outside WhatsApp'.[89] As regards the first scenario, the Commission concluded that even if Facebook introduced targeted advertising on WhatsApp, that would not affect competition and strengthen Facebook's position as there would continue to be a sufficient number of competitors offering targeted advertising.[90] The second scenario was not likely to be realized in the first place, as the decision noted. Facebook assured the Commission during the investigation that matching users' WhatsApp and Facebook profiles was not its plan and that such matching would not be easily achieved due to 'major technical obstacles'.[91] The Commission concluded that even if the matching took place, it would not distort competition as 'there will continue to be a large amount of Internet user data that are valuable for advertising purposes and that are not within Facebook's exclusive control'.[92]

Despite the potential and evidently negative data protection repercussions, the Commission took the same position as in *Google/DoubleClick*, noting that '[a]ny privacy-related concerns flowing from the increased concentration of data within the control of Facebook as a result of the Transaction do not fall within the scope of the EU competition law rules but within the scope of data protection rules'.[93] The transaction was also cleared by the FTC, following which Jessica Rich, Director of the FTC's Bureau of Consumer Protection, issued a letter obliging both companies to honour their privacy promises to consumers and warning that they would otherwise be liable for deceptive practice under Section 5 of the FTC Act.[94] Among the companies' promises was that information about WhatsApp users would not be used for advertising purposes or sold to third parties without users' consent. The letter also clarified that affirmative express consent would be required if the companies wanted to use the data collected by WhatsApp otherwise than compared to the use of that data pre-merger.

The data protection-related effects of the Facebook/WhatsApp merger became evident within a couple of years of its clearance. In August 2016, WhatsApp announced updates to its terms of service and privacy policy, which envisaged the possibility of sharing data within 'the Facebook family'.[95] Given that Facebook stated during the European Commission's initial investigation that it would not be able to establish a reliable automated matching of datasets, the Commission issued

[89] ibid para 167.
[90] ibid para 179.
[91] ibid para 185.
[92] ibid para 186.
[93] ibid para 164.
[94] Letter From Jessica L Rich, Director of the Federal Trade Commission Bureau of Consumer Protection, to Erin Egan, Chief Privacy Officer, Facebook, and to Anne Hoge, General Counsel, WhatsApp Inc (10 April 2014).
[95] WhatsApp Privacy Policy <https://www.whatsapp.com/legal/privacy-policy/revisions/20160825> accessed 14 April 2022.

a decision in 2017 fining Facebook €110 million for providing misleading information.[96] The Commission did not, however, reverse its 2014 decision, noting that the new updates did not change the legality of the merger.

As predicted, Facebook's post-merger data sharing policy posed data protection compliance challenges. In October 2017, the A29WP issued a letter to WhatsApp, noting that its terms of service and privacy policy had several shortcomings.[97] One troubling aspect was the consent mechanism employed by WhatsApp, which was neither informed (the information provided to individuals was insufficient and misleading) nor freely given (due to a 'take it or leave it' approach), specific, and unambiguous (due to a pre-ticked consent box). Legal action was also taken by individual national DPAs. In 2017, the French DPA found that WhatsApp had violated the French Data Protection Act by sharing data with Facebook without any legal basis, providing an insufficient notice to data subjects, and not cooperating with the authority throughout the investigative process. In 2018, the UK Information Commissioner's Office (ICO) obtained a signed undertaking from WhatsApp that it would not share personal data with Facebook until it could do so in compliance with the GDPR.[98]

The repercussions of the acquisition resurfaced in January 2021, when WhatsApp once again introduced changes to its terms and conditions. Although the changes focused predominantly on the app's business offerings, they also attracted attention to its already existing data sharing practices (eg sharing the phone numbers of WhatsApp users with Facebook). Besides triggering a general backlash that motivated users to switch to other messaging services such as Signal and Telegram, the policy change once again gave rise to a series of legal investigations. The Hamburg Commissioner for Data Protection and Freedom of Information, for example, reacted by issuing a three-month emergency order that prohibited Facebook from processing WhatsApp's user data for its own purposes, arguing that there was no valid legal basis for such data processing operations.[99] However, following the order, the EDPB, indicating lack of sufficient evidence, did not make the Hamburg Commissioner's order permanent.[100] Instead, it allowed the lead DPA (the Irish DPC) to continue its probe into WhatsApp's transparency obligations. In addition, the European Consumer Organisation (BEUC), together with its eight members, responded by issuing a complaint to the Commission and the European

[96] *Facebook/WhatsApp* (Case COMP/M.8228) Commission Decision of 18 May 2017.

[97] Letter from Isabelle Falque-Pierrotin, Chairwoman of A29WP, to Jan Koum, Co-Founder of WhatsApp (24 October 2017).

[98] Information Commissioner's Office, Data Protection Act 1998, Undertaking: WhatsApp Inc (12 March 2018).

[99] Hamburg Commissioner for and Data Protection and Freedom of Information, Anordnung des HmbBfDI gegen Facebook (11 May 2021).

[100] EDPB, Urgent Binding Decision 01/2021 on the Request under Article 66(2) GDPR from the Hamburg (German) Supervisory Authority for Ordering the Adoption of Final Measures Regarding Facebook Ireland Limited (12 July 2021).

network of consumer authorities, accusing WhatsApp of numerous breaches of EU consumer rights.[101] BEUC and its members took issue with WhatsApp's 'persistent, recurrent and intrusive' notifications pushing users to agree to its new policy.[102]

The new policy updates also alarmed jurisdictions outside Europe. Following the announcement of the updates, in March 2021 the Competition Commission of India ordered an investigation into WhatsApp, alleging that the updates—in particular the take-it-or-leave-it choice—constituted an abuse of a dominant position in the market of over-the-top messaging apps through smartphones in India under the 2002 Competition Act.[103]

The Facebook/WhatsApp saga provides the most illustrative example of how lack of coordination between data protection and competition law enforcement can result in violation of individuals' rights and exhaust the resources of enforcers. Merger assessments are future-oriented and, admittedly, it is not easy to envisage with certainty whether a merger will result in a breach of another legal field. Yet, whenever there is sufficient evidence to indicate a threat of potential future violations, the competition authorities should be able to pre-empt them either by integrating data protection concerns into theories of harm or at least by requiring relevant data protection remedies (see Chapter 4 Section C). It is difficult to estimate whether consumers would be better off today if the Facebook/WhatsApp transaction had been evaluated differently.[104] What is clear, however, is that the valuable resources of the enforcement authorities were and continue to be invested in correcting the avoidable data protection repercussions of the transaction.

2.2.2 Microsoft/LinkedIn

In the EU, a visible—yet not truly consequential—change of approach to transactions involving data protection considerations can be identified in a handful of decisions taken in the aftermath of the Facebook/WhatsApp merger. In the assessment of Microsoft's acquisition of LinkedIn,[105] the Commission expressed its concern that the merged entity would have the ability and incentive to foreclose competing providers of professional social networking services by: (2) pre-installing a LinkedIn application on Windows PCs or (2) integrating LinkedIn features into Microsoft Office and denying similar levels of integration to competing providers of professional social networks. As for the impact of such possible

[101] European Consumer Organisation, 'Consumer Groups File Complaint against WhatsApp for Unfairly Pressuring Users to Accept Its New Policies' (9 July 2021) <https://www.beuc.eu/press-releases/consumer-groups-file-complaint-against-whatsapp-unfairly-pressuring-users-accept-its> accessed 19 June 2022.

[102] ibid.

[103] Competition Commission of India, Suo Moto Case No 91 of 2021, Updated Terms of Service and Privacy Policy for WhatsApp Users.

[104] Maria C Wasastjerna, 'The Role of Big Data and Digital Privacy in Merger Review' (2018) 14 European Competition Journal 417, 431.

[105] *Microsoft/LinkedIn* (Case COMP/M.8124) Commission Decision 14 October 2016.

foreclosure strategies on effective competition, given the entry barriers resulting from the network effects and insufficient multi-homing, the market for professional social networking services could be expected to tip in favour of LinkedIn's services. The ensuing consumer harm would also consist in reduced consumer choice in relation to data protection. The Commission observed:

> [T]o the extent that these foreclosure effects would lead to the marginalisation of an existing competitor which offers a greater degree of privacy protection to users than LinkedIn . . ., the Transaction would also restrict consumer choice in relation to this important parameter of competition when choosing a PSN [professional social network].[106]

This theory of harm reflected the empirical findings of the market investigation, which showed that 'privacy is an important parameter of competition and driver of customer choice'[107] in the market for professional social networks. In the decision itself, the Commission mentioned the Hamburg-based social networking site XING, which is active in the German-speaking market and offers better privacy protections than LinkedIn.[108]

To mitigate these competition concerns, Microsoft offered a series of commitments. For example, in line with the pre-installation commitments, PC manufacturers and distributors would be free not to install LinkedIn on Windows and, in the case of a pre-installation, users would be permitted to remove LinkedIn from Windows.[109] Although such commitments were requisite in order to clear the transaction on competition grounds, they benefited data protection indirectly, as stressed by Vice-President Vestager. She maintained that 'by getting commitments from Microsoft that will keep the market open, we've helped to allow companies to compete to protect privacy more effectively'.[110] Thus, even though the data protection repercussions of the transaction were not as such determinative of the Commission's conclusion that commitments were required to give the acquisition the green light, acknowledging the relevance of competition on data protection was a welcome development.

2.2.3 *Google/Fitbit*

A transaction that raised serious data protection concerns and the investigation of which spanned several jurisdictions (including the EU, the US, Australia, Canada, Japan, and South Africa) was Google's purchase of Fitbit announced in 2019. As

[106] ibid para 350.
[107] ibid fn 330.
[108] ibid para 350.
[109] ibid paras 418–21.
[110] Margrethe Vestager, 'What Competition Can Do—and What It Can't' (Chillin' Competition Law Conference, Brussels, 25 October 2017).

Fitbit is a company active in the health and fitness sector (it produces and distributes wearable devices, software, and services), legitimate data protection issues surfaced in relation to the sharing of Fitbit's unique datasets (eg biometric data, including health and emotions[111]) with Google, which could materialize after the transaction.

In Europe, the Commission admitted in *Google/Fitbit*[112] that the transaction would indeed 'allow Google to combine its already very prominent datasets with those of Fitbit',[113] potentially strengthening Google's position in the markets of: (1) online search and display advertising services and ad tech services; (2) general search services; or (3) digital healthcare services, impeding effective competition in those markets.[114] As the decision also stressed, both companies were, however, obliged to comply with data protection law, including the GDPR.[115] Although the Commission even listed some relevant GDPR obligations (such as the purpose limitation principle, the transparency requirements, and a few additional rules governing the processing of health data[116]—a novel step as such), the question of the future compliance of the merged entity with data protection law in no way influenced the final outcome of the case. Rather, having identified a set of competitive concerns, the merger was approved conditional on the implementation of a remedial package valid for ten years that was aimed at addressing the identified competition issues.

In the EU, the approved package consisted of three sets of commitments, 'ads commitments' being the relevant ones for the purpose of the present discussion.[117] Under this commitment, which aimed at limiting Google's competitive advantage post-transaction, Google agreed not to use the health and wellness data collected by Fitbit's devices for Google Ads and agreed to store Fitbit's data in a 'data silo' which required the technical separation of Fitbit's user data. In addition, users' consent would be required for Google to be able to use the health and wellness data for other non-advertising services, such as Google Search, Google Maps, Google Assistant, or YouTube.

The same commitments package, including the ads commitments, was also the precondition for Google and Fitbit to obtain approval for the transaction in other jurisdictions, including in Japan[118] and South Africa.[119] However,

[111] Cristina Caffarra and Tommaso Valletti, 'Google/Fitbit Review: Privacy IS a Competition Issue' (*VoxEU*, 4 March 2020) <https://cepr.org/voxeu/blogs-and-reviews/googlefitbit-review-privacy-competition-issue> accessed 11 April 2022.

[112] *Google/Fitbit* (Case COMP/M.9660) Commission Decision of 17 December 2020.

[113] ibid para 402.

[114] ibid para 413.

[115] ibid para 404.

[116] ibid paras 405–07.

[117] ibid paras 964–73.

[118] Toko Sekiguchi, 'Google-Fitbit Deal Wins Approval from Japan with Its Global Remedies' *Mlex* (14 January 2021) <https://content.mlex.com/#/content/1256622> accessed 14 April 2022. Even though the transaction did not reach the thresholds for merger notification in Japan, the Japanese authority reviewed it under its new policy to scrutinize deals that could stifle future competition.

[119] Competition Commission South Africa, 'Competition Commission Conditionally Approves the Google/Fitbit Merger' (22 December 2020).

some authorities remained more sceptical. Although the companies closed the deal in January 2021, investigations by the ACCC in Australia and the US Department of Justice (DOJ) are still ongoing.[120] Rejecting the commitments package, the Australian authority noted that it still had concerns related, for example, to a possible consolidation of Google's leading position in relation to the collection of user data.[121] In addition, it stressed the difficulty of monitoring the proposed behavioural commitments, in particular given that the industry is complex and dynamic. Weller, the President and Co-founder of Sentinel, a tech company responsible for providing technical expertise to the ING Bank, a trustee appointed to monitor the remedies imposed in the EU, also noted that the commitments themselves were rather complex and monitoring them required staying constantly alert to future changes (eg changes to Google's ads or Fitbit's devices).[122]

The *Google/Fitbit* case also aptly illustrates the institutional controversy. In the EU, it was the first case in which the EDPB became more actively involved by adopting an official statement. In its statement, it expressed concerns about 'the possible further combination and accumulation of sensitive personal data' that 'could entail a high level of risk to the fundamental rights to privacy and to the protection of personal data'.[123] Unprecedentedly, the EDPB also urged both companies 'to conduct in a transparent way a full assessment of the data protection requirements and privacy implications of the merger'.[124] The novelty of that request lay in the fact that conducting a privacy assessment is not part of traditional merger proceedings and there is no obligation for the merging parties to review such implications. The EDPB's formal statement can be interpreted as signalling a willingness to engage in institutional cooperation in the course of competition proceedings. And yet, although the concerns around data concentration would justify strengthened—even if informal—cooperation between the Commission and the data protection authorities, Vice-President Vestager reportedly rejected the possibility of involving the latter in the proceedings. She noted that while '[w]e are very much aware that in cases there can be a privacy issue', '[w]e are just very careful not to see a competition issue where there is a privacy issue because, if that

[120] Reuters Staff, 'Google Closes Fitbit Deal as U.S., Australia Probes Continue' *Reuters* (14 January 2021) <https://www.reuters.com/article/us-fitbit-m-a-alphabet-idUSKBN29J1WR> accessed 14 April 2022.

[121] ACCC, 'ACCC Rejects Google Behavioural Undertakings for Fitbit Acquisition' (22 December 2020) <https://www.accc.gov.au/media-release/accc-rejects-google-behavioural-undertakings-for-fit bit-acquisition> accessed 4 September 2022.

[122] Ryan Chiavetta, 'How a "Technical Expert" Factors into the Google-Fitit Acquisition' *IAAP* (9 June 2021) <https://iapp.org/news/a/how-a-technical-expert-factors-into-the-google-fitbit-acquisit ion/> accessed 15 April 2022.

[123] EDPB, 'Statement on Privacy Implications of Mergers' (2020).

[124] ibid.

is the case, it's not for us'.[125] However, she provided no further justification for that institutional isolation. Even though the EU does not currently envisage a formal role and competence for data protection authorities to intervene in competition cases, and vice versa, nothing prevents the Commission from engaging in informal discussions, in particular where the expertise of other authorities might prove crucial to accurately grasp the market dynamics and possible future developments.

While *Google/Fitbit* provided momentum for tackling competition concerns in a more privacy-conscious way, for many the final decision proved far from satisfactory. Dismissing the opportunity to test novel data-related harm theories was the signal indicating that even in the most obvious cases with interlocking data and competition issues, there was no readiness to better align competition assessment frameworks with the new realities of digital markets.[126] At the same time, some authorities' reluctance to clear the merger illustrates growing scepticism to giving companies carte blanche to realize their business data strategies. In addition, the case offers a remedy-related precedent: the data silo remedy is a test for how effectively such data-related commitments can be monitored. If this commitment, as well as its monitoring system, prove functional despite the dynamic nature of digital markets, such behavioural solutions could be replicated in future cases linking competition and data protection obligations more tightly.

2.2.4 Meta/Giphy

The latest episode in the merger series that shows how differently jurisdictions might in future approach transactions in the digital economy is Meta's acquisition of Giphy, the world's leading provider of a library of free GIFs and stickers. While the merger was investigated by several jurisdictions, including Austria, Australia, and the US, the most noteworthy decision was issued by the UK's CMA which on 30 November 2021 required Meta to sell Giphy in order to address competition concerns identified by the CMA.[127] Given that Meta completed the transaction on 15 May 2020, the UK's competition authority could not block the merger, and instead issued an order requiring Meta's full divestiture of Giphy which, it concluded, was the only effective remedy.

The identified competition concerns leading to the divestiture decision were twofold. First, the CMA concluded that the merger would generate horizontal unilateral effects in that it would substantially lessen competition 'in the supply

[125] Aoife White and Hamza Ali, 'Google-Fitbit Probe Isn't for Data Watchdogs, Vestager Says' *Bloomberg* (25 February 2020) <https://www.bloomberg.com/news/articles/2020-02-25/google-fitbit-probe-is-for-me-not-data-watchdogs-vestager-says> accessed 5 May 2022.

[126] See eg European Consumer Organisation, 'Google's Fitbit Takeover: EU Merger Control Proves Unable to Protect Consumers in the Digital Economy' (17 December 2020) <https://www.beuc.eu/press-releases/googles-fitbit-takeover-eu-merger-control-proves-unable-protect-consumers-digital> accessed 14 June 2022.

[127] CMA, 'Completed Acquisition by Facebook, Inc (Now Meta Platforms, Inc) of Giphy, Inc Final report on the case remitted to the CMA by the Competition Appeal Tribunal' (18 October 2022).

of display advertising services in the UK'.[128] Concretely, Giphy had developed an innovative monetization model called Paid Alignment, which allowed commercial partners such as Pepsi to advertise their products through GIFs and other visual images. As this new way of advertising made Giphy a potential competitor in display advertising, Meta's decision to acquire Giphy was, in the view of the CMA, intended to eliminate a future competitive constraint posed by Giphy's innovative service. In this sense, one could argue that the transaction had some features resembling 'a killer acquisition', whereby one company acquires another to 'kill' an innovative idea and avoid potential competition. Besides restricting competition in display advertising, the transaction also generated vertical effects. Post-merger, Meta could foreclose other platforms by denying or limiting their access to Giphy's GIFs, affecting competition for user attention and leading to the further consolidation of Meta's power.

While these two main theories of harm were 'from the standard antitrust playbook',[129] the CMA also briefly analysed whether Meta's access to Giphy's data could be used to disadvantage Meta's competitors. Specifically, the concern was about Giphy's access to aggregated data about third-party platforms and user-level data (eg users' moods and sentiments)[130] and about Meta's future use of such data for its own advantage. As regards user-level data, the CMA noted that Meta 'could require larger partners, that currently do not return user-level identifiers to Giphy, to request such data as a condition of supply',[131] which might then be used by Meta for the purpose of targeted advertising. The decision explicitly recognized that Facebook's competitors might be unwilling to share such data on data protection grounds. As the CMA noted, Meta's requirement to share such data 'would thus be equivalent to raising the price of Giphy's services to third parties'.[132] As a result, platforms that value data protection would either need to stop using Giphy or switch to other providers, which would be challenging given the lack of effective alternatives. The decision further indicated that at least one platform reported that following the merger transaction it chose to switch away from Giphy on the ground that Meta would collect more data on its users. Another party expressed its readiness to switch, noting that 'instead of paying for additional measures to prevent "data leakage", ... it would rather stop using Giphy's service altogether'.[133]

In addition, Meta could use Giphy's data to gather additional insights about individuals and use those insights for advertising purposes. While the CMA decision did not elaborate on that scenario, the concern was that, for example, a user

[128] ibid para 7255.

[129] Cristina Caffarra, Gregory Crawford, and Johnny Ryan, 'The Antitrust Orthodoxy Is Blind to Real Data Harms' (*VoxEU*, 22 April 2021) <https://voxeu.org/content/antitrust-orthodoxy-blind-real-data-harms> accessed 14 May 2022.

[130] CMA (n 127) Appendix F, paras 24–26.

[131] ibid para 8.106.

[132] ibid para 8102.

[133] ibid para 8103.

searching for depression-related GIFs via Giphy might then see ads for antidepressants or counselling services on their Facebook or Instagram, which would fuel the surveillance- and tracking-based economy.[134]

The CMA's decision is unprecedented in two respects. First, it is the first decision in the field of digital mergers that has imposed structural instead of behavioural remedies: the full divestiture of Giphy by Facebook. As the consequences of this decision not only affect the UK market, but rather all jurisdictions where the merged entity would operate, structural remedies imposed by the CMA set a precedent for shaping the global digital marketplace through a merger decision. This bold move by the CMA is consistent with the Furman Report's recommendation that a merger assessment in digital markets 'needs a reset'.[135] The report suggested that the CMA takes 'more frequent and firmer action to challenge mergers that could be detrimental to consumer welfare through reducing future levels of innovation and competition'.[136]

While the imposition of structural remedies is the main novelty, the fact that the decision admitted the relevance of data protection concerns for competition demonstrates how these two go hand in hand in data-intensive markets.

2.3 Experimentation in abuse of dominance and monopolization cases

Merger control is not the only area where it becomes difficult to turn a blind eye to the interactions between personal data and competition. This section draws attention to a number of abuse of dominance and monopolization cases by showing how data protection has so far been incorporated into the assessments of exploitative abuses, exclusionary abuses, as well as how data protection-washing has become an emerging abuse-related competition issue.

2.3.1 Data protection and exploitative abuses

The most prominent decision that directly merges data protection and competition law through the concept of 'exploitation' is the decision against Facebook taken by the Bundeskartellamt on 7 February 2019.[137] The decision concluded that the platform abused its dominant position in the social media market in Germany by employing legally questionable data strategies. The decision's legal basis was Section 19(1) GWB, which is the national equivalent of Article 102 TFEU.

The Bundeskartellamt found that it was illegal for Facebook to collect data from Facebook-owned services such as WhatsApp and Instagram, as well as from

[134] Mike Swift, 'Facebook's History with Onavo Resonates for Privacy Experts Worried about Giphy Purchase' *Mlex* (23 June 2020) <https://mlexmarketinsight.com/news-hub/editors-picks/area-of-expertise/data-privacy-and-security/facebooks-history-with-onavo-resonates-for-privacy-experts-worried-about-giphy-purchase> accessed 13 May 2022.

[135] Furman (n 5) 12.

[136] ibid.

[137] Bundeskartellamt, Decision B6-22/16 of 6 February 2019 (*Facebook*).

third-party websites (ie websites that include interfaces such as 'like' or 'share' buttons), to subsequently assign them to a Facebook user account and use them without their lawful consent. The theory of harm posited that forcing individuals to accept Facebook's data-related terms and conditions deprived them of control over their data and affected their right to informational self-determination, constituting an exploitative abuse. The conclusion was that Facebook's data practices violated Articles 5(1)(a) and 6 GDPR, Facebook could not justify its extensive data processing on the grounds of performing a contract under Article 6(1)(b) GDPR, and its legitimate interests under Article 6(1)(f) GDPR did not outweigh the interest of individuals. Furthermore, given that Facebook has a dominant position and forces users to accept its data policies, the consent obtained by the company was not valid under Articles 6(1)(a) and 7 GDPR. Interestingly, the Bundeskartellamt noted that such merging of data protection and competition law issues 'does not in any way threaten the consistent interpretation of data protection law, but rather promotes consistency'.[138]

As the decision was taken under German competition law, the question emerged whether such a substantive stretching of competition law's traditional boundaries could also be replicated at the EU level.[139] Given that Chapter 5 features a detailed discussion on competition law theories of harm, it is for now sufficient to note that according to Article 3(2) of Regulation 1/2003, in the area of abuse of dominance (as opposed to anti-competitive agreements) Member States are not precluded from adopting stricter national competition laws compared to EU competition law.

Following Facebook's appeal to the Higher Regional Court of Düsseldorf, the court contested the Bundeskartellamt's decision and granted Facebook interim relief, suspending execution of the decision.[140] The court justified its decision by noting, inter alia, that there was no harm to competition and individuals did not incur any financial loss. It also indicated that the Bundeskartellamt had not proved any link between market dominance and the alleged abuse, and noted that individuals were not exploited because they willingly engaged with Facebook's services. The GDPR's violations, which were at the heart of the Bundeskartellamt's decision, were disregarded as irrelevant for the purpose of applying competition law.

The Bundeskartellamt appealed the Düsseldorf court's decision to the German Federal Supreme Court. In a rather unexpected and comprehensive interim decision of 23 June 2020, the Federal Supreme Court overruled the Düsseldorf court's judgment and upheld the Bundeskartellamt's Facebook decision. While the Federal Supreme Court agreed that Facebook's data policies were in principle illegal, its justification differed compared to that adopted by the Bundeskartellamt. While

[138] ibid para 541.

[139] On a parallel application of EU law in this case, see Wouter PJ Wils, 'The Obligation for the Competition Authorities of the EU Member States to Apply EU Antitrust Law and the Facebook Decision of the Bundeskartellamt' (2019) Concurrences No 3-2019, art no 91034 58.

[140] OLG Düsseldorf, Beschluss vom 26.08.2019—*VI-Kart 1/19* (*V*).

the latter pushed data protection concerns heavily to the forefront, the court formulated a competition-centred theory of harm based on an 'imposed extension of services' ('aufgedrängte Leistungserweiterung').[141] One of the main arguments was that given individuals' preference for Facebook not to use their data collected outside the social network platform ('off-Facebook' data), as the Bundeskartellamt's survey demonstrated, Facebook would also provide less 'data-intensive' alternatives in a more competitive setting.[142] The theory of harm was therefore not grounded in the concern for data protection, but rather pivoted around a lack of choice between the different models of service offered by a dominant company. As Seelinger rightly noted, this conclusion is, as such, rather novel for competition law and its significance extends beyond the Facebook case.[143]

Furthermore, the court noted that Facebook's data strategies harm competition in the social networks and advertising markets. Having considered both side of the market (platform users and advertisers), the court stated that Facebook's access to off-Facebook data allowed the company to improve its social network (eg by making it more personalized, which some users might value) and better design its future business strategies.[144] At the same time, it could also give Facebook an advantage over rivals competing for advertising contracts.[145] Thus, Facebook's functionalities based on off-Facebook data constituted 'an expanded service' imposed on individuals through an abuse dominance,[146] and the harm had two dimensions: a vertical one towards individuals, in particular as Facebook constitutes a crucial means of social communication and no alternative exists,[147] and a horizontal one towards competitors. As the Federal Supreme Court's justification focused its theory of harm on competition rather than on data protection, it was received in the competition community as relatively well grounded.

The court did not, however, disregard data protection issues entirely. As mentioned, one of the decision's grounds was consumer exploitation through data collection and processing, irrespective of whether it also violated the GDPR.[148] In that sense, impinging on users' privacy was presented as a competition-relevant harm, independent of any considerations under the GDPR. At the same time, the court

[141] Klaus Wiedemann, 'A Matter of Choice: The German Federal Supreme Court's Interim Decision in the Abuse-of-Dominance Proceedings *Bundeskartellamt v. Facebook* (Case KVR 69/19)' (2020) 51 International Review of Intellectual Property and Competition Law 1168, 1170. See BGH, Beschluss vom 23.06.20—*KVR 69/19*, para 58.

[142] Wiedemann (n 141) 1172.

[143] Daniela Seelinger, 'The Facebook Decision: Is Everything Clear Now?' (*D'Kart*, 27 June 2020) <https://www.d-kart.de/en/blog/2020/06/27/die-facebook-entscheidung-ist-jetzt-alles-klar/> accessed 14 May 2022.

[144] BGH (n 141) para 94.

[145] ibid.

[146] ibid para 97.

[147] ibid para 102.

[148] Ariel Ezrachi, *EU Competition Law: An Analytical Guide to the Leading Cases* (7th edn, Hart Publishing 2021) 346.

made explicit references to the GDPR. Stressing the political, social, and economic relevance of online communication, as well as the scope and sensitivity of information involved, personal data must be effectively protected in such markets, which the right to individual self-determination envisages.[149] The court thus asserted that the GDPR's values could be a relevant factor in the balancing of all interests at stake.[150]

The case took a curious turn when, in reaction to the decision issued by the Federal Supreme Court, the court in Düsseldorf filed a request for a preliminary ruling to the CJEU.[151] The request centred around a set of highly relevant questions, which would give the CJEU an opportunity—for the first time since the *Asnef-Equifax* case—to voice its view on the interaction between data protection and competition law. The questions referred touched upon a few institutional and substantive issues, such as the ability of a competition authority to declare that a company had violated the GDPR, the legality of Facebook's justification for its data processing terms on the grounds of the performance of the contract under Article 6(1)(b) GDPR, or the pursuit of its legitimate interests under Article 6(1)(f) GDPR, or on other grounds in individual cases (eg complying with a legal obligation, performing a public interest task), and the contexts in which the processing included sensitive data in line with Article 9(1) GDPR.

While the CJEU's judgment is eagerly awaited, in September 2022, Advocate General Rantos delivered an Opinion that essentially posited that competition law authorities could, in the course of a competition law investigation, consider lack of compliance with the investigated practice with the GDPR.[152] The nature of competition authorities' interpretation of the GDRP for the purpose of applying competition law should, however, be incidental. Overall, the Opinion can be considered a welcome step towards recognizing the role of data protection in competition enforcement.

Another recent and noteworthy enforcement action by the Bundeskartellamt that fuses competition and data protection considerations is the statement of objections issued against Google's data processing terms in January 2023.[153] While the agency relied in this case on the new Section 19a of the German Competition Act instead of the exploitation theory invoked in the *Facebook* decision, the proceedings against Google are similar in nature as they take issue with the data protection harm caused to individuals. In the *Google* case, the Bundeskartellamt expressed concern about Google's policy of combining personal data from its various services

[149] BGH (n 141) para 103.

[150] ibid para 109.

[151] Case C-252/21 *Facebook Inc and Others v Bundeskartellamt*, Request for a preliminary ruling from the Oberlandesgericht Düsseldorf (Germany) [2021] OJ C320/16.

[152] Case 252/21 *Meta Platforms and Others v Bundeskartellamt* [2022] ECLI:EU:C:2022:704, Opinion of AG Rantos.

[153] Bundeskartellamt, 'Statement of objections issued against Google's data processing terms' (2023).

such as Google Search, YouTube, Google Play, Google Maps, and Google Assistant, as well as from numerous third-party websites and apps, for various purposes (eg profiling, advertising). According to the allegation, Google's current terms do not provide users with 'sufficient choice as to whether and to what extent they agree to this far-reaching processing of their data across services', and the choices offered are not sufficiently transparent or are too general. This impedes users' ability to, for example, differentiate between the various processing purposes or to give free consent, and may prove to be anti-competitive.

A similar testing of competition law's boundaries can also be identified in other recent national cases. Reacting to the privacy terms and policies announced by WhatsApp in 2021, the Competition Commission of India issued an order announcing an investigation into WhatsApp's possible abuse of dominance under Section 4 of the Indian Competition Act 2002.[154] While WhatsApp questioned the CCI's jurisdiction, the CCI noted that in digital markets, 'unreasonable data collection and sharing thereof, may grant competitive advantage to the dominant players and may result in exploitative as well as exclusionary effects, which is a subject matter of examination under competition law'.[155] As regards the CCI's substantive assessment, having asserted WhatsApp's dominance in the market of over-the-top messaging apps through smartphones in India, the CCI maintained that individuals had no choice but to accept the new policy if they decided to use WhatsApp's services. In the CCI's view, the lack of opt-out options would lead to the collection of data that was 'unduly expansive and disproportionate'.[156] The take-it-or-leave-it approach also prevented WhatsApp from obtaining consent that would signify voluntary agreement: a strategy that is unfair and unreasonable.[157] In addition, information provided by WhatsApp regarding its data processing was too broad, vague, and unintelligible.[158] On that basis, the CCI concluded that WhatsApp's new data policy was exploitative vis-à-vis individuals and exclusionary vis-à-vis competitors.

As regards the exploitation theory, the CCI relied on the concept of quality, noting that the reduction of data protection and loss of control was equivalent to the reduction of quality.[159] These data protection harms would not occur in competitive markets, where users would have 'sovereign rights and control' over their data.[160] In that respect, the CCI's reasoning differs from that expressed by the German Federal Court of Justice, the latter formulating individuals' data-related exploitation as lack of choice instead of degradation of quality.

[154] Competition Commission of India (n 103).
[155] ibid para 13.
[156] ibid para 24.
[157] ibid para 29.
[158] ibid para 27.
[159] ibid para 32.
[160] ibid para 28.

Another relevant recent legal action that has the potential to shape the landscape of abuses in digital markets is the class action lawsuit against Meta, which was lodged with the UK's Competition Appeal Tribunal in London in mid-January 2022.[161] The case, led by Lovdahl Gormsen, alleged that Meta abused its dominant position in the market of (personal) social networks in the UK (alternatively, globally). Allegedly, the conduct violated individually and/or collectively Article 102 TFEU and section 18 of the UK Competition Act 1998.

The case advanced three exploitation-related allegations: (1) the unfair data requirement; (2) the unfair price; and (3) other unfair trading conditions. The first category included the claim that the nature, extent, and scope of personal data collected and processed by Meta was disproportionate and/or not necessary for the purpose of providing its services. This harms individuals because they have no choice but to agree to the company's data practices, and because there are no alternatives to Meta. The second set of allegations argued that the company 'demanded an unfairly high "price" or "payment in kind" for the provision of social networking services'.[162] While Meta's incremental costs of providing its services to each additional user is very low, its revenues from advertising by virtue of that data are high, leaving Facebook with supra-competitive profits that it would not obtain in a competitive market. The third group of allegations concerned the means of imposing data conditions and collecting and monetizing data. For example, what is unfair from a competition standpoint are excessively long and complex terms and conditions, as well as the lack of transparency regarding the nature, extent, and scope of data collection and ways of data use. If the action is successful, Meta will need to pay £2.3 billion in damages to its UK users.[163]

While the theory of exploitation has emerged as a way to challenge data practices under competition law, it is far from uncontroversial, as the German case shows. As it carries the risk of competition authorities filling the shoes of regulators, the approach towards exploitative abuses needs to be carved out carefully to respect the delicate balance between under- and over-enforcement. The book comes back to exploitative abuses in Chapter 5.

2.3.2 Data protection and exclusionary abuses

An alternative strategy to tackle abuse at the interface of competition and data protection—a strategy that centres on market exclusion rather than exploitation—has been adopted in a few equally noteworthy national cases.

[161] *Liza Lovdahl Gormsen v Meta Platforms, Inc and Others*, Notice of Application to Commence Collective Proceedings Under Section 47B of the Competition Act 1998, Case No 1433/7/7/22.

[162] ibid.

[163] Mike Butcher, 'UK Class Action Lodged against Meta Seeks £2.3 Billion in Damages to Facebook U.K. Users' *Techcrunch* (14 January 2022) <https://techcrunch.com/2022/01/13/uk-class-action-lodged-against-meta-seeks-3-1bn-for-breach-of-competition-law/> accessed 14 May 2022.

One example is a US civil antitrust lawsuit filed on 20 October 2020 by the DOJ along with eleven state Attorneys General against Google.[164] Relying on Section 2 of the US Sherman Act, the DOJ and the states alleged that Google maintained monopolies in three different markets: general search services, search advertising, and general search in the US. Among others things, Google did so by concluding exclusivity agreements forbidding pre-installations of competing search services, tying arrangements that forced pre-installation of Google's search applications in central locations on mobile devices and made them undeletable, long-term arrangements with Apple that required making Google a default search engine on the Safari browser and other search tools of Apple, and exploiting monopoly profits to buy preferential treatment for Google's search engine on multiple search access points. Relevant for the present discussion is how the complaint analysed the effects of these practices on the general search market, where it also reflected on privacy repercussions.

As a result of Google's conduct, competition in general search services was substantially foreclosed. This, in turn, harmed consumers 'by reducing the quality of general search services (including dimensions such as privacy, data protection, and use of consumer data), lessening choice in general search services, and impeding innovation'.[165] Thus, in line with the argument that as Google is 'the unchallenged gateway to the internet for billions of users worldwide', consumers are forced to agree to Google's privacy policies and its use of personal data, therefore new and innovative companies—including companies that would offer more privacy-friendly services—are unable to 'emerge from Google's long shadow'.[166]

Acknowledging privacy harms, which in line with the DOJ's argumentation is a competition-relevant dimension of the quality of search engines, is an aspect differentiating the US complaint from its EU counterpart, *Google Android*, which was decided by the Commission in 2018 and upheld on appeal by the CJEU in 2021.[167] In *Google Android*, the Commission concluded that Google had abused its dominant position by imposing a set of contractual restrictions on device manufacturers and mobile network operators, cementing its dominant position in the market for general search services. While both the US complaint and the *Google Android* decisions include assessments of the effects of Google's practices on rivals, the former is more precise as to the likely future repercussions.[168] For example,

[164] *US and Plaintiff States v Google LLC* (filed 20 October 2020).

[165] ibid para 167.

[166] ibid para 13.

[167] *Google Android* (Case AT.40099) Commission Decision of 18 July 2019; upheld on appeal in Case T-604/18 *Google and Alphabet v Commission (Google Android)* [2022] ECLI:EU:T:2022:541 (currently on appeal).

[168] Giorgio Monti, 'Taming Digital Monopolies: A Comparative Account of the Evolution of Antitrust and Regulation in the European Union and the United States' (2022) 67 Antitrust Bulletin 40, 53.

as mentioned, the US complaint considered how potential rivals that employ more privacy-protective business models (eg DuckDuckGo) might be affected by Google's practices. It was also more future-oriented as it assessed potential impacts on the development of alternative search engines on the next generation of search platforms such as smart speakers, home appliances, and smart cars. Comparing the two cases, Monti noted that there was nothing preventing the Commission from conducting a similarly forward-looking assessment, as EU competition law allows enforcers to scrutinize how potential competition might in the future be restricted as a result of abusive conduct.[169] Several reasons might explain this divergence. One of them can be the timing of the investigation: while the EU case against Google started in 2013, the US complaint was issued in 2020, hence the DOJ might simply have had a better understanding of the market's direction of development.[170] Furthermore, the EU, as opposed to the US, has bespoke data protection rules,[171] hence the Commission might have also in its *Google Android* decision embraced the view that it was data protection law that was responsible for correcting such market failures.

A more evident case integrating data protection and competition concerns around exclusionary abuse was the Bundeskartellamt's proceedings against Meta launched in late 2020. The German authority found it problematic that Meta: (1) decided to make the use of the Quest 2 VR headsets offered by Meta Quest conditional on having a Facebook or Instagram account ('combined use of services'), which was expected to result in (2) linking the data gathered from the use of the headset with other Meta services ('linking of data'). While the investigation was initially based on Section 19(1) GWB (abuse of a dominant position) and Article 102 TFEU, the Bundeskartellamt subsequently extended the scope of the proceedings when the new Section 19a came into force. In line with the latter, Meta became subject to the rules applicable to UPSCAM.

To understand the proximity of competition and data protection issues in this case, the two grounds for concern mentioned above need to be briefly explained. As regards the combined use of services, Section 19a(2) sentence 1 number 3(a) GWB prohibits an UPSCAM from automatically linking its various offers if such linking is unnecessary and does not give the user a choice. The thrust of the provision is to limit the UPSCAM's ability to expand its position and further strengthen its ecosystem: bundled offers 'trap' individuals in an ecosystem and raise barriers to entry for competitors.[172] While Meta addressed the authority's concern by removing the condition of having a Facebook or Instagram account (users are able to set up a separate Meta account), the Bundeskartellamt announced that it would

[169] ibid 54.
[170] ibid.
[171] Monti (n 168) 55.
[172] Bundeskartellamt, Decision B6-55/20 of 23 November 2022 (*Meta Quest*) Case Summary.

continue to examine the choice architecture provided to individuals, as well as further monitoring Meta's activities in the VR sector.

The second concern, namely linking data, is based on Section 19a(2) sentence 1 number 4(a) GWB. Under this provision, which visibly merges competition and data protection, it is prohibited for an UPSCAM to make 'the use of services conditional on the user agreeing to the processing of data from other services of the undertaking or a third-party provider', unless the user is given 'sufficient choice as to whether, how and for what purpose such data are processed'. As Meta's VR products and the social network are separate offerings, users need to be provided with choice as regards the processing of their data.[173] Although Meta confirmed that there would be no flow of data across its services, the Bundeskartellamt, awaiting the decision of the CJEU in the competition *Facebook* case, is yet to determine when combining data in such contexts can be permitted.

Last but not least, a case that sheds light of how the concept of abuse may be adapted to capture data practices is the Italian NCA's investigation into Google's conduct relating to data portability, which was opened in July 2022. According to the press release, Google may have abused its dominant position and violated Article 102 TFEU by hindering interoperability in sharing data on its platform with other platforms that offer innovative services (eg Weople APP, operated by Hoda, which developed an innovative data investment bank).[174] A twin concern, as the press release indicates, consists in data protection harm (ie hindering the effectiveness of the right to data portability laid down in art 20 GDPR) and restriction of competition given that the practice limits the ability of other operators to develop innovative services. The authority maintains that by restricting interoperability, Google impinged on Hoda's initiative to enhance user data protection and embark on innovative opportunities to use that data.

As the discussed cases illustrate, the data protection repercussions of exclusionary practices have on a few occasions been considered pertinent in elucidating a theory of harm. As opposed to exploitative abuses, exclusionary theories embrace data protection in a more indirect way: harm to competition might entail harm understood in a data protection sense.

2.3.3 *Data protection-washing as an emerging concern*

Recently, competition authorities in some jurisdiction have been confronted with a new type of conduct with data protection and competition repercussions: alleged improvements to data protection that at the same time trigger exclusionary concerns. Two recent business projects that provide an illustration of such strategies

[173] ibid.

[174] Autorità Garante della Concorrenza e del Mercato, 'Investigation Opened against Google for Abuse of Dominant Position in Data Portability' (14 July 2022) A552 <https://en.agcm.it/en/media/press-releases/2022/7/A552> accessed 18 July 2022.

are Google's Privacy Sandbox and Apple's App Tracking Transparency (ATT) project. In these cases, data protection is framed as the justification for an abuse rather than a finding of an abuse.

Google's Privacy Sandbox. Launched by Chrome (Google) in 2019, the Privacy Sandbox was presented as 'a collaborative, open-source effort to develop a set of new technologies in the form of web standards'.[175] Aimed at re-engineering how online advertising functions, the Sandbox project consisted in proposals for a set of browser application programming interfaces (APIs), which were supposed to replace third-party cookies by 2023. Instead of relying on cookies, advertisers could use APIs to receive aggregated data regarding their ads. As envisioned by Google, anonymized signals instead of cookies would provide advertisers with access to individuals' browsing habits—as opposed to personal data—as their behaviour would be tracked within their individual Chrome browsers. To guarantee privacy, data would be collected and stored on each user's device. The stated objectives of these proposed solutions were to 'prevent tracking as you browse the web', to 'enable publishers to build sustainable sites that respect your privacy', and to 'preserve the vitality of the open web'.[176]

Ever since its announcement, the Sandbox project has attracted criticism from within the industry and among regulators, in particular as regards its competition-related implications and the sincerity of its privacy justification. As the Electronic Frontier Foundation commented, '[t]he Sandbox isn't about privacy. It's about Google's bottom line. At the end of the day, Google is an advertising company that happens to make a browser.'[177]

Acting on complaints that Google's initiative to protect privacy might come at the cost of reduced market competition, in January 2021, the UK's CMA opened a competition investigation. The identified concerns were twofold: (1) if implemented without regulatory scrutiny and oversight, the initiative was likely to constitute an abuse of a dominant position by Google in the market for the supply of web browsers in the UK, and (2) the project's announcement itself and the steps taken by Google to implement it might amount to an abuse.[178] As regards the first claim, the Privacy Sandbox would allow Google to distort competition in the markets for the supply of ad inventory and ad tech services in the UK 'by restricting the functionality associated with user tracking for third parties, while retaining this functionality for Google'.[179] Relatedly, Google's project might imply self-preferencing of its own ad inventory and ad tech services. Furthermore, Google

[175] Google, Privacy Sandbox <https://privacysandbox.com/> accessed 4 September 2022.

[176] ibid.

[177] Bennett Cyphers, 'Don't Play in Google's Privacy Sandbox' (*Electronic Frontier Foundation*, 30 August 2019) <https://www.eff.org/deeplinks/2019/08/dont-play-googles-privacy-sandbox-1> accessed 4 June 2022.

[178] CMA, 'Notice of Intention to Accept Modified Commitments Offered by Google in Relation to Its Privacy Sandbox Proposals, Case Number 50972' (26 November 2021) 22.

[179] ibid 9.

would be able to exploit its dominant position by denying Chrome users' choice related to whether and how their data is used for the purpose of targeted advertising.

The second CMA claim was that Google's announcements and the steps it had taken had already caused harm to Google's rivals that rely on third-party cookies, weakening competition in display advertising. This was caused by market uncertainty about alternative solutions available to publishers and ad tech providers once third-party cookies were phased out. To address the CMA's twofold concern, Google offered a number of commitments. Having accepted Google's commitments in February 2022, the CMA's Chief Executive Coscelli stated that the CMA would 'keep a close eye on Google as it continues to develop these proposals'.[180]

Allegations that Google embarks on privacy-washing are also central to the ongoing US antitrust case launched by a multistate coalition led by Texas Attorney General Paxton.[181] The case is built on a number of allegations of competitively illegal conduct by Google in online advertising. Part of the complaint concerns two Google data strategies and initiatives: (1) Google's decision to restrict publishers' ability to access and share their ad server user IDs (information about website visitors) and (2) the Privacy Sandbox.

As regards the first practice, Google's ad server hashes or encrypts publishers' ad server user IDs, prohibiting publishers from sharing these IDs with non-Google ad exchanges and ad buying tools. This in turn results in a loss of profits for publishers, as such user IDs, in line with the complaint's argumentation, are essential for effective ad targeting and tracking of online advertising campaigns. The complaint also indicates privacy-washing by Google: it rejects Google's privacy justification of its conduct as Google's ad servers share these same user IDs with Google's exchange and buying tools. This means that Google is able to combine the datasets to create more detailed user profiles and provide improved targeted advertising, preventing privacy benefits for consumers. Google seems to have used privacy arguments in a pretextual manner, as a justification for engaging in monopolistic conduct.

The second allegation considers the Privacy Sandbox as potentially problematic under the US antitrust monopolization rules. The complaint describes it as 'building a walled garden out of the open web'[182] in the guise of protecting privacy. The main allegation is that Google's strategy will raise entry barriers in the markets for ad exchanges and ad buying tools, excluding competition and consolidating its power in the advertising sector. As the complaint notes, a small advertiser, for

[180] CMA, 'CMA to keep "close eye" on Google as it secures final Privacy Sandbox commitments' (11 February 2022) <https://www.gov.uk/government/news/cma-to-keep-close-eye-on-google-as-it-secures-final-privacy-sandbox-commitments> accessed 29 May 2022. The CMA publishes quarterly reports on updates of Google's compliance with the binding commitments. See the latest report: CMA, 'CMA third update report on implementation of the Privacy Sandbox commitments' (January 2023).

[181] *State of Texas and other States v Google LLC* (filed 15 March 2021).

[182] ibid para 265

example a local car dealership, will be unable to use cookies to advertise across small publishers such as *The Dallas Morning News*, but will be able to track and target ads across Google Search, YouTube, and Gmail. As Privacy Sandbox does not put an effective end to user profiling and targeting—on the contrary, Google Chrome will be at the centre of such practices—any privacy justifications serve only as a cover for an anti-competitive strategy.

The European Commission's *Google AdSense*[183] decision published in 2019—a de facto EU counterpart to the US complaint described above—in which the Commission fined Google €1.49 billion for abusive practices in online advertising, was silent on any possible privacy-related impacts.[184] Data protection concerns seem, however, to be part of the Commission's new investigation into Google's potentially anti-competitive conduct in the online advertising technology sector, which was opened in June 2021.[185] According to the press release, one of the focal points of the investigation is Google's strategy to restrict access by third parties to user data for the purpose of advertising, while using such data for its own purposes. Google's Privacy Sandbox and preventing advertisers or publishers from accessing data about user identity and behaviour (eg Doubleclick ID) are examples of practices that are part of such a general strategy. As regards the data protection dimension of the investigation, it merely notes that the Commission will take it into account and that competition law and data protection 'must work hand in hand to ensure that display advertising markets operate on a level playing field in which all market participants protect user privacy in the same way'.[186] This statement on the need to have both sets of rules aligned in the effort to ensure 'a level playing' field is rather new. How this relationship will be framed in the decision remains to be seen. It can be envisaged, though, that the Commission will present GDPR enforcement as one side of the coin, without advocating for or actually embarking on joint cooperation in the context of the case.

Apple's ATT. The second illustration of potential data protection-washing is Apple's version of its mobile operating system, iOS 14.5, launched in April 2021. A new feature that is particularly controversial is the ATT framework. Under this framework, Apple requires app developers to obtain the user's permission in order to track them and collect their data across different apps and websites. Contrary to the previous opt-out mechanism, tracking, with few exceptions, is according to the ATT framework only allowed if individuals actively opt-in through a standardized prompt, which requests permission 'to track your activity across other companies'

[183] *Google Search (AdSense)* (Case AT.40411) Commission Decision of 20 March 2019.

[184] Monti (n 168) 18.

[185] European Commission, 'Antitrust: Commission Opens Investigation into Possible Anticompetitive Conduct by Google in the Online Advertising Technology Sector' (22 June 2021) IP/21/3143 <https://ec.europa.eu/commission/presscorner/detail/en/ip_21_3143> accessed 25 March 2022.

[186] ibid.

apps and websites'.[187] Underneath this prompt, is information about the purposes of tracking that app developers can provide (eg 'Your data will be used to deliver personalized ads to you'). If users click on the option 'Ask app not to track', developers cannot access their ID for advertisers, hence are unable to track individuals' activity across apps.[188] Apple's stated rationale for ATT is to 'empower consumers by giving them greater transparency and ability to control the sharing of their own data'.[189]

Although some called this new feature requiring trackers to obtain consent 'an obvious baseline',[190] there were also voices concerned that Apple's ATT would entrench Apple's power to the detriment of smaller companies and publishers that rely on tracking to provide their services free of charge. According to Sokol and Zhu, '[w]hile thinly veiled as a privacy-protecting measure, Apple's iOS 14 policy changes harm the entire ad-supported ecosystem—from developers to advertisers to end consumers',[191] particularly as the transparency framework does not apply to Apple's own apps or proprietary ad products. Arguably, if opt-in rates are low, the new Apple's update might, for example, harm app developers' ability to monetize their apps through personalized ads, ultimately leaving consumers with fewer choices for apps.[192] Based on a similar set of arguments, Meta issued an announcement claiming that the 'new iOS 14 policy will have a harmful impact on many small businesses that are struggling to stay afloat and on the free internet'.[193] Although framed as defending smaller publishers, Meta's criticism was an attempt to (also) protect its own business. Reportedly, Apple's new features caused an estimated loss of $9.85 billion in revenues for Meta, YouTube, Twitter, and Snap in the second half of 2021.[194] Such losses might be more substantial for smaller publishers who cannot rely on first-party tracking data.

[187] Apple, 'User Privacy and Data Use' <https://developer.apple.com/app-store/user-privacy-and-data-use/> accessed 6 June 2022.

[188] Chaim Gartenberg, 'Why Apple's New Privacy Feature Is Such a Big Deal' *The Verge* (27 April 2021) <https://www.theverge.com/2021/4/27/22405474/apple-app-tracking-transparency-ios-14-5-privacy-update-facebook-data> accessed 4 June 2022.

[189] CMA, 'Mobile Ecosystems—Market Study Final Report' (2022) para 6.178.

[190] Andrés Arrieta, 'Facebook's Laughable Campaign Against Apple Is Really Against Users and Small Businesses' (*Electronic Frontier Foundation*, 18 December 2020) <https://www.eff.org/deeplinks/2020/12/facebooks-laughable-campaign-against-apple-really-against-users-and-small> accessed 18 June 2022.

[191] Daniel Sokol and Feng Zhu, 'Harming Competition and Consumers Under the Guise of Protecting Privacy: An Analysis of Apple's IOS 14 Policy Updates' (*Competition Policy International*, 27 May 2021) <https://www.competitionpolicyinternational.com/harming-competition-and-consumers-under-the-guise-of-protecting-privacy-an-analysis-of-apples-ios-14-policy-updates/> accessed 18 June 2022.

[192] ibid.

[193] Dan Levy (Facebook), 'Speaking Up for Small Businesses' (2020) <https://www.facebook.com/business/news/ios-14-apple-privacy-update-impacts-small-business-ads> accessed 18 June 2022.

[194] Patrick McGee, 'Snap, Facebook, Twitter and YouTube Lose Nearly $10bn after iPhone Privacy Changes' *Financial Times* (31 October 2021) <https://www.ft.com/content/4c19e387-ee1a-41d8-8dd2-bc6c302ee58e> accessed 18 June 2022.

In Europe, few competition authorities announced investigations into ATT. In March 2021, acting on received complaints, the French NCA concluded that there was no need to issue urgent interim measures blocking the implementation of Apple's new policy.[195] As the authority explained, there are two reasons why ATT is unlikely to be illegal under competition law. First, even if a company has a dominant position or is considered to be a 'structuring platform', it 'has the freedom in principle to set rules to access its services, subject to not disregarding the law and applicable regulation'.[196] Secondly, the data protection regulations do not preclude the implementation of such an obligation, the ATT policy does not appear to impose an unnecessary obligation or lack proportionality, and it facilitates choice and control for individuals over how their data is used. At the same time, the authority announced that it would continue to investigate the merits of the case, in particular whether there was any illegal 'self-preferencing' by Apple (ie imposing without justification strict rules on other companies as compared to how Apple treats its own similar operations).

In the course of its investigation, the competition authority consulted with the French DPA in relation to Apple's ATT. It was thus a curious development that several months later, in January 2023, the French agency imposed a fine of €8 million on Apple for collecting personal data from French users of Apple's App Store without their consent to receive targeted ads.[197]

In the UK, the CMA noted in the report that followed its market study of mobile ecosystems that ATT has privacy benefits: for example, it strengthens users' control of their data and improves app developers' compliance with data protection rules.[198] At the same time, it expressed competition concerns that ATT might prevent developers from finding consumers and monetizing their apps. Resulting price increases and the reduction of the quality and variety of apps might ultimately harm consumers.[199]

The Polish Competition Authority (UOKiK) expressed competition concerns about Apple's ATT in December 2021, when it launched an investigation with the aim of establishing whether ATT restricts competition in the market for personalized advertising services and constitutes an exclusionary abuse of market power.[200]

[195] Autorité de la concurrence, 'Targeted Advertising/Apple's Implementation of the ATT Framework. The Autorité Does Not Issue Urgent Interim Measures against Apple but Continues to Investigate into the Merits of the Case' (17 March 2021) <https://www.autoritedelaconcurrence.fr/en/press-release/targeted-advertising-apples-implementation-att-framework-autorite-does-not-issue> accessed 18 June 2022.

[196] ibid.

[197] Commission Nationale de l'informatique et des Libertés, Délibération de la formation restreinte no SAN-2022-025 du 29 décembre 2022 concernant la société Apple.

[198] CMA (n 189) para 6.163.

[199] ibid para 6.219.

[200] 'Poland Probes Apple Over App Tracking Transparency Rules' (*Competition Policy International*, 13 December 2021) <https://www.competitionpolicyinternational.com/poland-probes-apple-over-app-tracking-transparency-rules/> accessed 23 June 2022.

The latest competition authority to have expressed doubts about the legality of the ATT framework is the Bundeskartellamt.[201] Its investigation follows the proceedings opened by the Bundeskartellamt one year earlier, in June 2021 (still pending at the time of writing),[202] to determine whether Apple could be classified as having the status of an UPSCAM. If the conclusion is that Apple has such paramount significance, the Bundeskartellamt might prohibit Apple's new framework under Section 19a(2) GWB, in addition to its competition provision. According to sentence 1 of Section 19a(2) GWB, it is illegal for a company of paramount significance to favour its own offers above the offers of its competitors when mediating access to supply and sales markets. In Apple's case, the preliminary findings as outlined in the press release stress concern that Apple itself is not subject to its new rules in the ATT framework. Relevant for the investigation are therefore 'the possibilities for Apple itself to combine data across services and users' options regarding the processing of their data by Apple', as well as 'the question whether these rules may lead to a reduction of users' choice of apps financed through advertising'.[203]

As these two cases show, novel business strategies framed as necessary to protect personal data and users' privacy attract plenty of attention among competition enforcers, which are interested in establishing whether exclusionary competitive harm results from such strategies. While data protection motives underlying Google Sandbox and Apple's ATT are questionable, future cases might feature more genuine privacy justifications. In such an event, as Chapter 5 Section C will show, data protection arguments should be properly engaged with by competition authorities, and in some instances be able successfully to defend against harm to competition.

3. New policy and regulatory initiatives

The goal of this section is to shed light on the concrete legal initiatives that have followed the extensive reflection process on competition in the digital economy, and which affect the relationship between data protection and competition law. As will be shown, with a couple of exceptions, reforming ex post competition law has so far not been the primary trend, which may be attributed to the common view that

[201] Bundeskartellamt, 'Bundeskartellamt Reviews Apple's Tracking Rules for Third-Party Apps' (14 June 2022) <https://www.bundeskartellamt.de/SharedDocs/Meldung/EN/Pressemitteilungen/2022/14_06_2022_Apple.html;jsessionid=A8BB89473F8FEE64A25828B2829E6306.2_cid362?nn=3591568> accessed 4 June 2022.

[202] Bundeskartellamt, 'Proceeding against Apple Based on New Rules for Large Digital Companies (Section 19a(1) GWB)—Bundeskartellamt Examines Apple's Significance for Competition across Markets' (21 June 2021) <https://www.bundeskartellamt.de/SharedDocs/Meldung/EN/Pressemitteilungen/2021/21_06_2021_Apple.html;jsessionid=BB40E379A1063BE8F3AB4360E4182121.1_cid387?nn=3591568> accessed 4 June 2022.

[203] Bundeskartellamt (n 201).

the competition provisions as currently formulated are in many jurisdictions sufficiently flexible to capture new types of harm. Instead, a pronounced outcome of the policy debates has been a tendency to move towards ex ante regulation of large technology companies, which aims to complement competition law.

3.1 Abuse of a dominant position: between legal updates and soft law measures

A notable example of a jurisdiction that has modified its ex post rules on abuse of a dominant position as a reaction to the challenges posed by the digital economy is Germany. Entering into force in January 2021, the tenth amendment to the GWB includes a number of new provisions, among which are some that either directly or indirectly influence the relationship between competition law and data protection. For example, the GWB explicitly envisages in Sections 18 (art 3a(4)) and 19a (art 1(4)) that to determine a company's dominance or its paramount significance for competition across markets (UPSCAM), a competition enforcer must take into account 'its access to data relevant for competition'. Section 19 GWB lists examples of abusive conduct stipulating that a dominant company may under certain circumstances violate competition law if it refuses to supply another firm with objectively necessary goods or services, and 'in particular to grant it access to data, networks or other infrastructure facilities' (art 2(4)). The new Section 19a, addressing abusive conduct of UPSCAM, includes some provisions that are particularly relevant from a data protection standpoint. For example, according to Article 4(a) of Section 19(a), UPSCAM are prohibited from restricting competition 'by processing data relevant for competition that have been collected by the undertaking, or demanding terms and conditions that permit such processing'. Such conduct could include requiring the user to agree 'to the processing of data from other services of the undertaking or a third-party provider without giving the user sufficient choice as to whether, how and for what purpose such data are processed'. Also, impeding competition by refusing or restricting interoperability or data portability by UPSCAM is now classified as prohibited by Article 5 of Section 19(a). In introducing these provisions, Germany became the first jurisdiction specifically to recognize in its competition law the relevance of data and data protection.

An alternative and less far-reaching method for updating competition enforcement can be guidelines or other soft law instruments that provide interpretative instructions. This is the approach taken by the Japan Fair Trade Commission. In December 2019, it published guidelines clarifying the application of the Japanese competition provisions to data-related abuses of a superior bargaining position by digital platform operators.[204] The guidelines provide a non-exhaustive list of market practices relating to the acquisition and use of personal information that

[204] JFTC, 'Guidelines Concerning Abuse of a Superior Bargaining Position in Transactions between Digital Platform Operators and Consumers that Provide Personal Information' (2019).

are 'likely to impede fair competition'—an assessment to be conducted on a case-by-case basis. According to the guidelines, practices that may constitute an abuse of a superior bargaining position include: (1) an 'unjustifiable acquisition of personal information' (eg acquiring personal data without indicating the purpose of use; collecting data beyond that necessary for the purpose it has been collected; acquiring data without implementing the precautions necessary and appropriate for the safe management of data), and (2) an 'unjustifiable use of personal information' (eg using personal information 'against the intention of consumers beyond the scope necessary to achieve the purpose of use', for example, using data acquired for the purpose of targeted advertising, without obtaining the consumers' consent).

At the EU level, relevant for the area of abuse of dominance in digital markets is the Commission's ongoing revision of its Market Definition Notice of 1997. In the draft revised Notice,[205] which the Commission published in November 2022, several important updates were introduced to render the Notice a useful tool for market definition analyses in digital markets. The recognition of the multi-sided nature of digital business models, the acknowledgement that certain traditional tools, such as the SSNIP (small but significant and non-transitory increase in price) test, are not adequate to define zero-price markets, as well as a brief discussion of digital ecosystems are among the indicators of the Commission's changing approach to market definition in the digital era, even though it is hoped that the final version of the Notice will further clarify some of the remaining uncertainties, particularly those relating to the delineation of digital ecosystems.

3.2 Merger control: the focus on jurisdictional aspects

In the area of merger control, the key development has a jurisdictional dimension. At Member State level, the aim of capturing more mergers and acquisitions in digital markets motivated Germany and Austria in 2017 to introduce the new 'transaction value merger notification thresholds', which specify when a transaction needs to be notified to the respective authorities.[206] According to the new thresholds, a transaction is notifiable in Germany or Austria if it exceeds €400 million or €200 million respectively, and provided that additional criteria (ie specific revenue thresholds and the target have significant activities in one of those Member States) are fulfilled.[207] Moving away from the turnover-based threshold used previously had the aim of bringing under the scope of the national merger laws transactions that involve small innovative companies with competitive potential. An example would be a global company planning to acquire the new provider of a smartphone

[205] European Commission, 'Commission Notice on the definition of the relevant market for the purposes of Union competition law', Draft (2022).

[206] In India, a recommendation by the Competition Law Review Committee was to introduce 'data value' thresholds for merger notifications: Ministry of Corporate Affairs, Government of India, 'Report of Competition Law Review Committee' (2019) 131.

[207] See Section 35(1)(1) GWB and Section 9(4) Kartellgesetz 2005 (Cartel Act 2005).

communication app, which already attracts increasing numbers of users but still offers its services free of charge.[208] While it is likely that such a transaction would satisfy the turnover thresholds and would have to be notified, the new transaction value-based thresholds significantly increase the likelihood of the authorities being able to analyse the acquisition. These updates may also have implications for data protection, as many transactions occur in data-intensive markets.

As regards the EU, the Commission has not yet followed the precedent of modifying the thresholds set by Austria and Germany. It has recognized, however, that there have been a number of cross-border transactions with a potentially significant impact on competition in the EU internal market that have escaped review by both the Commission and the Member States.[209] Thus, in March 2021 the Commission issued guidelines reinvigorating the use of the so-called 'referral mechanism' laid down in Article 22 EUMR. The referral mechanism allows one or more Member States to request the Commission to examine any concentration that does not meet EU or national jurisdictional thresholds, but which fulfils two preconditions: it affects trade between Member States and 'threatens to significantly affect competition within the territory of the Member State or States making the request'. To justify the expansion of its powers to review a greater number of mergers, the Commission explicitly mentioned the potential risks generated by mergers in the digital economy. As it noted, there is 'a gradual increase of concentrations involving firms that play or may develop into playing a significant competitive role on the market(s) at stake despite generating little or no turnover at the moment of the concentration'.[210] Thus, the guidelines encourage referrals by Member States of mergers where the turnover of at least one of the involved undertakings 'does not reflect its actual or future competitive potential'.[211] This may materialize where, for example, the acquired undertaking is a start-up or a recent market entrant with significant competitive potential, an important innovator, or has access to competitively significant assets, including personal data.

While the nature of some of the factors that will be used to support the Commission's decision to review the referred concentration seem speculative and vague, leaving the Commission with substantive discretion, the decision to bring Article 22 EUMR back to life is a welcome step. The change to the referral policy has been also endorsed in the recent judgment of the CJEU issued in the context of the Illumina/Grail transaction.[212] Although the transaction concerned

[208] Bundeskartellamt, 'Guidance on Transaction Value Thresholds for Mandatory Pre-Merger Notification (Section 35(1)(1) GWB and Section 9(4) KartG)' (2018) para 88.

[209] European Commission, 'Commission Guidance on the Application of the Referral Mechanism Set out in Article 22 of the Merger Regulation to Certain Categories of Cases', COM (2021) 1959 final, para 10. See also European Commission, 'Evaluation of Procedural and Jurisdictional Aspects of EU Merger Control' (Staff Working Document) SWD (2021) 66 final.

[210] European Commission, 'Guidance on the Application of the Referral Mechanism' (n 209) para 9.

[211] ibid para 19.

[212] Case T-227/21 *Illumina v Commission* [2022] ECLI:EU:T:2022:447. For a commentary on the case, see eg Tilman Kuhn and others, 'EU General Court Confirms European Commission's Article

the healthcare sector rather than the digital sector, the Court's confirmation of the soundness of the new merger referral policy bodes well for future referrals of concentrations possibly affecting competition in the digital economy.

The CJEU's ruling in *Towercast*[213] is another noteworthy judicial pronouncement on the effective application of merger control. The question at stake in *Towercast*, on which the Paris Court of Appeal had requested a preliminary ruling, was whether Article 21(1) EUMR precludes NCAs and national courts from applying Article 102 TFEU to concentrations that have no Union dimension, fall below the national thresholds for mandatory ex ante control, and have not been referred to the Commission under Article 22 EUMR. In its response, the CJEU noted that the EUMR 'does not preclude ex post control of concentration operations that do not meet [the] threshold'.[214] At the same time, the mere finding that a merger has strengthened the position of an undertaking is not sufficient for a finding of abuse: the degree of dominance needs to result in a substantial impediment of competition.[215] The judicial assertion that non-notifiable mergers can be reviewed in an ex post manner under the heading of abuse of dominance is a promising development from the perspective of ensuring that harm resulting from mergers in the digital economy is effectively addressed, in particular as many of digital merger transactions, some of which appear competitively problematic, fall foul of the merger thresholds.

Whereas the jurisdictional dimension of merger control has been the focal point, some jurisdictions have also reflected on the adequacy of current substantive assessments. In 2021, the UK's CMA published revised merger assessment guidelines directly addressing the new digital challenges. For example, it stated that when conducting a merger assessment, the CMA would consider possible non-price aspects of competition, such as 'the level of privacy offered to users of digital services'.[216] The CMA may also reflect on how the merged entity can harm its competitors when supplying inputs: for example, how it can limit data access.[217]

In a similar vein, on 18 January 2022, the US Justice Department and the FTC launched a joint public inquiry that aims to modernize the merger guidelines in order to more effectively capture and address illegal merger deals. As the press release highlights, one of the areas where the agencies seek public input concern the 'unique characteristics of digital mergers', and in particular how to account

22 EUMR Referral Policy' (*Kluwer Competition Law Blog*, 18 July 2022) <http://competitionlawblog.kluwercompetitionlaw.com/2022/07/18/eu-general-court-confirms-european-commissions-article-22-eumr-referral-policy/> accessed 23 July 2022.

213 Case C-449/21 *Towercast v Autorité de la concurrence and Ministère de l'Économie* [2023] ECLI:EU:C:2023:207.
214 ibid para 41.
215 ibid para 52.
216 CMA, 'Merger Assessment Guidelines' (2021) 7.
217 ibid 56.

in merger assessment for 'zero-price products, multi-sided markets and data aggregation'.[218]

In 2021, the Competition and Consumer Commission of Singapore (CCCS) revised a number of its guidelines on the Competition Act 2004.[219] The Guidelines on Substantive Assessment of Mergers, for example, revisited the relevance of data as a barrier to entry and expansion.

3.3 Ex ante instruments complementing competition law

In light of the unprecedentedly entrenched power of a few companies and the weak contestability of digital markets, combined with the realization that ex post competition enforcement is not always an effective or adequate tool to promptly address harmful activities, some jurisdictions have expressed their readiness to introduce complementary ex ante regulatory regimes to promote competition.[220]

In the EU, the reflection process on a new tool for addressing the threefold problem of digital markets' incontestability, unfair business activities, and fragmentation of approaches across the Member States led to the adoption of the DMA.[221] Applicable as of May 2023, the DMA aims to ensure 'contestable and fair markets in the digital sector across the Union where gatekeepers are present'.[222] With this aim, it lays down a number of ex ante obligations and restrictions with which companies designated as gatekeepers—providers of core platform services such as online intermediation services, online search engines, or online social networking services[223] that satisfy a set of qualitative and quantitative criteria indicated in Article 3 of the DMA—need to comply. Among the largest technology companies that have entrenched positions and create bottlenecks between businesses and consumers, hence can be expected to obtain gatekeeper status, are Alphabet, Meta, Apple, Microsoft, and Amazon.

Out of many positive and negative obligations stipulated in the DMA, there are few that reflect the regulator's concern for how competition, data, and data protection

[218] US DOJ, 'Justice Department and Federal Trade Commission Seek to Strengthen Enforcement Against Illegal Mergers' (18 January 2022) <https://www.ftc.gov/news-events/news/press-releases/2022/01/federal-trade-commission-justice-department-seek-strengthen-enforcement-against-illegal-mergers> accessed 11 February 2022.

[219] Competition and Consumer Commission of Singapore, 'CCCS Revises Competition Guidelines for Greater Clarity and Guidance' (31 December 2021) <https://www.cccs.gov.sg/media-and-consultation/newsroom/media-releases/cccs-revises-competition-guidelines-for-greater-clarity-and-guidance.> accessed 11 February 2022.

[220] For a discussion on selected ex ante initiatives, see eg OECD, 'Ex Ante Regulation of Digital Markets' (2021) OECD Competition Committee Discussion Paper.

[221] See eg European Commission, 'Impact Assessment Report Accompanying Proposal for a Regulation of the European Parliament and of the Council on contestable and fair markets in the digital sector (Digital Markets Act)', SWD (2020) 363 final, paras 25–54.

[222] DMA, art 1.

[223] The list of core platform services indicated in art 2(2) DMA includes also video-sharing platform services, number-independent interpersonal communication services, operating systems, cloud computing services, and advertising services.

intersect, and some that explicitly refer to the GDPR. The relevant provisions can be broadly divided into those that restrict the data processing activities of gatekeepers and those that require gatekeepers to give other companies access to data—the latter set of rules evidently controversial from a data protection standpoint.[224]

One of the DMA's provisions that makes interactions between competition and data protection particularly evident, and is therefore worthy of note, is Article 5(2), according to which the gatekeepers shall not:

> (a) process, for the purpose of providing online advertising services, personal data of end users using services of third parties that make use of core platform services of the gatekeeper;
> (b) combine personal data from the relevant core platform service with personal data from any further core platform services or from any other services provided by the gatekeeper or with personal data from third-party services;
> (c) cross-use personal data from the relevant core platform service in other services provided separately by the gatekeeper, including other core platform services, and vice versa; and
> (d) sign in end users to other services of the gatekeeper in order to combine personal data, unless the end user has been presented with the specific choice and has given consent within the meaning of Article 4, point (11), and Article 7 of Regulation (EU) 2016/679.
>
> Where the consent given for the purposes of the first subparagraph has been refused or withdrawn by the end user, the gatekeeper shall not repeat its request for consent for the same purpose more than once within a period of one year.
>
> This paragraph is without prejudice to the possibility for the gatekeeper to rely on Article 6(1), points (c), (d) and (e) of Regulation (EU) 2016/679, where applicable.

Besides this provision, the DMA contains other rules that, although not strikingly similar to the GDPR's requirements, will contribute to shaping the impact of gatekeepers' competitive activities on data protection. According to Article 5(8), for example, gatekeepers are not allowed to require end users to subscribe to or register with their other core platform services as a condition for using any of that gatekeeper's core platform services. As the EDPS has opined, given that this requirement can be expected to 'reduce excessive collection and combination of personal data', it 'indirectly enhances the safeguards to data protection and privacy ... without encroaching upon the GDPR'.[225] There are other DMA

[224] See Konstantina Bania, 'Fitting the Digital Markets Act in the Existing Legal Framework: The Myth of the "Without Prejudice" Clause' (2022) European Competition Journal 1, 14–15.

[225] EDPS, 'Opinion 2/2021 on the Proposal for a Digital Markets Act' (2021) para 26.

provisions that, as the EDPS has stressed, demonstrate how competition law and data protection law can be complementary and mutually enhancing. For example, Article 6(3) DMA obliges gatekeepers to enable individuals to uninstall any software applications on their operating systems, and to easily change the default settings on their operating systems, virtual assistants, and web browsers, Article 6(6) DMA prevents gatekeepers from restricting the ability of end users to switch between various software applications and services accessed via the gatekeeper's services, and Article 6(9) obliges gatekeepers to provide users with effective portability of data. Also relevant is Article 15, according to which a gatekeeper needs to provide the Commission with 'an independently audited description of any techniques for profiling of consumers' that it applies across its core platform services, which shall then be shared with the EDPB. As such, an audit can help to reduce information asymmetries, as well as aiding DPAs in their assessment of the compliance of a gatekeeper's profiling activities with the GDPR. This is an example of how 'strong complementarity' can be introduced between a competition law tool and data protection law.[226]

Despite the DMA's potential to usefully complement data protection law, tensions may also arise. Article 6(10) and (11), which lay down the obligations to share data, including personal data, with business users or third parties, needs to be carefully applied in order not to result in outcomes conflicting with the GDPR.

Given the close proximity between the DMA's several provisions and data protection law, it remains to be seen how their interaction will take shape in practice. While the proposal for a DMA stated that it 'complements the data protection laws',[227] the DMA stipulates that its rules 'should apply without prejudice to the rules resulting from other acts of Union law', including the GDPR.[228] It does not, however, clarify how possible tensions should be solved. Article 40 DMA envisages cooperation between the Commission and other bodies, such as the EDPS and the EDPB, in the framework of a high-level group that is supposed to provide advice and expertise. Although formally establishing structured cooperation is welcome, seeking inputs from the relevant data protection authorities on an ad hoc and informal basis should become standard procedure whenever the DMA's enforcement poses a data protection challenge.

While the DMA is to date the most comprehensive ex ante regime complementing competition law, regulatory tools aimed at fostering competition have also been proposed or implemented in other jurisdictions, and have provisions that affect data protection. The Australian government, for example, was (as of February 2023) consulting on a new ACCC initiative to introduce a customized regulatory

[226] ibid para 36.

[227] European Commission, Proposal for a Regulation of the European Parliament and of the Council on contestable and fair markets in the digital sector (Digital Markets Act)', COM (2020) 842 final, 4.

[228] DMA, recital 12.

approach for digital platforms.[229] In its consultation paper, it explicitly stressed the need to coordinate this new regulatory approach with other regulatory initiatives, including a review of the Privacy Act 1988. As it observed, some trade-offs between competition and privacy goals might emerge with regard, for example, to regulating competitors' access to data.[230] In Japan, the Act on Improving Transparency and Fairness of Digital Platforms applicable as of February 2021 requires 'specified digital platform providers' (platforms designated so far include Amazon, Rakuten Group, Yahoo Japan, Apple, Goole) to disclose information to users such as the scope of data use.[231]

4. Preliminary conclusions

The amount of policy attention devoted over the past few years to competition law's enforcement in the digital economy is proof of how pronounced the empirical developments in digital markets are and how they can transform the legal landscape. The significance of data, and to a lesser extent data protection, is evident in various policy reflections on the necessary reforms that span several jurisdictions. Actual enforcement of competition law in digital markets is, however, far from treating concern for data protection with the seriousness and urgency it deserves. In particular, the silo approach underlies merger control, where the interactions between competition and data protection are most evident. While the DMA is a significant sign of progress as regards treating data protection and competition concerns with the same legal tool, competition law as we know it remains disturbingly reluctant to foster the much-needed coherence with data protection.

C. Competition–agnostic data protection law

To paint a holistic picture, this section complements the competition-focused angle presented previously with the perspective on how data protection law affects market competition. It is not possible to trace the evolution of integrating competition concerns into data protection law in a way similar to the analysis conducted in the previous section. The question 'How should data protection law be rethought to strengthen market competitiveness?' has never been seriously debated. It is also unheard of for an enforcement authority or a judge deciding a data protection case would explicitly consider the impacts of their decision on market competitiveness,

[229] Australian Government, 'Digital Platforms: Government Consultation on ACCC's Regulatory Reform Recommendations' (2022).

[230] ibid 7.

[231] Ministry of Economy, Trade and Industry (Japan), 'Key Points on the Act of Improving Transparency and Fairness of Digital Platforms' (2021).

or embark on a thorough balancing of data protection benefits against competitive harms. This explains the limited focus on 'competition-conscious' data protection in the current discourse. And yet, data protection law should not remain blind to the tangible impacts it has on shaping the competitive dynamics in digital markets—in particular, as markets' contestability and openness are prerequisites for data protection-friendly market alternatives to emerge and thrive.

This section's aim is to present the current position of the competition repercussions of data protection law in Europe. Section 1 explains why effective data protection law is vital for market competitiveness and flags two specific weaknesses of the present enforcement system: the inadequate functioning of the 'one-stop-shop' mechanism, and the uncertainties around the implementation of the right to effective judicial protection. Section 2 turns to the problem of fragmentation of the data protection landscape in the EU and compliance costs. While the book is premised on the conviction that strengthened, rather than weakened, data protection is vital for creating a competitive landscape where data protection is not continuously exploited, there are critical voices in the competition community regarding data protection law's impact on data-driven competition: this is the focus of Section 3. Finally, relying on the example of data portability, Section 4 shows that even though certain data protection notions have enormous potential to bring data protection and competition law closer together, the way they have been formulated and implemented diminish their unifying potential.

1. The lack of effective enforcement

1.1 Effective data protection enforcement as a precondition for well-functioning competition

Data protection law can be part of a concerted effort to promote market competitiveness and provide incentives to compete on data protection. Besides individual rights, obligations imposed on companies can also complement competition law in ensuring that data-driven competition races to the bottom are gradually replaced by business initiatives premised on meaningful data protection.

At first glance, it might seem counterintuitive to claim that strict data protection standards can support market competitiveness. Enabling wide access to data and ensuring greater freedom to use data in unrestricted ways seemingly squares better with the demands of competition. And yet, well-enforced data protection law should be approached precisely as the missing component needed to promote competitive dynamism and introduce diversity, transforming the current digital markets where the race for a data advantage and data exploitation inform the mode of competition. For example, stricter enforcement of data protection principles, such as purpose limitation as stressed by Caffarra and Ryan, can help to curb the power of large firms and pre-empt potentially anti-competitive conduct.

As they have noted, it 'would address the vast, unlawful data advantage that these tech giants gain from combining and cross-using the personal data of users'.[232] A similar point was made by Graef and Van Berlo, who submitted that stricter enforcement of the purpose limitation principle would not only foster data subjects' control, but also 'address concerns arising from the expansion of market power through the leveraging of personal data across services', promoting competition interests.[233] The claim that markets' contestability can be better achieved by effectively enforcing data protection law rather than weakening it is supported by the approach adopted in the DMA, which includes several important provisions that are in full synch with the GDPR (see Section A).

The reports and studies suggesting that the GDPR's effects on innovation and market competitiveness more broadly are solely negative and must be approached critically, especially if the goal is to stimulate privacy-respecting competitiveness. For example, Janßen and his colleagues analysed the GDPR's effects on the welfare of companies in the app market.[234] Their hypothesis was that while digitalization reduced entry costs, hence substantially induced market entry in various media markets, the GDPR 'may be like the digitalization in reverse'.[235] Having relied on data on 4.1 million apps in the Google Play Store in the period between 2016 and 2019, the authors concluded that the GDPR significantly reshaped Google's app market. While in the year following the GDPR's implementation, a third of apps exited the market and the entry rate of apps fell by 47.2 per cent after the regulation's enactment. Based on these observations, their article concluded that the GDPR has 'prevented the entry of a "lost generation" of valuable apps'[236] and 'produced the unintended consequence of slowing innovation'[237] to the disadvantage of consumers. This normative view that considers all forms of innovation valuable—even innovation that promotes intrusive data strategies—must be challenged. As the authors themselves admitted, apps' privacy-intrusiveness post-GDPR has declined.[238] Thus, this perceived loss of innovation does not seem to be an unintended outcome of the GDPR; on the contrary, the exit or the absence of entry of apps that are not compliant with data protection law is precisely what the GDPR intends to achieve. And, at the same time, it is precisely what a new competition paradigm in digital markets should strive for.

[232] Cristina Caffarra and Johnny Ryan, 'Ending the "Data Free-For-All": Antitrust vs GDPR Enforcement' *Euractiv* (22 January 2021) <https://www.euractiv.com/section/digital/opinion/ending-the-data-free-for-all-antitrust-vs-gdpr-enforcement/> accessed 3 June 2022.

[233] Inge Graef and Sean Van Berlo, 'Towards Smarter Regulation in the Areas of Competition, Data Protection and Consumer Law: Why Greater Power Should Come with Greater Responsibility' (2021) 12 European Journal of Risk Regulation 674, 692.

[234] Rebecca Janßen and others, 'GDPR and the Lost Generation of Innovative Apps' (2022) NBER Working Paper No 30028, 1.

[235] ibid.

[236] ibid.

[237] ibid 37.

[238] ibid 25–26.

Another illustration of the same phenomenon is the 2018 survey of merger and acquisitions professionals conducted by the Merrill Corporation.[239] The survey found that 55 per cent of respondents indicated that compliance with the GDPR and the data protection employed by the target company were the major stumbling blocks for the completion of mergers and acquisitions, and 66 per cent of the experts surveyed maintained that the GDPR rendered the deal-making process complex, as acquiring companies scrutinize the data protection policies and approaches of target companies. Rather than constituting an unintended consequence of the GDPR, these effects show that data protection law functions as intended.

The key to realizing the vision of data protection law as an instrument supporting market competitiveness is its effective enforcement. Before the entry into force of the GDPR, Albrecht optimistically noted: '[f]rom May 24 2018 the fragmented digital market of today and the lack of enforcement in the field of data protection provisions will end'.[240] However, as is alarmingly evident, the GDPR's enforcement is not sufficiently vigorous. This is worrisome not only from the viewpoint of data protection. At a conference in 2021, Coscelli, the chief executive of the UK's CMA, pointed directly to the undesirable spillover effects that the GDPR's under-enforcement might have on competition. As he noted, '[t]oday we are seeing the combined effect of changes in business models, potentially lack of regulations and potentially underenforcements of the regulations, and we as competition authorities are to some extent picking up the pieces of what happens'.[241] He added: 'I am a strong advocate for proper enforcement of privacy regulation because I think it will also help us.'[242]

As lack of effective enforcement is caused by a range of factors, the following sections shed light on two such factors: the inadequate functioning of the 'one-stop-shop' mechanism and the uncertainties around the implementation of the right to effective judicial protection.

1.2 The challenge of the one-stop-shop mechanism

Partially responsible for the current GDPR's enforcement challenge is the one-stop-shop mechanism introduced by the GDPR. As large technology companies such as Alphabet, Meta, Twitter, and Microsoft have their main establishments in

[239] Merill Corporation, 'GDPR Burdens Hinder M&A Transactions in the EMEA Region, According to Merill Corporation Survey' (13 November 2018) <https://www.datasite.com/us/en/company/news/press-releases/gdpr-burdens-hinder-m-a-transactions-in-the-emea-region.html> accessed 10 October 2022.

[240] Jan Philipp Albrecht, 'How the GDPR Will Change the World' (2016) 2 European Data Protection Law Review 287, 287.

[241] Victoria Ibitoye, 'Competition Regulators "Picking up Pieces" of Patchy GDPR Enforcement, Coscelli Says' *Mlex* (21 April 2021) <https://mlexmarketinsight.com/news/insight/competition-regulators-picking-up-pieces-of-patchy-gdpr-enforcement-coscelli-says> accessed 18 June 2022.

[242] ibid.

Ireland, the Irish DPC is responsible as the lead authority for a significant number of high-profile cases that affect individuals across Europe.[243] Although the DPC is not a large regulator, it is, as some have noted, 'technically regulating and enforcing privacy regulation on behalf of this massive market in Europe'.[244]

After the first few years of the GDPR's entry into force, there was a stark realization that the DPC's enforcement practice was not as effective as one would have expected. A European Parliament resolution issued in March 2021 expressed concerns over the one-stop-shop mechanism, in particular over the major role of the DPAs in Ireland and Luxembourg.[245] It noted that 'the Irish data protection authority generally closes most cases with a settlement instead of a sanction and that cases referred to Ireland in 2018 have not even reached the stage of a draft decision pursuant to Article 60(3) of the GDPR'.[246] In the same vein, at a hearing organized by Ireland's Oireachtas Joint Committee on Justice in April 2021, it was noted that the Irish DPC had decided only four out of 196 EU cases for which it was the lead authority, and that this 98 per cent backlog of cases was preventing progress in the EU.[247] According to Schrems, the DPC's approach is one 'of "micro debating" complaints and "negotiating" compliance with the law instead of enforcing it'.[248] Helen Dixon, head of the DPC, has regularly rebutted the criticism, stressing, for example, that the 'complexities of the decision-making involved in the "one stop shop", which multinationals may avail of under the GDPR, means the pace of delivery is not solely within the domain of the DPC'.[249]

The question of the division of competences and national authorities' cross-border powers to enforce the GDPR was at the heart of the landmark case of *Facebook v Belgian Data Privacy Commission*[250] decided by the CJEU. In this 2019 preliminary ruling, the Brussels Court of Appeal sought clarification from the CJEU on the one-stop-shop mechanism's effects on the competences of the Belgian DPA. One of the questions referred was whether it was compliant with the GDPR for the supervisory authority of a Member State to initiate or engage in legal proceedings before a court in its own Member State against an allegedly illegal practice with cross-border effects, even when the supervisory authority was not a

[243] Access Now, 'Three Years Under the GDPR. An Implementation Progress Report' (2021) 10.
[244] Ibitoye (n 241).
[245] European Parliament, 'Resolution on the Commission Evaluation Report on the Implementation of the General Data Protection Regulation Two Years after Its Application (2020/2717(RSP))' [2021] OJ C494/129, para 20.
[246] ibid.
[247] Houses of the Oireachtas, Joint Committee on Justice, 'Report on Meeting on 27 April 2021 on the Topic of GDPR' (2021) 35.
[248] Charlie Taylor, 'DPC Rejects Criticism of Its Regulation of Big Tech Companies' *The Irish Times* (27 April 2021) <https://www.irishtimes.com/business/technology/dpc-rejects-criticism-of-its-regulation-of-big-tech-companies-1.4549370> accessed 19 June 2022.
[249] ibid.
[250] Case C-645/19 *Facebook Ireland Ltd, Facebook Inc, Facebook Belgium BVBA* [2021] ECLI:EU:C:2021:483.

lead authority. Framed differently, the issue at stake was whether the Belgian DPA could bring an action against Facebook Belgium for a series of infringements of the GDPR even though the Irish DPC was the lead authority.

When looked at from the perspective of the inherent complexities caused by the one-stop-shop system, the question posed by the Brussels court was of significant practical relevance. Advocate General Bobek rightly observed in his Opinion that the one-stop-shop system introduced in the GDPR aimed to improve the previous enforcement system under the DPD. The previous system required companies to comply with various national data protection rules and to liaise with all national DPAs, which in the end proved 'not only costly, burdensome and time-consuming for the economic operators, but also an inevitable source of uncertainty and conflicts for those operators and their consumers'.[251] Addressing the criticism that leaving the enforcement in cross-border cases almost solely to a lead supervisory authority carries the risk of the GDPR's under-enforcement, Advocate General Bobek noted that 'as far as the layer of the *extant law* is concerned, the GDPR could be said to contain mechanisms aimed at avoiding such scenarios',[252] and 'as far as the *genuine operation and effects* of the new systems are concerned, such fears are, at this stage, premature and hypothetical'.[253]

He defended the one-stop-shop system, noting that making it optional or non-existent would severely affect the coherence of the whole system and result in a parallel 'race-to-the-first-judgment' by all supervisory authorities.[254] At the same time, he also observed that there should be close cooperation between the lead authority and other relevant authorities.[255] Furthermore, national DPAs are entitled to bring proceedings before national courts provided that they do so in the situations expressly indicated in the GDPR (eg the claim is outside the GDPR's material scope, the relevant undertaking has its establishment outside the EU, and the issue relates to data processing by public authorities in the public interest).[256] The Opinion thus upheld the one-stop-shop mechanism and posited that, as the GDPR was still in its infancy, 'one should give the infant the benefit of doubt, at least for the time being'.[257]

Following the Advocate General's reasoning, the CJEU concluded that, in principle, it is the lead DPA that is competent to take action in cases of cross-border data processing.[258] The CJEU also agreed that it is possible for an authority that is not

[251] Case C-645/19 *Facebook Ireland Ltd, Facebook Inc, Facebook Belgium BVBA* [2021] ECLI:EU:C:2021:5, Opinion of AG Bobek, para 77. For a short summary of the Opinion and a commentary, see eg Jos De Wachter and Charlotte Peeters, 'Advocate General Rules on the One-Stop Shop Mechanism' (2021) 7 European Data Protection Law Review 129.

[252] *Facebook Ireland Ltd*, Opinion of AG Bobek (n 251) para 109.

[253] ibid.

[254] ibid para 171.

[255] ibid para 55.

[256] ibid para 137.

[257] ibid para 128.

[258] *Facebook Ireland Ltd* (n 250) para 56.

the lead authority to bring an alleged infringement of the GDPR to the attention of a national court or, where necessary, to initiate or engage in legal proceedings.[259] Placing emphasis on the cooperation requirements, the CJEU—constrained by the legal boundaries and what the law prescribes—delivered a balanced decision that attempted to reconcile the competing standpoints. At the same time, in a relatively explicit manner—or at least more evidently than the Advocate General's Opinion—the CJEU expressed that vigilance is required in situations in which the primacy of the one-stop-shop mechanism may affect the effectiveness of enforcement. For example, the CJEU expressly addressed the risk of 'forum shopping' by data controllers: controllers might establish themselves in jurisdictions with a more lenient enforcement approach in order to circumvent fundamental rights.[260] Commenting on the divergences between the Advocate General's Opinion and the judgment, Woods observed that while the former posits that a high level of fundamental rights protection can be best achieved through the effective operation of a one-stop shop, the latter highlights the threat that under-enforcement of the GDPR may pose to the adequate protection of rights.[261]

Concerns about non-optimal functioning of the one-stop-shop mechanism are well grounded, even though evidence of under-enforcement is not yet solid enough to justify taking steps towards abolishing the current system, and establishing of a new, possibly more centralized, enforcement mechanism. In the meantime, less extreme solutions for boosting enforcement have emerged. A recent noteworthy development that can be expected to improve the effectiveness of the GDPR's enforcement is the decision of the European Ombudsman[262] and the subsequent comment by the Directorate-General for Justice and Consumers[263] issued in response to a complaint by the Irish Council for Civil Liberties. The complaint outlined the concern that the Irish DPC did not adequately enforce the GDPR, and inquired whether the European Commission provides sufficient information to monitor the problem. The Ombudsman's investigation found that the Commission's 'practice of obtaining bi-monthly overview from the Irish Data Protection Commission on the latter's handling of "big tech" cases, including cross border cases, is appropriate and in line with good administration',[264] and it issued a number of suggestions for improvement. To implement them, the Directorate-General for Justice and Consumers affirmed that it would request that all national

[259] ibid para 75.

[260] ibid para 68.

[261] Lorna Woods, 'Facebook Ireland and the One Stop Shop under the GDPR' (2021) 45 European Law Review 685, 691.

[262] European Ombudsman, 'Decision on whether the European Commission collects sufficient information to monitor Ireland's implementation of the EU's General Data Protection Regulation (GDPR)' (Case 97/2022/PB).

[263] Directorate-General for Justice and Consumers, 'Comments of DG Justice and Consumers on a request for information from the European Ombudsman—Complaint by the Irish Council for Civil Liberties (ICCL), ref 97/2022/PB' (2022).

[264] European Ombudsman (n 262).

supervisory authorities provide the Commission, on a bi-monthly and confidential basis, with information about large-scale cross-border GDPR investigations. In addition, the Commission would provide an account of that practice in its second report on the application of the GDPR. While the transition to centralized enforcement is not yet on the horizon, tasking the Commission with additional monitoring obligations is a first welcome step in the right direction. In addition, in February 2023, the Commission announced an initiative aimed at streamlining cooperation between national DPAs when they enforce the GDPR.[265] The aim is to improve enforcement by harmonizing certain aspects of the administrative procedure applied in cross-border cases.

While fixing the flawed operation of the one-stop-shop system should remain in the spotlight, the insufficient resources of the DPAs also merit attention. In order to effectively use their enforcement powers under the GDPR, DPAs need to have at their disposal sufficient human, financial, and technical resources. Yet, shortcomings in all these areas had already become evident a few years after the GDPR coming into force.[266] The Commission's 2020 stocktaking report noted that between 2016 and 2019 there had been a 42 per cent increase in staff and 49 per cent in the budget for all national DPAs taken together.[267] Despite this seemingly significant increase, the Commission concluded that the overall situation was not yet satisfactory and there were significant discrepancies across Member States.

1.3 Data subjects' access to justice: a legal limbo

One mechanism that is part of the GDPR's toolbox to ensure the law's effectiveness is access to justice by data subjects. According to Article 77, data subjects have the right to directly lodge a complaint with a supervisory authority. Article 78 GDPR envisages that each data subject has the right to an effective judicial remedy against any legally binding decision of a supervisory authority with which they are concerned,[268] or where a supervisory authority competent to handle a complaint that has been lodged does not do it or does not inform the data subject within three months of the progress or outcome of the complaint.[269] Where the data subject considers that their rights have been infringed as a result of non-compliance with the GDPR, as per Article 79 GDPR they also have the right to bring proceedings

[265] European Commission, 'Further specifying procedural rules relating to the enforcement of the General Data Protection Regulation' (2023) <https://ec.europa.eu/info/law/better-regulation/have-your-say/initiatives/13745-Further-specifying-procedural-rules-relating-to-the-enforcement-of-the-General-Data-Protection-Regulation_en> accessed 27 February 2023.

[266] See e.g. European Commission, 'Joint Statement Ahead of the 2nd Year Anniversary of the General Data Protection Regulation' (20 May 2020) Statement/20/913 <https://ec.europa.eu/commission/presscorner/detail/en/statement_20_913> accessed 24 March 2022.

[267] European Commission, 'Data Protection as a Pillar of Citizens' Empowerment and the EU's Approach to the Digital Transition—Two Years of Application of the General Data Protection Regulation', SWD (2020) 115 final, 6.

[268] GDPR, art 78(1).

[269] ibid art 78(2).

against a controller or a processor before the national courts. To exercise their rights under Articles 77, 78, and 79, data subjects have also the right to be represented by a not-for-profit body, organization, or association (art 80 GDPR). The right to an effective remedy is also enshrined in Article 47 of the EU Charter.

Despite the fact that effective access to justice is provided in the law 'on the books', data protection law 'on the ground' has major shortcomings in this respect. In 2022, González Fuster and her colleagues published a comprehensive study examining whether and how the current enforcement practices of national DPAs support or hinder data subjects' right to an effective judicial remedy.[270] Their findings point out several problematic practices. For example, even though DPAs are obliged to facilitate the submission of complaints by data subjects, insufficient information is provided on DPAs' websites about the possibility of lodging a complaint. The process of lodging a complaint is also rife with practical obstacles. In addition, data subjects do not obtain sufficient information on next steps once a complaint has been lodged (eg information about their right to a judicial remedy if they are not kept informed by the DPA about the progress or outcome of their complaint after three months). Importantly, the study highlighted significant discrepancies between DPAs' practices as regards fundamental aspects of submitting and handling a complaint, and suggested that such a fragmented and opaque system should be swiftly remedied. Obstacles pertaining to lodging a complaint with the DPA of a Member State in which the data subject does not reside, as well as the scarce information on DPAs' websites about data subjects' rights to be represented by a not-for-profit organization, were stressed as additional impediments to access to justice in the EU.

Remedying these fundamental data protection-related shortcomings should be approached not only as an urgently needed step to restore trust in the effectiveness of the data protection regime, but also as a vital means to stimulate competition. If notions of control and empowerment are to continue to underpin data protection law in Europe and to be considered relevant legal mechanisms for offering protection, the requisite mechanism of access to justice needs to be taken seriously.

2. The fragmentation of the data protection landscape

One of the GDPR's fundamental objectives was to harmonize the legal data protection landscape in Europe by replacing a directive with a regulation. This was also intended to improve the business environment by reducing compliance costs and administrative burdens for companies operating in several Member States, which before the GDPR were subject to different national legal requirements,

[270] Gloria González Fuster and others, 'The Right to Lodge a Data Protection Complaint: OK, But Then What? An Empirical Study of Current Practices under the GDPR' (Access Now 2022).

costing them close to €3 billion per year.[271] Boosting competitiveness through harmonization was explicitly recognized in the Commission's impact assessment of the GDPR: lower costs of making cross-border business, increased capacity to innovate thanks to consumer confidence in sharing data, and clearer rules were hoped to improve the business environment.[272] As the impact assessment stressed, the GDPR was supposed to improve competition in the internal market by clarifying data protection concepts and principles, harmonizing laws, and improving consistency of enforcement.[273] Competition in external markets was also supposed to benefit from a harmonized legal framework: 'EU based providers will be able to offer a service with higher quality in terms of data protection and security at competitive prices at a global scale',[274] as the Commission maintained.

Even though harmonization was one of the key drivers for data protection reform, diverging legal interpretations of the GDPR's provisions by national DPAs, prioritization inconsistencies, and cultural conflicts are some of the reasons that explain the continued fragmentation.[275] As the Commission stressed in the 2020 stocktaking report, another source of divergences is the fact that the GDPR allows the Member States to legislate in some areas and to further specify the GDPR's provisions in other instances.[276] Examples include the age at which children can provide consent for processing their personal data, and the different approaches of national jurisdictions to the reconciliation of data protection with the freedom of expression and information. Such remaining divergences risk complicating cross-border business activities and innovation.

Divergences also exist as regards the interpretation of key data protection provisions. An illustration of interpretative disparities is a recent disagreement between several national DPAs in regard to contracts as a legal basis for data processing for personalized ads. While the Irish DPC found that Meta's use of a contract as a legal basis was in that context legal, ten other DPAs disagreed, resulting in the EDPB's binding decision in which it overruled the conclusions of the Irish DPC.[277]

There are also notable differences relating to the intensity of enforcement. In line with the data provided by Access Now in its 2021 report on the implementation of the GDPR, in the period between May 2018 and March 2021, the DPAs in Europe imposed 596 fines and sanctions totalling €278,549,188.[278] Around 46 per cent of these GDPR fines targeted technology companies and telecommunication

[271] European Commission, 'Impact Assessment Accompanying Regulation (EU) 2016/679 and Directive (EU) 2016/680' (Staff Working Paper), SEC (2012) 72 final, 148.

[272] ibid 149.

[273] ibid 151.

[274] ibid.

[275] Jukka Ruohonen and Kalle Hjerppe, 'The GDPR Enforcement Fines at Glance' (2022) 106 Information Systems 101876, 2.

[276] European Commission (n 267) 7.

[277] EDPB, Binding Decision 3/2022 on the Dispute Submitted by the Irish SA on Meta Platforms Ireland Ltd and its Facebook Service (art 65 GDPR) (5 December 2022).

[278] Access Now (n 243) 2.

operators.[279] What the report also demonstrated, however, were significant divergences in how active individual DPAs are, with Spain having levied 223 fines during that period, and Luxembourg and Slovenia having issued no fines at all.[280]

In addition to differing with regard to their intensity of enforcement, the DPAs also diverge in their views on fines. The conundrum relating to the effective level of fines and the approach to enforcement was at the core of the proceedings against Twitter, for example, where the Irish DPC was the lead enforcement authority.[281] The investigation was launched following a data breach caused by a bug in Twitter's design in 2018 which affected around 88,726 (and most likely more) users in Europe and the impact of which was qualified as 'significant' in Twitter's Breach Notification Form.[282] The investigation focused on Twitter's failure to notify the breach without undue delay (art 33(1) GDPR) and to document personal data breaches (art 33(5)). The fine proposed by the DPC in its draft decision, which was communicated to other concerned supervisory authorities as required by Article 60 GDRP, was within the range of €135,000 to €275,000. The DPAs in a few Member States—including Austria, Italy, and Germany—raised several objections to the DPC's draft decision, including that the fine was insufficiently dissuasive. As a result, the DPC launched the dispute resolution mechanism envisaged in Article 65 GDPR, referring the case to the EDPB. In its binding decision, the EDPB concluded that the proposed fine 'is too low and therefore does not fulfil its purpose as a corrective measure, in particular it does not meet the requirements of Article 83(1) GDPR of being effective, dissuasive and proportionate',[283] and requesting the Irish DPC to reassess it.[284] Following the reassessment, the ultimate fine imposed by the DPC was €450,000, which in fact constituted only a small increase compared to the initial fine.

This case, which for the first time triggered the use of the GDPR's dispute resolution system, is illustrative of disagreements over fundamental concepts in Europe's multi-jurisdiction enforcement regime. As the GDPR's enforcement is not based on mutual recognition, nor does it envisage centralized enforcement, the current hybrid system that envisages a lead authority and a cooperation mechanism raises questions as to its effectiveness, efficiency, and its potential 'to support confidence in the rule of law in the EU'.[285] Furthermore, questions arise as to the

[279] ibid 7.

[280] ibid.

[281] Data Protection Commission, Decision of the Data Protection Commission Made Pursuant to Section 111 of the Data Protection Act 2018 in the matter of Twitter International Company, Case IN-19-1-1 (9 December 2020).

[282] ibid para 2.8.

[283] EDPB, Decision 01/2020 on the Dispute Arisen on the Draft Decision of the Irish Supervisory Authority Regarding Twitter International Company under Article 65(1)(a) GDPR (9 December 2020) para 199.

[284] ibid para 200.

[285] Christopher Hodges, 'Comments on GDPR Enforcement: EDPB Decision 01/2020' (2021) 9, <https://papers.ssrn.com/sol3/papers.cfm?abstract_id=3765602> accessed 2 July 2022.

interpretation of the GDPR's Article 83(1), which requires fines to be dissuasive and deterrent, and at the same time proportionate. As rightly noted by Hodges, the case also reveals a broader issue, namely 'the need for a fundamental reappraisal of the policy underlying the application and purposes of penalties under EU law generally, and certainly under the GDPR', adding that the entire EU's enforcement policy 'is ripe for reconsideration'.[286]

The lowering of compliance costs for firms operating in the EU, which the GDPR was supposed to achieve, does not seem to have materialized either: early evaluations of the GDPR's impact on firms' performance show a grim picture. In a recently published study covering thirty-five industries comprising all sectors of the economy, scholars examined how the GDPR had affected companies' profits and sales in sixty-one countries.[287] The authors concluded that in 2018 companies operating in the EU experienced on average an 8 per cent reduction in profits and a 2 per cent reduction in sales, attributing the losses to the implementation of the GDPR, and in particular to compliance costs.[288] Focusing on the technology sector, small firms with fewer than 500 employees proved to be particularly affected, as the decline in their profits was almost double the average. At the same time, the study found no statistically significant declines in sales or profits among large firms such as Facebook, Microsoft, Amazon, and Google. Such asymmetrical impacts raise concerns about the GDPR's effect of solidifying the market positions of the most powerful companies (see Chapter 6 Section D). On the other hand, even though the GDPR compliance costs prove burdensome and costly for small companies, this impact might be temporary, reflecting adjustment costs.[289] Higher compliance costs for smaller firms is not an idiosyncratic problem arising solely in the context of the GDPR: as Kerber noted, nearly all regulations create a relative advantage for large undertakings.[290]

3. Data protection law provisions that impede competition

The normative underpinnings of this book lie in the conviction that it is strengthened, rather than relaxed, data protection enforcement that can best complement competition law in a broader mission to create a competitive and data

[286] ibid 11.

[287] Chinchih Chen, Carl Benedikt Frey, and Giorgio Presidente, 'Privacy Regulation and Firm Performance: Estimating the GDPR Effect Globally' (2022) The Oxford Martin Working Paper Series on Technological and Economic Change Working No 2022-1.

[288] ibid 2. According to the authors, while compliance costs led to the reduction in profits, what caused the reduction in online purchases (and therefore sales) was the requirement to obtain consent.

[289] ibid 25.

[290] Wolfgang Kerber and Louisa Specht-Riemenschneider, 'Synergies between Data Protection Law and Competition Law' (2021) 36 <https://papers.ssrn.com/sol3/papers.cfm?abstract_id=3977039> accessed 24 June 2022.

protection-friendly digital economy in the long run. Others take a different perspective about how substantive rules for data protection restrict competition—a perspective centring on the repercussions of data protection law for 'data-driven competition'. Some go even further, saying that 'Europe's obsession with data protection is getting in the way of digital innovation', hampering efforts to develop digital solutions and making it impossible to use or develop technologies such as AI or blockchain.[291] While the reality is certainly more nuanced, some of the points stressed in this debate will be briefly outlined.

One of the most comprehensive accounts of the competitive effects of the GDPR can be found in the article by Gal and Aviv.[292] As the authors indicate at the outset, the competition-related effects that they observed are tied to 'the ability to realize economies in scale and scope in data analysis',[293] which they understand as enabling 'a well-functioning and social-welfare-enhancing digital economy'.[294] Having explored the different business models for data collection, the authors arrived at several conclusions on how the GDPR affects companies' choices of the business models they rely on. For example, organizations that seek to obtain data from an external firm might be constrained by the GDPR's requirement to base data processing on a lawful legal basis (eg consent), and those firms might incur additional compliance-related costs, disincentivizing the creation of joint data pools and data collection for the purpose of data sharing.[295] As a result, an undertaking might then abandon the idea of purchasing data from an external provider, resorting instead to internal data collection methods that might be inefficient.[296] Similar hurdles might surface in the context of merger transactions that some firms might see as a preferred business avenue for obtaining the necessary data. Gal and Aviv observed that because of the limitations imposed by data protection law, the merging of undertakings 'does not automatically imply that the merged entity can use data which were collected by one entity before the merger'.[297] This, in conjunction with the fact that the deal-making process might involve ensuring that the target company complies with the GDPR, implies higher costs of sharing data and makes potentially efficient mergers unprofitable.[298] While the these scenarios involve integrating or merging datasets that are interchangeable, data protection-related obstacles also emerge when the datasets that the firms seek to combine create synergies—that is, when the insights derived from both sets of data are significantly more valuable as compared to relying on just one database. For example,

[291] Axel Voss, 'How to Bring GDPR into the Digital Age' *Politico* (25 March 2021) <https://www.politico.eu/article/gdpr-reform-digital-innovation/> accessed 24 June 2022.
[292] Gal and Aviv (n 1).
[293] ibid 350.
[294] ibid.
[295] ibid 370–71.
[296] ibid.
[297] ibid 371.
[298] ibid 371–72.

as the authors illustrate, if the dataset of the target company includes sensitive data, the acquiring company will need to comply after the transaction with strengthened data protection requirements,[299] which might have competition implications.

Others have similarly stressed the obstacles that the GDPR creates for data sharing initiatives, even though the data protection framework does not as such forbid the sharing of personal data.[300] The purpose limitation principle, for example, implies that if data sharing, which is a new processing activity, has a purpose other than the one for which the data was originally collected, a new lawful basis is required. In conducting an assessment of the compatibility between the purpose of data sharing and the initial purpose, the reasonable expectations of data subjects must be duly considered.[301] The principle of data minimization may pose another obstacle to data sharing as it limits the categories and amounts of data that can be shared to those that are necessary to achieve the indicated purpose.[302] The impacts of these two principles on data sharing are exacerbated due to the increasing technological possibilities for re-identify a data subject, and categorizing data as personal implies the need to comply with the GDPR's principles.[303]

Those who consider data-driven competition and innovation to be the preferred future trajectory of the digital economy might react with dismay about how data protection law restraints certain data collection and processing activities. Another view on such limitations—one that sees them as an opportunity rather than a disadvantage—can also be adopted. Having conducted an inquiry into whether and how data protection law considers data-driven efficiencies and innovation, Zingales noted that 'data protection requires any strive for efficiency to take a back seat to individual autonomy'.[304] While this approach 'may limit some kind of innovation, ... it permits and indeed promotes responsible and human-centric innovation in accordance with Article 8 of the EU Charter'.[305]

4. Data protection law provisions that (allegedly) support competition

While several data protection law provisions might trigger divergent views on whether they support or limit competition, there is a consensus that there are

[299] ibid 375–76.

[300] Inge Graef, Thomas Tombal, and Alexandre de Streel, 'Limits and Enablers of Data Sharing. An Analytical Framework for EU Competition, Data Protection and Consumer Law' (2019) TILEC Discussion Paper No DP 2019-024, 11.

[301] ibid.

[302] ibid.

[303] ibid 12.

[304] Nicolo Zingales, 'Data Protection Considerations in EU Competition Law: Funnel or Straightjacket for Innovation'? (2018) 41 <https://papers.ssrn.com/sol3/papers.cfm?abstract_id=3158008> accessed 4 June 2022.

[305] ibid.

certain concepts that resonate equally well with data protection and competition law. Data portability is a notable example. As this section will show, however, the unifying force of the right to data portability as currently conceptualized in data protection law is weaker than commonly assumed.

While the notion of data portability is fluid and can be interpreted differently depending on the context,[306] one possible way to define it is 'the ability of people to reuse data across interoperable operations'.[307] In the EU, data portability is formulated as a right of data subjects that aims to empower them and strengthen their right of access. Although traces of data portability can be detected in other EU legislation,[308] the GDPR was the first to conceptualize it as a more comprehensive and enforceable right.

As Article 20 GDPR stipulates, the right to data portability is two-pronged. The first dimension is established in Article 20(1) and gives data subjects the right to obtain their data from the controller and transfer that data to another provider. This occurs in a business to business to consumer (B2C2B) relationship, and individuals should be able to exercise their rights without any hindrance such as fees, lack of interoperability, lack of access to a data format or API, unwarranted delay or complexity of retrieving the dataset, its deliberate obfuscation, or excessive sectorial standardization.[309] The types of data that can be ported include both data provided by individuals knowingly and actively, and personal data generated by their activity, as long as the basis for data processing is consent or contract. In line with the second right's dimension stipulated in Article 20(2) GDPR, data subjects can request to have their data transmitted directly from one controller to another one, in a more direct business to business (B2B) relationship. This is arguably weaker than the first sub-right in that it can be exercised only where technically feasible.[310]

Although the right to data portability was introduced with a view to enhancing control, its potential to foster competitiveness in the digital market environment is beyond doubt[311]—at least in theory. As it can lead to decreased switching costs and

[306] Helena U Vrabec, *Data Subject Rights under the GDPR* (OUP 2021) 159.

[307] <http://dataportability.org> accessed 22 March 2022.

[308] eg Directive 2002/22/EC of the European Parliament and of the Council of 7 March 2002 on universal service and users' rights relating to electronic communications networks and services (Universal Service Directive) [2002] OJ L108/51, art 30; Directive 2002/21/EC of the European Parliament and of the Council of 7 March 2002 on a common regulatory framework for electronic communications networks and services (Framework Directive) [2002] OJ L108/22, recital 31. More recently, data portability was introduced eg in Regulation 2018/1907 of the European Parliament and of the Council of 14 November 2018 on a framework for the free flow of non-personal data in the European Union [2018] OJ L303/59, art 6.

[309] A29WP, 'Guidelines on the Right to Data Portability' (2017) 15.

[310] Jan Krämer, Pierre Senellart, and Alexandre de Streel, 'Making Data Portability More Effective for the Digital Economy' (2021) <https://papers.ssrn.com/sol3/papers.cfm?abstract_id=3866495 18> accessed 3 March 2022.

[311] Paul De Hert and others, 'The Right to Data Portability in the GDPR: Towards User-Centric Interoperability of Digital Services' (2018) 34 Computer Law & Security Review 193, 194.

lock-in effects, as well as lowering entry barriers, data portability is among the key tools for ensuring market contestability. In addition, it can facilitate data fluidity, hence stimulate competition and innovation in secondary markets.[312] The fact that data portability is now also enshrined in the DMA (art 6(9)) is another indicator of data portability's close resonance with competition law. According to Cyphers and Doctorow, portability 'is as much about user rights as it is about interoperability between businesses'.[313] According to others, providing users with 'control of data where it resides allows them to invite third parties to compete to create benefits with the host site, prompting greater sharing of value'.[314] The Commission has noted that an effective opportunity to port data becomes particularly relevant in light of the increased uptake of IoT devices, as consumers generate more and more data, and without data portability they might experience 'lock-in' effects and be subject to unfair practices[315]—concerns that are well recognized from a competition law standpoint.

As is becoming increasingly clear, however, the potential of the data portability right to deliver enhanced control and market contestability has not been fully realized.[316] For example, according to two recent surveys conducted with German internet users (predominantly students) on their knowledge of the GDPR and on users' motivations for switching between online service providers, the right to data portability is the GDPR's least known right (less than a third of participants had heard of it), while at the same time there is 'a significant need for simple and user-friendly data portability solutions'.[317] As the study showed, what mainly motivates users' willingness to switch are concerns related to data privacy and security and lack of trust in the current service providers, with 66.4 per cent of participants indicating that the inability to port their data from their current provider to another was a major obstacle to switching providers.[318]

The framing of the right to data portability by agencies is also not promising when considered from a competition perspective. In its comment on data portability, A29WP noted that 'the GDPR is regulating personal data and not competition', thus the GDPR's Article 20 should not be mistaken for a competition tool.[319] That Article 20 does not directly pursue the goals of competition can also be inferred from the scope of the right: portable data are not limited to those that can

[312] Simonetta Vezzoso, 'Competition Policy in Transition: Exploring Data Portability's Roles' (2021) 12 Journal of European Competition Law & Practice 357, 361.

[313] Bennett Cyphers and Cory Doctorow, 'Privacy Without Monopoly: Data Protection and Interoperability' (2021) Electronic Frontier Foundation, 16.

[314] Geoffrey Parker, Georgios Petropoulos, and Marshall Van Alstyne, 'Platform Mergers and Antitrust' (2021) 30 Industrial and Corporate Change 1307, 1323.

[315] European Commission (n 267) 8.

[316] ibid.

[317] Sophie Kuebler-Wachendorff and others, 'The Right to Data Portability: Conception, Status Quo, and Future Directions' (2021) 44 Informatik Spektrum 264, 267.

[318] ibid.

[319] A29WP (n 309) 6.

enable switching services.[320] The right does not apply to inferred data, which significantly limits its scope of application.[321] Furthermore, it applies only to data processing based on consent or contract, and does not mandate interoperable formats, which led Vrabec to conclude that the right has 'an ambitious goal but a narrowly defined scope'.[322] Others have observed that the GDPR's right to data portability 'has not been drafted to facilitate multi-homing or the offering of complementary services, which frequently relies on continuous and potentially real-time data access'.[323] This has repercussions not only for data protection, but also indirectly for competition law.

Overall, while it is important to acknowledge the objective limitations of the GDPR's portability formulations in achieving competition goals, it seems less justified to stress the need to compartmentalize the two areas of law in this context, as the previous comment by A29WP illustrated. Jurisdictions that are yet to introduce the right to data portability should be more mindful of its competition-stimulating potential. Alternatively, new rights can be established to facilitate data access along the lines of what the right to data portability aims to achieve. Parker, Petropolous, and Van Alstyne, for example, put forward the idea of an *in situ* data right, which is 'a new user right of information access that obligates gatekeeper platforms to allow third-party access to a user's raw data upon that user's request'.[324]

5. Preliminary conclusions

This section drew attention to a range of GDPR's weaknesses that prevent it from actively and positively supporting competition law in creating markets where competition, in particular competition on data protection, has a chance to emerge and thrive. Particular attention was devoted to enforcement challenges, stressing that adequate enforcement of data protection law is not only a data protection issue, but might also have severe repercussions for market dynamics. Continued fragmentation of legal approaches to several data protection provisions prevents market harmonization that is urgently needed to facilitate competition in the Digital Single Market. While many express disappointment with the GDPR's impacts on the current model of data-driven competition, the premise underlying this section was that it is time to refocus this debate and reflect on the GDPR's potential to create business incentives to compete on data protection instead. Whereas the analysis highlighted that data protection concepts such as data portability would need to be

[320] ibid.
[321] Vrabec (n 306) 187.
[322] ibid 189.
[323] Crémer, de Montjoye, and Schweitzer (n 2) 8–9.
[324] Parker, Petropoulos, and Van Alstyne (n 314) 1323.

revisited to better cohere with competition, more substantive suggestions will be presented in Chapter 6.

D. The lack of institutional bridges

In the wake of a gradual understanding that the overlaps between data protection and competition law are manifold and require attention, calls for abandoning the prevailing institutional silo approach have intensified. While some of these calls suggest creating new institutions with far-reaching powers to regulate various online or data-related business activities, others focus on strengthening institutional cooperation. As this section shows, however, concrete efforts to improve the institutional set-up are underwhelming, falling short of what the advocates of better institutional synchronization call for. This section will first review the institutional proposals outlined in various policy reports, and will then turn to the actually implemented institutional reforms.

1. Institutional reforms in the policy discourse

Suggestions to create institutional bridges have surfaced in many recent reports and policy recommendations. In the UK, the proposal was put forward to establish a Digital Markets Unit (DMU) with powers to govern companies with a 'strategic market status'. Having a single authority would minimize the risk of substantive fragmentation: as the Furman Report noted, the powers of institutions such as the Ofcom, the ICO, and the CMA 'are fragmented and have not been designed to deliver a coherent, ongoing, engaged pro-competition policy approach across digital markets'.[325] In a similar fashion, the US Stigler Report introduced the idea of creating a US Digital Authority, ideally introduced as a sub-division of the FTC to avoid capture by the industry.[326] The Digital Authority would need to have overarching powers and oversee all aspects of digital platforms: centralized enforcement would ensure that various concerns related to data power were addressed in a holistic manner. It should have powers to review mergers and propose a standard for data exchange, and should also be able to conduct investigations and obtain information from companies. The German Commission Competition 4.0 recommended establishing at the EU level a Digital Markets Board, which would be responsible for 'permanent coordination and harmonisation of the various policy areas in the interest of an overarching and coherent European digital policy'.[327]

325 Furman (n 5) 55.
326 Stigler Committee on Digital Platforms (n 6) 18.
327 German Federal Ministry of Economic Affairs (n 3) 78.

Other reports have advocated less sweeping institutional reforms, highlighting the benefits of cooperation rather than the need for creating a new authority. For example, the Canadian Competition Bureau has maintained that its mandate partially overlaps with that of Canada's Office of the Privacy Commissioner (eg in ensuring that personal data collection is not misleading or deceiving), and has stressed the importance of ad hoc collaborations in such cases.[328] The Japan Fair Trade Commission, referring directly to the position expressed on a few occasions by the EDPS, observed that personal data markets, competition, data protection, and consumer protection require coordination, a balanced approach, and the need to be approached as a whole.[329] The Brazilian Competition Authority has stressed the relevance of pursuing 'an active co-operation for coordinated work between competition and other related authorities', including the National Secretariat for Consumer Protection (SENACON) and the Brazilian DPA.[330] The Competition Commission of India has highlighted the importance of reaching a consensus across agencies on balancing data-based innovations and cross-border data flows with consumers' increasing demands for privacy.[331]

2. Institutional initiatives

When it comes to concrete steps, there are, regrettably, only a few noteworthy efforts to improve the institutional landscape. In the EU, the most concrete institutional endeavour so far has been the establishment of the Digital Clearinghouse, which was recommended by the EDPS in 2016[332] and launched in the same year. With the mission to more effectively and coherently protect individuals in an era of Big Data and AI, the Clearinghouse aims to create a platform for 'cooperation, dialogue and exchange of insights and best practices between regulatory authorities, policy makers, researchers and other stakeholders'.[333] Conceptualized as a voluntary network of national and EU authorities responsible for regulating the digital sector, the Clearinghouse is expected to be joined by those who share the aim of 'mutually enhancing their respective enforcement activities', and are willing to exchange information and cooperate within the boundaries of their legal competences.[334] This cooperative initiative was also endorsed by the European

[328] Competition Bureau of Canada (n 8) 13.
[329] JFTC (n 9) 25.
[330] BRICS Competition Authorities (n 11) 23.
[331] ibid.
[332] EDPS, 'Opinion 8/2016 on Coherent Enforcement of Fundamental Rights in the Age of Big Data' (2016). Establishing 'a forum of cooperation between competent authorities' was mentioned by Giovanni Buttarelli in a speech a few months earlier: Giovanni Buttarelli, 'Keynote Speech' (BEUC DIGIFORUM, Brussels, 20 June 2016).
[333] <https://www.digitalclearinghouse.org/> accessed 29 March 2022.
[334] EDPS (n 332) 15.

Parliament, which noted that the Clearinghouse 'can help deepen the synergies and the safeguarding of the rights and interests of individuals'.[335] In the period 2017 to 2018, the EDPS facilitated four meetings between the regulatory authorities whereas the Digital Clearinghouse is currently jointly hosted by two academic institutions and a not-for-profit think tank.[336] While the initiative is to be applauded, the voluntary nature of participation in the Clearinghouse's initiatives, as well as the fact that its origins are 'one-sided' (eg it was not established in collaboration with the Directorate-General for Competition), creates the risk that essential stakeholders, namely competition enforcers, might not be fully on board.

In the UK, the Digital Regulation Cooperation Forum (DRCF) was set up in 2020 to bring together key UK regulators tasked with regulating digital markets: the CMA, the Financial Conduct Authority, the ICO, and Ofcom. The DRFC has the mission to ensure intensified cooperation, particularly in the face of the unique challenges in the online platform economy. Following the Furman Report's recommendation, in April 2021 the UK also launched the DMU, which so far is the most prominent example of a new institution responsible for coherently regulating digital markets. Housed within the CMA, the DMU is conceptualized 'as a centre of expertise for digital markets, with the capability to understand the business models of digital firms, including the role of data and the incentives driving how these firms operate'.[337] Once the UK's new regulatory framework for online companies with a strategic market status is in force, the DMU will have a mandate to oversee the new regime, promote competition and innovation in digital markets, as well as protect consumers and businesses from unfair practices. Although it is not yet clear what provisions the new regulatory regime will contain, the initiative to create an institution whose mandate will most likely span various legal areas—and predominantly competition and data protection—is the most notable institutional reform implemented to date. The question that remains is the extent to which the DMU will be involved in enforcing competition law and data protection vis-à-vis companies that are dominant but do not have a strategic market status.

Choosing less far-reaching options, some jurisdictions have introduced cooperation initiatives. In Australia, already in 2002 the ACCC and the Office of the Federal Privacy Commission had signed a memorandum of understanding providing a framework for cooperation. The memorandum aimed to improve privacy compliance and envisaged cooperation among authorities in the case of overlapping responsibilities, as well as mutual assistance in the areas of

335 European Parliament, 'Fundamental Rights Implications of Big Data: Data Protection, Non-Discrimination, Security and Law Enforcement (2016/2225(INI))' [2018] OJ C263/82.

336 The Digital Clearinghouse is currently hosted by the Research Centre in Information, Law and Society at the University of Namur, the Tilburg Institute for Law, Technology, and Society at Tilburg University, and the European Policy Centre in Brussels.

337 <https://www.gov.uk/government/collections/digital-markets-unit> accessed 29 March 2022.

enforcement, investigation, litigation, training, and education.[338] There is, however, little evidence of actual collaboration on these issues.[339] The need to intensify institutional exchanges was also acknowledged in a more recent memorandum between the ACCC and the Office of the Australian Information Commissioner concluded in July 2020. The area of focus of consultation and cooperation between the authorities is 'the consumer data right', in relation to which both institutions have regulatory roles and responsibilities.[340]

In Singapore, the competition regulator and the data protection enforcer have also declared a willingness to cooperate in order to understand the boundaries of their respective areas and assess the legitimacy of business claims that might include both competition and data protection factors.[341]

In Canada, in 2019 the Canadian Competition Bureau appointed its first Chief Digital Enforcement Officer (CDEO) to assist the Bureau in monitoring the digital landscape and identifying new investigative and intelligence-gathering techniques.[342]

While some of the mentioned institutional initiatives reflect the need to develop a unified approach to various policy and legal fields governing the digital economy, more institutional efforts are required to revamp the current institutional set-up and ways of cooperating. These are requisite if decisions on the interface of various areas of law are to be viewed holistically and sensibly.

E. Conclusions

In the opinion of Zanfir-Fortuna and Ianc, the recent legal developments on the interface of data protection and competition enforcement, and the positions of various authorities indicating their willingness to more seriously consider emerging interfaces between these two sets of concerns, signal the 'dawn of Uberprotection'.[343] The authors defined the concept in the following way:

338 ACCC, 'Regulators cooperate to improve privacy compliance' (12 March 2002) <https://www.accc.gov.au/media-release/regulators-co-operate-to-improve-privacy-compliance> accessed 29 March 2022.

339 Samson Y Esayas and Dan Svantesson, 'Digital Platforms Under Fire: What Australia Can Learn From Recent Developments in Europe' (2018) 43 Alternative Law Journal 275, 281.

340 ACCC, 'Consumer Data Right (CDR). Memorandum of Understanding with the Office of the Australian Information Commissioner' (2020).

341 Competition Commission Singapore, 'Data: Engine for Growth—Implications for Competition Law, Personal Data Protection, and Intellectual Property Rights' (2017) 98.

342 Matt Richards, 'Canada Hires Chief Digital Enforcement Officer' *Global Competition Review* (3 July 2019) <https://globalcompetitionreview.com/article/canada-hires-chief-digital-enforcement-officer> accessed 30 March 2022.

343 Gabriela Zanfir-Fortuna and Sînziana Ianc, 'Data Protection and Competition Law: the Dawn of 'Uberprotection' (2018) <https://papers.ssrn.com/sol3/papers.cfm?abstract_id=3290824> accessed 30 March 2022.

> [T]he protection of the rights of individuals and their welfare as data subjects, participants to the market and consumers, afforded by concerted enforcement and facilitated by coherent policymaking of competition authorities, data protection authorities and consumer protection authorities.[344]

While some signs of synergetic substantive and institutional approaches can be detected and warrant (cautious) optimism, Uberprotection is nowhere near being realized. Competition cases actually adopting an integrated approach are scarce and contested: a prominent example being the German *Facebook* case, where the CJEU's judgment is highly awaited, and which scholars have described as a case that 'goes significantly beyond EU abuse of dominance law'.[345] When it comes to ex ante regulation complementing competition law, while the DMA is a breakthrough piece of legislation with a number of prohibitions merging competition-style theories of harm with data protection issues, it should be borne in mind that the DMA does not apply to all dominant companies but only to companies that have gatekeeper status.

Data protection law, on the other hand, is riddled with enforcement problems that must be urgently addressed to avoid the GDPR becoming an ineffectual tool, not to mention that proper enforcement also has enormous potential to complement competition law in promoting competition on data protection. Harmonization, the objective on which the GDPR promised to deliver, is a precondition for creating a competitive EU digital single market.

From an institutional viewpoint, initiatives such as the Digital Clearinghouse have led to many acknowledging the importance of a dialogue between different enforcers, and other institutional reforms, notably those implemented in the UK, have illustrated that new agencies with more holistic mandates should be an integral part of a coherent enforcement vision in the digital economy. There is, however, enormous institutional progress that still needs to be made before the dialogue between the various relevant authorities governing the digital economy—not to mention actual enforcement collaboration or new institutional structures—acquires the desired shape.

[344] ibid 21.

[345] Eleanor M Fox and Philipp Baschenhof, 'History of (In)Equality in Competition Law and Its Guide to the Future' in Jan Broulik and Kati Cseres (eds), *Competition Law and Economic Inequality* (Hart Publishing 2022) 112.

4

Sectional Coherence as a New Paradigm

A. Introduction

The concept of coherence is commonly invoked in the discourse on narrowing the disconnect between data protection and competition law. The EDPS, for example, referred to the concept of coherence in one of its opinions on the subject, emphasizing 'an urgent need for coherent enforcement of digital rights in all domains of law regulating online markets'.[1] Similarly, in the UK, the ICO, the CMA, and Ofcom seek to strengthen their collaboration in examining the interaction between competition and data protection 'with the goal of supporting a coordinated and coherent approach to digital regulation'.[2] In the view of the Irish DPC, 'coherence between data protection, competition, and consumer law will be necessary to deliver a fair deal to service users'.[3] From an academic perspective, Lynskey, for example, recommended that cooperation is requisite 'to ensure a coherence approach between different regulators working in data-related fields'.[4] Schweitzer and her colleagues suggested that in the process of developing a legal framework for the data economy, the EU should ensure 'coherence across its various legal projects, both with regard to the legal terminology and conceptually'.[5] Wiedman asserted that where market dominance is to a significant extent based on personal data processing, 'EU competition law should be applied in a coherent and consistent way'.[6] In their analysis of instances where competition, data protection, and consumer law can be applied more coherently, Graef, Clifford, and Valcke defined coherence 'as an effective application and enforcement of the three regimes whereby

[1] EDPS, 'Opinion 8/2016 on Coherent Enforcement of Fundamental Rights in the Age of Big Data' (2016) 15.

[2] CMA and ICO, 'Competition and Data Protection in Digital Markets: A Joint Statement between the CMA and the ICO' (2021) para 88.

[3] Data Protection Commission, 'Annual Report 2017' (2018) 9.

[4] Orla Lynskey, 'Towards a Holistic Approach to Effective Data Protection' (*LSE Business Review*, 7 June 2022) <https://blogs.lse.ac.uk/businessreview/2022/06/07/towards-a-holistic-approach-to-effective-data-protection/> accessed 22 August 2022.

[5] Heike Schweitzer and others, 'Data Access and Sharing in Germany and in the EU: Towards a Coherent Legal Framework for the Emerging Data Economy. A Legal, Economic and Competition Policy Angle' (2022) 302.

[6] Klaus Wiedemann, 'Data Protection and Competition Law Enforcement in the Digital Economy: Why a Coherent and Consistent Approach Is Necessary' (2021) 52 International Review of Intellectual Property and Competition Law 915, 915.

Coherence between Data Protection and Competition Law in Digital Markets. Klaudia Majcher, Oxford University Press.
 DOI: 10.1093/oso/9780198885610.003.0005

substantive protections and enforcement actions build upon and strengthen each other, as such protecting the different dimensions of consumer welfare in a unified way'.[7]

While the idea of coherence has gained traction, a more thorough investigation of the concept is needed to elucidate its boundaries and implications, providing better theoretical underpinnings for the discussion on how data protection and competition law can be rendered more coherent. With this aim, and given that coherence has been discussed thoroughly by legal theorist, Section B relies on these theoretical accounts to define the concept, discuss its scope, and present its normative strength. The section also introduces a new notion of 'sectional coherence', which is a leading paradigm proposed in this book.[8] The subsequent Section C turns to EU law to investigate how it perceives and qualifies coherence as a legal principle. It puts in the spotlight Article 7 TFEU, which, as this chapter argues, can be understood as providing the legal foundations for the principles of consistency and coherence in the EU.

B. Coherence in legal theory

1. Definition of coherence

Coherence has been discussed extensively by legal theorists. Three decades ago, expressions such as 'coherence is in vogue'[9] or 'we are all coherentists now'[10] signalled the emergence of a new trend, which consisted in relying more frequently on the concept of coherence when theorizing about legal systems and adjudication. Adopting an increasingly attentive approach towards exploring coherence as a normative concept in law resulted in the emergence of new theories and propositions.

Coherence theories can be divided into two broad categories: coherence in a legal system and coherence in adjudication. Coherence in a legal system focuses on the relationships between its various components, such as legal rules and principles. Coherence in adjudication deals, in a narrow sense, with how arguments in a legal decision are connected or 'how to form coherent cumulations, chains, or nets of reasons'.[11] In a wider sense, it is an inquiry into how the process of adjudication

[7] Inge Graef, Damian Clifford, and Peggy Valcke, 'Fairness and Enforcement: Bridging Competition, Data Protection, and Consumer Law' (2018) 8 International Data Privacy Law 200, 203.

[8] The theory of sectional coherence was first introduced in my PhD: Klaudia Majcher, 'Coherence between EU Data Protection and Competition Law in the Digital Market' (PhD in Law, Vrije Universiteit Brussel, 2020).

[9] Joseph Raz, *Ethics in the Public Domain: Essays in the Morality of Law and Politics* (Clarendon Press 1994) 277.

[10] William A Edmundson, 'Comments on Coherence Theory in the Philosophy of Law' (1994) 1 <https://papers.ssrn.com/sol3/papers.cfm?abstract_id=1147392> accessed 4 January 2023.

[11] Leonor Moral Soriano, 'A Modest Notion of Coherence in Legal Reasoning. A Model for the European Court of Justice' (2003) 16 Ratio Juris 296, 297.

may help to introduce or restore coherence in a legal system. Given the focus of this book, namely interactions between data protection and competition law, coherence as a concept that describes the connections between the different elements of one legal system, and how adjudication may contribute to (re-)establishing it, are the relevant areas. Thus, the narrow account of adjudicative coherence will not be discussed further.

In line with the common kernel of coherence conceptions, 'coherence is a justificatory relation among principles and a certain set of rules to which such principles supposedly underlie'.[12] MacCormick, who formulated one of the most influential theories in this context, defined coherence between different elements of a legal system (more specifically, between legal norms), as 'a function of its justifiability under higher order principles or values'.[13] Accordingly, a set of norms contained in a legal system is coherent, and hence 'makes sense', if it is instrumentally or intrinsically related to the realization of a common value or values. To phrase it differently, failing to make sense results directly from there being 'no common value or value-cluster which the enactment of such laws serves'.[14] Such values constitute 'actually pursued or possible pursued states of being or of affairs which are conceived to be legitimate, desirable, worthy or even … mandatory for pursuit as standing purposes, aims, goals or ends'.[15] Hence, for any value there is a principle according to which that value may, should, or must be pursued or realized. As other scholars summarized MacCormick's theory, 'principles make rules coherent'.[16] MacCormick was not the only prominent theorist who delved into the question of relations between different elements of legal systems. Dworkin's 'law as integrity' is another theory that strongly resonates with MacCormick's concept of normative coherence.[17]

In short, theorists propose that different elements of a legal system can be claimed to be coherent if they serve the same higher order value(s). The basic schematic representation of this theory can be seen in Figure 4.1.

[12] Giovanni Battista Ratti and Jorge Luis Rodríguez, 'On Coherence as a Formal Property of Normative Systems' (2015) 27 Journal for Constitutional Theory and Philosophy of Law 131, 141. Although theorists generally agree on the essence of coherence, there is no complete consensus on all coherence's demands.

[13] Neil MacCormick, 'Coherence in Legal Justification' in Aleksander Peczenik, Lars Lindahl, and Bert van Roermond (eds), *Theory of Legal Science* (D Reidel Publishing 1984) 238.

[14] Neil MacCormick, *Rhetoric and the Rule of Law* (OUP 2005) 197.

[15] MacCormick, 'Coherence in Legal Justification' (n 13) 237.

[16] Aleksander Peczenik, *Scientia Juris: Legal Doctrine as Knowledge of Law and as a Source of Law* (Springer 2005) 138.

[17] See Aleksander Peczenik, 'Coherence, Truth and Rightness in the Law' in Patrick Nerhot (ed), *Law, Interpretation and Reality. Essays in Epistemology, Hermeneutics and Jurisprudence* (Springer 1990) 58; Ronald Dworkin, *Law's Empire* (Hart Publishing 1998) 176–84.

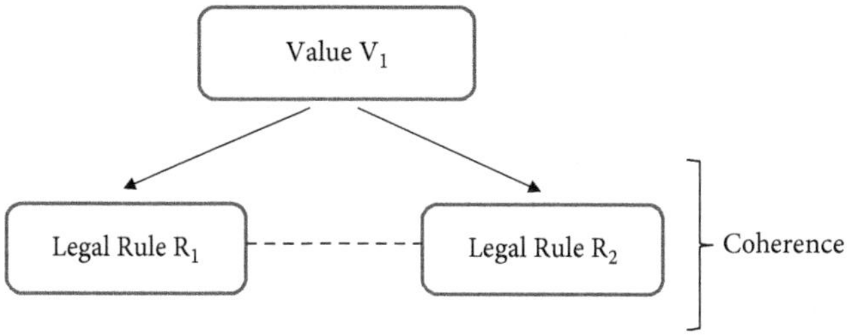

Fig 4.1 Coherence in law

2. Horizontal dimension of coherence

2.1 Global and local coherence

The scope of legal rules that demonstrate coherence is an inherent part of this book that looks at two different fields of law. This is a new dimension of coherence, as so far the legal theory has focused either on 'global coherence', which implies coherence of the entire legal system through a set of common principles or values,[18] or proposed employing the notion of coherence to one branch of law only, which can be defined as 'local coherence'.[19]

A disagreement on whether coherence should have a local or a global dimension derives from conflicting views on the existence of the plurality of values in a legal system and their reducibility. Commenting on this issue, Kress observed that '[h]istorical, strict, rationalist, idealist coherence theories flow from a single principle', whereas '[m]odern normative coherence theories tend to be pluralistic'.[20] Among the adherents of the theory that coherence in law has a global dimension is Dworkin. In his opinion, integrity in law is undermined 'whenever a community enacts and enforces different laws each of which is coherent in itself, but which cannot be defended together as expressing a coherent ranking of different principles of justice or fairness or procedural due process'.[21] Although integrity with a global dimension remained for Dworkin an ideal vision of law, he acknowledged that it might be unfeasible to 'bring all the various statutory and common-law rules our judges enforce under a single coherent scheme of principle'.[22]

The majority of propositions in the scholarship contradict the global vision of coherence.[23] MacCormick, for example, refers to rules and precedents that deal with

[18] Dworkin ibid.

[19] MacCormick, *Rhetoric and the Rule of Law* (n 14) 199.

[20] Ken Kress, 'Coherence' in Dennis Patterson (ed), *A Companion to Philosophy of Law and Legal Theory* (Blackwell 1999) 521.

[21] Dworkin (n 17) 184.

[22] ibid.

[23] Moral Soriano (n 11) 300.

the same subject matter within the same area of law.[24] Thus, in his view, coherence functions as a possible constraint on legislative and judicial actions solely within a specific branch of law. Similarly, Levenbook claimed that certain decisions could be supported by values that are specific to one area of law, and extraneous from the perspective of another legal branch.[25] Raz expressed his scepticism towards global accounts that impose coherence on an entire legal system by indicating two ways in which such accounts err.[26] First, a global dimension disregards value pluralism or, put differently, wrongly presupposes that the plurality of values should be subsumed under a few supreme principles. Secondly, it unnecessarily strives to idealize or prettify law that is untidy due to the reality of politics.[27] Indeed, law is frequently an outcome of a collective conflict 'among many different wills and imaginations, interests and visions',[28] which makes it unachievable to base an entire legal system on a single justificatory rationale.[29]

2.2 Sectional coherence as a new dimension

The question of coherence between EU competition and data protection law concerns two legal areas, hence does not square with a global or a local account of coherence. Although useful as such, the existing theories cannot be relied on to address the issue at stake. The book therefore proposes to move away from this purely binary distinction between global and local accounts and introduces a new type of coherence, which in this book is referred to as 'sectional coherence'. This new type of coherence can be defined as coherence between legal rules that belong to two or more different fields in the same legal system. Thus, the scope of sectional coherence differs from the scope of coherence accounts that already exist in the legal theory: its reach is more limited than that of global coherence, but wider and more encompassing as compared to local coherence that relates to one area of law only.

Sectional coherence is grounded in scepticism towards subsuming all legal rules enshrined in a legal system under a few supreme principles. By endorsing the position that a legal system consists of a plurality of irreducibly independent and possibly conflicting supreme values or principles, it proposes moving away from the monistic premise on which global coherence accounts are largely based. Indeed, the EU legal system can be considered as an embodiment of a pluralistic conception. Rather than emanating from one or very few supreme values, it embraces many frequently irreducible and equally weighty ones.

[24] MacCormick, *Rhetoric and the Rule of Law* (n 14) 199.

[25] Barbara B Levenbook, 'The Role of Coherence in Legal Reasoning' (1983) 3 Law and Philosophy 355, 304.

[26] Raz (n 9) 314.

[27] ibid.

[28] Roberto Mangabeira Unger, *What Should Legal Analysis Become* (Verso Books 1996) 65–66.

[29] John McGarry, 'The Possibility and Value of Coherence' (2013) 34 Liverpool Law Review 17, 19.

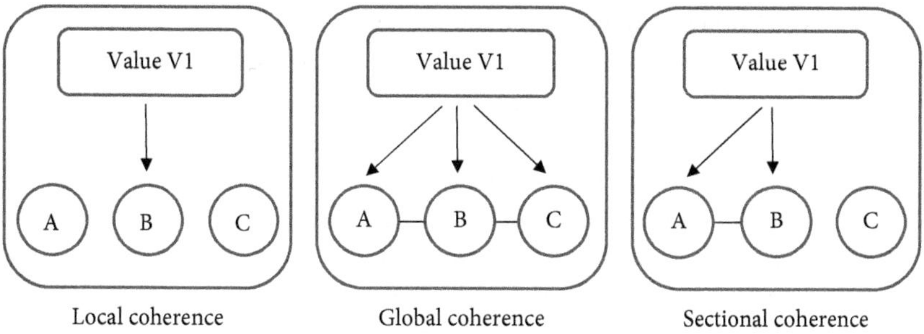

Fig 4.2 The distinction between local coherence, global coherence, and sectional coherence

Simultaneously, sectional coherence challenges the narrow view that it is possible to establish coherence predominantly in local contexts, within one specific branch of law. Although it is incontestable that different legal areas embrace distinguishable considerations, there is no reason to assume that values served by these different areas exhibit some sort of inherent exclusivity. Ascribing exclusivity to values would lead to creating an artificial system of distinct blocks of law. To frame it differently, sectoral coherence assumes that the legal rules of two or more fields of law might be able to exhibit coherence by serving the same value or set of values. As Chapter 2 explained, data protection and competition law already share a common set of values such as individual welfare, individual sovereignty, and fairness.

Visually, a distinction between local, global, and sectional coherence can be presented as shown in Figure 4.2 (A, B, and C represent different areas of law belonging to the same legal system).

3. The normative force of coherence

Although coherence invokes positive connotations, contradicting views have surfaced in relation to its normative force and the extent to which coherence should be decisive in legal interpretation and justification. Having introduced the notion of sectional coherence, it is therefore relevant to outline why establishing coherence might be desirable in a normative sense. While the discussion in this section is theoretical, subsequent chapters complement this theoretical overview by demonstrating how the concrete instances of coherence between data protection and competition law will be of benefit to the society and the economy.

3.1 Formal and moral significance of coherence

Theorists suggesting that coherence is of limited importance have claimed that a coherent legal system is desirable merely in a formal sense, logically entailing that there exist other standards that should additionally be considered by those entrusted with interpretation. Accordingly, the claim is that coherence-oriented decision making is considered as representative of a rather formalistic (formally rational) and relativistic approach to interpretation and justification.[30] For them, the coherence theory has an inherent flaw, as it accepts describing as coherent a set of rules that serve certain values, even if those values are undesirable.[31] Coherence as an internal value of actual positive law cannot in itself guarantee any justice,[32] as it does not distinguish between a wicked legal system and a well-founded one.[33] Put differently, a legal system can be perfectly coherent while simultaneously morally pernicious or dysfunctional, according to some.[34] In that sense, coherence is likely to compete with other the normative premises of a legal system, such as moral merit.[35]

It seems, therefore, indisputable that coherence has an important formal dimension. Viewed positively, it can eliminate arbitrariness in formulating certain interpretations, and can also be considered one of the core ideas behind the rule of law.[36] Linking coherence to the rule of law, MacCormick identified legal certainty, the protection of legitimate expectations, as well as protection from arbitrary intervention as important considerations.[37] Such demand that arbitrariness should be avoided and interpretation be predictable and based on rational discretion are the criteria of the legitimacy of decisions as formulated by Aarnio.[38] But they are not the only criterion. Another postulates that interpretative decisions must also reflect material rightness, which means that they must fulfil some axiological (moral) criteria.[39] Only then can an interpretative statement receive 'rational acceptability' in the legal community in question, which for Aarnio is an ideal that allows for evaluating the legitimacy of legal interpretation. Thus, the following question arises: besides its formal relevance, does coherence have a moral force that can help to achieve the material rightness of interpretative statements?

Some theorists have claimed that coherence does also have a moral dimension.[40] Responding to Hart's claim that 'evil aims may have as much coherence and inner

[30] MacCormick, 'Coherence in Legal Justification' (n 13) 243.
[31] ibid.
[32] MacCormick, *Rhetoric and the Rule of Law* (n 14) 203.
[33] Aldo Schiavello, 'On "Coherence" and "Law": An Analysis of Different Models' (2001) 14 Ratio Juris 233, 237.
[34] Kenneth Ehrenberg, 'Pattern Languages and Institutional Facts: Functions and Coherence in the Law' in Michał Araszkiewicz and Jaromir Šavelka (eds), *Coherence: Insights from Philosophy, Jurisprudence, and Artificial Intelligence* (Springer 2013) 158.
[35] Raz (n 9) 307.
[36] Mark Dawson, 'Better Regulation and the Future of EU Regulatory Law and Politics' (2016) 53 Common Market Law Review 1209, 1229.
[37] MacCormick, *Rhetoric and the Rule of Law* (n 14) 16.
[38] Aulis Aarnio, 'On Rational Acceptability. Some Remarks on Legal Justification' in Nerhot (n 17) 80.
[39] ibid.
[40] Kress (n 20) 533.

logic as good ones', Fuller expressed his disagreement by stating: 'I shall have to rest on the assertion of a belief that may seem naïve, namely, that coherence and goodness have more affinity than coherence and evil.'[41] The affinity between coherence and goodness would express itself in the moral acceptability of the values or principles that underlie coherence. Interestingly, although MacCormick seemed to consider coherence incapable of guaranteeing substantive justice, he expressed at the same time the fact that values and principles that condition coherence must 'in their totality … be conceived as expressing a satisfactory form of life'.[42] It can thus be suggested that coherence ensures material rightness in that it accepts only values that are morally right. That notwithstanding, coherence seems unhelpful in choosing one out of several morally acceptable interpretations.

As most of the arguments indicated previously have been formulated in relation to the local type of coherence (ie coherence within one area of law), it is essential to establish whether they are transposable to the new account of sectional coherence proposed in this book.

3.2 Maximum rational acceptability of coherence-based interpretations

As sectional coherence used in interpretations of competition and data protection differs in scope from local coherence, its normative appeal can also be assumed to differ and needs to be briefly examined.

Regarding the formal dimension, it is more straightforward to concur with the claim that one area of law needs to be subordinate to a value or a set of values as only then is it coherent and 'makes sense', rather than asserting that two legal fields must be coherent in order to make sense. Interpretation I_1 of a provision enshrined in legal field A (eg competition law) does not necessarily need to be coherent with other provisions in legal field B (eg data protection law) to be formally rational, unless they share the same value basis. Although it would enhance the legitimacy of I_1, it is sufficient that I_1 coheres with other provisions enshrined in field A and with past court decisions. Thus, although achieving sectional coherence between two legal fields might not always be essential for achieving formal rationality, there could be instances where formal factors such as legal certainty or predictability are boosted by formulating common interpretations across different fields of law.

What about coherence's moral force? It can occur that a provision belonging to legal field A has two semantically and legally possible interpretations I_1 and I_2. I_1 is locally coherent with other rules in legal field A, predictable, and on that basis satisfies the criterion of formal rationality. It is also morally acceptable. I_2, on the other hand, is an alternative semantically and legally possible interpretation. It differs from I_1 in that it is not an interpretation as predictable and formally rational as I_1,

[41] Lon L Fuller, 'Positivism and Fidelity to Law: A Reply to Professor Hart' (1958) 71 Harvard Law Review 630, 636.

[42] MacCormick, *Rhetoric and the Rule of Law* (n 14) 193 and 202.

which means that to some extent it may even frustrate local coherence. Suppose, however, that in contrast to I_1, I_2 ensures the highest level of coherence between legal areas A and B. The question that inevitably arises is whether and when choosing I_2 instead of I_1 can be legitimate.

To address this issue, one must verify the second criterion of legitimacy, namely the material rightness of suggested interpretations. This book proposes that to be legitimate, I_2 needs to achieve a greater rational acceptability in the legal community than I_1 'thanks to' its moral superiority/rightness and 'despite' its formal inferiority (decreased level of local coherence) as compared to I_1. This would entail that sectional coherence through a higher order value may generate an outcome that is axiologically preferable and receives maximum rational acceptability. Although it is unlikely that sectional coherence can always be qualified as a strongly justifying argument in a formal sense, it might be conducive to achieving a more substantively (morally) desirable outcome, overruling local coherence.

C. Coherence in EU law

In EU law, coherence remains an ambiguous legal concept. The English language versions of the EU Treaties do not contain an explicit reference to the notion of coherence in their core provisions. Article 7 TFEU indicates, however, the principle of 'consistency', which in other official languages figures as Kohäranz (German), coherencia (Spanish), cohérence (French), or coerenza (Italian). This provision states that '[t]he Union shall ensure *consistency* between its policies and activities, taking all of its objectives into account and in accordance with the principle of conferral of powers'.[43]

Article 7 TFEU remains 'a rather under-analysed element of the Treaties'.[44] As regards the concept of consistency, it converted from a political objective to a legally binding one.[45] The first reference to the principle of consistency was in the Single European Act (SEA)[46] in relation to the EU's external relations. Article 30(5) SEA stated that 'the external policies of the European Community and the policies agreed in European Political Co-operation must be consistent'. This understanding of consistency as an external matter was solidified by the Maastricht Treaty and the introduction of the pillar system in the EU, after which European Political Cooperation (EPC) was replaced by the Common Foreign and Security Policy (CFSP).[47] Article 3 placed dual emphasis on an institutional framework that

[43] Emphasis added.
[44] Dawson (n 36) 1227.
[45] For a more comprehensive analysis, see Christian Franklin, 'The Burgeoning Principle of Consistency in EU Law' (2011) 30 Yearbook of European Law 42.
[46] Single European Act [1987] OJ L169/25.
[47] Franklin (n 45) 44.

should ensure the consistency and continuity of Union's activities as well as the consistency of the Union's 'external activities as a whole in the context of its external relations, security, economic and development policies'.

As regards Article 7 TFEU specifically, commentators interpreted it as requiring 'an inter-sectoral coordination of the decision makers in respect to common objectives, and the likewise consistent formulation of their political agendas'.[48] Thus, the provision should be read in keeping with the Union's objectives, such as those indicated in Article 3 of the Treaty on European Union (TEU) (eg internal market, environmental protection, combating social exclusion and discrimination, and promoting social justice and equality) and with the 'mainstreaming' provisions, such as Article 9 TFEU (social exclusion), Article 10 TFEU (non-discrimination), or Article 11 TFEU (environmental protection).[49] As observed by Dawson, for example, this implies that 'market-making policies should be conditioned by a number of non-market objectives, from social exclusion to environmental protection and non-discrimination to animal welfare'.[50] Although not explicitly envisaged, consistency might also encompass the principle of continuity, which prohibits spontaneous policy changes in one field without carrying out consultations with decision-makers in other fields.[51]

The CJEU has not brought much clarity to the meaning of the principles of consistency and coherence in EU law. Over the past years, it has invoked both notions—often interchangeably—in cases dealing with various subject matter, painting a fragmented conceptual picture. For example, both concepts figured prominently in cases dealing with national legislation restricting free movement for the purpose of pursuing a public interest objective. As Advocate General Maduro observed in his Opinion in *Blanco Pérez and Chao Gómez*, in such cases one needs to 'understand the increased importance that the requirement of *consistency* and *coherence* has acquired in the case-law of the Court in reviewing how national legislation pursues its stated goals'.[52] This requirement, as the Court asserted in *Hartlauer*, lays down the idea that restrictive national legislation is 'appropriate for ensuring attainment of the objective pursued only if it genuinely reflects a concern to attain it in a *consistent* and systematic manner'.[53] Although the Court does not define it in

[48] Markus Kotzur, 'Article 7 [Principle of Coherence]' in Rudolf Geiger, Daniel Erasmus-Khan, and Markus Kotzur (eds), *European Union Treaties. A Commentary* (Hart Publishing 2015) 214.

[49] Dawson (n 36) 1227.

[50] ibid.

[51] Kotzur (n 48) 215.

[52] Joint Cases C-570 and 571/07 *Blanco Pérez and Chao Gómez* [2009] ECLI:EU:C:2009:587, Opinion of AG Maduro, para 21 (emphasis added).

[53] Case C-169/07 *Hartlauer* [2009] ECLI:EU:C:2009:141, para 55 (emphasis added). See also Case C-169/08 *Presidente del Consiglio dei Ministri* [2009] ECLI:EU:C:2009:709, para 42; Case C-42/07 *Liga Portuguesa de Futebol* [2008] ECLI:EU:C:2008:560, para 61; Case C-341/08 *Petersen* [2009] ECLI:EU:C:2009:513.

more detail, consistency in this sense seems to require that there are no contradictions in pursuit of such an objective.[54]

In another line of case law, the CJEU has invoked coherence requirements when arguing for the hierarchical ranking of laws within the EU legal system, asserting in *Werhof* that this principle requires secondary legislation 'to be interpreted in accordance with the general principles of Community law'.[55] At the same time, the CJEU has relied on consistency, rather than coherence, to hold that national courts are under an obligation not to apply national legal rules that conflict with EU law.[56] In another case, the Court referred to 'the necessary *coherence* of the system of judicial protection established in the Treaty'[57] to argue for its jurisdiction to declare void or invalid an act of an EU institution. In this set of cases, as commentators have observed, 'the Court promulgated its very own principle of coherence as a means for carrying out its self-perceived role as the EU's constitutional gap-filler'.[58]

The concepts of consistency and coherence have also been invoked in case law relating to the field of the EU's external relations, where the Court held that there is a duty of close cooperation between the Member States and the EU institutions to 'facilitate the achievement of the Community tasks and to ensure the *coherence* and *consistency* of the action and its international representation'.[59]

The Court's interchangeable use of the concepts of consistency and coherence, as well as the introduction of different tests to satisfy their requirements, show that there is no one definitive understanding ascribed to these concepts under EU law, rather their meaning is determined on a case-by-case basis. As regards the main provision laying down the principle of consistency—Article 7 TFEU—the essential interpretative question that remains open is whether the provision has a narrow meaning implying solely a 'lack of contradictions' between different laws or policies, or whether it should be read as a broader and more demanding principle implying the 'presence of positive connections' between different elements of a legal system in pursuing certain objectives. In fact, these two requirements are so materially different that scholars have used different terms to describe them: consistency for a lack of contradictions and coherence for the presence of positive connections between different elements

[54] Gjermund Mathisen, 'Consistency and Coherence as Conditions for Justification of Member State Measures Restricting Free Movement' (2010) 47 Common Market Law Review 1021, 1023; Werner Haslehner, '"Consistency" and Fundamental Freedoms: The Case of Direct Taxation' (2013) 50 Common Market Law Review 737, 744.

[55] Case C-499/04 *Hans Werhof v Freeway Traffic Systems GmbH & Co KG* [2005] ECLI:EU:C:2005:686, para 32.

[56] Case C-106/77 *Amministrazione delle finanze dello Stato v Simmenthal* [1978] ECLI:EU:C:1978:31.

[57] Case 314/85 *Foto-Frost v Hauptzollamt Lübeck-Ost* [1987] ECLI:EU:C:1987:452 (emphasis added).

[58] Franklin (n 45) 52.

[59] Case C-266/03 *Commission v Luxembourg* [2004] ECLI:EU:C:2004:750, para 60 (emphasis added); Case C-433/03 *Commission v Germany* [2005] ECLI:EU:C:2005:153, para 66 (emphasis added); Case C-247/07 *Commission v United Kingdom* [2008] ECLI:EU:C:2008:682, para 75 (emphasis added).

of a legal system, as described earlier.[60] Defined in this way, consistency is generally argued to be an essential requirement for rationality, and a requisite condition for coherence.[61] Although necessary, consistency is not, however, sufficient to achieve coherence.[62] As MacCormick observed in relation to coherence within a single area of law, '[o]ne can imagine a random set of norms none of which contradict each other but which taken together involve the pursuit of no intelligible value of policy'.[63] Also contemporary EU law scholars have acknowledged that coherence is 'something more than logical consistency of propositions'[64] in that 'elements of a coherent structure are mutually supporting and reinforcing'[65] and 'coherence is a broader and more flexible concept than consistency'.[66]

Thus, differentiating between consistency and coherence under EU law is not linguistic pedantry but rather a necessity for ensuring that these two concepts can be used predictably, as clear and functional principles in cases and analyses. In discussions on interactions between data protection and competition law, conflating consistency with coherence carries the risk of confusing two very different objectives: merely striving to eliminate conflicts between these two fields of law (consistency), or establishing a higher degree of their convergence and positive connections through common principles and values (coherence).

D. Conclusions

Sectional coherence introduced in this chapter provides a new paradigm and offers a theoretical means of researching on how to place competition and data protection law on a more synergetic path.[67] As Chapter 2 illustrated, data protection and

[60] Franklin (n 45) 46–47. See also Mathisen (n 54) 1024.

[61] Peczenik, 'Coherence, Truth and Rightness in the Law' (n 17) 297.

[62] ibid; Aleksander Peczenik, *On Law and Reason* (Springer 2009) 158.

[63] Neil MacCormick, *Legal Reasoning and Legal Theory* (Clarendon Press 1978) 106.

[64] Stefano Bertea, 'The Argument from Coherence: Analysis and Evaluation' (2005) 25 Oxford Journal of Legal Studies 369, 373.

[65] ibid.

[66] See Marise Cremona, 'Coherence Through Law: What Difference Will the Treaty of Lisbon Make?' (2008) 3 Hamburg Review of Social Sciences 11, 14. In Cremona's opinion, coherence is a multi-layered concept: a first level of coherence is consistency, encompassing 'rules of hierarchy' (ie primacy of EU law), a second level is 'rules of delimitation' (ie effective allocation of tasks between actors), and a third level implies 'principles of cooperation and complementarity' (ie synergy between the norms, actors, and instruments).

[67] For a discussion on sectional coherence in relation to competition law and data protection, and competition law and the value of environmental sustainability, see Klaudia Majcher and Viktoria HSE Robertson, 'Protecting Personal Data and the Environment: Doctrinal Challenges for EU Competition Law in Our Day and Age' (2022) 47 European Law Review 622.

competition law already share a panoply of values—a conclusion that forms the basis for formulating the claim that they cohere on a broader level of values. The question that remains to be explored in the next two chapters is how this coherence through values can translate into coherence on a more granular level of concrete provisions and their enforcement.

5
A Competition Law Perspective on Sectional Coherence

A. Introduction

Operationalizing sectional coherence requires examining competition and data protection law separately, and inquiring how the interpretation of their provisions and their enforcement might need to be modified to ensure a more synergetic approach. This chapter is devoted to competition law, and its aim is to identify and discuss the multiple ways in which competition law can better integrate data protection. It submits that a new coherence-oriented outlook is required in relation to establishing the power of undertakings (Section B), in the area of abuse of a dominant position (Section C), and in merger control (Section D). While both the concept of market definition and the area of anti-competitive agreements may also reveal noteworthy tensions or congruity between competition and data protection law, they are left out of the chapter given that coherence-related issues are for the time being less prominent in these contexts.

B. Data power

The position of power enjoyed by large technological firms is rooted—at least partially—in their ability to collect and process large amounts of data. This section reflects on power in digital markets and how to redefine it from a competition perspective. While accurately conceptualizing and measuring power is a requisite for ensuring the soundness of competition decisions, whether and how the strength of companies that they infer from data is considered in competition law also has indirect repercussions for data protection. If all relevant dimensions of power are effectively incorporated into a competition law's power assessment framework, the chances of bringing a powerful undertaking within the scope of competition law increase. While the possession of power is not as such problematic under competition law in the EU and in several other jurisdictions, if data-related harm is subsequently proved, competition enforcement offers a powerful tool for tackling an abusive exercise of power.

This section has a threefold aim. First, it introduces 'data power' as a subcategory of market power. It then creates a taxonomy of data power, differentiating

Coherence between Data Protection and Competition Law in Digital Markets. Klaudia Majcher, Oxford University Press.
 DOI: 10.1093/oso/9780198885610.003.0006

between 'economic data power', 'political data power', and 'individual data power'. Finally, it provides suggestions on how data power and its consequences can be considered in competition assessments.

1. Data power as a sub-category of market power

In competition law, an analysis of market dominance aims to establish whether a company has a sufficient degree of immunity in the market and is therefore not susceptible to the usual disciplining market forces, for example from rivals or consumers.[1] In the vast majority of jurisdictions, market dominance is a key precondition for applying the law on abuse. Dominance is also a relevant concept in the area of merger control: a merger can be considered detrimental to competition when it leads to the creation or strengthening of a dominant position.[2]

In EU law, the notion of dominance as defined by the CJEU[3] (ie a position of economic strength that enables the prevention of effective competition; see Chapter 1 Section D) slightly differs from how dominance is understood in economic terms: from an economic perspective, dominance is associated with the concept of market power, which refers to the ability of undertakings to set supra-competitive prices.[4] Firms may also be considered to have market power if they are able to restrict output, or to influence other recognized parameters of competition, including quality, variety, and innovation. Even though there are nuanced differences between the concepts of market power and market dominance, they will be used interchangeably in this section, as the same core idea represented by both notions is the economic strength of an undertaking.

In the digital economy, access to personal data offers unique value for many firm. Naturally, the question that this poses for competition law is whether and how to factor personal data as a source of corporate power into an overall market power assessment, and what weight should be accorded to it. It is a moot point whether 'data power' ought to be included in the competition law glossary and, if so, how its evaluation should be conducted.

Data power, which this book understands as a sub-category of competition-relevant power, is concerned with power that results from access to personal data as well as other structural features that data enables, such as the creation of digital ecosystems. A similar conceptualization of data power figures in Lynskey's analysis: she defines data power as 'a multifaceted form of power available to digital

[1] Robert O'Donoghue and Jorge Padilla, *The Law and Economics of Article 102 TFEU* (3rd edn, Hart Publishing 2020) 185.
[2] EUMR, art 2(3) and recital 26.
[3] Case 27/76 *United Brands Co and United Brands Continental BV v Commission* [1978] ECLI:EU:C:1978:22, para 65; see also Chapter 1.
[4] O'Donoghue and Padilla (n 1) 186.

platforms, arising from their control over data flows'.[5] As she explains, 'it is control over data that is decisive to this power'.[6] The notion of data power is thus different from, but partially related to, various new concepts coined in recent years to capture the strength of technology companies, such as 'ecosystem power',[7] 'platform power', 'intermediation power', or 'bottleneck power'.[8] In a conceptual sense, data power has the closest resemblance to 'informational power', which was referred to by the EDPB in its statement on the data protection impacts of economic concentration.[9]

2. A taxonomy of data power

From a competition perspective, a common framing of the problematic repercussions of power focuses on its economic costs. This section submits that in addition to having economic repercussions, data power might have a profound influence on non-economic spheres. A similar observation was made by Jacobides and Lianos in relation to ecosystem power. As they claimed, such power can have both social (eg harm to democracy, privacy, fairness) and economic costs (eg high prices, lack of innovation, inequality of opportunity).[10]

In an attempt to challenge the boundaries of the traditional market power notion, a broader taxonomy of data power is introduced to bring into the limelight the scope of influence of modern technology companies. The following discussion of data power taxonomy is based on three categories: 'economic data power', 'political data power', and 'individual data power'.[11] Having presented the taxonomy, the chapter explores what methods can be used to assess data power at the stage of establishing a dominant position under competition law.

2.1 Economic data power

Economic power that businesses acquire thanks to access to data is undisputed. As already described in detail in Chapter 2 Section C, data is at the centre of the

[5] Orla Lynskey, 'Grappling with "Data Power": Normative Nudges from Data Protection and Privacy' (2019) 20 Theoretical Inquiries in Law 189, 196.

[6] ibid 197.

[7] Michael G Jacobides and Ioannis Lianos, 'Ecosystems and Competition Law in Theory and Practice' (2021) CLES Research Paper Series UCL No 1/2021, 22.

[8] OECD, 'The Evolving Concept of Market Power in the Digital Economy' (2022) OECD Competition Policy Roundtable Background Note, 22–25.

[9] EDPB, 'Statement of the EDPB on the Data Protection Impacts of Economic Concentration' (2018).

[10] Jacobides and Lianos (n 7) 22.

[11] A taxonomy of power of the big tech companies introduced by Gerbrandy and Phoa distinguishes between 'instrumental power', 'structural power', and 'discursive power'. As the authors claim, power can also manifest itself in the political, social, and personal domain: Anna Gerbrandy and Pauline Phoa, 'The Power of Big Tech Corporations as Modern Bigness and a Vocabulary for Shaping Competition Law as Counter-Power' in Michael Bennett, Huub Brouwer, and Rutger Claassen (eds), *Wealth and Power: Philosophical Perspectives* (Routledge 2022).

ad-based business model that dominates the modern digital economy. In our day-to-day online activities, the likelihood of using services that do not rely on any personal data collection and processing—whether for the purpose of offering targeted ads, personalizing content, or furthering the other economic goals of companies—is disturbingly low. Drawing insights from data, companies are able to improve their economic performance by boosting consumer engagement and customizing their experiences. Although some of these actionable data insights help to create products and services for which there is individual demand (eg some users may genuinely prefer personalized ads or social network timelines), due to the lack of alternatives, many consumers use them despite feeling uneasy about the scale of data processing, whilst companies' bottom lines continue to improve.

In addition to underlying the core business model, access to data helps companies in their efforts to enter related or unrelated markets, build ecosystems, lock in consumers, and potentially foreclose rivals. The innovation costs of such foreclosing strategies cannot be disregarded: as argued by Ezrachi and Stucke, while large technological firms might continue to provide sustained innovation that secures their profits and growth, value-creating disruptive innovation that challenges the existing business models, products, and services suffers as a result.[12] This is regrettable, as in the author's view it is precisely disruptive innovation that has the highest potential for delivering the kind of turbulence that is needed to change the established models of resourcing and competition in the digital economy.

In addition to limiting the economic opportunities of rivals and harming individuals indirectly, personal data processing might also have direct economic repercussions for individuals. Data-based price discrimination (see Section C) or exacerbated inequalities related to economic opportunities illustrate how data-based decision making might cause individual-level economic damage.

2.2 Political data power

In addition to having economic implications, the political dimension of data power is noteworthy. Revealing in this context and representative of the problem is the way in which companies with data power continue to shape the media landscape, for example. The media is a highly impactful institution in any democratic system[13] and a core knowledge infrastructure that enhances citizens' political agency. Participatory and deliberative democracy that values critical reflection and active engagement in public discourse cannot flourish without a well-functioning information environment. In the words of Helberger, '[o]nly when

[12] Ariel Ezrachi and Maurice E Stucke, *How Big-Tech Barons Smash Innovation—And How To Strike Back* (HarperCollins 2022) 24–26.

[13] Jack M Balkin, 'Free Speech in the Algorithmic Society: Big Data, Private Governance, and New School Speech Regulation' (2018) 51 UC Davis Law Review 1149, 1210.

citizens are aware of the different perspectives, interests and concerns in a society and are able to tolerate and even further them, is political participation deserving of the name'.[14]

The debate on how personal data and data power influence the political sphere is not new. The Snowden and Cambridge Analytica scandals, as well as the repeated occurrences of large-scale disinformation campaigns and 'fake news' that span the online domain, have provided solid evidence that the power of technological companies to influence politics is unparalleled. The phenomenon of 'platformization' of information, which means that an online platform performs the role of the manager of communication 'that enables, directs and channels specific flows of information',[15] as well as decides what content is meaningful and should feature more prominently on user interfaces, is one prominent development that fuels the political power of online businesses. Reuter's *Digital News Report 2022* indicated that as regards the main gateways to digital news, social media preference (28 per cent) has recently surged ahead of direct access (23 per cent), marking a tipping point.[16] As Klonick noted, companies such as Google and Facebook have in the past years dominated the public sphere by becoming de facto news curators as well as 'the architecture for publishing new speech and the architects of the institutional design that governs it'.[17] Social networking platforms 'organise not just a single element of communication, but the entire process of political persuasion'.[18] Arguably, this makes them 'social editors' or 'data-driven, social forms of opinion power' that have so far been largely neglected in traditional policies.[19] These development have implications for traditional publishers which have limited control over how the news is curated and prioritized, as well as on citizens who are exposed to algorithmically-selected personalized narratives or unverified content.

Conceptually, political data power can be grounded in epistemology. The term 'epistemology' is derived from the Greek words 'epistēmē', which can be translated as 'knowledge' or 'understanding', and 'logos', which means 'reason'.[20] In philosophy, epistemology commonly refers to the theory of knowledge. In relation to individuals, political power can be equated with their 'epistemic welfare'—their

[14] Natali Helberger, 'On the Democratic Role of News Recommenders' (2019) 7 Digital Journalism 993, 1002.

[15] Ganaele Langlois, 'Participatory Culture and the New Governance of Communication: The Paradox of Participatory Media' (2013) 14 Television and New Media 91, 100.

[16] Reuters Institute, 'Digital News Report' (2022) 23.

[17] Kate Klonick, 'The New Governors: The People, Rules, and Processes Governing Online Speech' (2018) 131 Harvard Law Review 1598, 1603–04.

[18] Natali Helberger, 'Facebook Is a New Breed of Editor: Social Editor' (*LSE Media Policy Project*, 15 September 2016) <https://blogs.lse.ac.uk/mediapolicyproject/2016/09/15/facebook-is-a-new-breed-of-editor-a-social-editor/> accessed 3 May 2022.

[19] ibid.

[20] Stanford Encyclopaedia of Philosophy, 'Epistemology' <https://plato.stanford.edu/entries/epistemology/> accessed 6 July 2022.

'right to know' and receive trustworthy, independent, and varied information. Problematizing these 'conditions of our knowing', as expressed by Dahlgren, 'takes us in the realm of epistemology, and today democracy is facing … a growing epistemic crisis',[21] as human agency remains thoroughly dependent on the knowledge process.[22] In a similar vein, others have referred to the political power of tech companies as 'opinion power'[23] or 'media power',[24] which represents the same core idea as 'epistemic power'.

2.3 Individual data power

Companies with access to users' personal data have at their disposal a powerful tool to influence the numerous dimensions of individual well-being. Among non-economic and non-political repercussions of data power are various forms of discrimination, limited individual autonomy, dignity, control, and reputation.

While there are numerous overlaps between individual data power on the one hand, and economic and political power on the other—all these forms of power can indeed be employed vis-à-vis individuals—the notion of individual data power captures the effects that economic and political power categories may not grasp. For example, discrimination based on gender, race, or sexual orientation may have economic repercussions, but can also affect individuals psychologically (stigma, shame, loss of esteem).[25] Similarly, loss of autonomy can take the form of political influencing, but it can also prevent people from making other, non-political, choices though manipulation, coercion, or failure to inform.[26] There is thus an expansive range of individual states that might be deeply influenced by data power.

Data power's influence on individuals also has evident spillover effects on society as a whole. As Frischmann and Selinger warned, in the digital domain, individuals are increasingly confronted with 'techno-social engineering', the processes where the compound of technological and social forces impacts the way they think, perceive, and act.[27] The foregoing of human agency may not only have a disruptive effect on how people develop personal skills and abilities, but also on how they interact with others.

[21] Peter Dahlgren, 'Media, Knowledge and Trust: The Deepening Epistemic Crisis of Democracy' (2018) 25 Journal of the European Institute for Communication and Culture 20, 20.

[22] ibid 21. See eg Albert Bandura, 'Toward a Psychology of Human Agency' (2006) 1 Perspectives on Psychological Science 164.

[23] See eg Natali Helberger, 'The Political Power of Platforms: How Current Attempts to Regulate Misinformation Amplify Opinion Power' (2020) 8 Digital Journalism 842.

[24] Robin Mansell, 'Platforms of Power' (2015) 43 Intermedia 20.

[25] Danielle K Citron and Daniel J Solove, 'Privacy Harms' (2022) 102 Boston University Law Review 793, 855.

[26] ibid 845–46.

[27] Brett M Frischmann and Evan Selinger, *Re-Engineering Humanity* (CUP 2018).

3. Assessing data power in digital markets

There are multiple factors that competition authorities traditionally consider for measuring power and establish dominance. While market shares 'provide a useful first indication'[28] of a company's economic strength, there are a number of other relevant factors: the existing market conditions and market structure, the position of other competitors, barriers to expansion and entry, or countervailing buyer power. The fact that market shares alone cannot always correctly reflect the degree of power is commonly acknowledged in the context of digital markets,[29] where additional indicators need to be carefully scrutinized. In particular, network effects combined with strong economies of scale and scope in digital environments may contribute to consumer lock-in, reduce multi-homing of consumers, strengthen the position of incumbents, and discourage the market entry of new businesses. The existence of ecosystems that data helps to create is another indicator that should be accounted for in an assessment of dominance.

While there is a relatively wide consensus that the factors mentioned above are reliable benchmarks against which to measure digital power, the idea of including access to data as an indicator of power—possibly as contributing to or creating barriers to market access or expansion—they does not have an unequivocal support. What is fiercely debated is not whether companies such as Meta or Alphabet derive an advantage from the data they collect, but rather, as Graef has framed it, whether 'the effort required to collect the data necessary to be able to compete on equal footing with the incumbent amounts to a sustainable advantage and barrier to entry'.[30]

Sceptics of ascribing a competitive relevance to data at the stage of a market power assessment commonly point to certain qualities of data, including their non-economic nature, their ubiquity, the fact that they are cheap to obtain, that historic data are of little relevance, or that data are subject to diminishing returns.[31] These features of data allegedly support the conclusion that personal data might not deliver a competitive advantage as rivals can obtain similar datasets.

[28] European Commission, 'Guidance on the Commission's enforcement priorities in applying Article 82 of the EC Treaty to abusive exclusionary conduct by dominant undertakings' [2009] OJ C45/1, para 13.

[29] See eg Case T-79/12 *Cisco Systems, Inc and Messagenet SpA v European Commission* [2013] ECLI:EU:T:2013:635, para 69.

[30] Inge Graef, *EU Competition Law, Data Protection and Online Platforms: Data as Essential Facility* (Wolters Kluwer 2016) 250.

[31] See eg Darren S Tucker and Hill B Wellford, 'Big Mistakes Regarding Big Data' (2014) The Antitrust Source <https://papers.ssrn.com/sol3/papers.cfm?abstract_id=2549044> accessed 10 July 2022; Anja Lambrecht and Catherine E Tucker, 'Can Big Data Protect a Firm from Competition?' (2015) <https://papers.ssrn.com/sol3/papers.cfm?abstract_id=2705530> accessed 10 July 2022. Authors presented similar arguments in the context of data power in merger control: see eg Paul Gilbert and Richard Pepper, 'Privacy Considerations in European Merger Control: A Square Peg for a Round Hole' (2015) CPI Antitrust Chronicle 6–7.

Invoking just a few examples (eg the market entry of the dating app Tinder), Sokol and Ma concluded that 'low entry barriers are a *common* attribute in online data markets',[32] which in their view offers a significant policy lesson. As they claimed, 'new entrants are unlikely to be at a significant competitive disadvantage relative to incumbents in terms of data collection or analysis': instead of first relying on data, they can enter the market by offering innovative services, and only then start collecting data on users.[33] Admittedly, such an entry strategy might in some markets prove effective, even though subsequent expansion attempts could turn out to be problematic. Generic and often unverified assumptions about the ease of entry into digital markets, some of which are based on vaguely described features of data and do not introduce a contextual nuance, must, however, be approached critically.

A case-by-case assessment of specific datasets reveals a much more nuanced picture of the competitive value of data. The need to conduct case-specific evaluations of digital market power and of the role of data was stressed in the Special Advisers' Report, for example. The report indicated that 'any discussion of market power should analyse, case by case, the access to data available to the presumed dominant firm but not to competitors, and the sustainability of any such differential access to data', and that an analytical framework ensuring the objectivity of the analysis was necessary.[34] The view that data can confer power in the competition sense has also been expressed in reports published in other jurisdictions. The discussion paper authored by the Australian Competition and Consumer Commission mentioned a few types of competitive advantage of data access, including data's role in product improvement or development, positive user and monetary feedback loops resulting from data-based innovation, enhanced targeting services, and opportunities to forecast product demand and market trends.[35] Other reports, for example the UK's Furman Report[36] and the report published jointly by the French and German NCAs,[37] also clearly reflect the understanding that personal data has the potential to raise entry barriers, in particular for smaller companies.

There are also important scholarly attempts to determine what concretely should be considered in a market power assessment in the context of data. For example, focusing on Big Data, Rubinfeld and Gal provided a taxonomy of access barriers to

[32] Daniel Sokol and Jingyuan Ma, 'Understanding Online Markets and Antitrust Analysis' (2017) 15 Northwestern Journal of Technology and Intellectual Property 43, 47 (emphasis added).
[33] ibid 49.
[34] Jacques Crémer, Yves-Alexandre de Montjoye, and Heike Schweitzer, 'Competition Policy for the Digital Era' (2019) Report for the European Commission 49.
[35] ACCC, 'Updating Competition and Consumer Law for Digital Platform Services' (2022) Discussion Paper for Interim Report No 5, 33–34.
[36] Jason Furman, 'Unlocking Digital Competition' (2019) Report of the Digital Competition Expert Panel 33–35.
[37] Autorité de la concurrence and Bundeskartellamt, 'Competition Law and Data' (2016) 11–13.

data.[38] They introduced four categories of barriers: barriers to collection, barriers to storage, barriers to synthesis and analysis, and barriers to the usage of big data.

Besides paying attention to market shares and several additional factors, including access to data, the analysis of power and dominance may also consider behavioural elements. As such, the conduct of a company is part of the analysis of abuse, which follows that of establishing a dominant position. In the EU, however, both the Commission and the Courts have asserted that behavioural facts may also be considered as indicators of power. In *United Brands*, the CJEU stated that in order to find out whether United Brands had a dominant position on the relevant market, 'it may be advisable to take account if need be of the facts put forward as acts amounting to abuses without necessarily having to acknowledge that they are abuses'.[39] Similarly, the Commission said in *Hilti* that the undertaking's conduct is a 'witness to its ability to act independently of, and without due regard to, either competitors or customers'.[40] In its reasoning in *AstraZeneca*, the CJEU held that the ability of AstraZeneca to maintain prices higher than those offered by its competitors, while retaining very high market shares, evidenced its significant market power in respect of price.[41]

In relation to data power, the question arises whether enforcers could use behavioural evidence—how a company influences economic, political, or individual spheres—to draw a conclusion on power. In her discussion on gatekeepers, Lynskey noted that 'the analysis of political, social, and cultural dimensions of gatekeepers must accompany an economic analysis of their role'.[42] According to O'Donoghue and Padilla, accounting for behavioural factors would be most useful in the context of exploitative, rather than exclusionary, abuses. This is because most companies, no matter whether they are dominant or not, can embark on some form of exclusion. Dominance may at the same time be a likely explanation for exploitative conduct, for example when companies offer excessive prices over a long period and the market is resistant to change.[43] Others are more sceptical. The weakness of relying on behavioural factors is that it implies circular thinking: 'an undertaking is dominant because it has adopted a course of conduct which amounts to an abuse, yet certain courses of conduct only amount to an abuses because the undertaking which has adopted them is dominant'.[44] As mentioned earlier, both the Commission and the CJEU maintained, however, that certain market acts can

[38] Daniel L Rubinfeld and Michal S Gal, 'Access Barriers to Big Data' (2017) 59 Arizona Law Review 229.

[39] *United Brands* (n 3) para 68.

[40] *Eurofix-Banco v Hilti* (Cases IV/30.787 and 31.488) Commission Decision of 22 December 1987, para 71.

[41] Case T-321/05 *AstraZeneca AB and AstraZeneca plc v European Commission* [2010] ECLI:EU:T:2010:266, para 266.

[42] Orla Lynskey, 'Regulating "Platform Power"' (2017) LSE Law, Society and Economy Working Papers No 1/2017.

[43] O'Donoghue and Padilla (n 1) 214.

[44] Van Bael & Bellis, *Competition Law of the European Union* (6th edn, Wolters Kluwer 2021) 134.

be considered at the stage of a dominance assessment without reaching a conclusion on potential abuse.

Thus, some of data power's impacts on economic, political, and individual dimensions could already at the stage of a dominance assessment offer valuable insights or evidence. While using evidence of the economic repercussions of power might not be too controversial, harmful manifestations of political or non-economic individual power as potential proof of power for competition purposes are more contentious. That notwithstanding, updating the competition approach along these lines should be explored as it might more accurately grasp the scope of influence—hence, power—that data helps to expand. Given that some of the economic, political, and individual repercussions of power explained in the previous section might be more complex to integrate at the stage of establishing abuse, reflecting on them in the course of conducting an analysis of dominance would signal an important development. One caveat to be stressed is that an analysis of market dominance is preceded by establishing a product and geographical market definition[45]—a step that might have a profound influence on which factors are relevant or irrelevant to subsequently establish power in the specific market.

C. Abuse of a dominant position

Abuse of a dominant position is one of the central areas of competition law, and one where interlocking data protection and competition concerns are at their most evident. This section provides an insight into how competition assessments should reflect on data protection at three different analytical steps: formulating theories of harm, examining justifications, and designing remedies.

1. Theories of harm

Once a dominant market position is established, the next key step in a competition law assessment of abuse of a dominant position is the formulation of a theory of harm, which aims to demonstrate what type of abuse is at stake and why it harms competition and consumers. The following sections discuss two main categories of abuse—exploitation and exclusion—to show how data-based market strategies challenge the interpretation of the concept of abuse and what the response could be. Discriminatory abuses with an exploitative or exclusionary character are also discussed in the respective sections.

[45] For an extensive analysis of market definition as an analytical tool of competition law in dynamic, innovation-driven markets, see Viktoria HSE Robertson, *Competition Law's Innovation Factor: The Relevant Market in Dynamic Contexts in the EU and the US* (Hart Publishing 2020).

Before delving into the various data- and data protection-relevant theories of harm, one caveat should be made as to their novelty. Some of the theories presented here are new, while others are partially or fully anchored in the notions established in competition law, but have been over time been interpreted differently depending on context (eg fairness, proportionality). Thus, some of the suggested interpretations do not have solid legal precedents. That said, Article 1(3) of Regulation 1/2003 states that '[t]he abuse of a dominant position referred to in Article [102] of the Treaty shall be prohibited, *no prior decision to that effect being required*'.[46] The generic and broad formulation of Article 102 TFEU allows competition enforcers to expand or reformulate its scope to capture new forms of problematic conduct. As Temple has said in relation to exclusionary abuses, if Article 102 TFUE 'was confined to classical restraints on trade or to any given list of types of behaviour, it would be open to dominant firms to devise new exclusionary practices and practise them with impunity'.[47]

At the same time, experimenting with theories of harm should respect the principle of legal certainty. O'Donoghue and Padilla warned that it 'would be highly problematic if the EU Courts' statements that the abuses mentioned in Article 102 TFEU are not exhaustive were applied in unthinking way'.[48] Moving towards an 'open-ended' or 'nebulous' notion of abuse,[49] thereby broadening the scope of Article 102 TFEU, might carry important risks. Also, as Monti and Feases observed, EU cases are usually designed in a way that fits within one of the categories listed in paragraphs (a)–(d).[50] Thus, while a certain leeway exists in competition law to sanction new types of problematic conduct, safeguards—or methods of balancing between the need to adapt competition law to new empirical developments and create a predictable business environment—need to accompany innovative interpretations of the established concepts and provisions.

1.1 Exploitative abuses and data protection

In competition law, direct exploitation of customers and consumers as stipulated in Article 102(a) TFEU is expressed through the notion of fairness. Specifically, dominant undertakings are not allowed to directly or indirectly impose 'unfair purchase or selling prices or other unfair trading conditions'. This section explains the

[46] Council Regulation (EC) No 1/2003 of 16 December 2002 on the implementation of the rules on competition laid down in Articles 81 and 82 of the Treaty [2003] OJ L1/4 (emphasis added). See also Wouter PJ Wils, 'The Obligation for the Competition Authorities of the EU Member States to Apply EU Antitrust Law and the Facebook Decision of the Bundeskartellamt' (2019) No 3-2019 Concurrences 58, 63.

[47] John Temple Lang, 'Monopolisation and the Definition of "Abuse" of a Dominant Position under Article 86 EEC Treaty' (1979) 16 Common Market Law Review 345, 350.

[48] O'Donoghue and Padilla (n 1) 314.

[49] Robert O'Donoghue, 'The Death of the Theory of Everything Under Article 102?' (Global Competition Law Centre Conference, Brussels, February 2016).

[50] Giorgio Monti and Alexandre Ruiz Feases, 'The Case Against Google: Has the U.S. Department of Justice Become European?' (2021) 35 Antitrust Magazine 26.

meaning of these prohibited forms of conduct by extracting the values and notions through which the Commission and the CJEU have analysed fairness in varying factual circumstances. Building on that, the analysis demonstrates the potential relevance of Article 102(a) TFEU for strengthening data protection.[51] Even though the following sections reflect on personal data in the context of 'trading conditions' or 'prices', the proposals contained therein should not be mistaken for a suggestion that personal data can be conceptualized as a tradeable commodity.[52]

1.1.1 Unfair 'personal data trading conditions'

There are only a few cases at the EU level that refer to unfair trading conditions. Although the interpretations of anti-competitive trading conditions that they contain have been criticized for their vagueness and imprecision,[53] they deserve a brief overview before addressing fairness in digital markets specifically.

Unfair trading conditions under EU competition law. One of the first instances where the CJEU interpreted unfair trading conditions was the *SABAM* case concerning copyright.[54] The Court linked fairness to the notion of 'necessity', even in its stringent form of 'absolute necessity'. It ruled that trading conditions are unfair when a dominant company exploiting copyrights 'imposes on its members obligations which are not absolutely necessary for the attainment of its object',[55] as it undermines their freedom to exercise copyrights. This interpretation was subsequently implemented by the Commission in *GEMA*.[56]

In *Duales System Deutschland (DSD)*, the Commission decided that DSD, which owned the recycling trade mark GREEN DOT, had abused its dominant position by applying unfair trading conditions in the market for sales packaging waste in Germany.[57] The Commission pointed out that the licence fee was imposed on the customers of DSD irrespective of whether or not they used the company's waste recovery services. Fairness was again associated with the necessity of the clauses in terms of the object of DSD's licensing contract.[58] The Commission also stated

[51] The analysis in this section is to a large extent based on my co-authored article exploring the linkages between competition and data protection law in the context of fairness: Harri Kalimo and Klaudia Majcher, 'The Concept of Fairness: Linking EU Competition and Data Protection Law in the Digital Marketplace' (2017) 42 European Law Review 210.

[52] See eg Bart Custers and Gianclaudio Malgieri, 'Priceless Data: Why the EU Fundamental Right to Data Protection Is at Odds with Trade in Personal Data' (2022) 45 Computer Law & Security Review 1, 2.

[53] Kati Cseres, 'Towards a European Model of Economic Justice: The Role of Competition Law' in Hans-Wolfgang Micklitz (ed), *The Many Concepts of Social Justice in European Private Law* (Edward Elgar 2011) 427.

[54] Case C-127/73 *Belgische Radio en Televisie v SV SABAM and NV Fonior* [1974] ECLI:EU:C:1974:25.

[55] ibid 15.

[56] *GEMA statutes* (Case IV/29.971) Commission Decision of 4 December 1981, para 36.

[57] *DSD* (Case COMP/34.493) Commission Decision of 20 April 2001. The decision was upheld on appeal in Case T-151/01 *Der Grüne Punkt-Duales System Deutschland GmbH v Commission* [2001] ECLI:EU:T:2007:154; C-385/07 P *Der Grüne Punkt-Duales System Deutschland GmbH v Commission* [2009] ECLI:EU:C:2009:456.

[58] Robert O'Donoghue and Jorge Padilla, *The Law and Economics of Article 102 TFEU* (2nd edn, Hart Publishing 2013) 856.

that 'unfair commercial terms exist where an undertaking in a dominant position fails to comply with the principle of proportionality'.[59] It referred to *United Brands*, where the CJEU ruled that a dominant firm violates the principle of proportionality when it refuses to continue supplies to its customer on account of the latter's participation in the advertising campaign of the dominant company's competitor. The CJEU explained that such a 'counter-attack' by a dominant firm would be acceptable only if it were 'proportionate to the threat taking into account the economic strength of the undertakings confronting each other'.[60] Thus, in both *DSD* and *United Brands*, fairness was understood 'in the sense that the interests of the contracting parties are balanced'[61] in a vertical relationship.

In *Alsatel*, the CJEU asserted that contractual practices concerning the unilateral fixation of the price of supplements through contractual modifications, as well as automatic renewals of contracts for a fifteen-year term, constituted unfair trading conditions.[62] The case implied that the factors of unfairness could be defined broadly as '*oppressiveness and one-sidedness* of the contract for the consumer'.[63]

Finally, one of the aspects examined in *Michelin II* concerned the fact that dealers were mandated to 'to enter into quantitative commitments to Michelin ... before they had even received the quantity rebates for the previous year'.[64] The Commission considered this practice unfair not only because of the weak psychological position of the dealers in the negotiation process, but also because the dealers were unable to reliably estimate their cost prices and could not freely decide on their business strategy.[65] A bonus programme introduced by Michelin was also unfair. Although it was presented as being based on an agreement, it actually constituted 'a requirement unilaterally imposed by the manufacturer to increase purchases of Michelin tyres on the market'.[66]

It can be inferred from these various cases and decisions that the concept of fairness in the context of trading conditions is understood as encompassing a set of values or factors rather than a single determining quality. Akman noted that fairness has been applied as 'an umbrella notion', its meaning depending on the context.[67] Despite the fact that the notion of fairness is thus left vacuous,[68] there is a set of concepts through which the CJEU and the Commission have aimed to define fairness, as the previous cases illustrate. Among them are absolute necessity, one-sidedness, equality, proportionality, balance of interests, transparency, objectivity,

59 *DSD* (European Commission) (n 57) para 112.
60 *United Brands* (n 3), para 190.
61 Pinar Akman, *The Concept of Abuse in EU Competition Law* (Hart Publishing 2012) 155.
62 Case C-247/86 *Alsatel v SA Novasam* [1988] ECLI:EU:C:1988:469, para 10.
63 Akman (n 61) 155 (emphasis added).
64 *Michelin* (Case COMP/36.041) Commission Decision of 20 June 2001, para 223.
65 ibid, para 223.
66 ibid, para 265.
67 Akman (n 61) 157.
68 ibid.

and certainty.[69] The analysis that follows relies on some of these notions to reflect on fairness of personal data trading conditions.

Unfair personal data trading conditions under EU competition law. First, fairness of data-related trading conditions understood in terms of proportionality and necessity needs to be analysed. In both *SABAM* and *GEMA*, fairness was considered compromised when dominant undertakings imposed requirements that were unnecessary in relation to the pursued objectives. Proportionality and absolute necessity may therefore limit the types and amounts of data a company can collect in light of the purpose of their collection. This interpretation displays similarities to the concept of data minimization (art 5(1)(c) GDPR). The notion of necessity also finds its expression in Article 7(4) GDPR in the context of freely given consent. The GDPR requires that the provision of a service is not made conditional on consent to the processing of data that is not necessary for the provision of a service.

The conceptualization of fairness through the notions of one-sidedness and oppression in competition law is more debatable. In the context of data processing, there are indeed substantial limitations to users' self-determination.[70] Schwartz, for example, observed that negotiations in relation to privacy may be unfeasible due to data collectors' bargaining power and ability to influence the playing field on which individual decisions are determined.[71] Yet, it needs to be stressed that Article 102 TFEU prohibits abuse of market power, not market power itself. As the CJEU has remarked, 'a finding that an undertaking has a dominant position is not in itself a recrimination'.[72] The argument that a company violates competition law simply because it has greater bargaining power and its conduct is one-sided would be difficult to substantiate. Economic strength entails a special responsibility on the part of a company to ensure that its conduct does not impair competition, but it does not affect its business freedom to unilaterally set fair and non-exploitative terms of the bargain, such as prices and trading conditions. Insofar as such terms are substantively fair, the aspects relating to the abilities of consumers to negotiate seem to be of limited relevance in establishing abusive conduct. Yet, if such one-sided conduct amounts to a drastic breach of standards of fairness in terms of data protection, the arguments might bear more weight.

Finally, although the notion of transparency has thus far not been invoked in the EU case law as a factor determinative of unfairness of trading conditions—the *Facebook*[73] decision issued by the Bundeskartellamt being a national-level

[69] ibid 156.

[70] See also Alessandro Mantelero, 'Competitive Value of Data Protection' (2013) 3 International Data Privacy Law 229, 232.

[71] Paul M Schwartz, 'Property, Privacy, and Personal Data' (2004) 117 Harvard Law Review 2056, 2081.

[72] Case C-322/81 *NV Nederlandsche Baden-Industrie Michelin v Commission* [1983] ECLI:EU:C:1983:313.

[73] Bundeskartellamt, Decision B6-22/16 of 6 February 2019 (*Facebook*).

exception—transparency seems a relevant consideration in the context of exploitative abuses. It can be argued that a company processing data can be condemned on the basis of fairness where it provides unclear, or even misleading or deceptive, information about its data practices. Article 102 TFEU does not contain an outright prohibition of dishonest or misleading conduct.[74] Yet, scholars have observed that 'a general prohibition may be inferred from the recognition of the character of unfairness of other trading conditions as any type of dishonest or unfair business strategy broadly defined'.[75] Such a conceptualization of fairness in competition law would align with the understanding of the data protection law provision requiring 'fair data processing' (art 5(1)(a) GDPR), which is concerned, among others, with the provision of information to data subjects, as well as the prohibition of misleading or deceptive practices and rebalancing asymmetrical power relationships.

The challenge that arises in this context is to determine the threshold that could trigger competition law liability. Valuable insights may be derived from *AstraZeneca*,[76] in which the CJEU decided that the company's notification of misleading information to patent offices with the intention of maintaining its monopoly violated Article 102 TFEU. Although the case concerns an exclusionary rather than exploitative abuse, it offers suggestions as regards the benchmarks for competition liability. The Court emphasized that a dominant undertaking does not have to be infallible and that not 'each objectively wrong representation made by such an undertaking' constitutes an abuse of its position.[77] It ruled, however, that AstraZeneca's conduct was incompatible with competition on the merits because it was consistently linear, highly misleading, featuring a manifest lack of transparency, and deliberate.[78] The transposition of these conditions of liability to data practices would suggest that a dominant undertaking behaves unfairly, and might therefore exploit individuals and violate Article 102(a) TFEU, if it deliberately, consistently, and manifestly relies on a misleading strategy with regard to data practices.

As the analysis shows, consumer detriment identified through the concept of fairness of digital trading conditions under Article 102(a) TFEU can be linked at the initial stage of data processing to notions of transparency, and misleading or deceptive behaviour. Additionally, fairness can, through the requirements of (absolute) necessity and proportionality, be evoked as regards the types and amounts of data collected by companies for specified purposes. Yet, notwithstanding these possible conceptualizations of fairness of personal data trading conditions, one

[74] Anca Daniela Chiriţă, *The German and Romanian Abuse of Market Dominance in the Light of Article 102 TFEU* (Nomos 2011) 365.
[75] ibid.
[76] Case C-457/10 P *AstraZeneca AB and AstraZeneca plc v European Commission* [2014] ECLI:EU:C:2014:28.
[77] ibid para 99.
[78] ibid para 93.

needs to be mindful that they would imply a partial departure from the established case law and create a precedent in digital competition law.

1.1.2 Unfair 'personal data prices'

Besides unfair trading conditions, Article 102(a) TFEU also covers unfair purchase or selling prices. The notion of unfair prices has been interpreted in EU law as excessive prices.[79] Excessive pricing is, however, an abuse that is difficult to prosecute. The complexity is to distinguish between high, yet still tolerable, and unreasonably high prices.[80] Framed differently, the dilemma pertains to the methods employed to discern and prove an excessive price.[81]

Unfair prices under EU competition law. To provide guidance, the CJEU explained in *United Brands* that a company might violate competition law if it is 'charging a price which is excessive because it has no reasonable relation to the economic value of a product supplied'.[82] The Court put forward two cumulative conditions to classify a price as excessive, which were subsequently followed by the Commission in the *Port of Helsingborg* decision:[83] 'whether the difference between the costs actually incurred and the price actually charged is excessive and, if the answer to this question is in the affirmative, to consider whether a price has been imposed which is either unfair in itself or when compared to competing products'.[84]

Unfair personal data prices under EU competition law. The question therefore arises whether unfair 'personal data prices' fall within the scope of Article 102(a) TFEU, and when such unfair data prices might be deemed illegal. In digital markets, there are a large number of companies that operate in two-sided markets. Economic theory establishes that a two-sided platform offers services and products 'below average variable cost, below marginal cost, or even below zero'[85] on a subsidy side and recoups its losses on a paid side of the market. Only one side of the market can be rationally discounted at a time.[86] The profits of a two-sided platform and the volume of transactions more generally depend on a breakdown of the prices between the two sides, not only on the prices independently. The definition

79 See eg OECD, 'Policy Roundtable: Excessive Prices' (2011) DAF/COMP(2011)18; *United Brands* (n 3); *Deutsche Post AG* (Case COMP/36.915) Commission Decision of 20 March 2001.

80 Giorgio Monti, *EC Competition Law* (CUP 2007) 218; Jonathan Faull and Ali Nikpay, *The EU Law of Competition* (3rd edn, OUP 2014)192.

81 Massimo Motta and Alexandre de Streel, 'Excessive Pricing in Competition Law: Never Say Never?' (Conference organized by the Swedish Competition Authority, Stockholm, 9 November 2007) 32.

82 *United Brands* (n 3) para 250.

83 *Scandlines Sverige v Port of Helsingborg* (Case COMP/36.570) Commission Decision of 23 July 2004.

84 *United Brands* (n 3) para 252. See also Monti (n 80) 218–19.

85 David S Evans and Richard Schmalensee, 'The Industrial Organization of Markets with Two-Sided Platforms' (2007) 3 Competition Policy International 151, 176.

86 Geoffrey Parker and Marshall Van Alstyne, 'Two-Sided Network Effects: A Theory of Information Product Design' (2005) 51 Management Science 1494, 1501.

of an optimal price structure is at the core of a successful business strategy for a platform.

These economic features need to be considered in competition assessments of potentially unfair pricing strategies in order to reach sound conclusions. This is particularly so when confronted with allegations of one-sided predation on the subsidized market side and/or excessive pricing on the paid side. Accordingly, while evaluating pricing on the subsidized market side, a 'presumption that below-cost pricing by two-sided platforms is anticompetitive is simply not valid',[87] as firms have the prospect of recouping the (predatory) losses.[88] Correspondingly, high prices can emerge in a stable market equilibrium on the paid side of the market,[89] yet should not be classified as excessive under the assumption that there are corresponding below-costs prices on the other side.

Competition law evaluations of pricing strategies on the free market side may, however, need to be reconsidered in digital markets if one assumes that transactions in such markets are performed in exchange for data.[90] It is well established that in multi-sided markets where there is a free service on the subsidy side; users often pay a 'hidden, non-monetary price'[91] in the form of giving away personal data. In a similar fashion, Gebicka and Heinemann claimed that 'an undue increase in the use of personal data' or 'an unreasonable expansion of the data use policy' could be paralleled with price exploitation.[92] Thus, possible Article 102(a) TFEU violations pertaining to excessive pricing on the allegedly free market side merit examination, and the analysis needs to factor personal data into price exploitation.

The first part of the unfair pricing test delineated by the CJEU in *United Brands* entails performing price–costs comparisons to verify whether the price is excessive. To evaluate the fairness of 'data prices' under Article 102 TFEU, one would first need to establish the monetary price of personal data on the subsidized side of the market. In this respect, the methodologies envisaged in the OECD report *Exploring the Economics of Personal Data*[93] appear insightful. In particular, the methodology based on market valuation can prove helpful. It stipulates that the value of personal data can be estimated, for example, by analysing 'the financial results of a company such as market capitalization, revenues and net income on a

87 Evans and Schmalensee (n 85) 176.

88 OECD (n 79) 13.

89 Evans and Schmalensee (n 85) 176.

90 Waltraut Kotschy, 'The Proposal for a New General Data Protection Regulation—Problems Solved?' (2014) 4 International Data Privacy Law 274, 280. See also Alessandro Acquisti, 'The Economics and Behavioural Economics of Privacy' in Julia Lane and others (eds), *Privacy, Big Data, and the Public Good: Frameworks for Engagement* (CUP 2014) 80.

91 Dirk Auer and Nicolas Petit, 'Two-Sided Markets and the Challenge of Turning Economic Theory Into Antitrust Policy' (2015) 60 Antitrust Bulletin 426, 430.

92 Aleksandra Gebicka and Andreas Heinemann, 'Social Media & Competition Law' (2014) 37 World Competition 149, 165.

93 OECD, 'Exploring the Economics of Personal Data: A Survey of Methodologies for Measuring Monetary Value' (2013) OECD Digital Economy Papers No 220.

per-user or per-record basis'.[94] Another indicator of market valuation is the market price for data, delineated as a 'price per data entry offered on the market by data brokers',[95] who often mediate business transactions between data collectors and advertisers.[96] Once the monetary value of personal data has been analysed against the costs of providing digital goods or services, competition assessments need to determine whether the difference is excessive, and indicate an anti-competitive price exploitation of consumers.

Moving to the second prong of the *United Brands* fairness test, the price will need to be either 'unfair in itself or when compared with competing products' to constitute an infringement. Unfairness 'in itself' would require the specification of what the notions of 'undue' or 'unreasonable' collection of data connote.[97] Referring once more to the OECD, the exploitation threshold could be estimated through individual valuations of data protection as revealed in surveys and economic experiments. This would establish the amount of money that should be offered to individuals for disclosing personal data or the price that they would be willing to pay to have their data protected from disclosure.[98] Alternatively, fairness of 'data prices' charged by a dominant company could be established by making comparisons with the prices imposed on digital users by competing undertakings (ie the amount of personal data collected and processed by a similar digital service), which would, however, be burdensome.

There may thus be methods for satisfying the analytical requirements of the *United Brands* excessive pricing test in the context of Article 102 TFEU, even if the test also obviously has inherent limitations.[99] Because it does not determine what 'excessive' is, or the ratio between the costs and price that is excessive,[100] the test does not by itself establish a clear definition of fairness. The second prong of the test of whether the price is unfair in itself or when compared with competing products is, admittedly, subjective.[101] Referring, for example, to individual valuations of data protection while estimating an anti-competitive price excess can, due to subjectivity, trigger concerns related to legal certainty and the clarity of the standard of proof.

Other—and preferred—benchmarks that might be used to establish the excessiveness of a data price under competition law can be derived directly from data protection law, and specifically from the requirements of data minimization and

[94] ibid 20.

[95] ibid.

[96] EDPS, 'Opinion 8/2016 on Coherent Enforcement of Fundamental Rights in the Age of Big Data' (2016) 10–11.

[97] Gebicka and Heinemann (n 92) 165.

[98] OECD (n 79) 30.

[99] *Deutsche Post AG* (n 79) para 142.

[100] Nils Wahl, 'Exploitative High Prices and European Competition Law: A Personal Reflection' (Conference organized by the Swedish Competition Authority, 9 November 2007) 60.

[101] O'Donoghue and Padilla (n 58) 758.

the purpose limitation enshrined in Article 5(1) GDPR. Accordingly, if a firm violates the GDPR by collecting personal data beyond that which is necessary to achieve a specific purpose, or by keeping the data for a period longer than necessary, such data extraction could be perceived as excessive and exploitative under competition law. This legal avenue, while certainly controversial to some, would prevent second-guessing by competition authorities and allow competition law to integrate already established data protection benchmarks in its assessments. It would also provide an opportunity for joint competition and data protection evaluations of cases where excessive data is a concern.

1.1.3 Price discrimination as another type of exploitation

Exploitation within the meaning of Article 102(a) TFEU may surface in many different shapes and forms, as the preceding analysis has shown. This section zooms in on discrimination-based infringements, specifically on price discrimination. It provides insights on whether data-based price discrimination can be addressed by competition law, and how competition law might interact in this context with data protection.

Price discrimination. The concept of 'price discrimination' is not new in competition law. As traditionally understood, it represents various types of pricing practices, such as rebates, discounts, selective price cuts, or discriminatory input prices set by vertically integrated operators.[102] It also most commonly refers to either primary line injury (ie discrimination vis-à-vis competitors) or secondary line injury (ie discrimination vis-à-vis trading partners).[103] The latter is directly referred to in Article 102(c) TFEU, which prohibits a dominant undertaking from applying 'dissimilar conditions to equivalent transactions with other trading partners, thereby placing them at a competitive disadvantage'. The present analysis, which is concerned with discrimination of individuals, introduces a novel dimension to the established concept of abusive discrimination. Rather than relying on Article 102(c) TFEU, this section frames discrimination as a possible violation of Article 102(a) TFEU.

Whish and Bailey define price discrimination as 'the sale or purchase of different units of a good or service at prices not directly corresponding to differences in the cost of supplying them'.[104] The traditional taxonomy of price discrimination introduced by Pigou indicates three categories: first-degree (perfect), second-degree (nonlinear), and third-degree price discrimination.[105] First-degree price

[102] Damien Geradin and Nicola Petit, 'Price Discrimination under EU Competition Law: The Need for a Case-by-Case Approach' (2005) GCLC Working Paper No 07/05, 2.

[103] Alison Jones and Brenda Sufrin, *EU Competition Law: Text, Cases, and Materials* (6th edn, OUP 2016) 381–82.

[104] Richard Whish and David Bailey, *Competition Law* (7th edn, OUP 2012) 759.

[105] Hal R Varian, 'Price Discrimination' in Richard Schmalensee and Robert D Willig (eds), *Handbook of Industrial Organization*, vol 1 (Elsevier 1989) 600.

discrimination occurs when the price charged for each unit equals the consumer's maximum willingness to pay for that specific unit. Second-degree discrimination means that the price depends on the number of units of the product purchased (eg quality discounts).[106] Third-degree price discrimination involves charging a different price to identifiably different consumers or consumer groups (eg discounts for students).[107]

It has been mainstream to perceive the first category, perfect price discrimination, as theoretical and unlikely to occur in practice, hence not deserving much attention in the competition law discourse.[108] Transactions related to perfect price discrimination can be described as cost prohibitive, which means that it is difficult for companies to discriminate in a perfect manner.[109] Armstrong observed that 'the information needed for first-degree price discrimination (e.g. perfect discrimination) makes it more of a theoretical benchmark than a realistic business strategy'.[110] Yet, with the increased potential of technologies to enable perfect discrimination, revisiting the practice seems essential.

Perfect and almost-perfect price discrimination in digital markets. There exist various impediments for companies to perfectly discriminate in digital markets. For example, due to insufficient amounts of data, an algorithm may not be able to single out all relevant variables that affect the reservation price, therefore to correctly predict or infer that price for each individual.[111] Accurately identifying the reservation price, which is the least favourable price that a consumer is willing to pay, is a prerequisite for perfect discrimination. Absent such data, an algorithm would need to assume the reservation price. Another obstacle to engaging in perfect price discrimination is the fact that the assumptions can be erroneous due to 'multiple dispositional and situational factors that can affect purchasing decisions', such as consumers' bounded rationality and their imperfect willpower.[112] Overall, as scholars have noted, substantial investments would need to be made, for example in tracking consumers, collecting data on their behaviour, categorizing them into groups, establishing their demand elasticities and increasing their search costs, reducing market transparency, hindering the growth of anti-tracking technology, or lobbying against greater data protection.[113]

That aside, algorithms coupled with tracking technologies are claimed to unprecedentedly facilitate 'almost perfect' price discrimination in online retailing, a phenomenon referred to as 'personalized pricing'. Ezrachi and Stucke observed that

[106] Mark Armstrong, 'Price Discrimination' (2007) MPRA Paper No 4693, 3.

[107] ibid.

[108] Geradin and Petit (n 102) 4.

[109] Richard Posner, *Economic Analysis of Law* (9th edn, Wolters Kluwer 2014) 345.

[110] Armstrong (n 106) 3.

[111] Ariel Ezrachi and Maurice E Stucke, *Virtual Competition: The Promise and Perils of the Algorithm-Driven Economy* (Harvard UP 2016) 96–97.

[112] ibid 97–98.

[113] ibid 121.

almost perfect behavioural discrimination 'will involve labelling you in countless ways and placing you in smaller groupings of consumers with common situational and dispositional factors'.[114] Thus, the question emerges whether competition law can respond to this type of discrimination.

Personalized pricing under EU competition law. The effects of price discrimination on consumer welfare depend on the context and type of price discrimination. Personalized pricing can be discussed as a practice corresponding to first-degree (perfect) or third-degree price discrimination, the level of correspondence being contingent upon the quality and completeness of information that companies have about consumers' willingness to pay.

In a monopolistic market in which an online platform has almost-complete information about consumers' willingness to pay, and is therefore able to perfectly price-discriminate, welfare is likely to decrease. Armstrong claims that in such a scenario 'the firm appropriates the entire gains from trade and consumers are left with nothing',[115] giving rise to the 'appropriation effect'. As a result, companies are better off and consumers with a high willingness to pay are worse off. Although such transactions might be beneficial in view of the total welfare standard (ie the sum of consumer and producer surplus), it can be classified as exploitative if considered from the viewpoint of the consumer welfare standard. This standard refers solely to the consumer surplus, more precisely to the difference between consumers' valuations (ie their willingness to pay) and the actual price.[116] Put differently, if it is acknowledged that competition law takes into account the distributional issue of wealth transfers between companies and customers, imposing different prices on the consumer market side based on personal data could in specific circumstances raise a competition concern relating to exploitation.

1.2 Exclusionary abuses and data protection

Exploitation-based theories provide the most direct way for competition law to remedy data protection harms. Given the limitations of exploitative abuses and the authorities' hesitance to pursue exploitative cases due to their proximity to regulatory interventions, exclusionary theories can be an alternative in cases with intersecting data protection and competition issues.

While the digital economy has in the past years witnessed the emergence of a few companies embracing alternative business models not centred on extracting personal data, none have so far managed to cause a notable market disruption. For example, between 2012 and 2021, the global market shares of DuckDuckGo, a search engine that offers privacy-friendly and non-personalized searches,

114 ibid 102; Armstrong (n 106) 5.

115 Armstrong (n 106) 7.

116 Louis Kaplow, 'On the Choice of Welfare Standards in Competition Law' (2011) Harvard Law and Economics Discussion Paper No 693, 2.

increased merely from 0.01 to 0.63 per cent.[117] There are a number of reasons that might explain this inability to disrupt. Consumer preferences as revealed through market choices naturally play a role, even though they cannot be assumed to reliably represent normative preferences. Market features that give the incumbents an advantage, such as network effects and related lock-in effects, as well as limited multi-homing, offer an alternative explanation. Importantly, what can prevent the emergence and stifle the growth of alternative providers are the market strategies employed by incumbents. Large technology companies have a strong interest in preserving the status quo relating to the dynamics, structures, and features of digital markets. Carefully orchestrated digital ecosystems where personal data plays a key role are so profitable that any interference by new entrants that offers potentially disruptive services needs to be forestalled. Depending on the area of activity (eg search, social networking services, e-commerce), there are a range of anti-competitive methods that incumbent firms may be incentivized to employ to prevent competition from potentially disruptive services, some of which are worthy of discussion.

This section discusses three established types of abuse—tying, refusals to deal, and predation—to illustrate how their implementation in competition law decisions may affect data protection, and how they can be reinterpreted to more suitably capture data protection-relevant exclusion in digital markets. The aim is not to exhaustively outline all forms of exclusion that might have a data protection relevance, but rather to provide an illustration of the problem by offering a glimpse into the selected forms of exclusionary conduct.

1.2.1 Tying

Tying as a concern for competition and data protection. Tying, which may be either contractual or technological, is a common business strategy.[118] While contractual tying occurs when a seller makes the sale of one product (the tying product) conditional upon the purchase of another product (the tied product), technological tying involves integrating separate products (eg Microsoft's strategy to tie its Windows operating system to the Internet Explorer web browser).[119]

When employed by an undertaking dominant in the tying product market, tying might give rise to a competition concern as it restricts buyers' freedom to make their own choices.[120] In digital markets, for example, tying can take the form of pre-installations of certain apps (eg the requirement to pre-install the Google

[117] Brian Dean, 'DuckDuckGo Usage Stats for 2022' *Backlinko* (5 April 2021) <https://backlinko.com/duckduckgo-stats> accessed 5 July 2022.

[118] A strategy similar to tying is 'bundling', which means that two or more products are sold together as a bundle.

[119] John M Newman, 'Antitrust in Zero-Price Markets: Foundations' (2015) 164 University of Pennsylvania Law Review 149, 155.

[120] Daniel Mandrescu, 'Tying and Bundling by Online Platforms—Distinguishing between Lawful Expansion Strategies and Anti-Competitive Practices' (2021) 40 Computer Law & Security Review 1, 11.

Search app in *Android*[121]). As a result, buyers' freedom and competition might be inhibited given that pre-installations are de facto default settings, and default bias is a well-known phenomenon. Indeed, consumers' lack of willingness or their inability to actively change defaults typically results in their passive deference to the default option, making the default an actual choice[122]—whether or not the default aligns with consumers' normative preferences. As with data protection law where the problem of defaults is recognized as relevant from a regulatory standpoint (eg pre-ticked boxes do not constitute valid consent[123]), default choices and how they bias consumer judgement make them a potential competition issue. In particular, large online firms' strategies to make their services default options for consumers can lead to the exclusion of other firms, including potential disruptors that employ data protection-friendly business models.

Tying can also have other negative repercussions for data protection. For example, tying-enabled platform envelopment provides an opportunity for firms to expand their datasets and, relatedly, data power: 'consumer data gathered through the provision of a new service is added to an already existing trove of data,'[124] as Mundt observed while discussing an envelopment strategy. Such 'data consolidation' resulting from an expansion strategy poses obvious data protection risks. It might also lead to the exclusion of potential entrants, even as-efficient competitors, in the market into which a dominant firm expands: such entrants might have a limited ability to take advantage of cross-subsidizing or offering similar bundles of products and services in the first place.[125]

Competition law's approach to tying. In EU law, tying is captured by Article 102(d) TFEU. While a literal reading of this provision indicates a narrow understanding of tying—contractually tying two separate products—the case law and the Commission's decisions have expanded this notion. In *Android*,[126] as mentioned earlier, the theory of tying was applied to the pre-installation of apps, whereas in

[121] *Google Android* (Case AT.40099) Commission Decision of 18 July 2019; upheld on appeal in Case T-604/18 *Google and Alphabet v Commission (Google Android)* [2022] ECLI:EU:T:2022:541 (currently on appeal).

[122] Mary Steffel, Elanor F Williams, and Ruth Pogacar, 'Ethically Deployed Defaults: Transparency and Consumer Protection Through Disclosure and Preference Articulation' (2016) LIII Journal of Marketing Research 865, 866.

[123] GDPR, recital 32. The issue of pre-ticked boxes and implicit consent as methods to obtain (cookie) consent was addressed by the CJEU in Case C-673/17 *Bundesverband der Verbraucherzentralen und Verbraucherverbände—Verbraucherzentrale Bundesverband eV v Planet49 GmbH* [2019] ECLI:EU:C:2019:801. Stressing the phenomenon of 'default inertia,' AG Szpunar expressed in his Opinion in this case that 'empirical evidence overwhelmingly demonstrates that people rarely change default settings': Opinion of AG Szpunar [2019] ECLI:EU:C:2019:246, para 37.

[124] Andreas Mundt, Interview by Richard Whish and Amelia Fletcher in anticipation of the 4th Innovation Economics Conference for Antitrust Lawyers [2020] Concurrences.

[125] Manu Mohan, 'Platform Mergers: Tips for Getting the Deal Through' (*Kluwer Competition Law Blog*, 16 May 2019) <http://competitionlawblog.kluwercompetitionlaw.com/2019/05/16/platform-mergers-tips-for-getting-the-deal-through/#_ftn1> accessed 14 July 2022.

[126] *Google Android* (European Commission) (n 121).

the earlier *Microsoft* case,[127] tying an operating system with software was classified as an abuse. Holzweber noted that 'hardly any doctrine of competition law was broadened more markedly with the advent of the internet economy than the concept of tying and bundling'.[128]

While there are not many competition cases that address tying, the conclusion in the pre-*Android* cases was that tying is per se (ie by object) prohibited under competition law unless it is objectively justified.[129] In the early decisions such as *Hilti*[130] and *Tetra Pak*,[131] the Commission clarified that no anti-competitive effects needed to be shown to consider tying an abuse under Article 102 TFEU. This approach has evolved over time. In *Microsoft*, the Commission noted that tying Windows and Windows Media Player did not by its nature foreclose competition, stressing the need to analyse tying's anti-competitive effects and potential counterbalancing efficiencies.[132] The same view was expressed in the Commission's 2009 Guidance Paper,[133] and confirmed later by the CJEU in *Android*. In the US, the tying doctrine has evolved in a similar way: the courts have moved from classifying tying as a per se violation towards analysing it using a rule of reason approach.[134]

The EU *Android* case is illustrative of how the tying doctrine is currently applied in competition law. Google's anti-competitive strategy consisted in a set of contractual restrictions aimed at expanding its dominant position in the online search market from the PC to the mobile environment. One of the restrictions that deserves a brief overview are the Mobile Application Distribution Agreements (MADAs): Alphabet required manufacturers of mobile devices such as Samsung to pre-install the Google search app and the browser app Chrome as a condition for obtaining a licence to use Play Store on their devices. Thus, Google leveraged its power to cement its dominance on the search market on mobile devices. Falling under the scope of the 'tying' category, these contractual requirements, and the way the Commission and the CJEU assessed them from a competition standpoint, triggered a heated debate on whether tying as a theory of harm continues to make sense in the digital economy. While supporters of the Commission's approach in

[127] *Microsoft* (Case COMP/37.792) Commission Decision of 24 March 2004; upheld on appeal in Case T-201/04 *Microsoft Corp v Commission* [2007] ECLI:EU:T:2007:289.

[128] Stefan Holzweber, 'Tying and Bundling in the Digital Era' (2018) 14 European Competition Journal 342, 343.

[129] Pablo Ibáñez Colomo, 'Beyond the "More Economics-Based Approach": A Legal Perspective on Article 102 TFEU Case Law' (2016) 53 Common Market Law Review 709, 717.

[130] *Eurofix-Bauco v Hilti* (n 40).

[131] *Tetra Pak II* (Case IV/31.043) Commission Decision of 26 July 1988.

[132] *Microsoft* (European Commission) (n 127) para 841

[133] Commission's Guidance Paper (n 28) para 62.

[134] The change of approach was largely influenced by the Chicago School, which put forward the 'single monopoly profit theorem' to explain why tying and bundling may generate efficiencies or other pro-competitive effects. The theory posits that a monopolist in one product market cannot increase its monopoly profits through tying and gaining a monopoly in another product market. On the theory and its criticism, see eg Einer Elhauge, 'Tying, Bundling, And the Death of the Single Monopoly Profit Theory' (2009) 123 Harvard Law Review 397.

Android argued that, for example, tying and bundling deserve competition oversight, as such practices are more prevalent in the digital economy, sceptics pointed out that Google's strategy benefits consumers and that the intervention intrudes into the legitimate product design decisions of Google.[135] The outcome of this debate, as the analysis will show, is poised to not only determine the future competition law approach to tying, but also digital markets and the prospect of alternative data protection-friendly services emerging.

One of the steps in the Commission's assessment of Google's tying strategy was whether it was capable of restricting competition, leading the authority to conclude that the practice gave it a significant competitive advantage, one that alternative providers of search services on smart mobile devices were unable to offset. Among the reasons justifying this conclusion was the fact that pre-installation is a significant distribution channel for search services on mobile devices, in particular because users are likely to 'stick' to the pre-installed apps.[136] Hence, Google ensured for itself a market position that would be almost impossible to contest by other providers: for example, between 2011 and 2016, alternative search apps were downloaded only on 0–5 per cent of devices on which the Google Search app was pre-installed.[137] The conclusion about Google's competitive advantage resulting from tying on mobile devices is consistent, as the Commission observed, with the evolution of Google's share of general search queries, which were higher on mobile devices as compared to PCs.[138] Rebutting Google's claim that the reason for the Google Search app's success was its superior quality, the Commission noted that in 2018, Google's app was ranked the same as that of DuckDuckGo, for example.[139] Relatedly, in the context of analysing another, non-tying abuse, namely Google's payments to large device manufacturers and mobile network operators (MNOs) to exclusively pre-install the Google Search app on their devices, the decision also explicitly noted that the manufacturers and MNOs 'may have wanted to offer differentiated products to improve user experience': for example, they may have wanted to pre-install search apps other than Google Search to 'target a specific group of users that devote more attention to certain issues such as privacy (e.g. DuckDuckGo, Qwant)'.[140] Pre-installation of other general search services would have increased traffic to those alternative services.[141] This concurs with Stucke's observation that defaults result in stifled growth of 'smaller, more privacy-friendly

[135] See Alison Jones, Brenda Sufrin, and Niamh Dunne, *EU Competition Law: Text, Cases, and Materials* (7th edn, OUP 2019) 480.

[136] *Google Android* (European Commission) (n 121) paras 778–800.

[137] ibid para 808.

[138] ibid para 836.

[139] ibid para 849.

[140] ibid para 1213.

[141] ibid para 1214.

search engines'.[142] Although in the *Android* decision the exclusion of data protection-friendly alternative providers of search and browser services was not the focus—the Commission was naturally concerned about the foreclosure of all types of providers of competing services—the case illustrates how a competition law approach to tying may fundamentally affect the opportunities of privacy-friendly browsers or search engines to contest the markets.

Rethinking the approach to tying. The digital economy provides opportunities to implement tying practices not only using traditional contractual methods, but also through technical means and product design. As described earlier, the tying doctrine has evolved from treating tying in a rather strict manner—as anti-competitive 'by object'—towards approaching it as a strategy that does not always produce harmful results, hence an analysis of effects in some tying instances is required.[143] Scholars advocate a further relaxation of competition law's approach to some instances of tying in digital markets. Ibáñez Colomo, for example, criticized the *Android* decision on the ground that it unjustifiably interfered with Google's business model. As he claimed, traditional 'competition law in general, and tying in particular, typically interferes with *how products are sold*' and 'is generally wary not to second-guess *how products are made*'.[144] As Google's tying of the App Store with the search app was in his view inherent in how Google monetizes its services, rather than a practice designed to exclude rivals, the scope of competition law intervention could in this case be disputed.

An opposite view is that making the concept of tying effective in the digital economy implies precisely the need 'to extend competition law scrutiny to the product design of market dominant undertakings'.[145] Leaving various forms of non-contractual tying outside the reach of competition law would inevitably create a blind spot that dominant firms could easily use to their advantage.

The direction and the final outcome of this debate should be influenced not only by how the approach to tying affects the internal coherence and the soundness of competition law, but also how sectional coherence and markets' contestability are affected as a result. From the perspective of the latter, relaxing the approach to tying and excluding from its scope certain forms of tying that are considered to be a business model rather than exclusionary conduct, are far from desirable.

[142] Maurice E Stucke, 'Addressing Personal Data Collection as Unfair Methods of Competition' (2022) University of Tennessee Legal Studies Research Paper No 439, 31 <https://papers.ssrn.com/sol3/papers.cfm?abstract_id=4186226> accessed 14 October 2022.

[143] Pablo Ibáñez Colomo, 'The Notion of Abuse after the Android Judgment (Case T-604/18): What Is Clearer and What Remains to Be Clarified (I)' (*Chillin' Competition*, 28 September 2022) <https://chillingcompetition.com/2022/09/28/the-notion-of-abuse-after-the-android-judgment-case-t%e2%80%91604-18-what-is-clearer-and-what-remains-to-be-clarified-i/> accessed 11 October 2022.

[144] ibid (emphasis added).

[145] Holzweber (n 128) 345.

1.2.2 Refusals to deal

Refusal to deal as a concern for competition and data protection. The competition law discourse on how to improve the contestability of digital markets frequently invokes the reawakening of the 'essential facilities doctrine'.[146] In a nutshell, the doctrine implies that a refusal by a dominant undertaking to give another company access to some type of essential input may be abusive and violate competition law. In relation to technology companies, there are at least two types of facilities that might be considered essential for other businesses to compete: the data generated on or by the platform and the company's services themselves. Given that the way in which competition law can approach refusals to give access to either of these facilities might have data protection implications, they merit a short overview.

As regards access to personal data, there can be instances where the data collected by or on the platform is essential for a company on a related downstream market to offer its services. An illustration of this type of essential facility is the US case *hiQ Labs v LinkedIn*,[147] which involved a data analytics company offering to business clients services such as identifying employees who were at risk of being headhunted. In order to provide its services, hiQ Labs had to be able to scrape personal information (eg name, job title, work history) from LinkedIn. As in this type of case there is no direct competitive relationship between the company seeking access and the dominant firm's main product, the essential facilities doctrine, as will be discussed later, can be used if access to the data is refused.

When it comes to access to a company's services, there are multiple practices by dominant firms that may fall under the umbrella of refusals to grant access to an essential facility. As suggested by Bostoen and Mândrescu, examples include removals or refusals of apps from Apple's App Store or Google's Play Store, as well as restricted interoperability with Apple's mobile ecosystem.[148] The emergence of online platforms that act as 'gatekeepers with substantial control over the access to . . . digital markets'[149] may indeed imply that some of their services can be classified as essential facilities—a point to which this section will return.

Restricting or granting access to either of these facilities—the data or the company's services—not only had competition consequences, but can also be expected to affect data protection. In cases of data access, the implication might be twofold: restricted access to personal data can either generate positive impacts as

[146] Nikolas Guggenberger, 'The Essential Facilities Doctrine in the Digital Economy: Dispelling Persistent Myths' (2021) 23 Yale Journal of Law & Technology 301. See also eg Inge Graef, 'Rethinking the Essential Facilities Doctrine for the EU Digital Economy' (2019) 53 Revue juridique Thémis de l'Université de Montréal 33; Ofcom, 'Data, Digital Markets and Refusal to Supply' (2022)Economic Discussion Paper Series No 6.

[147] *HiQ Labs, Inc v LinkedIn Corp*, No 17-16783 (9th Cir 18 April 2022).

[148] Friso Bostoen and Daniel Mândrescu, 'Assessing Abuse of Dominance in the Platform Economy: A Case Study of App Stores' (2020) 16 European Competition Journal 431, 459.

[149] European Commission, 'Proposal for a Regulation of the European Parliament and of the Council on contestable and fair markets in the digital sector (Digital Markets Act)', COM (2020) 842 final, 1.

the risk that data is shared in a way that is non-compliant with data protection law is reduced, or negative, when such restricted access impedes the right to data portability, for example. Whereas in the former scenario data protection could be used as justification for a potentially illegal refusal to grant access, in the latter, mandating data access through competition enforcement may facilitate the right to data portability, strengthening coherence between competition and data protection law.

Similarly, a refusal to grant access to a company's services can lead to coherence or conflict with data protection law. For example, if Apple refuses to give an app access to its App Store on genuine privacy grounds, and that refusal proves to be anti-competitive at the same time, Apple's refusal may cause a conflict between competition and data protection—a conflict that might be resolved if data protection is accepted as providing a justification for anti-competitive conduct. If, on the other hand, there is a privacy-friendly app that is eliminated from the market as a result of Apple's refusal to deal, a competition law intervention would be aligned with the data protection interests of individuals.

Competition law's approach to refusals to deal. Originally, the essential facilities doctrine was formulated in the US case of *Terminal Railroad*,[150] which the Supreme Court decided under Section 2 of the Sherman Act in 1912.[151] In the EU, the origins of the essential facilities doctrine can be traced back to 1974, when the CJEU upheld the Commission's decision in *Commercial Solvents* that concerned a refusal to supply raw materials to a downstream firm, Zoja.[152] In a series of subsequent cases, the legality of refusals to deal was addressed mostly in the context of access to essential physical facilities and infrastructure, including airline computer reservation systems,[153] interlining facilities (facilities combining flights from different carriers),[154] and port facilities.[155]

A seminal case where the Court formally introduced the 'essential facilities doctrine' and clarified its scope of application was *Bronner*,[156] a case based on a preliminary reference from an Austrian court. The question at the core of the case was

150 *United States v Terminal Railroad Association of St Louis US*, 224 US 383 (1912).

151 Graef (n 30) 157.

152 Joined Cases 6 and 7/73 *Istituto Chemioterapico Italiano SpA and Commercial Solvents Corporation v Commission* [1974] ECLI:EU:C:1974:18. The Court's reasoning presented in *Commercial Solvents* was further developed in Case 311/84 *Centre belge d'études de marché—Télémarketing (CBEM) v SA Compagnie luxembourgeoise de télédiffusion (CLT) and Information publicité Benelux (IPB)* [1985] ECLI:EU:C:1985:394.

153 *London European—Sabena* (Case IV/32.318) Commission Decision of 4 November 1988.

154 *British Midland v Aer Lingus* (Case IV/33.544) Commission Decision of 26 February 1992.

155 *Sea Containers v Stena Sealink—Interim Measures* (Case IV.34.689) Commission Decision of 21 December 1993.

156 Case C-7/97 *Oscar Bronner GmbH & Co KG v Mediaprint Zeitungs- und Zeitschriftenverlag GmbH & Co KG, Mediaprint Zeitungsvertriebsgesellschaft mbH & Co KG and Mediaprint Anzeigengesellschaft mbH & Co KG* [1998] ECLI:EU:C:1998:569. For a commentary on the *Bronner* case, see eg Albertina Albors-Llorens, 'The "Essential Facilities" Doctrine in EC Competition Law' (1999) 58 Cambridge Law Journal 490.

whether Mediaprint, a large newspaper group that had developed a nationwide home-delivery scheme for daily newspapers in Austria, had abused its dominant position in the market for newspapers distribution by refusing to grant Bronner, a small Austrian publisher, access to its distribution network. While Bronner claimed that Mediaprint's scheme was an essential facility and the refusal to grant access to it violated Article 102 TFEU, the CJEU, largely following the opinion of Advocate General Jacobs, disagreed and introduced a number of limiting principles applicable to essential facilities cases. For example, the Court maintained that the input to which a downstream competitor seeks access needs to be '*indispensable* to carrying on that person's business, inasmuch as there is no actual or potential substitute in existence'.[157] Furthermore, one has to consider whether there are any technical, legal, or economic obstacles making it impossible or unreasonably difficult for a competitor to develop an indispensable infrastructure—in this case, for Bronner to develop its own home-delivery scheme. Hence, in the aftermath of *Bronner*, the benchmark for finding an abuse in essential facilities cases became significantly higher.

Besides dealing with physical properties, the case law and decisions on refusals to deal also include instances of refusals to license intellectual property. The Court and the Commission had a chance to clarify their position on this matter in a number of cases, such as *Magill*,[158] *Ladbroke*,[159] *IMS Health*,[160] and *Microsoft*,[161] which complement the legal landscape of essential facilities.

While the case law on essential facilities is not extensive and there are disagreements on the scope of its application, consensus exists that there are six cumulative minimum criteria that need to be satisfied:[162] (1) two markets (upstream and downstream); (2) refusal to deal; (3) indispensability of the input for competition; (4) exclusion of effective competition on the downstream market; (5) prevention of the introduction of a new product or limitation of technical development (applicable only in cases of refusals to license intellectual property (IP)); and (6) lack of objective justification.

In the recent *Slovak Telekom*[163] case, the CJEU had the chance to revisit these criteria and the earlier *Bronner* case. The main takeaway from *Slovak Telekom* is that the refusal to deal doctrine does not apply to cases where a dominant undertaking gives access to the essential facility but attaches 'unfair conditions' (imposing

[157] *Oscar Bronner* (n 156) para 41 (emphasis added).
[158] Case T-69/89 *Raidió Teilifís Éireann (RTE) v Commission* [1991] ECLI:EU:C:1995:98.
[159] Case T-504/93 *Tiercé Ladbroke SA v Commission* [1997] ECLI:EU:T:1997:84.
[160] *IMS Health/NDC—Interim Measures* (Case COMP/38/044) Commission Decision of 3 July 2001.
[161] *Microsoft* (European Commission) (n 127).
[162] O'Donoghue and Padilla (n 1) 631.
[163] Case C-165/19 P *Slovak Telekom v Commission* [2018] ECLI:EU:C:2021:239. For a short analysis of the case, see eg Katarzyna Czapracka, 'The Essential Facilities Doctrine and the *Bronner* Judgment Clarified: Case C-165/19 P *Slovak Telekom v Commission*' (2022) 13 Journal of European Competition Law & Practice 278.

unfair conditions does not, however, preclude the application of art 102 TFEU, where another theory of harm can be relevant).

Before exploring how these criteria can be applied to cases in digital markets, a distinction between the 'essential facilities doctrine' formalized in *Bronner* and the concept of a 'refusal to deal', which was relied on in earlier cases, should be briefly explained.[164] Their key distinguishing feature is that the former refers to refusals to deal with a company with which an incumbent has never had any business relationship (cases of first contracts, 'an absolute refusal to deal'[165]), while the later can also encompass cases where a dominant firm discontinues its existing business relationship ('a discontinuation of supply'). Furthermore, it has been argued that the requirements for finding an abuse in the second scenario are less stringent as compared to the cases where an incumbent refuses to share an essential facility with a 'new' company.[166] Both an absolute refusal to deal (ie the essential facilities doctrine) and a discontinuation of supply might occur in the contexts of data sharing and access to a platform. The remainder of this section refers to the essential facilities doctrine: if the more stringent conditions of this doctrine are met, it can be inferred that abuse would also be found in cases involving a discontinuation of supply.

The application of the essential facilities doctrine in digital markets. The first condition of the essential facilities doctrine is the existence of two markets: an upstream market where a vertically integrated firm has a dominant position, and a downstream market. In refusal to supply cases, a dominant firm leverages its power from the upstream market to refuse access to an input necessary for its downstream rival. The rationale behind the two-markets condition is that forcing a dominant firm to deal with a horizontal rival might minimize its incentives to invest and innovate. For example, even though a small search engine might be interested in obtaining access to Google's data in order to earn more profits on the advertising market side, the two-markets requirement makes such cases fall outside of the scope of the essential facilities doctrine. Sharing an essential input with a downstream competitor, however, can occasionally be mandated to prevent the monopolization of another market.

While the two-markets condition is an essential limiting principle that should be preserved, it might restrict the ability of the doctrine to facilitate the right to data portability, for example. Individuals may be incentivized to port data from one service (eg an incumbent social network) to an alternative platform that might be a direct rival of that incumbent. Although the essential facilities doctrine can as such be an interesting avenue to challenge an incumbent that restricts the

164 See eg Cyril Ritter, 'Refusal to Deal and "Essential Facilities": Does Intellectual Property Require Special Deference Compared to Tangible Property?' (2005) 28 World Competition 281, 285.

165 Both terms, 'an absolute refusal to deal' and 'a discontinuation of supplies', were introduced by Graef (n 30).

166 O'Donoghue and Padilla (n 1) 631.

individual's ability to reuse their personal data and port it to another service, the doctrine cannot be applied to scenarios where the second service is provided by a horizontal rival. On the other hand, if the doctrine could be applied to horizontal contexts, data protection would likely suffer as a result: access to data granted to horizontal rivals under competition law would heighten the risk of personal data being exploited by other businesses.

The second condition for applying the doctrine is the existence of a refusal to deal. The refusal may take various forms: 'unduly delaying or otherwise degrading the supply of the product' and imposing 'unreasonable conditions in return for the supply' are the examples provided by the Commission in its Guidance Paper.[167] As *Slovak Telekom* has recently made clear, however, for the essential facilities doctrine to apply, there needs to be a refusal rather than merely an imposition of unfair conditions for access. As mentioned, a refusal to deal in digital markets might take various forms. Less obvious cases of refusals, for instance violating the right to data portability in non-horizontal contexts, should not be excluded from the scope of competition law if its effectiveness is to be preserved.

The third requirement, input's indispensability, is satisfied when the input at stake is essential for a downstream rival to compete, no alternatives exist (even less advantageous), and it is not economically viable for a company seeking access to an essential input to create it itself. When it comes to data, for example, not all types of data are equally valuable from a competition standpoint: its value is indeed 'contextual to its use'.[168] It is also a case-by-case assessment if a competitor is able to obtain a similar dataset itself. In considering this criterion, an additional factor that competition authorities could consider is whether a rival can obtain the indispensable data in full compliance with data protection law.

In addition, as others have suggested, 'the threshold for finding that a refusal to supply data constitutes an abuse may be somewhat lower than the threshold for finding an abuse in cases of a refusal to grant access to infrastructures or to intellectual property rights'[169]—particularly when a dominant platform has gathered data incidentally and without considerable investment. While this is a justified proposition from a competition standpoint, lowering the threshold for intervention might be harmful for data protection.

According to the fourth requirement, which is directly related to the indispensability condition, a refusal to deal should eliminate all effective competition on the downstream market to be illegal. If the input's indispensability is established, one can assume that competition will be eliminated.

[167] Commission's Guidance Paper (n 28) para 79.

[168] Ioannis Lianos and Bruno Carballa-Smichowski, 'A Coat of Many Colours—New Concepts and Metrics of Economic Power in Competition Law and Economics' (2022) Journal of Competition Law & Economics 1, 45.

[169] Heike Schweitzer and others, 'Modernising the law on abuse of market power' (2018) Report for the German Federal Ministry for Economic Affairs and Energy, 5.

According to the fifth criterion, which applies to refusals to license IP, a refusal to deal is problematic if it prevents the emergence of a new product or limits technical development. In other words, it is unlikely that a refusal to deal is abusive if a downstream rival that seeks access to the input plans to use it to create a product or a service identical to already existing offerings. This criterion may be applicable to some interoperability-related cases. In such cases, the analysis of the innovativeness of the product or the service that access to the essential facility would enable should also take into consideration the data protection dimensions. For example, as Hoffmann and Gonzalez Otero noted, '[a]nalysing how firms use APIs [application programming interfaces] for data transfers and what happens if sensitive data is exposed or the API is hacked are important within the data sharing debate'.[170] In the course of evaluating the essential facilities doctrine, the risks resulting from mandated interoperability, for example, should be discussed jointly by competition and data protection enforcers.

The last condition postulates that there are no objective reasons that justify refusal. While the EU case law is not entirely clear on the scope of this requirement, a number of possible defences can be identified.[171] These include capacity limitation, quality degradation or security, the input being phased out, shortage of supply, a dominant firm's intention to market the new product itself, or the creditworthiness of the requesting party.[172] In cases of refusals to give access to personal data, the question to consider is whether data protection can offer a valid justification for a dominant firm's refusal.

In fact, this question has already surfaced in the US case *hiQ Labs v LinkedIn*,[173] which provides an interesting case study of how privacy arguments should be integrated in an analysis of a refusal to deal. The case was put into motion in 2017 when hiQ Labs, a data analytics company with a business model focused on scraping member personal data from LinkedIn, complained that LinkedIn's cease-and-desist letter restricting hiQ Lab's access to LinkedIn's data was anti-competitive. Seeking injunctive relief, hiQ claimed that to be able to continue offering its 'people analytics' services to business clients (ie identifying employees who were at risk of being headhunted), it must be allowed to scrape information that LinkedIn's users include on their public profiles, such as name, job title, work history, or skills. Without access to LinkedIn's data, as hiQ argued, the company would go out of business, in particular given that no alternatives to LinkedIn's database existed. LinkedIn justified its decision to restrict data access by asserting that hiQ Lab's data-scraping relating to publicly available profiles was done without permission

[170] Jörg Hoffman and Begoña Gonzalez Otero, 'Demystifying The Role of Data Interoperability in the Access and Sharing Debate' (2020) 11 Journal of Intellectual Property, Information Technology and E-Commerce Law 252, 254.

[171] O'Donoghue and Padilla (n 1) 657–58.

[172] ibid 658–63.

[173] *HiQ Labs, Inc v LinkedIn Corp* (n 147).

or authorization, in violation of LinkedIn's User Agreement as well as the US Computer Fraud and Abuse Act (CFAA). It also expressed concerns about users' privacy, noting that the popularity of its 'Do not Broadcast' feature (ie no notification of a profile change to other users) demonstrated that LinkedIn's members wished to keep some of their information private.

Defending the business model of data scraping, the US Ninth Circuit of Appeals confirmed in its judgment of April 2022 the district court's ruling that hiQ should be granted a preliminary injunction.[174] It thus rejected LinkedIn's justification. As regards LinkedIn's privacy arguments, the court observed that 'there is little evidence that LinkedIn users who choose to make their profiles public actually maintain an expectation of privacy with respect to the information that they post publicly'.[175] There was also no evidence that LinkedIn members choose the 'Do Not Broadcast' option for privacy reasons. Notably, the court stated that LinkedIn's own actions undercut its privacy justification: LinkedIn explicitly enables recruiters to provide analytics services similar to the ones offered by hiQ.[176] Hence, even if there were some privacy interests to consider, they were, according to the court, not 'significant enough to outweigh hiQ's interest in continuing its business'.[177] Drawing attention to the possible risks to competition, it also noted that 'giving companies like LinkedIn free rein to decide, on any basis, who can collect and use data—data that they do not own . . .—risks the possible creation of *information monopolies* that would disserve the public interest'.[178]

The argumentation in *HiQ Labs v LinkedIn* is reflective of how the US courts engage with a plurality of arguments, taking account of various legal areas and policy considerations: the outcome of the proceedings was indeed based on a balancing of various factors, including privacy, public interest, freedom to conduct business, and competition. Commenting on this decision, Tene noted that irrespective of whether or not one agrees with the judgment, 'a synthesis of all these factors . . . yields results that are more grounded than decisions based on just one line of reasoning'.[179] It is difficult to predict what the final outcome would look like if a similar case were brought before the CJEU. Privacy advocates and commentators would likely argue that data protection arguments should be engaged with in more depth in the EU given the status of data protection as a fundamental right. Determining whether there is any legitimate legal basis listed in Article 6 GDPR that hiQ could invoke for its data scraping activity, which happens without individuals' consent, knowledge, or any contract between them and hiQ, would

[174] ibid.
[175] ibid 18.
[176] ibid 18–19.
[177] ibid 19.
[178] ibid 43 (emphasis added).
[179] Omar Tene, '*LinkedIn v. HiQ* and the Trans-Atlantic Privacy Divide' (*IAPP*, 22 April 2022) <https://iapp.org/news/a/linkedin-v-hiq-and-the-transatlantic-privacy-divide/> accessed 20 July 2022.

alone hopefully trigger an extensive legal assessment. A potential violation of the GDPR could be a solid argument to support LinkedIn's decision to block access to its members' public profiles. While engagement with a number of other arguments (eg competition, freedom to conduct business, public interest) would provide for a grounded outcome, data protection's status in the EU should justify giving data protection considerations more weigh in an overall balancing.

All in all, refusals to deal have a complex link to data protection as they might benefit it in some instances and negatively affect it in others. How the specific conditions to be interpreted to lead to coherence-supportive outcomes is thus contingent on the specific facts of the case. Particularly interesting will be assessments of potential data protection justifications—a topic that this chapter will come back to.

1.2.3 Other types of exclusion

Tying and refusals to license are just two illustrations of exclusionary strategies with potential data privacy implications. The aim of this section is to briefly outline other examples of conduct that might exclude rivals and simultaneously harm data protection.

Predatory practices. In competition law, the term 'predation' is commonly associated with the pricing strategy of a dominant firm that consist in below-cost pricing (eg setting excessively low purchase prices). 'Predatory pricing' might be anti-competitive if it does not aim to achieve any economic objective other than eliminating competitors.[180] While discussed less frequently, there is also non-price predation that dominant firms may seek to implement with the sole intention of excluding competitors.[181] One example of non-price predation that relates to product tactics and can prove relevant in digital markets is 'predatory innovation'. In a nutshell, predatory innovation occurs when a company deliberately designs its product with the aim of raising rivals' costs, providing no advantage to consumers.[182]

As regards predatory pricing, it might seem at first glance that this theory of harm is inapplicable in the digital context. Even though zero-price products are commonly encountered in the digital economy, it is widely acknowledged that pricing below cost on one side of the market (eg free search services) needs to be considered in a more holistic way, taking into account the multi-sided nature of digital markets.[183] As Bostoen noted, 'somewhere, somehow, someone is

[180] Van Bael & Bellis (n 44) 863.

[181] For a taxonomy of predatory strategies, see Gregory T Gundlach, 'Predatory Practices in Competitive Interaction: Legal Limits and Antitrust Considerations' (1990) 9 Journal of Public Policy & Marketing 129.

[182] ibid 132. For an extensive discussion on predatory innovation, see also Thibault Schrepel, 'Predatory Innovation: The Definite Need for Legal Recognition' (2018) 21 Science and Technology Law Review 19.

[183] See eg Miguel Rato and Nicolas Petit, 'Abuse of Dominance in Technology-Enabled Markets: Established Standards Reconsidered?' (2013) 9 European Competition Journal 1, 49–53. See also, Jones, Sufrin, and Dunne (n 135) 412–13.

paying'.[184] Thus, the fact that a company prices above cost on the other market side (eg on the advertising side) in order to recoup losses on the free market side makes the rationale behind illegal predatory pricing less relevant in multi-sided markets. Similarly, a 'freemium' model whereby the losses incurred by offering a service free of charge are compensated by users who pay for a 'premium' version might not be captured by the theory of predatory pricing.

On closer scrutiny it is, however, possible to single out instances where the argument against applying predatory pricing to multi-sided data-driven markets can be challenged. One obvious scenario is where a dominant firm prices its product in a way that it makes a loss at the margin, irrespective of whether its pricing structure involves one- or multi-sided markets.[185] A more intriguing suggestion was put forward by Fletcher, who rightly highlighted the need to recognize predation by a dominant undertaking that materializes though asymmetrical pricing between two or more market sides. A predation-relevant question that emerges is 'whether a given pricing structure can affect market structure, and specifically whether low pricing on one side of a market can prevent entry into both sides'.[186] For example, a small search engine might be unable to collect data about individuals to the same extent as a dominant company, making its services both less attractive for consumers who value personalized search results, as well as for advertisers seeking to deliver targeted ads. The ecosystemic structure of a dominant platform that collects and combines data from various sources further impinges on the ability of smaller rivals to enter or expand on the market where an incumbent relies on asymmetrical pricing. While operationalizing Fletcher's proposal would require a reformulation of the test laid down in the *AKZO* case (eg moving from the average variable cost benchmark to an opportunity cost standard),[187] it is an effort worth pursuing as the result might be negative incentives to apply exclusionary pricing structures in the first place. Such negative incentives can in turn prompt the emergence of alternative business models in digital markets to the advantage of data protection.

The type of predation that in the digital economy finds a more evident application is predatory innovation. As the concept can as such encompass a variety of practices, Crane stressed the need to clarify its boundaries, and defined a 'pure' predatory innovation claim as involving 'allegations that the design of a new product or service itself impedes competition'.[188] Among design decisions that may be labelled predatory is creating a search algorithm that demotes rival products

[184] Friso Bostoen, 'Online Platforms and Pricing: Adapting Abuse of Dominance Assessments to the Economic Reality of Free Products' (2019) 35 Computer Law & Security Review 263, 266.

[185] For a comprehensive analysis of this scenario, see eg Stefan Behringer and Lapo Filistrucchi, 'Areeda–Turner in Two-Sided Markets' (2015) 46 Review of Industrial Organization 287.

[186] Amelia Fletcher, 'Predatory Pricing in Two-Sided Markets: A Brief Comment' (2007) 3 Competition Policy International 221, 223.

[187] ibid 224.

[188] Daniel A Crane, 'Legal Rules for Predatory Innovation' (2013) Concurrences No 4-2013, art no 58811, 2.

or designing an operating system code in a way that it obstructs a programmer's ability to write applications.[189] Predatory innovation can also be conceptualized narrowly or broadly depending on the importance attached to the condition of 'profit sacrifice'. Accordingly, a narrowly defined predatory innovation encompasses only innovation strategies that are implemented 'even if their implementation entails a sacrifice of a part of the profit'[190]—for Ordover and Willig, this is 'the hallmark' of a predatory strategy. A more encompassing understanding of predatory innovation implies that a profit sacrifice does not need to be shown in order to categorize an innovation as predatory. If the latter conceptualization of predation in particular finds support from a competition perspective, a range of allegedly innovative tactics that have exploitation of personal data at their core might be captured by the predation-based theory of harm.

Market envelopment. The strategy of platform envelopment that consists in leveraging market power and exploiting the features of digital markets has already been discussed in Chapter 2 Section C. Under competition law, the legality of envelopment strategies must be scrutinized on a case-by-case basis as they may have pro-competitive (eg facilitated entry in target platform markets, improved services) and anti-competitive effects.[191] Yet, enforcement authorities should remain cautious in cases where tipping is likely in the market and the envelopment strategy includes a coercive tying of privacy policies.[192] This scenario was discussed by Condorelli and Padilla: as they noted, a platform operating across many platform markets with a common user side might engage in 'privacy policy tying'.[193] Such tying occurs 'when the (conglomerate) firm's privacy policies in each of those platform markets request users to grant consent so that it can combine the data they generate when using its multiple platforms to improve its offerings in one or more of them'.[194] Arguably, the objective is to monopolize the unique data produced in the target platform and combine that data with those in the origin platform, and the ultimate aim is to monetize the merged datasets and obtain an advantage in the origin platform market or to extract more surplus in that market. One example is Google's entry into the mobile operating systems market, which gave the company the opportunity to combine, among others, users' search histories from Google search and the location data from Android devices to construct superior profiles and enable advertisers to better target consumers.[195] Recently, the

[189] ibid.

[190] Janusz A Ordover and Robert D Willig, 'An Economic Definition of Predatory Product Innovation' (1987) 17 Journal of Reprints for Antitrust Law and Economics 301, 308.

[191] Daniele Condorelli and Jorge Padilla, 'Harnessing Platform Envelopment in the Digital World' (2020) 16 Journal of Competition Law & Economics 143, 173–74.

[192] ibid 176. See also Gregor Langus and Vilen Lipatov, 'Does Envelopment through Data Advantage Call for New Regulation?' (2021) CESifo Working Papers No 8932, 3.

[193] Condorelli and Padilla (n 191).

[194] ibid 145.

[195] ibid 172.

Bundeskartellamt has highlighted in its analysis of linking Meta Quest with the Facebook network that in data-driven markets, 'there is often a close link between the combined use of services and data linkage across sources'.[196]

This scenario, whereby a powerful firm in a data-intensive primary market enters another data-intensive market with a view to combining user data through privacy-policy tying, might pose concerns not only for competition, but also, or even primarily, for data protection.

Exclusionary discrimination. The gatekeeper nature of large technological companies, and specifically the fact that many third-party firms that offer competing or complementary services are highly dependent on them, have triggered the question of the anti-competitiveness of some of the strategies employed by incumbents in this respect. One of them, which similarly to the practice of tying can fall into the category of power leveraging, consists in discrimination between business partners and own services.

The way in which exclusionary discrimination can manifest itself in the digital economy is exemplified by *Google Shopping*.[197] In the decision taken in 2017, the Commission imposed on Google a fine of €2.4 billion for abusing its dominant position as a search engine by favouring another Google product, its comparison shopping service, over competing comparison shopping services. Google did so by displaying and positioning its own service more favourably and demoting the competing services in the generic results. While in discussions on the case the contentious new concept of 'self-preferencing' is commonly used to label the type of the conduct at stake,[198] the CJEU repeatedly referred in its *Google Shopping* judgment to the more established principle of 'non-discrimination'.[199] Accordingly, companies that have a dominant position—or are 'ultra-dominant', as in the case of Google—cannot negatively influence the equality of opportunity for various economic operators through favouring practices.[200]

The repercussions of discriminating practices for data protection are not immediately evident: they might, however, materialize when the economic dependencies prevalent in digital markets lead to the exclusion of more privacy-friendly services from the market. This type of impact on the market opportunities of economic operators who rely on data protection as a distinguishing feature, or simply provide

[196] Decision B6-55/20 of 23 November 2022 (*Meta Quest*) Case Summary 2.

[197] *Google Search (Shopping)* (Case AT.39740) Commission Decision of 26 June 2017; upheld on appeal in Case T-612/17 *Google LLC, formerly Google Inc and Alphabet, Inc v European Commission (Google Shopping)* [2021] ECLI:EU:T:2021:763.

[198] For a discussion on the concept of 'self-preferencing' in competition law, see eg Pablo Ibáñez Colomo, 'Self-Preferencing: Yet Another Epithet in Need of Limiting Principles' (2020) 43 World Competition 417.

[199] *Google LLC, formerly Google Inc and Alphabet, Inc v European Commission (Google Shopping)* (n 197) paras 71, 180, 244.

[200] ibid para 180. For a discussion on the various forms of self-preferencing, see Patrice Bougette, Olivier Budzinski, and Frédéric Marty, 'Self-Preferencing and Competitive Damages: A Focus on Exploitative Abuses' (2022) 67 Antitrust Bulletin 190.

improved products or services in that regard, might also result from a number of other actual and potential exclusionary strategies that this section, due to considerations of space, is not able to discuss.

2. Justifications

Data protection can be relevant not only at the stage of formulating theories of harm, but also in the context of arguments put forward by dominant firms to justify their prima facie abusive conduct. Even though there are recent business strategies such as Google Privacy Sandbox and Apple's ATT that have raised questions in relation to justification (see Chapter 3 Section B), the viability of data protection justifications has not occupied centre stage in the academic and policy discourse on coherence between competition and data protection law. This inattention constitutes a gap that this section aims to fill by discussing the concept of objective justification in the area of abuse of dominance, and subsequently applying it to possible data protection justifications.

2.1 An objective justification defence

Even though the text of Article 102 TFEU does not envisage that otherwise abusive conduct can be justified, there is a consensus that an objective justification plea can be put forward in the context of various abusive practices.[201] This is the approach adopted not only in the EU, but also in other jurisdictions.

In EU competition law, the specific grounds that a dominant firm can invoke to successfully defend its conduct are open to question. The types of defences that have so far been considered as possible justification pleas can be divided into three broad categories:[202] (1) objective necessity; (2) the efficiency defence; and (3) protection of commercial interests.

The first category encompasses scenarios where conduct is objectively necessary because of factors external to a dominant undertaking.[203] Such external factors might include public policy goals such as public health and safety,[204] as well

[201] Commission's Guidance Paper (n 28) paras 28–31. The CJEU has confirmed on multiple occasions that objective justification is available under art 102 TFEU: eg Case C-413/14 P *Intel v Commission* [2017] ECLI:EU:C:2017:632, para 140. See also eg Ekaterina Rousseva, 'The Concept of "Objective Justification" of an Abuse of a Dominant Position: Can It Help to Modernise the Analysis under Article 82 EC?' (2006) 2 Competition Law Review 27; Albertina Albors-Llorens, 'The Role of Objective Justification and Efficiencies in the Application of Article 82 EC' (2007) 44 Common Market Law Review 1727.

[202] Commission's Guidance Paper (n 28). A similar typology was introduced in Philip Lowe, 'DG Competition Review of the Policy on Abuse of Dominance' in Barry E Hawk (ed), *International Law & Policy: Annual Proceedings of the Fordham Corporate Law Institute 2003* (Juris Publishing 2004) 170–71.

[203] Commission's Guidance Paper (n 28) para 29.

[204] Case T-30/89 *Hilti AG v Commission* [1991] ECLI:EU:T:1991:70, para 118; Case T-83/91 *Tetra Pak v Commission* [1994] ECLI:EU:T:1994:246, para 83.

as other considerations. For example, in *Android*, Google claimed that its abusive conduct consisting in anti-fragmentation agreements was objectively necessary 'to protect the integrity and quality of the Android platform against the risks inherent in any incompatibilities'[205]—a plea that the CJEU ultimately rejected. To succeed, the objective necessity test needs to show that the conduct is both necessary and proportionate to the professed objective pursued by a dominant undertaking.[206] An objective necessity defence does not, however, require balancing between the benefits resulting from the conduct and its adverse impact on competition.[207]

Efficiency gains are the second type of justification. Efficiencies capable of justifying the problematic conduct must be 'sufficient to guarantee that no net harm to consumers is likely to arise',[208] as the Commission expressed in its Guidance Paper. An efficiency justification defence can be accepted under Article 102 TFEU only if the four cumulative criteria that mirror Article 101(3) TFEU are fulfilled:[209] (1) efficiencies such as quality improvement or cost reduction are realized as a result of the conduct; (2) consumers receive a fair share of the resulting benefit; (3) the conduct is indispensable for realizing the efficiencies and no less anti-competitive conduct is capable of achieving the same efficiencies; and (4) the conduct does not eliminate effective competition. A caveat stressed by the Commission is that if anti-competitive conduct helps to maintain, create, or strengthen a near-monopoly position, an efficiency defence is unlikely to succeed.[210]

The third category of available justification pleas is the protection of own commercial interests, which includes strategies that can be labelled 'competition on the merits',[211] or simply reflect the reasonable conduct of a profit-oriented, non-dominant company.[212] An early case that considered a legitimate business interest plea was *United Brands*, where the CJEU established that a company can in theory adopt defensive measures to protect its commercial interests unless the genuine aim of the conduct is to strengthen and abuse its dominant position, and the adopted measures are disproportionate.[213] Defending one's own commercial interest as an acceptable justification has been confirmed in a few other cases.[214]

[205] *Google LLC, formerly Google Inc and Alphabet, Inc v European Commission (Google Android)* (n 120) para 867.

[206] Commission's Guidance Paper (n 28) para 29; O'Donoghue and Padilla (n 1) 344.

[207] Faull and Nikpay (n 80) para 4.219.

[208] Commission's Guidance Paper (n 28) para 30.

[209] ibid para 30.

[210] ibid para 30.

[211] Tjarda van der Vijver, 'Objective Justification and Article 102 TFEU' (2012) 351 World Competition 55, 75.

[212] Jones, Sufrin, and Dunne (n 135) 388, referring to Roberto Nazzini, *The Foundations of European Union Competition Law: The Objectives and Principles of Article 102* (OUP 2011) 300.

[213] *United Brands* (n 3) paras 189–90.

[214] *BBI/Boosey & Hawkes: Interim Measures* (Case IV/32.279) Commission Decision of 29 July 1987; Cases C-468–78/06 *Sot Lélos kai Sia EE and Others v GlaxoSmithKline AEVE Farmakeftikon Proïonton, formerly Glaxowellcome AEVE* [2008] ECLI:EU:C:2008:504, para 68. See also Case C-53/03 *Synetairismos Farmakopoion Aitolias & Akarnanias (Syfait) and Others v GlaxoSmithKline plc and GlaxoSmithKline AEVE* [2004] ECLI:EU:C:2004:673, Opinion of AG Jacobs.

Yet, as Albors-Llorens rightly noted, the challenge with this type of justification is to distinguish between a dominant firm's commercial interests and 'conceal[ed] attempts to foreclose the market'.[215]

As regards burden of proof, both the CJEU and the Commission made clear that while proving the existence of prima facie abuse is the task of a competition authority, '[i]t is incumbent upon the dominant undertaking to provide all the evidence necessary to demonstrate that the conduct is objectively justified'.[216] In practice, the hurdle for justifying an abusive practice is high,[217] and the efficiency defence in particular has been a theoretical construct rather than a plea likely to be successfully invoked. Nevertheless, as the law does envisage an objective justification, it is worth reflecting on how possible defences grounded on data protection claims could be approached in abuse of dominance cases in the future.

2.2 Data protection as an objective justification

Many business initiatives aimed at protecting personal data and privacy in digital markets reflect genuine efforts to respond to individuals' demand or regulatory requirements. At the same time, there are increasingly concerns that companies might be incentivized to pursue less noble objectives, such as excluding rivals and harming competition, under the guise of strengthening privacy or data protection—a practice that can be labelled 'privacy washing' or 'data protection washing' (see Chapter 3 Section B).[218] Even where the protection of privacy or personal data is not intentionally used as a pretext for harming competition, a negative impact on competition might follow as an undesirable side effect. For example, in their joint statement on interactions between competition law and data protection, the UK's CMA and the ICO noted that tensions might arise when 'there is a risk of data protection being interpreted by large integrated digital businesses in a way that leads to negative outcomes in respect of competition, e.g. by unduly favouring large, integrated platforms over smaller, non-integrated suppliers'.[219] From a competition law standpoint, both dubious and genuine instances of privacy and data protection strategies that result in anti-competitive restrictions require homing in on the following question: when and how can the protection of personal data or privacy serve as a credible justification of a prima facie abuse of a dominant position?

[215] Albors-Llorens (n 201) 1745.

[216] Commission's Guidance Paper (n 28) para 31; *Microsoft Corp v Commission* (n 127) para 688.

[217] Jones, Sufrin, and Dunne (n 135) 382.

[218] See also Timothy Cowen, '"Privacy Fixing" After *Texas et al v. Google* and *CMA v. Google (Privacy Sandbox)*: Approaches to Antitrust Considerations of Privacy' (*Competition Policy International*, 26 January 2021) <https://www.competitionpolicyinternational.com/privacy-fixing-after-texas-et-al-v-google-and-cma-v-google-privacy-sandbox-approaches-to-antitrust-considerations-of-privacy/> accessed 11 November 2021.

[219] CMA and ICO, 'Competition and Data Protection in Digital Markets: A Joint Statement between the CMA and the ICO' (2021) 24.

In an attempt to consider how data protection pleas might square with the three justification categories available in the context of abuse of dominance—objective necessity, efficiency gains, and the protection of commercial interest as described in the previous section—it is useful to introduce a typology of possible data protection and privacy justifications based on their connection to the extant data protection and privacy laws in a given jurisdiction, for example the GDPR in the EU. The reason for choosing compliance as a distinguishing factor is that adherence to the external regulatory obligations, as the following paragraphs will argue, will play an important role in reviewing the justifying potential of data protection pleas in competition law.

On the basis of compliance, two core categories can be distinguished: (1) compliance and (2) beyond compliance and over-compliance. The first category encompasses initiatives necessary to ensure that a company's data-related conduct does not violate data protection law. An example is a social media platform that limits the amount of data it collects in order to comply with the data minimization principle. Practices going beyond compliance, which belong to the second category, occur when a company deliberately aims at exceeding the requirements of data protection laid down in the law. The beyond compliance attitude towards data protection is generally normatively encouraged. Commenting on the obligation to conduct impact assessments, for example, Koops noted that doing so, and in particular translating the findings into data protection-friendly designs and default settings (art 23 GDPR), 'requires an attitude that looks beyond legal compliance, a vision that sees the logic behind the many legal rules of data protection, a mindset that is aware of the rationale of data protection.'[220] Finally, over-compliance, which for the purpose of this section can be discussed jointly with strategies that go beyond compliance, occurs when in striving to comply with data protection rules a dominant company incidentally achieves more than legally required. This may be the effect of specific technological solutions implemented to achieve compliance.

How the aforementioned types of data protection strategies can justify otherwise abusive conduct is an unexplored issue, and deserves attention. To start with the first category, namely compliance, it can be asserted that it should constitute the strongest type of data protection plea justifying prima facie abuse insofar as it satisfies the requirements of necessity and proportionality. Given that competition law already envisages an objective necessity justification because of factors external to the dominant undertaking, as explained earlier, the proposal that compliance with external data protection and privacy obligations is capable of justifying anticompetitive conduct is not controversial. The question that should be at the core of the analysis of objective necessity is the following: is the restriction of competition strictly necessary and proportionate to ensure compliance with data protection

[220] Bert-Jaap Koops, 'The Trouble with European Data Protection Law' (2014) 4 International Data Privacy Law 250, 255.

law? If the answer is yes, the presented data protection plea should be accepted and the conduct justified. Conversely, if there exist measures that can achieve the same level of data protection law compliance without having an adverse effect on competition—even if such alternative measures are more costly or burdensome for a dominant firm to implement—the compliance-related justification should be rejected under competition law.

Cases of over-compliance and beyond compliance fall into the grey zone of justifications and require careful scrutiny. Thus, the question that needs to be addressed is whether the instances of over-compliance and beyond compliance might fall under the category of objective necessity, the efficiency defence, or protection of commercial interest.

As regards objective necessity defences, it was suggested earlier that the conduct of a dominant firm implemented to ensure compliance with data protection law and meeting the necessity and proportionality tests could justify prima facie abuse. Whether the category of objective necessity should encompass a business strategy that pursues a privacy or data protection aim, but is not as such required under data protection law, is more contentious. The case law dealing with public interest goals as a potential objective necessity is not conclusive on the issue of exactly when going beyond the externally required minimum can be accepted as a justification. However, in *Hilti*,[221] the Commission made clear that public interest goals (in *Hilti*: safety considerations that went beyond legal requirements) can constitute a valid justification if they represent a genuine concern for a dominant company—and that the Commission is prepared to go to great lengths to assess the genuineness of the investigated company's intentions. To establish whether Hilti's abusive conduct 'was motivated purely by safety considerations',[222] the Commission presented detailed evidence indicating that the company's overall behaviour did not reveal its commitment towards the allegedly pursued goal of ensuring product safety. Among the evidence suggesting that safety was not a genuine aim of Hilti's conduct was the fact that Hilti never complained to the responsible authorities about the safety or reliability of products sold by other companies nor communicated its concerns directly to those companies.[223]

Applying this logic to data protection justifications, a competition authority would need to scrutinize the overall conduct of the dominant firm to establish how genuine its data protection motivations were. For example, if a search engine's consistent respect for data protection is manifest, the genuineness of its privacy or data protection motivations behind implementing a potentially abusive practice would naturally be easier to establish. Conversely, if a firm has a track record of violating

221 *Eurofix-Banco v Hilti* (n 40).

222 ibid para 89.

223 ibid. The Court agreed with the Commission's reasoning and upheld the decision on appeal: *Hilti AG v Commission* (n 204), paras 115–19.

data protection law requirements or the spirit of the rights to privacy and data protection, the trustworthiness of its business intentions must be called into question. As demonstrated in *Hilti*, a competition authority can use various types of evidence to support its argument. A recent example involving Google provides an illustration: Google removed dozens of apps (eg several Muslim prayer apps) from its Play Store after researchers discovered that they included a hidden code to surreptitiously gather personal data—Google noted, however, that those apps could be reinstalled once the code had been removed.[224] In a hypothetical scenario, if Google's decision to remove the apps had anti-competitive repercussions, allowing their reinstallation once the data protection concern was resolved, could serve as an indication that Google's data protection intentions were genuine, even though the general approach by Google to data protection should also be scrutinized in order to draw reliable conclusions.

Ascertaining the genuineness of a company's intent is a pivotal step to minimize the risk of accepting privacy and data protection washing as a valid justification. To provide negative incentives for privacy and data protection washing, the ultimate fine imposed for abusing a dominant position should be increased if a company offers a privacy or data protection justification that proves to be a sham.

In addition to genuinely aspiring to improve data protection, a business initiative that represents over-compliance or beyond compliance should pass both the necessity and proportionality tests to be accepted as an objective necessity. Furthermore, balancing should be conducted between the benefits resulting from the conduct and the identified harm to competition. Although the balancing requirement would raise the hurdle of satisfying the objective necessity test, it is a necessary safeguard to ensure that abusive conduct has net gains for individuals. In scenarios of over-compliance or beyond compliance, conduct, even if data protection-friendly, is not as such legally required from an undertaking. As the potential rejection of the presented justification plea in such cases would not result in the violation of data protection law, data protection benefits should be weighed against harm to competition.

As shown, over-compliance and beyond compliance with data protection law may serve as objective necessity if they genuinely pursue a legitimate data protection goal, meet the necessity and proportionality criteria, and outweigh harm to competition. An alternative avenue for considering them at a justificatory stage in a competition analysis is to approach them as efficiency gains, in which case they would need to meet the four cumulative criteria mirroring Article 101(3) TFEU as indicated in the previous section.

[224] Byron Tau and Robert McMillan, 'Google Bans Apps With Hidden Data-Harvesting Software' *The Wall Street Journal* (6 April 2022) <https://www.wsj.com/articles/apps-with-hidden-data-harvesting-software-are-banned-by-google-11649261181> accessed 11 July 2022.

In analysing the first criterion, namely that the conduct of a dominant firm must result in efficiency gains, the key question is whether the protection of data resulting from over-compliance or beyond compliance can be equated with the competition law concept of efficiency. The Commission's Guidance Paper, for example, specifically refers to 'technical improvements in the quality of goods' to illustrate the types of acceptable efficiencies.[225] Moreover, in its Draft Horizontal Guidelines published in 2022, the Commission formulated a broad definition of the concept of efficiencies: they encompass 'not only reductions in production and distribution costs but also increases in product variety and quality, improvements in production or distribution processes, and increases in innovation'.[226] Although the Draft Horizontal Guidelines concern the interpretation of Article 101(3) TFEU in the context of agreements, there is no reason why such a more-encompassing understanding of efficiencies could not be applied to objective justifications under Article 102 TFEU. Accepting a broad definition of efficiencies would leave no doubt that data protection can be a competition-relevant category of efficiencies.

The second criterion requiring that consumers receive a fair share of the benefit resulting from anti-competitive conduct would also be straightforward to satisfy in cases of genuine data protection initiative.

In the third step, the test transposed from Article 101(3) TFEU requires proof that the over-compliance or beyond compliance is indispensable for realizing the stated efficiencies—for example technological improvements ensuring better protection of personal data—and no less anti-competitive conduct is capable of realizing the same efficiencies. This is a test akin to the necessity and proportionality requirements described earlier.

The third step consists in proving that the efficiencies outweigh harm to competition, a requirement that was already discussed in the preceding paragraphs.

Finally, a dominant firm would need to show that its conduct does not eliminate 'effective' competition, which can be interpreted as 'existing' competition. This is an additional criterion inherent in an efficiency defence plea that does not exist in the objective necessity test discussed previously. This criterion is, however, of an inherently problematic nature when applied to exclusionary conduct: for example, if exclusionary conduct such as a refusal to deal is prima facie abuse, the implication is that it probably eliminates effective competition. This, in conjunction with the other requirements of an efficiency-based justification, renders an efficiency defence plea based on data protection very unlikely to succeed.

The third possibility for a dominant firm to justify prima facie abuse in cases of over-compliance and beyond compliance is to invoke the protection of own

[225] Commission's Guidance Paper (n 28) para 30.

[226] European Commission, 'Approval of the content of a draft for a Communication from the Commission "Guidelines on the applicability of Article 101 of the Treaty on the Functioning of the European Union to horizontal co-operation agreements"' (Communication), COM (2022) 1159 final, para 577.

commercial interests. If a business seeks to employ data protection as its distinguishing feature, it might rely on a range of techniques and market strategies that improve the protection of the personal data of its users, going even beyond that prescribed by law, but that might also have a foreclosing effect on the market. As long as such implemented measures are strictly proportionate and constitute the reasonable behaviour of a business-oriented firm, they might justify the violation of Article 102 TFEU. The reason why this type of justification merits vigilance on the part of competition enforcers is the inherent difficulty of distinguishing between a genuine business interest and an exclusionary strategy disguised as competition on the merits.

By way of conclusion, it is worth stressing that the empirical reality is yet to confront competition enforcers with cases where meaningful data protection business efforts create a conflict with competition law along the lines described earlier. Yet, in the hope that that the future of the digital economy is one where data protection becomes a business aspiration, it is helpful to anticipate the response that such genuine, albeit potentially anti-competitive, data protection effort might receive under competition law. As the analysis presented previously illustrates, the defence mechanisms already envisaged under competition law offer a conceptual framework for data protection to occasionally justify a dominant firm's conduct that is otherwise illegal from a competition standpoint. At the same time, it has shown that the mechanism for detecting data protection washing and for distinguishing it from genuine strategies should be developed to ensure sound assessments. Cooperation between competition and data protection authorities would, in this respect, offer a crucial procedural safeguard.

3. Remedies

The effectiveness of antitrust enforcement efforts is to a large extent contingent on the remedies envisaged for addressing the identified concerns. In EU law, the powers of the Commission to impose remedies have their legal basis in Regulation 1/2003. Whereas Article 7 of Regulation 1/2003 envisages remedies to be imposed on a dominant firm by the Commission following a finding of an infringement, Article 9 establishes that a dominant firm might offer commitments where the Commission intends to adopt an infringement decision. Article 7(1) of Regulation 1/2003 stipulates that remedies may take a behavioural or structural form, and need to be '*proportionate* to the infringement committed and *necessary* to bring the infringement effectively to an end'.[227] Behavioural remedies require a dominant company to act or to refrain from acting in a specific way in the future (eg licensing

[227] Emphasis added.

IPRs, providing access to an essential facility),[228] which entails the need to monitor their implementation for a specified period. Conversely, structural remedies are one-off measures that mandate specific changes to the firm's structure and do not require monitoring.[229]

As both behavioural and structural remedies can be powerful tools to shape the market, their potential impacts on data protection are noteworthy. It is not the aim of this section to discuss each and every competition law remedy that might conflict or resonate with data protection. Instead, the following discussion relies on a number of examples to illustrate how competition law remedies can be carved out to consider data protection.

3.1 Behavioural remedies

To date, multiple types of behavioural remedies have been imposed following competition investigations in digital markets in Europe and beyond. Scholars have grouped these remedies into five broad categories: (1) establishing non-discrimination obligations and limiting self-preferencing; (2) limiting contractual arrangements (eg exclusivity); (3) limiting the use of parity clauses; (4) mandating interoperability; and (5) limiting exploitative practices.[230] As explained in the section on theories of harm, even cases that do not pivot around a data or data protection harm (eg certain types of tying cases) might affect data protection indirectly by shaping the digital business environment. It can thus be claimed that successful design and enforcement of all the categories of remedies mentioned earlier are, at least indirectly, is of interest to data protection. To narrow down this section's discussion, the focus is placed on two types of behavioural remedies with an explicit data protection dimension: supply side data remedies and demand side data remedies.

3.1.1 Supply side data remedies

The remedies that belong to this category are competitor-facing. Disparities as regards companies' access to personal data may generate competition issues where powerful platforms exploit data to their own advantage, as already shown. Authorities have at their disposal at least two types of competitor-facing remedies that represent opposite ends of the spectrum: restricting a dominant firm's access to data or requiring a dominant undertaking to share personal data with its competitors.[231]

[228] O'Donoghue and Padilla (n 1) 1126.

[229] Frank P Maier-Rigaud, 'Behavioural versus Structural Remedies in EU Competition Law' in Philip Lowe, Mel Marquis, and Giorgio Monti (eds), *European Competition Law Annual 2013: Effective and Legitimate Enforcement of Competition Law* (Hart Publishing 2016) 209–10.

[230] Filippo Lancieri and Caio Mario S Pereira Neto, 'Designing Remedies for Digital Markets: The Interplay Between Antitrust and Regulation' (2021) 18 Journal of Competition Law & Economics 613, 617.

[231] See eg CMA and ICO (n 219) 22.

The first remedy consisting in restricted data access can be designed in various ways, one of which is to mandate data separation—so-called 'data silos'. This suggestion was put forward by the UK's CMA in its market study of online platforms and digital advertising, and a data silo remedy had already been imposed by the Commission in the *Google/Fitbit* merger decision (see Chapter 3 Section B). In the antitrust context, the view of the CMA is that imposing a data silo remedy will prevent firms with a 'strategic market status' from combining data and using data from services where they have power in other related or unrelated markets where using such data might restrict competition.[232] Mandating data separation is a justified tool where the negative effects on competition outweigh efficiency gains.[233] This scenario might materialize where, for example, the linking of the various datasets creates entry and expansion barriers, a data combination poses data protection concerns, or data has been collected through power leveraging.[234] This course of action would certainly signal a progressive approach to remedies and one that coheres with data protection. As the CMA stressed, data silo interventions 'could in principle deliver strong synergies between the interests of competition and data protection, since they involve restricting the ability to combine and process personal data, at the same time as creating a more level playing field for all businesses to compete fairly'.[235]

Another way of designing remedies with the view of restricting data access or use can be through direct reference to data protection law. The purpose limitation principle, compliance with which could be mandated as part of a competition remedy package, was suggested as a way to 'scrupulously ring face data for specific purposes'.[236] Given that as a result a dominant firm would need to obtain user consent for each purpose, this would, allegedly, give data subjects 'the power to functionally break up Google by withdrawing their consent for granular purposes', constituting 'a consumer-led functional separation of Google'.[237] Mandating a purpose limitation remedy, while coherent with data protection law, might not alone deliver the desired outcome, however. It is increasingly recognized that consumer empowerment through consent does not necessarily result in genuine control, and rendering consumers partially responsible for making this remedy a functional mechanism risks overburdening them.[238] Mandating compliance with other data protection principles and provisions that centre on imposing the responsibility for limiting data processing on organizations rather than on data subjects—data minimization being one example—could provide an alternative solution. As designing

232 CMA, 'Online Platforms and Digital Advertising, Market Study Final Report' (2020) para 8.237.
233 ibid.
234 CMA (n 232) para 8.238.
235 CMA and ICO (n 219) 22–23.
236 Johnny Ryan, 'Formal GDPR Complaint against Google's Internal Data Free-for-All' (16 March 2020) <https://brave.com/google-internal-data-free-for-all/> accessed 20 July 2022.
237 ibid.
238 CMA (n 232) para 8.239.

remedies requires a case-by-case approach, the key question while doing so is whether compliance with data protection alone can deliver the expected competition outcomes, or whether more stringent data separation measures should be envisaged. All in all, however, depriving the law violating companies of data—which, using Khan's words, can be described as 'the fruits of their misconduct and the instrumentalities used in the violation'[239]—is the preferred way forward. To this end, also other, more 'proactive' or 'affirmative' measures (eg requiring companies to modify certain elements of their business models) could be mandated as part of an effort to create future-proof solutions[240]—insofar as such remedies satisfy the requirements of proportionality and necessity laid down in Article 7(1) of Regulation 1/2003.

Highly contentious, yet present in the current debates, is the idea of an antitrust remedy focused on sharing data, including personal data, with competitors—a remedy that is the exact opposite of the one just discussed. Vice-President Vestager suggested that if competition enforcers 'find that some businesses are using their control of data to deny others a chance to compete, then those companies might have to share the data they hold—in a way that's fully in line with the data protection rules'.[241] Yet, ensuring that a data sharing remedy is fully compliant with data protection is precisely the conundrum to which there might be no viable solution.[242] Some have suggested that the reliance on 'effective' data anonymization could be a way forward, arguing that this might 'open up the door to a broad range of security-based techniques allowing large-scale datasets to be used anonymously', and, as a result, make data access remedies likely compliant with data protection law in Europe.[243] Yet, the difficulties of creating genuinely anonymous datasets while simultaneously retaining the valuable information are by now well acknowledged.[244] Other dilemmas might emerge too. For example, how to proceed in cases where the investigated companies have not obtained the data on the merits or obtained them illegally in the first place (eg by violating data protection rules)?

[239] Lina M Khan, 'Remarks of Chair Lina M. Khan' (CRA Conference, Brussels, 31 March 2022) <https://www.ftc.gov/news-events/news/speeches/remarks-chair-lina-m-khan-charles-river-associates-conference-competition-regulation-disrupted-times> accessed 20 July 2022.

[240] For criticism of this approach, see Raphael Reims, 'The Problem of Requiring Firms to Develop an Alternative Monetisation Strategy through Competition Law' (*LSE Business Review*, 30 March 2022) <https://blogs.lse.ac.uk/businessreview/2022/03/30/the-problem-of-requiring-firms-to-develop-an-alternative-monetisation-strategy/> accessed 20 July 2022.

[241] Margrethe Vestager, 'Privacy and Competition in an Age of Data' (IAPP Europe Data Protection Congress, Brussels, 21 November 2019).

[242] For a discussion on this topic, see eg Thomas Tombal, 'The GDPR: A Shield to a Competition Authority's Data Sharing Remedy?' in Jean Herveg (ed), *Deep Diving into Data Protection: 1979-2019 : Celebrating 40 Years of Research on Privacy and Data Protection at the CRIDS* (Larcier 2021).

[243] Crémer, de Montjoye, and Schweitzer (n 34) 78.

[244] See eg A29WP, 'Opinion 05/2014 on Anonymisation Techniques' (2013), cited in Asunción Esteve, 'The Business of Personal Data: Google, Facebook, and Privacy Issues in the EU and the USA' (2017) 7 International Data Privacy Law 36, 46. On the difficulties related to the anonymization of unstructured data, see Emily M Weitzenboeck and others, 'The GDPR and Unstructured Data: Is Anonymization Possible?' (2022) 12 International Data Privacy Law 184.

In such instances, a data sharing remedy might need to be rejected upfront by virtue of not meeting the broader legitimacy standards. Also, wherever restoring competition would require continuous access to data—a conceivable requirement if a rival company is to make effective use of the shared datasets—additional data protection, as well as other, more practical hurdles, would inevitably arise.

3.1.2 Demand side data remedies

As the market's demand side—essentially market behaviour of consumers—influences competition in numerous respects, it might be justified to focus remedies on consumer-facing measures. Consumer-facing remedies, while envisaged to shape the demand side, are commonly imposed on undertakings.[245] An illustrative example is one of the remedies offered by Microsoft to resolve the Commission's concern that its power leveraging strategy distorted competition in the web browser market;[246] the remedy envisaged making available for five years a 'Choice Screen' enabling Windows customers to choose the web browser they wished to install.[247]

Competition authorities have at their disposal a large repertoire of demand side data remedies. Fletcher and Hansen created a useful taxonomy of possible remedies, grouping them around four actions required from consumers to make informed and engaged market decisions: 'attend, 'access', 'assess', and 'act'.[248] Attending remedies aim to influence consumers' engagement with the market: examples include introducing 'attention triggers' or changing choice architecture (eg changing default options).[249] Devising ways to stimulate a greater uptake of alternative products and services can certainly be expected to facilitate market expansion of smaller providers, including data protection-friendly ones. The second type of remedies, namely accessing remedies, include measures to access the information necessary to make an informed choice.[250] In data-related contexts, such remedies should be employed in ways aligned with the data protection transparency requirements, or go beyond them. Remedies focused on assessment, which belong to the third category, strive to improve the chances that consumers are not only provided with information, but that they are also able to assess it: standardized

[245] Amelia Fletcher and David Hansen, 'The Role of Demand Side Remedies in Resolving Competition Concerns' in Damien Gerard and Assimakis Komninos (eds), *Remedies in EU Competition Law* (Wolters Kluwer 2020) 30.

[246] *Microsoft (Tying)* (Case COMP/39.530) Commission Decision of 16 December 2009.

[247] European Commission, 'Antitrust: Commission accepts Microsoft commitments to give users browser choice' (16 December 2009) IP/09/1941 <https://ec.europa.eu/commission/presscorner/detail/en/IP_09_194> accessed 6 September 2022. In 2013, Microsoft was fined for non-compliance with these commitments: European Commission, 'Antitrust: Commission Fines Microsoft for Non-Compliance with Browser Choice Commitments' (6 March 2013) IP/13/196 <https://ec.europa.eu/commission/presscorner/detail/en/IP_13_196> accessed 12 July 2022.

[248] Fletcher and Hansen (n 245) 21.

[249] ibid 24–25.

[250] ibid 26–27.

disclosures or information collation (eg through comparison services) exemplify this type of remedy.[251] The GDPR already mandates that controllers provide information to data subjects 'in a concise, transparent, intelligible and easily accessible form, using clear and plain language'.[252] If a competition remedy offered further guarantees that that requirement was thoroughly complied with, sectional coherence would be at its most evident. Finally, acting remedies should be implemented where consumers face switching barriers. Mechanisms aimed at fostering data portability and interoperability are of particular value. As regards data portability, remedies designed to strengthen users' ability to port data could also indirectly address the current weaknesses of the right to data portability enshrined in the GDPR (Chapter 3 Section C). They could also offer a way to implement new ideas for effective porting of data. One such idea proposed by Parker, Petropolous, and Van Alstyne envisages introducing an 'in situ data right', which is 'a new user right of information access that obligates gatekeeper platforms to allow third-party access to a user's raw data upon that user's request'.[253] When it comes to interoperability, Cyphers and Doctorow, for instance, proposed creating a 'federated social networking': taking Facebook as an example, in order to federate, the company could be required to design an interface allowing Facebook users to be able to add off-platform identities as friends, being able to interact with them, and seeing on the Facebook feed social media content that off-platform users generate on another service.[254] As a result, alternative providers would get a chance to enter or expand. At the same time, the design of interoperability-centred remedies must account for potential data protection risks. As the EDPS recently remarked, 'a technological environment with information systems that are not inter-operable with each other has provided a very strong safeguard against the violation of the fundamental data protection principle of purpose limitation'.[255] Framed differently, '[t]echnical non-feasibility has made it harder to use large amounts of data for purposes for which they were nor collected'.[256]

While consumer-facing remedies should be an inherent part of a remedy package in digital markets where various impediments to consumer behaviour are prevalent and well recognised (eg behavioural biases), the risk of overburdening consumers and placing on them an asymmetrical responsibility should be borne in mind. Such remedies should be considered a complement, rather than a substitute, for supply side remedies.

[251] ibid 27–28.

[252] GDPR, art 12(1).

[253] Geoffrey Parker, Georgios Petropoulos, and Marshall Van Alstyne, 'Platform Mergers and Antitrust' (2021) 30 Industrial and Corporate Change 1307, 1323.

[254] Bennett Cyphers and Cory Doctorow, 'Privacy Without Monopoly: Data Protection and Interoperability by Electronic Frontier Foundation' (2021) 18.

[255] EDPS, 'Opinion 1/2023 on the Proposal for an Interoperable Europe Act' (2023) 7.

[256] ibid 7.

3.1.3 *Institutional and other considerations*

The previous discussion on supply and demand side remedies is by no means exhaustive. New technologies and new ways of interacting with technologies, as well as novel market strategies, require agencies to be vigilant and innovative as regards their remedial approaches. From an institutional angle, any competition remedy design that envisages data-related behavioural measures must include the involvement of data protection experts. From the perspective of sectional coherence, it would be hard to legitimize any data-based antitrust remedy that might restore competition in the market, but be at the same time a questionable fix from a data protection standpoint. Envisaging the role for data protection experts is even more pertinent when the abuse takes the form of a data protection violation. In such cases, acknowledging overlapping mandates of competition and data protection authorities—and the substantive knowledge that the latter can contribute—is precisely what is needed to minimize the risk of a remedy failure. As Lancieri and Pereira Neto noted, in certain cases an optimal remedy design framework should leverage the different strengths of various regulatory authorities.[257] There are in their view no reasons why a 'vertical integration of authorities', which means that it is the same authority that identifies the problem, designs a remedy, and monitors its implementation, should not be broken up if doing so would benefit policy-making.[258]

3.2 Structural remedies

In *Standard Oil*,[259] a foundational US antitrust case, the US Supreme Court ordered the company to be broken up into thirty-seven smaller companies. Nowadays, a structural remedy is not a measure that in the antitrust context competition authorities make use of to restore competition. While in the area of merger control ex ante break-ups have long been relied upon to authorize mergers that would otherwise be prohibited, divestitures imposed on dominant companies in an ex post manner are much more intrusive and in principle avoided.[260] In EU law, Article 7(1) of Regulation 1/2003 states explicitly that 'structural remedies can only be imposed either where there is no equally effective behavioural remedy or where any equally effective behavioural remedy would be more burdensome for the undertaking concerned than the structural remedy'.

While structural remedies are extremely rare in the area of abuse of dominance in Europe and beyond and have a 'residual nature',[261] digital markets have brought

[257] Lancieri and Pereira Neto (n 230) 650.

[258] ibid.

[259] *Standard Oil Co v United States*, 221 US 1 (1911). See also *United States v Paramount Pictures, Inc*, 85 F Supp (SDNY 1949); *United States v AT&T Co*, 552 F Supp 131 (DDC 1982).

[260] For a discussion on these different approaches to remedies in antitrust and merger control, see eg Wei Wang, 'Structural Remedies in EU Antitrust and Merger Control' (2011) 34 World Competition 571.

[261] Alessandro Tajana, 'If I Had a Hammer ... Structural Remedies and Abuse of Dominant Position' (2006) 1 Competition and Regulation in Network Industries 3, 5.

them to the fore as many reflect on the need to break up big tech companies to ensure markets' contestability. The calls for break-ups of large online firms are premised on the conviction that concentration in the online economy is reaching a tipping point.[262] Although subject to discussion in expert antirust circles, the subject of breaking up digital monopolies has also surfaced in the political discourse. In her 2020 US presidential campaign, Senator Elisabeth Warren put antitrust into the spotlight by making the break-ups of firms such as Amazon, Facebook, and Google—which she described as 'platform utilities'—one of her key pledges.[263]

The appeal of structural remedies is grounded in the conviction that behavioural remedies are simply not always effective. A hurdle related to behavioural remedies that might compromise their effectiveness is the need to constantly monitor undertakings' remedial compliance. For example, it was not until approximately fourteen months after Microsoft unintentionally stopped displaying the choice screen—a behavioural remedy imposed in the abuse of dominance case—that the Commission detected and investigated the company's failure to comply.[264] The questionable effectiveness of certain behavioural remedies also became evident in the aftermath of the Commission's *Google Shopping* decision.[265] Thus, while structural remedies require careful design and might take time to implement,[266] they are, in the longer run, easier to administer and enforce as they do not need any monitoring and oversight. Also appealing is the fact that they are more difficult to circumvent—the risk of circumvention being an evident problem in complex markets with information asymmetries between companies and authorities—and better ensure that the infringement will not be repeated.[267] Importantly, a recent study conducted by Watzinger and Schnitzer shows evidence of the positive impact of break-ups on innovation.[268] The authors analysed the effects of the 1984 divestiture of Bell System, the US monopolist in telephone services, imposed in the US under Section 2 of the Sherman Act in *Standard Oil*. Having considered the remedy's implications for the rate, diversity, and direction of US innovation, they

[262] Francesco Ducci and Michael Trebilcock, 'Structural vs. Behavioural Remedies in Big Tech Sectors' (2020) CPI Chronicle 2.

[263] Elizabeth Warren, 'Here's How We Can Break up Big Tech' *Medium* (8 March 2019) <https://medium.com/@teamwarren/heres-how-we-can-break-up-big-tech-9ad9e0da324c> accessed 14 July 2022; Daniel Trotta, 'Wall Street Critic Warren Vows to Break up Amazon, Facebook, Google' *Reuters* (8 March 2019) <https://www.reuters.com/article/us-elizabethwarren-technology-idUSKCN1QP1M0> accessed 14 July 2022.

[264] Lancieri and Pereira Neto (n 230) 2–3. European Commission, 'Antitrust: Commission Fines Microsoft for Non-Compliance with Browser Choice Commitments' (6 March 2013).

[265] For a detailed discussion on the remedies in *Google Shopping*, see eg Philip Mardsen, 'Google Shopping for the Empress's New Clothes—When a Remedy Isn't a Remedy (and How to Fix It)' (2020) 11 Journal of European Competition Law & Practice 553; Marek Krzysztof Kolasinski, 'Interpretation of the Remedy in the *Google Shopping* Decision and Its Consequences' (2020) 4 European Competition and Regulatory Law Review 4.

[266] O'Donoghue and Padilla (n 1) 1198.

[267] ibid.

[268] Martin Watzinger and Monika Schnitzer, 'The Breakup of the Bell System and Its Impact on US Innovation' (2023) Center for Economic Policy Research, Discussion Paper No 17635.

concluded that innovation increased—a conclusion that in their view extends beyond that particular setting.

From a substantive and coherence angle, the central issue is whether and how structural remedies can positively support data protection. It is beyond doubt that splitting large technology companies into smaller units might benefit data protection by reducing the risk of combining personal data from various services without a legal basis, or exploiting the resulting insights in ways questionable from an individual welfare perspective. Simultaneously, these positive repercussions might prove temporary. It is not illegal for companies to internally grow and develop new services, hence they can recreate the economic structures that gave rise to competition and data protection concerns in the first place. Behavioural remedies designed along the lines described earlier might thus hold greater potential for rendering specific beneficial conduct more prevalent in digital markets.

D. Merger control

The past few years have witnessed a wave of mergers and acquisitions in digital markets, bringing merger control to the forefront of discussions on how to effectively integrate data protection into merger appraisals. From reflecting on the effects that the accumulation of personal data might have on competition and data protection, to expressing a renewed interest in conglomerate mergers as well as rethinking jurisdictional thresholds, the discourse on how merger control should be improved to be fit for purpose in the digital economy is multifaceted. Taking some of these facets into account, this section endeavours to analyse how the law and enforcement practice in the area of merger control might need to adapt to better respond to calls for its coherence with data protection. Building on Chapter 3 Section B that discussed prominent mergers on the interface of competition and data protection, this section looks into theories of harm, justification, and remedies.

1. Theories of harm

The SIEC ('significant impediment to effective competition') test is the cornerstone of merger control. It is the main test applied in substantive appraisals of horizontal, vertical, and conglomerate mergers in the EU as well as in several other jurisdictions, including almost all EU Member States, the US, Canada, and Turkey.[269] Going beyond the notion of dominance, the SIEC test aims to catch a wide range of anti-competitive transactions: a merger should be prohibited if it significantly

[269] Hanna Stakheyeva, 'Test SIEC' in *Global Dictionary of Competition Law*, Concurrences art no 89155.

impedes effective competition. While the EUMR explicitly notes that such an impediment to competition results in particular from the 'creation or strengthening of a dominant position',[270] the SIEC test also helps to detect the anti-competitive effects of a transaction between undertakings that would not lead to market dominance. Market structure, actual or potential competition, the market positions of the undertakings concerned, their economic and financial power, barriers to entry, supply and demand trends, consumers' interests, and technical and economic progress are among factors to consider in substantive merger appraisals. In relation to digital markets, the question arises how access to personal data and data protection should influence the outcome of merger assessments. The next two sections reflect first on the theories of harm based on a data advantage, and then on harm linked to data protection. The third section is devoted to a broader analysis of conglomerate mergers.

1.1 Theories of harm based on a data advantage

Many of the mergers in the digital economy are either partially or fully motivated by the desire to gain access to new datasets.[271] Part of a competition appraisal of such mergers involving personal data is the question whether post-transaction data accumulation significantly impedes effective competition. For example, when a party to a transaction has an ad-based business model, its access to new types of data after the transaction might improve its ability to offer targeted advertising, thereby harming rivals who are not in a position to obtain a similar volume and variety of data. This enforcement logic, as Lynskey noted, shows that in a competition appraisal, personal data are commonly approached 'solely as an economic asset, with the proliferation of data viewed positively'.[272] The mergers described in Chapter 3 Section B illustrate well this approach, which is a common cause of inconsistency between competition and data protection. For example, while competition law sees the availability of personal data on secondary markets (eg through data brokers) as 'a boon', the availability of such data might be incompatible with the data protection principles of purpose limitation and data minimization.[273]

From a broader conceptual viewpoint, it can be asserted that a competition-driven logic underpinning such cases might create a conflict with data protection. At the same time, one could argue that a formulation of a competition law theory of harm based on a data advantage might also create synergies between the two legal fields in an indirect way. If a relevant post-transaction competitive data advantage

[270] EUMR, art 2(3).

[271] Samson Y Esayas, 'Data Privacy in European Merger Control: Critical Analysis of Commission Decisions Regarding Privacy as a Non-Price Competition' (2019) 40 European Competition Law Review 166, 166.

[272] Orla Lynskey, 'A Legal Response to Data-Driven Mergers' in Emre Bayamlioğlu and others (eds), *Being Profiled: Cogitas Ergo Sum. 10 Years of Profiling the European Citizen* (Amsterdam UP 2018).

[273] ibid.

is identified during the course of a merger review, that merger will not be cleared without companies offering commitments to minimize the competition risk brought about by a data advantage. For example, as discussed in Chapter 3 Section B, the commitments in *Google/Fitbit* included an agreement that Google would not use Fitbit's data for advertising purposes, and that Fitbit's user data would be stored in a 'data silo' and technically separated. Even though the reliance on a data advantage theory of harm is not underpinned by a concern for data protection, future data protection risks that such a merger potentially entails can be mitigated as a result of a competition intervention. This conclusion holds true as long as the relevant remedies are centred on addressing the data advantage of the post-merger entity by restricting its data usage rather than imposing data sharing obligations.

1.2 Theories of harm based on data protection

A dearth of merger cases with theories of harm that comprehensively reflect the transactions' impacts on data protection illustrates the problem of a continuous disconnect between competition law and data protection. While the more recent decisions (eg *Microsoft/LinkedIn*) made evident that data protection can be a relevant factor when it is a parameter of competition, the progress made so far in relation to capturing mergers' potential harm to data protection is, regrettably, negligible.

1.2.1 Data protection as a dimension of competition

There is a growing consensus that data protection repercussions of merger transactions can be a factor to consider when there is competition on data protection in the relevant market. In this sense, data protection can be approached as an independent dimension of a product or service that is valued by individuals, a dimension of quality, or a matter of choice (ie a restriction of competition could simultaneously impede a consumer's ability to choose the most data protection-friendly service). In *Microsoft/LinkedIn*, for example, the Commission observed that 'data privacy is an important parameter of competition' between providers of professional social networks,[274] hence data protection is a relevant parameter of competition to consider in merger review. While acknowledging the pertinence of competition on data protection in merger control represents already a more progressive attitude, a twofold criticism can be expressed as to: (1) the operationalization of this approach and (2) its disregard for the nature of data protection as a fundamental human right.

As regards the first point of criticism, some have stressed that it remains unclear how to correctly identify instances of competition on data protection and, once such instances are identified, how to formulate a theory of harm (eg what

[274] *Microsoft/LinkedIn* (Case COMP/M.8124) Commission Decision of 6 December 2016.

constitutes a reduction in data protection, or when a transaction reduces competition on data protection).[275] With regard to establishing competition on data protection, Esayas distinguished between two scenarios: when merging firms have similar privacy policies, and when their privacy policies differ—both of which can signal that competition on data protection exists.[276] He then rightly criticized the approach in *Facebook/WhatsApp*, where the Commission's treatment of WhatsApp and Facebook Messenger as complementary rather than competitive services was partially based on the premise that firms with dissimilar privacy approaches (which was the case here) compete less fiercely on data protection compared to companies with similar privacy policies.[277] Indeed, the quality of data protection offered by companies cannot be used to determine the existence of competition on this parameter. For example, a privacy-friendly service may exert competitive pressures on other companies which offer poorer privacy protection. Even though competitors' reactions to such pressures might not always lead to genuine privacy initiatives, the claim that competition on data protection does not exist in such cases, or is not strong enough to be relevant for a merger analysis, risks being flawed. For example, as suggested by Gilbert and Pepper, the removal 'of an important "maverick" that has developed innovative data protection and control systems could potentially raise competition issues by reducing innovation in data privacy, even if the merging firms were not otherwise competitors'.[278]

The second key problem with treating data protection as merger-relevant only if competition on data protection can be established is the fact that this approach elevates data protection to a valuable consideration only if firms de facto choose to make data protection their competitively distinguishing feature. In other words, in such scenarios it is the market that emerges as a reference point for establishing the value of data protection. And yet, inferring that individuals do not value data protection by observing the markets may lead to flawed conclusions. As the OECD observed, 'a current lack of differentiation among firms in terms of data protection does not necessarily mean that privacy is not a valued dimension of quality for consumers; indeed, it may instead suggest a lack of competition in the market'.[279] Mindful of the fact that the right to data protection is in the EU a fundamental and inalienable human right, it can be claimed that individual valuation of data protection should not determine whether or not personal data is worthy of protection. This assertion serves as a bridge to the next section, where data protection as a stand-alone consideration in merger control is considered.

[275] Esayas (n 271) 167.

[276] ibid. According to the OECD, 'a current lack of differentiation among firms in terms of data protection does not necessarily mean that privacy is not a valued dimension of quality for consumers': OECD, 'OECD Competition Trends 2021, Volume II, Global Merger Control' (2021) 29.

[277] Esayas (n 271) 168.

[278] Gilbert and Pepper (n 31) 5.

[279] OECD (n 276) 29.

1.2.2 Data protection as a stand-alone consideration

The second approach—one that would introduce sectional coherence between competition law and data protection, but is controversial—is to classify data protection as a stand-alone factor in merger assessments. As opposed to the scenario presented above, this approach assumes data protection's relevance in merger control irrespective of whether or not competition on data protection can be identified. In practical terms, this implies prohibiting a merger that can be expected to have undesirable data protection consequences, unless the parties to the transaction offer commitments to remedy the identified data protection concerns. Adopting this approach would require complementing the SIEC test with a test that can help to detect a data protection harm, and which can be called a 'significant impediment to data protection' (SIDP).

Thus far, merger enforcement practice has not revealed approval for the idea of considering data protection implications in this way, relegating non-competition impacts to data protection law instead. In a similar vein, the literature has highlighted a paradigm shift that treating data protection as a stand-alone concern would imply for merger control. For example, in his analysis of data protection in merger review, Esayas rejected this approach upfront due to the fact that it 'does not consider purely competition concerns' such as price increase, or output or quality reduction, and that 'it would have to overcome insurmountable challenges to succeed'.[280] The risk of 'injecting subjectivity and unrelated policy objectives into competition analysis'[281] is feared as another consequence if such an approach is pursued.

While resistance to including non-competition harms in merger assessments prevails, the idea of expanding the scope of substantive merger analyses has recently also gained some ground. The chair of the FTC, Lina Khan, noted for instance that new business practices require the authorities to 'look beyond concepts like foreclosure and exclusion when trying to cognize harm'.[282] Acknowledging that a narrow approach to mergers may in the past have created 'blind spots' that enabled harmful mergers, in September 2021, the FTC suggested that in its 'second request'—a counterpart to a Phase II investigation in the EU—the agency investigates additional areas affected by a merger. These might include the effects of the filed merger on labour markets or its possible cross-market effects. Although privacy was not mentioned, the expansion of the substantive range of investigated concerns signalled the agency's readiness to look beyond the traditional boundaries of merger assessments. The proposal to consider non-competition factors in merger control is also in tune with the EDPB's suggestion that the evaluation of mergers' non-competition impacts (eg on privacy, freedom of expression) should

[280] Esayas (n 271) 166.
[281] OECD (n 276) 29.
[282] Khan (n 239).

accompany a competition assessment either as an independent appraisal or as integrated into a competition assessment.[283] Scholars similarly opined that the case for such a non-competition assessment should be made.[284] From a normative viewpoint, as already mentioned, it is difficult to fathom why a fundamental right to data protection is considered worth pursuing only if business operators decide to make it their competitively distinguishing feature.

To provide a blueprint for integrating data protection as a stand-alone value, the remainder of this section addresses the following two-pronged question: what type of a data protection impact would a merger need to generate to be prohibited by a competition authority, and what procedural tools should be used to identify such problematic transactions?

Violation of data protection law as a concern. As regards the type of repercussion that should trigger a prohibition decision for a transaction, it should be limited to a likely violation of data protection law. Thus, if a merger is likely to give a post-merged entity the incentives and the ability to embark on a data protection violation in the future, or strengthen its incentives and ability to do so, prohibiting such a transaction should be seriously considered, even if a post-transaction accumulation of data does not raise competition concerns. Conversely, if a transaction is expected to result in a deterioration of data protection standards, but a violation of data protection law is unlikely, that alone should not provide a ground for a prohibition decision.

There are two reasons for limiting competition law interventions to the likely instances of a breach of data protection law. First, data protection law provides reliable benchmarks, limiting the discretion of a reviewing authority and preventing fuzzy and unpredictable theories of harm. Secondly, restricting the scope of the SIDP test in this way would mitigate concerns about unjustifiably expanding the purview of merger control. Admittedly, intervening in transactions that result in degraded data protection standards, but do not breach data protection law, is difficult to defend. It is, at the same time, inconceivable that one authority expressly authorizes a transaction that would likely lead to a violation of another branch of law. Not only does such an enforcement strategy create an undesirable lack of coherence, but it also implies that additional resources will then need to be invested to address the negative spillovers that the enforcement might have on other areas of the law. This is a realistic scenario, as already demonstrated by a range of data protection enforcement actions taken after the authorization of the *Facebook/WhatsApp* transaction in the EU.

Restricted in this way, the SIDP test has, however, a significant shortcoming. While the limited version of the SIDP test can be applied in jurisdictions with data protection or privacy laws, it would need to be rethought to be of use in

[283] EDPB, 'Statement on Privacy Implications of Mergers' (2020).
[284] Lynskey (n 272).

jurisdictions with no such comprehensive legal frameworks in place. Absent data protection law, an alternative could be to rely on the privacy principles as defined by the OECD.[285]

New procedural tools. Given the prospective nature of a merger analysis, establishing a likely risk of a data protection violation is certain to involve a challenge. To render the final conclusions as reliable as possible, a new tool that should be introduced is a Merger Data Protection Impact Assessment (MDPIA). Accordingly, if a transaction involves parties that collect and process personal data, they should submit to competition authorities an assessment of their transaction's implications for data protection—an assessment akin to a Data Protection Impact Assessment (DPIA) required under Article 35 GDPR or a Privacy Impact Assessment (PIA),[286] which is more common in other jurisdictions. An MDPIA should then be considered by a reviewing authority alongside other, more established factors indicative of the merged entity's incentives and abilities to embark on practices violating data protection law (eg the structure of all relevant markets and the company's financial strength) to draw a conclusion.

In the EU, the EUMR already entrusts the Commission with substantial investigation powers to ensure that the final appraisal of the notified mergers relies on comprehensive and reliable information.[287] Gathering information about the future data strategies of the post-merger entity does not in any way extend those powers, and has already been used in the course of merger investigations in data-intensive contexts. The added value of a mandatory MDPIA therefore lies not in the novelty of obtaining information about companies' data-related future approaches, but rather in the fact that they would render impacts on data protection an inherent part of a merger analysis, institutionalize that analysis, and require companies to thoroughly consider data protection law compliance while preparing their post-merger data strategies.

As regards the content of an MDPIA, competition and data protection authorities should cooperate to develop a harmonized template. Mirroring a DPIA mandated under the GDPR, a MDPIA should contain information on the envisaged data protection operations, their purposes, necessity, and proportionality. In addition, the submitted document should contain an elaborate review of any intended merging of datasets, their possible risks to the rights and freedoms of individuals, and the envisaged safeguards to ensure compliance. Any further information

[285] OECD, 'Guidelines on the Protection of Privacy and Transborder Flows of Personal Data' (1980).

[286] As of the mid-1990s, PIAs became more common in jurisdictions such as Australia, Canada, New Zealand, the US, and the UK: Roger Clarke, 'An Evaluation of Privacy Impact Assessment Guidance Documents' (2011) 1 International Data Privacy Law 111, 111. For a detailed discussion on data protection and privacy impacts assessments, see eg David Wright and Paul De Hert, *Privacy Impact Assessment* (Springer 2012).

[287] EUMR, recital 38.

required in the context of an MDPIA should serve the key objective of evaluating the likelihood of a post-transaction data protection law violation.

As such, an MDPIA should be a complementary tool to facilitate decision making. In addition to considering data processing-related information included in the submitted MDPIA, the SIDP test should also, as already mentioned, reflect on other exogenous parameters to evaluate the likelihood of a data protection violation. As regards an MDPIA itself, the authorities should remain critical towards its content. The likelihood of the parties submitting misleading or incomplete information is not a theoretical scenario: as already discussed, in 2014 the Commission fined Facebook €110 million for providing misleading information about its plans relating to the automated matching between Facebook's and WhatsApp's accounts of users.[288] Although the Commission may impose fines for submitting incorrect information, such fines are not substantial, hence do not serve as a deterrent. If the Commission issues a clearing decision based on the information inferred from the submitted MDPIA, and the analysis of additional exogenous factors, but the merged entity breaches data protection rules in any event, such a clearance decision should be revoked, as envisaged by Article 8(6)(a) EUMR.

In addition to the substantive information included in an MDPIA, it would also need to be further determined when exactly companies need to submit an MDPIA in the context of a merger notification. A DPIA—on which an MDPIA could be modelled is—according to Article 35 GDPR—required only where data processing 'is likely to result in a high risk to the rights and freedoms of natural persons'. The indication of 'high risk' as a filtering threshold implies that a substantive amount of processing operations would be exempt.[289] To ensure the effectiveness of the new MDPIA tool, it would be desirable to introduce the MDPIA obligation for all notifiable mergers in data-intensive markets.

To use the resources in the most efficient way, an MDPIA should only be required when a reviewing authority has preliminary concerns after the 'Phase I'[290] analysis, and moves the assessment of the proposed merger to 'Phase II',[291] where a more detailed investigation would be conducted. This would also resonate in other jurisdictions, the vast majority of which follow a two-phase investigation procedure.[292] It can be the case that data protection concerns can already be resolved after the Phase I analysis if companies offer adequate commitments. If, however,

[288] European Commission, 'Mergers: Commission fines Facebook €110 million for providing misleading information about WhatsApp takeover' (18 May 2017) IP/17/1369 <https://ec.europa.eu/commission/presscorner/detail/en/IP_17_1369> accessed 11 June 2022.

[289] Reuben Binns, 'Data Protection Impact Assessments: A Meta-Regulatory Approach' (2017) 7 International Data Privacy Law 22, 28.

[290] EUMR, art 10(1): Phase I analysis needs to be conducted within twenty-five working days (extendable to thirty-five).

[291] EUMR, art 10(3): Phase II analysis needs to be conducted within ninety days (extendable to 105 days).

[292] According to the OECD report, forty-seven out of fifty-seven jurisdictions in the OECD CompStats database adopt a two-phase approach: OECD (n 276) 14–15.

the case requires a more thorough examination, the likely risk of a data protection breach should warrant the opening of Phase II investigation, where an MDPIA would be of help. If a transaction does not raise any competition concerns, a Phase II analysis should concentrate solely on data protection.

It cannot be overstated that the SIDP test requires data protection expertise. A competition authority should work alongside data protection experts (either in-house experts or data protection organizations, eg the EDPS or the EDPB) to evaluate the likelihood of a future infringement of data protection law. Conducting such a prospective analysis of whether intended data processing by a data controller would violate the GDPR is not new for national DPAs: for example, Article 58(2)(a) provides DPAs with powers to issue warnings about the future likelihood of an infringement.

1.3 A stricter approach to conglomerate mergers

Over the past years, powerful technological companies have been growing and building their digital ecosystems by relying to a significant extent on acquisition strategies. In some of these transactions, the targets are not competitors, but rather innovative small firms offering complementary services—making these transactions fall into the category of conglomerate mergers.

From a competition standpoint, the operational assumption has long since assumed that non-horizontal mergers in general, and conglomerate mergers in particular, are less likely to pose harm to competition as compared to horizontal transactions. The reason for that, as framed by Witt, is that '[t]hey neither reduce the number of competitors in the market nor do they involve the danger of the merged entity cutting off a competitor's access to key inputs or distributions'.[293] This more lenient approach to conglomerate deals, which are usually considered benign, or even efficiency-enhancing, is now being revisited in light of their harmful potential in the digital era.[294] Although conglomerate harm theories have not yet been widely or consistently applied by the competition authorities—conglomerate effects have, for example, played a relatively negligible role in digital merger decisions issued in the US—a substantial part of all digital mergers reviewed by the Commission has taken into account conglomerate effects (eg *Google/Fitbit*, *Microsoft/LinkedIn*, *Apple/Shazam*).[295] Concerns relating to conglomerate mergers include in particular the acquiring company's ability and incentive to leverage its power and embark on anti-competitive tying and market envelopment.[296] Potential future strategies of the merged entity, such as limiting interoperability and imposing pre-installations or defaults, can also be a source of

[293] Anne C Witt, 'Who's Afraid of Conglomerate Mergers?' (2022) 67 Antitrust Bulletin 208, 210.
[294] OECD (n 276) 27.
[295] Witt (n 293) 220–26.
[296] James Mancini, 'Making Online Markets More Competitive: The Benefits and Challenges of Conglomerate Merger Review' (2021) OECD Going Digital Toolkit Notes No 3, 6–8.

concern. In addition, conglomerate mergers can be a strategy to eliminate a potential future competitive threat.[297]

If followed by bold enforcement, this renewed interest in conglomerate mergers not only has the potential to spur competitiveness, but might also indirectly create an improved data protection environment. Pre-empting expansionist strategies of powerful firms implies that their future ability to collect and merge data from various sources, as well as embark on other potentially harmful data strategies, will be restricted.

2. Justifications

In merger control, the primary dilemma relevant for this book's discussion is how to approach transactions that are likely to have harmful data protection implications, in particular when they do not restrict competition. A reverse scenario—one that should be touched upon even though it has not surfaced in merger practice so far—is when the transaction harms competition but the parties seek to justify it on data protection grounds. Unlikely as such scenarios seem to be at present, it cannot be excluded that they could materialize in the future, making it worthwhile to briefly reflect on how competition law should respond.

2.1 An efficiency defence in the area of merger control

In the EU, the harmful effects of a transaction might in certain instances be counterbalanced by the efficiencies it brings about. Next to a 'failing firm defence' that is irrelevant for the present discussion, an efficiency claim is the only type of justification specifically mentioned in the EUMR and the merger guidelines.[298] To be taken into account in a merger assessment, the efficiencies need to: (1) benefit consumers; (2) be merger-specific; and (3) be verifiable. As regards the first condition, the benefit can take the form of lower prices resulting from cost savings in production or distribution,[299] or new or improved products or services thanks to efficiency gains resulting from R&D and innovation.[300] To have a chance to succeed, efficiencies need to be timely (materialize in the near future),[301] and a transaction should not lead to a near-monopoly.[302] The second criterion submits that the stated

[297] ibid 9.

[298] EUMR, recital 29; European Commission, 'Guidelines on the assessment of horizontal mergers under the Council Regulation on the control of concentrations between undertakings' [2004] OJ C31/03 (hereafter: Horizontal Merger Guidelines) paras 76–88; European Commission, 'Guidelines on the assessment of non-horizontal mergers under the Council Regulation on the control of concentrations between undertakings' [2008] OJ C265/6 (hereafter: Non-Horizontal Merger Guidelines') para 53.

[299] Horizontal Merger Guidelines (n 299) para 80.

[300] ibid para 81.

[301] ibid para 83.

[302] ibid para 84.

efficiencies need to directly result from a merger, and cannot be achieved through less anti-competitive means.[303] The non-horizontal merger guidelines note that vertical and conglomerate mergers 'provide a substantial scope for efficiencies'.[304] According to the third and final requirement, namely verifiability, the Commission must 'be reasonably certain that the efficiencies are likely to materialise, and be substantial enough to counteract the merger's potential harm to consumers'.[305] It is the task of the notifying parties to present a solid efficiency claim—ideally one quantifying a consumer benefit and showing a clearly identifiable (rather than marginal) positive impact on consumers.[306]

2.2 Data protection as an efficiency defence

In theory, a data protection justification might be able to satisfy the three requirements presented above, namely efficiency gains, merger specificity, and verifiability. As the boundaries of the efficiency concept have been expanding over the past years—a development described in Section C discussing justifications in antitrust—it is conceivable that some type of data protection improvement might fall under its scope.

As regards merger specificity, some of the digital mergers scrutinized thus far have raised, rather than removed, risks to data protection. How a merger can be a tool to enhance compliance with data protection rules is thus hard to envisage. At the same time, just as there might be forms of collaboration between companies that render data protection efforts more efficient or cost-effective,[307] for example, it can be envisaged that some merger transactions may in the future be underpinned by a similar motivation.

The last criterion, namely verifiability, is highly contextual. It does not seem, however, that data protection efficiencies would have peculiarities making them less likely to be verifiable as compared to other types of efficiencies. Thus, while competition authorities should remain open to data protection justifications, they must also stay vigilant to the problem of data protection washing.

3. Remedies

A merger posing a competition concern may still be declared compatible with competition law if companies implement modifications, the aim of which is

[303] ibid para 85.

[304] Non-Horizontal Merger Guidelines (n 299) para 13

[305] Horizontal Merger Guidelines (n 299) para 86.

[306] ibid.

[307] Anne Federle, 'The Interplay of Data Protection and Competition Law—Issues Beyond the *Facebook* Case' (*Bird & Bird*, 19 March 2019) <https://www.twobirds.com/insights/2019/global/the-interplay-of-data-protection-and-competition-law-issues-beyond-the-facebook-case> accessed 2 September 2022.

to eliminate the identified concern. Commonly referred to as 'commitments' or 'remedies', such modifications are expressly envisaged in the EUMR (Arts 6(2) and 8(2)).[308] As the remedial stage can prove crucial in bringing competition law and data protection closer together, and given an intense merger activity in data-driven digital markets, this section sheds light on how merger remedies should be designed in a coherence-oriented way. Similarly to antitrust remedies, remedial measures in merger control can be broadly divided into structural and behavioural.

3.1 Structural remedies

In contrast to the area of abuse of a dominant position, merger control usually relies on structural remedies and in particular on 'divestitures' (ie a commitment by a company to sell one or more of its units). In the EU, in the period between 2011 and 2019, over 70 per cent of the cases cleared by the Commission involved a divestiture.[309] Structural remedies in merger control are also the preferred method of resolving competition concerns in other jurisdictions.[310] The reason for favouring structural over behavioural remedies is the ability of the former to effectively address the identified concerns in a durable way.[311] Structural remedies are also not flexible enough to reflect the complexity of digital markets. High monitoring costs, market uncertainty, information asymmetries, lack of appropriate ex post evaluation, or spillovers into neighbouring markets are among the risks carried by behavioural remedies that justify a preference for structural solutions.[312] A joint statement issued in 2021 by the CMA, the ACCC, and the Bundeskartellamt noted that structural remedies are preferred given that complex behavioural remedies are 'unlikely to recreate the pre-merger competitive intensity of the market, can raise significant circumvention risks, ... can quickly become outdated as market conditions change', as well as may imply the burden of monitoring.[313]

Even though favoured in general, structural remedies might not, however, be the right choice when the aim is to resolve new concerns arising in digital markets. In a 2022 report on merger review in digital and technology markets commissioned by the European Commission, Robertson analysed ninety-seven recent national merger cases from various EU Member States and the UK and concluded that '[i]t is notable that very few cases resorted to structural remedies in order to

[308] See also European Commission, 'Commission Notice on Remedies Acceptable under Council Regulation (EC) No 139/2004 and under Commission Regulation (EC) No 802/2004' [2008] OJ C267/01 (hereafter: Remedies Notice).

[309] OECD, 'Conglomerate Effects of Mergers—Note by the European Union' (2020) DAF/COMP/WD(2018)47, para 29.

[310] For a US perspective, see eg Charles F Rule and Daniel J Howley, 'Structural Remedies' (2021) Global Competition Review <https://globalcompetitionreview.com/guide/the-guide-merger-remedies/fourth-edition/article/structural-remedies> accessed 5 December 2022.

[311] Remedies Notice (n 308) para 15.

[312] Jéssica Nemeth, 'Blockchain, Behavioural Remedies, and Merger Control: How Can Access Remedies Do Better?' (2022) 13 Journal of European Competition Law & Practice 167, 167.

[313] CMA, ACCC, and Bundeskartellamt, 'Joint Statement on Merger Control Enforcement' (2021).

address competition concerns'.[314] Behavioural remedies—in particular, access and interoperability commitments—constituted the prevalent method for resolving competition concerns.[315] Several reasons might explain this shift. As many digital mergers are vertical or conglomerate rather than horizontal, mandating a divestment, for example, might be disproportionate for addressing the concerns that these transactions potentially entail and risk eliminating the efficiencies they bring about.[316] Snoep, the chairman of the Dutch NCA, observed that behavioural remedies help to strike the right balance between over-enforcement and under-enforcement.[317] Markets' complexity, incentives to innovate, and urgency are among other considerations that might tilt the balance in the favour of behavioural remedies.[318]

Whether or not structural measures can aptly eliminate a data protection concern posed by a digital merger is contingent on the specific circumstances of the case. While divesting part of a business that is data-intensive might be an effective fix, it is highly unlikely that competition authorities will have recourse to such a stringent measure just to remedy a concern that is commonly not considered competition-related.

3.2 Behavioural remedies

As structural remedies might have important weaknesses as implemented to remedy competition concerns posed by digital mergers, quasi-structural and behavioural remedies emerge as sounder alternatives. The Commission Vice-President Vestager expressly noted that in many vertical or conglomerate mergers, 'the only alternative to behavioural or quasi-structural remedies is often to block the merger', mentioning a 'data silo' commitment (ie keeping data separated, as implemented in *Google/Fitbit*) as an example of a quasi-structural remedy fit for the digital age.[319] Open access and interoperability are other examples of remedies that might be better suited to digital mergers as compared to structural solutions.

In relation to data and data protection, the data silo remedy accepted by the Commission in *Google/Fitbit* is an excellent illustration of how competition and data protection law can display sectional coherence at a remedial stage, even though the remedy was designed to address a purely competition concern of data merging. The package of behavioural remedies in *Google/Fitbit* also garnered the

[314] Viktoria HSE Robertson, 'Merger Review in Digital and Technology Markets: Insights from National Case Law' (2022) Report for Directorate-General for Competition, para 270.

[315] ibid 271.

[316] Thomas Wilson, 'Merger Remedies—Is It Time to Go More Behavioural?' (*Kluwer Competition Law Blog*, 21 February 2021) https://competitionlawblog.kluwercompetitionlaw.com/2020/02/21/merger-remedies-is-it-time-to-go-more-behavioural/#_ftn25 accessed 5 December 2022.

[317] Martijn Snoep, 'Speech' (CRA Conference, Brussels, 10 December 2019), cited n ibid.

[318] Thomas Hoehn, 'Challenges in Designing and Implementing Remedies in Innovation Intensive Industries and the Digital Economy' in Gerard and Komninos (n 245).

[319] Margrethe Vestager, 'Defending Competition in a Digital Age' (Florence Competition Summer Conference, Florence, 24 June 2021).

approval of the vast majority of NCAs in the advisory committee meeting preceding the adoption of the Commission's decision, with only two out of fifteen NCAs voting against.[320] At the same time, Robertson noted that a remedy consisting in separating datasets has not been imposed in any national case analysed in her report,[321] which demonstrates either that data combination concerns do not emerge in national merger cases, or that NCAs are simply not ready to have recourse to this remedy that is relatively novel and requires thorough monitoring to be effective, even though the NCAs approve of it in theory. The access and behavioural remedies accepted in *Google/Fitbit* were rejected for example in Australia. The ACCC justified its decision by claiming: 'we are not satisfied that a long term behavioural undertaking of this type in such a complex and dynamic industry could be effectively monitored and enforced in Australia'.[322] In the EU, to monitor compliance with the behavioural commitments accepted in *Google/Fitbit* for the ten-year period, the Commission appointed ING Bank NV (London branch) as an independent monitoring trustee, which in turn selected the company Sentinel as a technical expert to assist with the monitoring.[323] Commenting on this assignment, Sentinel President Weller stressed the privacy dimension. As he said, '[t]here are a lot of adjacencies and skills where you may not think of being able to look at an API and understand how it works as being a core privacy skillset', adding that this 'really goes to the rise of privacy engineering as a discipline as well'.[324] All in all, it is still to be seen whether this type of complex behavioural remedy proves successful.

Instead of mandating data to be kept in silos, a similar commitment, yet less technically demanding, can take the form of a pledge not to merge data from various services. For example, in a recent Greek case involving the acquisition of four food service companies by the online food-delivery platform Delivery Hero, the platform committed to not using personal data it collected from its food-delivery (e-food) service to offer personalized advertising for its restaurant-booking (e-table) services, and vice versa, unless users consented to the practice.[325] A monitoring

[320] Gerwin Van Gerven and others, 'Data and Privacy in EU Merger Control' (2022) Global Competition Review, fn 49 <https://globalcompetitionreview.com/guide/digital-markets-guide/second-edition/article/data-and-privacy-in-eu-merger-control#footnote-014> accessed 5 December 2022.

[321] Robertson (n 314) para 273.

[322] ACCC, 'ACCC Rejects Google Behavioural Undertakings for Fitbit Acquisition' (22 December 2020) <https://www.accc.gov.au/media-release/accc-rejects-google-behavioural-undertakings-for-fitbit-acquisition> accessed 4 September 2022.

[323] Ryan Chiavetta, 'How a "Technical Expert" Factors into the Google-Fitbit Acquisition' (*IAPP*, 9 June 2021) <https://iapp.org/news/a/how-a-technical-expert-factors-into-the-google-fitbit-acquisition/> accessed 10 September 2022.

[324] ibid.

[325] *Delivery Hero/Alfa Distributions/Inkat/Delivery.gr/E*-table, Decision 775/2022 (18 April 2022); Hellenic Competition Commission, 'Press Release—the HCC approves Delivery Hero's acquisition of four companies subject to commitments' (20 April 2022) <https://www.epant.gr/en/enimerosi/press-releases/item/2189-press-release-the-hellenic-competition-commission-approves-delivery-hero-s-acquisition-of-four-companies-subject-to-commitments.html> accessed 30 August 2022.

trustee was also appointed to ensure compliance. Whereas such a purely behavioural remedy might have the same end result as a data silo if effectively monitored, a silo remedy is certainly more adequate to mitigate the risk of circumventing approved commitments. In addition to restricting the ability to process personal data from various services by a post-merged entity, the competitor- or consumer-facing behavioural remedies outlined in the previous section can also, where suitable, be part of a merger commitment package.

From a procedural standpoint, cooperation with the EDPS or DPAs should be an inherent part of the process of accepting proposed commitments where the remedy might have repercussions, positive or negative, on data protection. Any ex post evaluation of the remedies should equally involve data protection expertise.

E. Conclusions

As the analysis in this chapter has shown, sectional coherence across the competition and data protection fields brings prospects for mutually beneficial interpretations and common approaches to evolve, both from practical and theoretical perspectives, in cases involving data-related practices by technology companies. Sectional coherence through concepts (eg fairness, discrimination, power), norms and rules (eg prohibition of abuse, justification), and other legal tools (eg remedies) would offer a useful standard for compatible, potentially even combined, legal assessments.

Moving forward, the basic assumptions underpinning competition law should be verified for this legal field to become more responsive to socio-economic realities, hence an up-to-date legal instrument. How to establish consumer normative preferences and consider their multiple preference-orderings, how to approach new types of harm that materialize in digital markets and the ways they affect market structures, competitors, and individuals, and how to formulate legal responses that are future-proof and take into account possible market developments, are among the pressing matters that competition law should thoroughly reflect upon. An in-depth understanding of the present empirical phenomena and technologies is also crucial for decisions to be grounded in solid factual assessments. At the same time, envisaging future market developments needs to be an inherent part of competition analysis, particularly as competition law interventions are capable of leaving a long-lasting mark on the markets. The developmental trajectory of the online economy provides sufficient evidence that the companies operating therein tend to be one step ahead of the regulators and policy-makers. Thus, a proactive rather than a reactive approach is vital to remedy this concern.

Above all, it is key to bear in mind that any progress can only be achieved through actual enforcement. Johannes Leitenberger, Judge at the CJEU and former Director-General of the Commission's Directorate-General for Competition, stressed the need for tackling new cases to gain experience in digital markets: this should not mean rushing 'to new cases without a solid factual grounding', but rather 'when there is enough evidence, we must be ready to revisit assumptions and theories in light of new facts'.[326] Framed in more philosophical terms, 'we should not link competition law to a scholastic approach but subject it to Popper's thorough exercise of verification, falsification and then maybe confirmation'.[327]

[326] Johannes Leitenberger, 'Keynote Speech' (14th Annual Conference of the GCLC on Remedies in EU Competition Law, Brussels, 31 January 2019).
[327] ibid.

6

A Data Protection Law Perspective on Sectional Coherence

A. Introduction

Competition law, albeit having a vital role in fostering sectional coherence, is not the only building block of an effective transition towards a more synergetic approach to data protection and competition. Data protection law is competition law's counterpart in a broader effort to reach the sectional coherence objective. While the previous chapter introduced a number of substantive amendments that competition law would need to undergo to enhance coherence, the starting point in the present analysis is much more straightforward. The hypothesis is that it is effective enforcement of the extant data protection law, rather than a large-scale reform of its substantive provisions, that is vital for data protection to cohere better with competition demands (see Chapter 3 Section C). Proposals that zero in on making data protection authorities fit for purpose, converting the current enforcement system into a more centralized one, and rethinking fines and remedies, deserve attention not only because of their potential to improve data protection, but also due to their likely positive repercussions for the competitiveness of the digital economy.

While effective enforcement should thus be prioritized, there are a few substantive adjustments of data protection law in Europe that might contribute to achieving sectional coherence. This chapter discusses three such possible improvements. Section B suggests that data protection assessments should better consider market power in two specific contexts: conducting a risk analysis and performing balancing. The focus in Section C is on the notion of individual empowerment and on control-oriented mechanisms: specifically, how the approach to them should be re-examined to foster competition on data protection. Section D sheds light on the need to limit the unintended consequences of data protection law, in particular its negative spillover effects resulting in market consolidation. Concluding reflections are offered in Section E. While the substantive proposals laid out in this chapter are far from constituting a comprehensive mapping of the possible readjustments needed for data protection to positively support competition, they can be approached as a point of departure for this much-needed debate.

Coherence between Data Protection and Competition Law in Digital Markets. Klaudia Majcher, Oxford University Press.
 DOI: 10.1093/oso/9780198885610.003.0007

B. Accounting for market power in data protection assessments

It is widely acknowledged that the entrenched market power of a few technology companies—and other market transformations that are inherently linked to this phenomenon, including the emergence of digital ecosystems—creates fertile ground for data-related and other harms. In competition law, the notion of market power and how to adapt the benchmarks to measure it spark regular debate (see Chapter 5 Section B). The recent regulatory frameworks including the DMA and the DSA also reflect concern for the unprecedented power of a few technology giants.

Even though increasing economic power in digital markets has been an impetus for a few policy and regulatory revisions and developments in the EU and beyond, data protection appears to be shielding itself from the question how the interpretation of its provisions might need to be adjusted in light of the distinctive features of digital markets, in particular the extraordinary consolidation of power. In an important contribution on this topic, Lynskey noted that 'EU data protection law is ostensibly ambivalent towards data power'.[1] At the same time, however, it provides 'a clear normative nudge that such power merits particular attention'.[2] This normative cue to consider power can be detected in the legal context of defining the scope of companies' data protection obligations, as well as measuring the impact of data processing on the rights and interests of individuals.[3]

Building on this insight, this chapter explores how the 'normative nudge' in data protection law to allow for power should convert into an explicit recognition of power—as well as of the factors that contribute to power—as relevant parameters in interpreting a range of data protection provisions. The main premise, namely that there needs to be a stronger link between power and data protection requirements, aligns with the reasoning of Advocate General Bobek, for example, who noted in *Fashion ID* that 'there ought to be, perhaps not always an exact match, but at least a reasonable correlation between power, control, and responsibility'.[4] Accounting for power in data protection law would not only bring its rules closer to the empirical digital reality, enhancing their effectiveness, but also indirectly benefit competition. In line with the proposition that effective data protection can be a tool for improving market competition, it can be assumed that a competition-conscious approach to data protection can help to pre-empt the emergence of potentially anti-competitive practices.

[1] Orla Lynskey, 'Grappling with "Data Power": Normative Nudges from Data Protection and Privacy' (2019) 20 Theoretical Inquiries in Law 189, 209.
[2] ibid.
[3] ibid 200.
[4] Case C-40/17 *Fashion ID GmbH & Co KG v Verbraucherzentrale NRW eV* [2018] ECLI:EU:C:2019:629, Opinion of AG Bobek, para 91.

The subsequent proposals on how to interpret data protection law in a 'power-conscious' way focus on two types of data protection mechanisms with the greatest potential to directly incorporate the power factor: (1) the risk-based approach and (2) balancing.

1. The risk-based approach: defining the scale of obligations

The scale of several data protection obligations of data controllers is contingent upon the likelihood and severity of risks that their data processing activities pose to individual rights and freedoms. This section first outlines how the risk-based approach currently embraced in the GDPR replaced the size-based approach, and subsequently explores what role the power factor could have in establishing risk.

1.1 From reckoning with size to reckoning with risk

The early vision for the GDPR envisaged a partially asymmetrical data protection regime, which the regulator intended to achieve by relying on the size of an organization as a factor in determining its data protection obligations.[5] The proposal for a GDPR stipulated, for example, the Commission to consider specific measures for small and medium-sized enterprises (SMEs) in the context of obtaining verifiable consent for processing a child's personal data,[6] and when laying down standard forms and specifying procedures for exercising the rights of a data subject.[7] Establishing specific obligations for SMEs was also envisaged in relation to the information to be provided to the data subject,[8] the responsibility to adopt policies and appropriate measures to demonstrate compliance,[9] and the obligation to carry out a DPIA.[10] In relation to administrative sanctions, the proposal for the GDPR specified that in the case of a first and non-intentional GDPR violation, no sanctions should be imposed on an organization employing fewer than 250 persons and when data processing was only its ancillary activity.[11] Organizations with fewer than 250 employees would also not need to designate a Data Protection Officer (DPO)[12] or a Union representative.[13]

The initial idea to create an asymmetrical data protection regime based on the size of an organization was subject to severe criticism. Even though the burden that the GDPR would create for SMEs was an important consideration throughout the

5 Lynskey (n 1) 205.
6 Proposal for a GDPR, art 8(3).
7 ibid art 12(6).
8 ibid art 14(7).
9 ibid art 22(4).
10 ibid art 33(6).
11 ibid art 79(3)(b).
12 ibid art 35(1).
13 ibid art 25(2)(b).

legislative process, critical voices stated that using size as a derogation criterion would create a legal blind spot, as even small organizations might be able to process large amounts of data.[14] This was reflected in the European Parliament's draft report,[15] which introduced several changes to widen the scope of the GDPR's application. For instance, the report took issue with the exemption of SMEs from the obligation to designate a DPO. As the report noted, given that in the age of cloud computing 'even very small controllers can process large amounts of data through online services, the threshold for the mandatory designation of a data protection officer should not be based on the size of the enterprise, but rather on the relevance of data processing'.[16] Thus, the amendment suggested relying on the number of affected individuals (above 500 per year) as a factor in determining an exemption.

As a result, considering 'the specific needs of micro, small and medium-sized enterprises' is currently explicitly required in just a few of the GDPR's provisions, for example in those that relate to the drawing up of the codes of conduct (art 40) and the establishment of data protection certification mechanisms, seals, and marks (art 43). The sole provision directly stipulating that the size of a company determines the required level of compliance is Article 30 GDPR. According to this provision, organizations with fewer than 250 employees do not have to comply with the obligation to keep records of data processing, unless such processing is likely to result in a risk, the processing is not occasional, or it includes special categories of data.[17]

Despite the departure from the size-based approach, a partial asymmetry of some of the GDPR's obligations was preserved, albeit in a different form: instead of focusing on the size of an organization, the policy-maker gave more prominence to the notion of risk.[18] While the risk-based approach to data protection had existed in a more limited form in the DPD, the GDPR extended the notion of risk to other provisions.[19] As a result, a number of data protection rules currently in place, such as those governing general accountability (art 24), data protection by design and by default (art 25), security of processing (art 32), notification of a personal data breach (art 33), and DPIAs (art 35) stipulate that a risk to the rights and

[14] See Christopher Kuner, Lee A Bygrave, and Christopher Docksey, 'Background and Evolution of the EU General Data Protection Regulation (GDPR)' in Christopher Kuner, Lee A Bygrave, and Christopher Docksey (eds), *The EU General Data Protection Regulation (GDPR): A Commentary* (OUP 2020) 20; Lynskey (n 1) 206.

[15] European Parliament, 'Report on the proposal for a regulation of the European Parliament and of the Council on the protection of individual with regard to the processing of personal data and on the free movement of such data (General Data Protection Regulation)' (2013).

[16] ibid.

[17] This provision gives effect to recital 13 of the GDPR. See also AWP29, 'Position paper on the derogations from the obligation to maintain records of processing activities pursuant to Article 30(5) GDPR' (2018).

[18] Lynskey (n 1) 207.

[19] See A29WP, 'Statement on the Role of a Risk-Based Approach in Data Protection Legal Frameworks' (2014) 2.

freedoms of natural persons needs to be considered. The practical implication is that high-risk data processing requires the implementation of stricter measures as compared to processing that poses a lower risk to the rights and freedoms of individuals. The risk-based approach is thus not a replacement of the rights-based approach, but rather 'a scalable and proportionate approach to compliance'.[20] This approach was adopted even though, as noted by Yeung and Bygrave, relying on the concept of risk for the purpose of regulating data processing may seem contradictory: while data protection has the dignitarian basis, risk assessments are usually conducted in the context of numerical assessments of the likelihood and severity of tangible harm.[21] That notwithstanding, the risk-based approach also found support in other jurisdictions. For example, the draft Data Protection and Digital Information Bill introduced in the UK in 2022 relies on the notion of risk in a number of provisions.[22]

1.2 Approximating the concepts of risk and power

The GDPR remains silent as to the specific factors that should be considered in an assessment of the likelihood and severity of the risk. Recital 76 of the GDPR notes broadly that this assessment needs to be objective and conducted 'by reference to the nature, scope, context and purposes of the processing'. Recital 75 includes a non-exhaustive list of risky data processing operations that cause 'physical, material, or non-material damage' to data subjects. Among the listed examples is data processing that deprives data subjects of their rights and freedoms or prevents them from exercising control, reveals racial or ethnic origins or political opinions, enables profiling and prediction of the economic situation, health, or personal preferences, or involves a large amount of data and affects a large number of individuals.

When looked at through a competition lens, the examples mentioned above epitomize the types of risky data processing that concentrated markets with limited contestability and featuring few powerful technological companies facilitate. Relatedly, market power inevitably has a bearing on the nature, scope, context, and purposes of personal data processing—the relevant parameters mentioned in recital 76 of the GDPR. Thus, the question arises whether data protection law that remains oblivious to the broader concerns related to the economic strength of a data controller and the market context in which it operates might result in a false negative—that is, an incorrect conclusion that a data processing operation does not pose a risk to the rights and freedoms of individuals.

[20] ibid.

[21] Karen Yeung and Lee A Bygrave, 'Demystifying the Modernized European Data Protection Regime: Cross-Disciplinary Insights from Legal and Regulatory Governance Scholarship' (2021) 16 Regulation & Governance 137, 143.

[22] Support for the risk-based approach has also been expressed in the UK: see Department for Digital, Culture, Media & Sport, 'National Data Strategy' (2020).

Conceptually, a distinction can be introduced between 'endogenous' and 'exogenous' risk factors. Factors endogenous to data processing, such as its nature, scope, and purposes, are the ones that the GDPR refers to directly in the context of establishing risks. At the same time, certain exogenous factors related to the data controller itself and the broader market setting in which it operates could undoubtedly influence both the likelihood and severity of a risk in a data protection sense. It can therefore be suggested that such factors should be recognized as equally relevant in establishing risk and, relatedly, companies' data protection obligations. While certain exogenous factors might be reflected indirectly in the analysis of the endogenous ones (eg market power can translate into a wide scope of data processing), an explicit reflection on exogenous risk factors would minimize the likelihood of legal blind spots rendering the outcome of a data protection risk assessment inaccurate. To ascertain which exogenous risk factors to incorporate in a risk analysis, data protection law can learn from the extensive enforcement experience in the area of competition law and the academic debates on market power, as well as from the emerging competition discourse on new phenomena that facilitate power (eg digital ecosystems). In other words, market power and related factors can serve as proxies for risk for the purpose of applying the GDPR. Greater engagement of data protection law with exogenous risk factors would make the data protection notion of risk analogous—or at least closer—to that of the 'special responsibility' of a dominant undertaking, which is the premise embraced in the competition law area of abuse of a dominant position. While in competition law powerful firms have a special responsibility not to distort competition, data protection law would extend their special responsibility to the protection of the rights and freedoms of individuals.[23] The very fact that data processing by powerful undertakings makes the protection regime fragile (eg it almost inevitably creates prominent power asymmetries between organizations and data subjects), justifies the imposition of strengthened the data protection obligations for such organizations.

By way of comparison, the distinction between the endogenous and exogenous risk factors introduced here is somewhat comparable to the logic underlying Mantelero's discussion of the risk assessment requirement under the DSA.[24] While the risk assessment requirements embraced by the GDPR and the DSA diverge in several notable respects (eg the DSA is a size-based regulation and embraces several categories of risk), the lack of explicit recognition of the relevance of exogenous factors in establishing risk is a unifying characteristic. Commenting on

[23] For a discussion on how the concept of 'special responsibility' could be integrated into consumer protection and data protection law, see Inge Graef and Sean Van Berlo, 'Towards Smarter Regulation in the Areas of Competition, Data Protection and Consumer Law: Why Greater Power Should Come with Greater Responsibility' (2021) 12 European Journal of Risk Regulation 674.

[24] Alessandro Mantelero, Fundamental Rights Impact Assessment in the DSA' in Joris von Hoboken and others (eds), *Putting the Digital Services Act into Practice: Enforcement, Access to Justice, and Global Implications* (Varfassungsbooks 2023).

the DSA, Mantelero suggested that an analysis of risk should include 'contextual elements other than the features of the system'.[25] As he explained, 'the prejudice to fundamental rights is not limited to the design and functioning of platforms, but also concerns the context in which a given system is used'.[26]

On a final note, a short observation on the interpretation of the very notion of risk is warranted. While the 'role' of the risk-based approach, namely ensuring effective compliance with the data protection principles enshrined in Article 5(1),[27] is relatively clear, the 'type' of risk has spurred discussions. For example, while Demetzou maintained that the concept of risk is broad in scope and relates to the rights and freedoms of natural persons,[28] Gellert expressed support for approaching it as a 'non-compliance' risk.[29] If one follows the literal wording of the GDPR—one that indicates the risk 'to the rights and freedoms of natural persons' as suggested by Demetzou—the relevance of scrutinizing market power in order to establish risk becomes blatantly obvious. This broad formulation suggest that not only the risk to data protection is at stake, but also to other rights and freedoms, which may include freedom of expression or the right to non-discrimination. As Chapter 5 analysed in more detail, data power has implications that go well beyond economic harm and may affect individuals in multifaceted ways, including when they act as participants of democracy, for example. As taking a position in this polemic is not this section's objective, it is sufficient to note that the market power of companies would be a relevant risk indicator irrespective of which of the two previously mentioned types of risk is accepted as an accurate understanding of risk in data protection law.

2. Balancing: measuring the scope of interference

Balancing—a method used to weigh conflicting interests and rights—is the cornerstone of data protection law and underlies a range of key concepts that span the GDPR, including fairness and proportionality.[30] Yet, despite being a commonly recognized tool both in the context of the EU Charter as well as under the GDPR,

[25] ibid 113.

[26] ibid.

[27] Katerina Demetzou, 'Risk to the "Rights and Freedoms": A Legal Interpretation of the Scope of Risk under the GDPR' in Dara Hallinan and others (eds), *Data Protection and Privacy*, vol 12 (Bloomsbury Publishing 2021) 139.

[28] ibid 138.

[29] Raphaël Gellert, 'Why the GDPR Risk-Based Approach Is about Compliance Risk, and Why It's Not a Bad Thing' in Erich Schweighofer, Franz Kummer, and Christoph Sorge (eds), *Trends and Communities of Legal Informatics, Proceedings of the 20th International Legal Informatics Symposium* (Austrian Computer Society 2017).

[30] Jeff Ausloos, 'Balancing in the GDPR: Legitimate Interests v. Right to Object' (*CiTiP*, 2017) <https://www.law.kuleuven.be/citip/blog/balancing-in-the-gdpr-legitimate-interests-v-right-to-object/> accessed 26 September 2022.

the legal principle of balancing is as such 'too vague to offer sufficient guarantees of rationality, objectivity, transparency and legal theoretical coherence',[31] as scholars have noted. It therefore needs other tools to clarify how the balancing should be performed, as otherwise intuition, obscurity, and subjectivity might creep in.[32]

One such tool that may help to interpret data protection provisions in a sounder manner is the notion of power. Authors have already noted that power might be a determinative, or at least an impactful, factor in data protection assessments. Having distinguished between the procedural and substantive balancing—the former being 'the construction/mechanics of the balance itself, and the latter relating to 'the actual content in each of the scales'—Ausloos noted that one must pay particular attention to the procedural aspects, especially where strong power asymmetries mean that one party controls the operation of the balance.[33] Referring to Gutwirth, Ausloos stressed that it is precisely the role of data protection law to mitigate undesirable power imbalances, which continue to grow dramatically, and to advance the position of individuals vis-à-vis ever-powerful data controllers.[34]

In discussing the role of power in data protection-related balancing, this section centres on balancing in the context of establishing a valid legal basis, zooming in on legitimate interest and consent. It should, however, be noted that there are also other GDPR provisions that embrace the balancing method either explicitly or implicitly. One example is Article 21(1) GDPR which lays down the right to object: the controller should no longer process the data unless it 'demonstrates compelling legitimate grounds for the processing which override the interests, rights and freedoms of the data subject'. Thus, some of the rationale behind considering power presented in this section can be extended to other instances of data protection balancing.

2.1 Balancing and data protection legal bases

To be lawful, data protection needs to be based on one of the six legal bases set out in Article 6(1) GDPR: consent of the data subject (art 6(1)(a)), performance of a contract (art 6(1)(b)), legal obligation of the controller (art 6(1)(c)), necessity to protect the vital interests of the data subject (art 6(1)(d)), necessity to perform a task carried out in the public interest or the exercise of official authority (art 6(1)(e)), or the legitimate interest of the controller (art 6(1)(f)). The logic underpinning all these legal bases is balancing between individuals' rights and interests on the one hand, and the interests of data controllers on the other. Although balancing

[31] Christina Angelopoulos, 'European Intermediary Liability in Copyright: A Tort-Based Analysis' (PhD Thesis, University of Amsterdam 2016) 284 <https://dare.uva.nl/search?identifier=a406e67d-b537-49ae-9f46-80e831b988d4> cited in Jeff Ausloos, *The Right to Erasure in EU Data Protection Law. From Individual Rights to Effective Protection* (OUP 2020) 278.

[32] ibid.

[33] Ausloos (n 31) 278–79.

[34] ibid 293.

is explicitly required only when an organization relies on the legitimate interest basis, other legal bases represent instances where the interest in data processing 'prevails by default'.[35] In light of the entrenched power of a few technology companies, the urgent question that emerges is whether explicit balancing required in the context of establishing a legitimate interest, as well as the default premise that the controller's interest prevails in the context of the remaining legal bases, should be re-examined to better reflect data power. This is a pertinent normative issue, as data power may result in a greater scope of interference with the rights and freedoms of individuals.

2.2 Legitimate interest

Article 6(1)(f) GDPR stipulates that data processing is permitted if it is necessary for the purposes of the controller's or third party's legitimate interests except where those interests 'are overridden by the interests or fundamental rights and freedoms of the data subject which require protection of personal data, in particular where the data subject is a child'.[36]

In practice, the test requires a three-step assessment: (1) the legitimacy of the data controller's interest and the necessity and proportionality of the data processing; (2) the impact on the interests or rights of the data subject; and (3) balancing.[37] As regards the interest of controllers that can be considered legitimate, examples in recital 47 of the GDPR include data processing for the purpose of preventing fraud or for direct marketing purposes, the latter arguably falling under the scope of the right to conduct business. As observed by Kotschy, the rights and freedoms recognized in the EU Charter are 'potential sources of legitimate interests'.[38] As the impacts on data subjects that need to be evaluated next relate to a wide range of their rights and interest, individuals enjoy, at least in theory, extensive protection.[39] Finally, a balancing test needs to be performed between the opposing interests of the controller and the data subject. In this context, A29WP noted that while profiling can be based on a legitimate interest, relying on this ground may be difficult to justify if the controller embarks on 'intrusive profiling and tracking practices for marketing or advertising purposes' (eg tracking individuals across various websites, locations, devices, or services), as the balancing would

[35] Ausloos (n 30).

[36] For a critical analysis of the legitimate interest legal ground, see eg Federico Ferretti, 'Data Protection and the Legitimate Interest of Data Controllers: Much Ado about Nothing or the Winter of Rights?' (2014) 51 Common Market Law Review 843.

[37] See eg A29WP, 'Opinion 06/2014 on the notion of legitimate interests of the data controller under Article 7 of Directive 95/46/EC' (2014) 29–30; Irene Kamara and Paul De Hert, 'Understanding the Balancing Act Behind the Legitimate Interest of the Controller Ground: A Pragmatic Approach' (2018) 4 Brussels Privacy Hub 5.

[38] Waltraut Kotschy, 'Article 6. Lawfulness of Processing' in Kuner, Bygrave, and Docksey (n 14) 337.

[39] ibid 338.

in this case tilt towards the data subject.[40] In performing balancing, due account should be taken of the safeguards implemented by the controller to reduce the impact on the data subject.[41]

The second step—measuring the impacts on the rights and interest of data subjects—is one where the consideration of data power should arguably play a role in order to accurately envisage such consequences. Already in its 2014 Opinion on the legitimate interest basis in the DPD, which can be relied on in interpreting the GDPR, A29WP had noted that in order to assess the potential or actual impacts on the data subject, the status of the data controller should be scrutinized alongside other factors such as the nature of the data, the means of processing it, the data subject's reasonable expectations, and the status of a data subject.[42] It is revealing that this Opinion also invoked the concepts of dominance and power.[43] Thus, what counts as relevant are the dominant firm's resources and negotiating power vis-à-vis the data subject, which gives it the possibility to impose on that individual what it believes to be its legitimate interest. As A29WP noted, '[j]ust as consumer protection and competition laws ensure that this power will not be misused, data protection law could also play an important role in ensuring that the rights and interest of the data subjects will not be unduly prejudiced'.[44] Competition law could thus prove to be a useful point of reference for the purpose of establishing power in the context of investigating the lawfulness of data processing. If, (partially) due to its power, a dominant or an otherwise powerful organization cannot rely on the legitimate interest legal basis to justify its processing, that can also have positive repercussions in a competition sense as it might pre-empt potentially harmful practices and strengthen sectional coherence between the two legal fields. Even though a company could still rely on another legal basis, at least the legitimate interest ground would not provide a possible avenue.

A29WP also opined that the analysis of the impacts under Article 6(1)(f) GDPR is akin to a traditional risk assessment (ie the likelihood and severity of risk). This assertion reinforces the argument made in Section 1, namely that the status of a data controller and its power should also be taken into account, *mutatis mutandis*, in a data protection assessment of risk.

From an enforcement perspective, *Google Spain* is a noteworthy case in this respect. To assess whether the legitimate interest was a justified legal ground for Google's data processing activities, the CJEU carried out a balancing exercise, noting that the effect of the interference with the rights to privacy and data

[40] A29WP, 'Guidelines on Automated individual decision-making and Profiling for the purposes of Regulation 2016/679' (2018) 14–15.

[41] See A29WP (n 37) 31.

[42] ibid 36. See also Paolo Balboni and others, 'Legitimate Interest of the Data Controller New Data Protection Paradigm: Legitimacy Grounded on Appropriate Protection' (2013) 3 International Data Privacy Law 244, 147, cited in Kamara and De Hert (n 37) 9.

[43] A29WP (n 37) 40.

[44] ibid.

protection of data subjects 'is heightened on account of the important role played by the internet and search engines in modern society, which render the information contained in such a list of results ubiquitous'.[45] Given the gravity of the interference caused by Google's data processing, the CJEU judged that it 'cannot be justified by merely the economic interest which the operator of such an engine has in that processing'.[46] Although the case does not make explicit reference to the notions of dominance or power, it implies that asymmetrical relationships created by economic power can tilt the balance towards a data subject. In her comment on the case, Lynskey noted that 'the harm suffered by an individual would be greater when her name is entered into Google Search than into DuckDuckGo given the significantly higher number of users of the former'.[47]

While it can thus be safely stated that in many cases the impacts on data subjects may be more likely and severe when their personal data is processed by an organization with power, the crux of the issue is to ensure that this factor is properly considered in day-to-day assessments. Conducting a balancing test for the purpose of relying on the legitimate interest basis is the task of a data controller, and the only way to know whether the controller has in fact conducted the balancing is to challenge it in court.[48] Thus, the EDPS, for example, ideally in consultation with the Commission's Directorate-General for Competition, could issue guidance on how the power factor should be reckoned with in assessments of the impacts of data processing on the rights and interests of data subjects. A set of presumptions could even be developed to ensure more clarity. Any such presumptions should, however, take into consideration the contextual nature of the balancing exercise in data protection. As the CJEU stressed in *Rīgas*, 'balancing the opposing rights and interests ... depends in principle on the specific circumstances of the particular case'.[49]

2.3 Consent

According to Article 6(1)(a) GDPR, data processing should be deemed lawful if the data subject has given consent to the processing of their data for one or more specific purposes. To be compatible with the GDPR's requirements laid down in Article 4(11), consent through which data subjects indicate their wishes needs to be freely given, specific, informed, and unambiguous, and should take the form of a statement or clear affirmative action.

[45] Case C-131/12 *Google Spain SL, Google Inc v Agencia Española de Protección de Datos (AEPD), Mario Costeja Gonzalez* [2014] ECLI:EU:C:2014:317, para 80.

[46] ibid para 81.

[47] Lynskey (n 1) 208.

[48] Bits of Freedom, 'Why the "Legitimate Interest" Test Fails to Protect the Interests of Users and the Regulation Needs to Be Amended' (2011) Section 4 <https://www.bof.nl/live/wp-content/uploads/20121211_ onderzoek_legitimate-interests-def.pdf> accessed 3 December 2022; cited in Kamara and De Hert (n 37) 9.

[49] Case C-13/16 *Valsts policijas Rīgas reģiona pārvaldes Kārtības policijas pārvalde v Rīgas pašvaldības SIA 'Rīgas satiks* [2017] ECLI:EU:C:2017:336, para 31.

As mentioned in the introductory remarks, to rely on consent as a legal basis, it is not mandatory to conduct any explicit balancing between the interests of the data controller and the interests and rights of the individual. Yet, the balancing is implicit: if all the conditions for consent indicated in the GDPR are satisfied, the balance tilts by default towards the interest in data processing.[50] This prompts the question whether the conditions for valid consent that should guarantee a fair outcome of the balancing are achievable when a data subject is in a highly asymmetrical relationship with a powerful technology company. While such a power imbalance may affect all the conditions for valid consent—free, specific, informed, and unambiguous—one that goes to the core of the issue is the 'freedom' of consent. Thus, the normative questions in the spotlight of this section are the following: can consent be considered free if an individual is in an asymmetrical power relationship, especially with an undertaking that has a dominant position in the market? If yes, when? This legal puzzle underpins a broader discussion on the interconnections between the competition law notion of power and the data protection law concept of freedom.

Recital 43 of the GDPR notes that consent cannot be freely given 'where there is a clear imbalance between the data subject and the controller', the imbalance at issue being one of power.[51] As repeatedly stressed by A29WP, data subjects need to have a real choice, and there must be 'no risk of deception, coercion or significant negative consequences if he/she does not consent'.[52] Any pressure, compulsion, or a limited ability to exercise free will directly contradict the idea of freedom in the context of consent.[53] Examples of power imbalances provided in the GDPR and by AWP29 include situations where the controller is a public authority[54] or an employer.[55] In addition, and importantly, Article 7(4) and recital 43 of the GDPR address the instances of 'bundling/'tying': the former indicates that in establishing freedom of consent, 'utmost account' should be taken of whether the contract's performance (eg the provision of a service) is conditional on consent to the processing of data that is not needed for the performance of that contract.

In discussing the relationship between the freedom of consent and power, it is thus useful to distinguish between two scenarios: where (1) consent is the condition for a service and (2) the conditionality is not present in relation to consent.

[50] See also Serge Gutwirth, 'Short Statement about the Role of Consent in the European Data Protection Directive' (2012) <http://works.bepress.com/serge_gutwirth/80/> accessed 1 October 2022.

[51] Lee A Bygrave and Luca Tosini, 'Article 4(11). Consent' in Kuner, Bygrave, and Docksey (n 14) 182.

[52] A29WP, 'Opinion 15/2011 on the definition of consent' (2011) 12. See also AWP29, 'Guidelines on consent under Regulation 2016/679' (2018) 7.

[53] AWP29, 'Guidelines on consent under Regulation 2016/679' (n 52) 7.

[54] GDPR, recital 43.

[55] AWP29, 'Guidelines on consent under Regulation 2016/679' (n 52) 7.

2.3.1 Consent as the condition for a service

The first scenario can be illustrated by reference to the German *Facebook* case,[56] which, as Fox and Baschenhof observed, 'is a good example of law protecting the vulnerable from the powerful in the digital economy'.[57] At the core of the case was the legality of Facebook's terms of use to which individuals had to agree in order to use the service: specifically, these terms required users to consent to Facebook's intrusive data processing activities (ie combining Facebook data with the data from other Facebook's services such as WhatsApp and Instagram, and from third-party websites). As the provision of Facebook's services was conditional on consenting to the data processing, the only choice left for users was to agree to Facebook's intrusive data policy, or otherwise refrain from using Facebook. Importantly, the data processing that users had to consent to was not necessary for the provision of Facebook's service.

In its decision, the Bundeskartellamt ruled that the consent obtained by Facebook to its comprehensive data processing was not free, this lack of freedom being causally related to Facebook's dominant position.[58] Largely agreeing with the Bundeskartellamt's conclusion, the German Federal Court of Justice noted that given that no alternative providers of social media existed, the decision of consumers to use Facebook 'can only be considered autonomous to the extent that *they are able to dispense with the use of a service that is non-essential*'.[59] This was not the case here, as Facebook's communication service is, for some consumers, 'to a significant extent decisive for their participation in social life and has particular relevance for the public debate on political, social, cultural and economic issue'.[60] For all these reasons, a dominant company with an essential function has, in the view of the German Federal Court of Justice, '*a special responsibility* with regard to the right to informational self-determination when laying down the terms and conditions for the use of its platform'.[61]

On the basis of the reasoning outlined in the German court's decision, one can formulate a 'power–freedom test'. It appears that four cumulative criteria would need to be satisfied to conclude that consent is not free, hence potentially illegal, from a competition perspective: (1) the data controller has a dominant market position; (2) it provides an essential service; (3) the provision of its service is conditional on consent; and (4) the data subject is required to consent to data processing

[56] Bundeskartellamt, Decision B6-22/16 of February 2019 (*Facebook*).

[57] Eleanor M Fox and Philipp Baschenhof, 'History of (In)Equality in Competition Law and Its Guide to the Future' in Jan Broulik and Kati Cseres (eds), *Competition Law and Economic Inequality* (Hart Publishing 2022) 112.

[58] ibid.

[59] BGH, Beschluss vom 23.06.20—*KVR 69/19*, para 102 (emphasis added). The quotes are from the unofficial translation of the case provided by the Bundeskartellamt: 'Courtesy translation of Decision KVR 69/19 rendered by the Bundesgerichtshof (Federal Court of Justice) on 23/06/2020 provided by the Bundeskartellamt' (2020).

[60] BGH (n 59) para 124.

[61] ibid (emphasis added).

that is not necessary for the provision of the service. While criteria (3) and (4) are straightforward and have been commented on in the context of Article 7(4) and recital 43 of the GDPR, the first two requirements that can be inferred from the reasoning of the German Federal Court of Justice are noteworthy and merit a short analysis.

Where consent is the condition for a service, the aim of the criteria of 'dominance' and 'the essential nature of the service' is to prevent a situation in which an individual who refuses to consent to an unfair bargain, and as a result is denied access to the essential service, does not have any 'fall back' option. Framed differently, if a service (eg a social network) is essential, the problem arises when a refusal to give consent to a dominant data controller that provides it leads to the inability to use such essential service. Thus, at stake are not any power asymmetries, but rather asymmetries that result in a high level of dependency on a given service. Bietti noted that freedom of consent implies 'that there must be *at least one viable and morally acceptable alternative* in the form of a viable option to walk away'.[62] The idea of 'free will', which is a dimension of control that the mechanism of consent must guarantee, should encompass 'the freedom to do otherwise'.[63] Walking away is not, however, a viable choice in a market monopolized by a powerful firm. Criteria (1) and (2) should be thus interpreted in light of their objective to ensure that not using a specific service is a sound alternative, in particular because other options exist. As regards the criterion of dominance, competition parameters for establishing market power can be of assistance. The requirement that the service needs to be essential in nature (at least for some users) would need to be further clarified to be of practical relevance.

How does this power–freedom competition law test square with the presumption of illegality laid down in Article 7(4) in conjunction with recital 43 of the GDPR? And is this test of use in data protection law? As mentioned, these GDPR provisions already contain the presumption that the consent to unnecessary data processing is not free where it is the condition of a service. On the one hand, the power–freedom test seems therefore to be more stringent than the GDPR in that it stipulates two additional criteria, namely dominance and the essential nature of the service provided, for the consent to be considered not free and arguably illegal from a competition perspective. On the other hand, the problem with the presumption of illegality laid down in the GDPR is precisely that it is formulated as a presumption that can in theory be rebutted. As mentioned by Advocate General Szpunar in *Planet49*, the prohibition laid down in Article 7(4) GDPR 'is not absolute in

[62] Elettra Bietti, 'The Discourse of Control and Consent over Data in EU Data Protection Law and Beyond' (2020) Stanford University Aegis Paper Series No 2001, 323.

[63] Stanford Encyclopedia of Philosophy, 'Free Will' <https://plato.stanford.edu/entries/freewill/> accessed 2 October 2022.

nature'.[64] Thus, the GDPR does not 'fully and utterly' prohibit the practice, as Kosta explained,[65] even though rebutting the presumption of its illegality would in the view of A29WP be 'highly exceptional'.[66] Even if possible only in exceptional instances, a rebuttal is an option. The power–freedom test, on the other hand, if it is formulated in strictly prohibitory terms—that is, implying that if all its conditions are cumulatively met, then the consent is not free, and the conclusion cannot be rebutted—would arguably provide better protection of personal data as compared to the GDPR's presumption contained in Article 7(4). It could even be relied on in a data protection assessment of consent in the context of monopolized markets.

2.3.2 The conditionality is not present in the context of consent

Even in situations where consent is not tied to the provision of a service, the power of data controllers might need to be scrutinized in assessing freedom of consent. One of the questions referred to the CJEU by the Higher Regional Court of Düsseldorf in *Facebook* sought clarity on this issue. The court asked: 'Can consent within the meaning of Article 6(1)(a) and Article 9(2)(a) of the GDPR be given effectively and, in accordance with Article 4(11) of the GDPR in particular, freely, to a dominant undertaking such as Facebook Ireland?'[67]

Even though the context of the preliminary reference is the *Facebook* case where the consent was the condition for the service, the question asked of the CJEU is formulated in a more encompassing way—and so is the Opinion of Advocate General Rantos in the case.[68] It thus seems correct to reflect on the remarks of the Advocate General in the present section that explores the relevance of power where consent is not a condition to obtain access to a service.

While the judgment in this preliminary reference case is yet to be delivered, Advocate General Rantos rendered an Opinion dealing with the interface of data protection and competition law. Explaining the link between freedom of consent and a dominant position, he asserted that 'any dominant position on the market held by a personal data controller operating a social network *is a factor* when assessing whether users of that network have given their consent freely'.[69] Market power, as he noted, could result in a 'clear imbalance' of power between a data subject and a controller.[70] Yet, for the market power factor to be relevant under the GDPR, 'it need not necessarily be regarded as a dominant position within the

[64] Case C-673/17 *Bundesverband der Verbraucherzentralen und Verbraucherverbände—Verbraucherzentrale Bundesverband eV v Planet49 GmbH* [2019] ECLI:EU:C:2019:246, Opinion of AG Szpunar, para 98.

[65] Eleni Kosta, 'Conditions for Consent' in Kuner, Bygrave, and Docksey (n 14) 352.

[66] AWP29, 'Guidelines on consent under Regulation 2016/679' (n 52) 9.

[67] Case-252/21 *Meta Platforms and Others v Bundeskartellamt* [2021] Request for a preliminary ruling from the Oberlandesgericht Düsseldorf (Germany) [2021] OJ C320/16.

[68] Case 252/21 *Meta Platforms and Others v Bundeskartellamt* [2022] ECLI:EU:C:2022:704, Opinion of AG Rantos.

[69] ibid para 75 (emphasis added).

[70] ibid.

meaning of Article 102 TFEU'.[71] At the same time, the mere fact that a company has a dominant position 'cannot, on its own, render invalid the consent'[72] of a data subject, and the validity of consent has to be assessed on a case-by-case basis and in light of other factors.

Two points made by Advocate General Rantos deserve further comment. First, he maintained that market power is a factor to be taken into account while performing an analysis of the consent's validity, even when a company does not have a dominant position in a competition law sense. In other words, the degree of market power able to create power asymmetries problematic from the perspective of data protection law can be lower as compared to the degree of power needed for a dominant position to arise under competition law. It is a sound conclusion, in particular given that the finding of dominance in the context of Article 102 TFEU is not straightforward. Importantly, however, the nature of power that shall be taken into account in a data protection assessment of the freedom of consent slightly differs from the type of power that is at stake in competition assessments: while the former is concerned with individuals being able to freely express their will, the latter concentrates on power that makes it possible for companies to behave independently from their competitors, customers, and consumers. While these two types of power might overlap in a significant number of instances, thus data protection authorities may 'borrow' certain assessment benchmarks used to establish power under competition law, it will be of utmost importance for data protection law to thoroughly reflect on and propose its own parameters to measure data protection-relevant power.

The second central point made by the Advocate General is that the finding of a dominant position cannot alone trigger the conclusion that the consent is not freely given. Other circumstances of the case would need to be examined for such a finding to be justified. While determining the exact extent to which dominance should play a role in the assessment of the freedom dimension of consent requires further research, and constitutes a case-by-case analysis, it would be unwarranted not to give the fact of dominance appropriate weight.

To conclude, it is indisputable that the premise of consent lies in allowing individuals to act with free will. Advocate General Szpunar stressed that consent enables choice relating to the use and processing of personal data and 'at the same time protects [the data subject] in situations which are by their very nature asymmetrical'.[73] Some scholars have expressed that 'notice and consent normalizes platform power, operating as a discourse of control which subtly burdens users with intractable governance responsibilities without empowering them', and

[71] ibid.
[72] ibid para 77.
[73] Case C-61/19 *Orange România SA v Autoritatea Națională de Supraveghere a Prelucrării Datelor cu Caracter Personal (ANSPDCP)* [2020] ECLI:EU:C:2020:901, para 37.

that consent, which 'acts as a free pass for corporate action', should be replaced with other tools.[74] This section has proposed a less radical path forward: to live up to its promise, the mechanism of consent—and in particular the requirement of freedom—must reflect the power structures in concentrated digital markets. Having so asserted, Section C presents a more critical view of the very idea of control and the related notion of empowerment.

C. Stimulating competition on data protection: beyond individual empowerment

The previous section pivoted around the question how the competition law concept of power can be streamlined more directly into a number of data protection assessments. The nature of the problem examined in this section is different, and somewhat broader. Instead of asking how data protection can play a role in promoting competition, it embraces a more normative take on competition, and explores how data protection can promote a specific type of competition, namely competition on data protection. With that aim, it investigates whether this can be achieved through the control-oriented mechanisms of data protection, or whether more responsibility should be placed on data controllers and data protection enforcers to create incentives for organizations to more fiercely compete on the parameter of data protection.

1. The empowerment ideal

Promoting individual empowerment is an important touchpoint for data protection and competition law, as Chapter 2 Section B illustrated. To briefly recall the essence of that argument, it can be claimed that, if effective, individual empowerment that underpins data protection law in the EU translates into consumer sovereignty, ideally resulting in greater control over their market choices. Revealed preferences, including those that concern data protection, can indeed provide an impetus for market competition—and it is then the role of competition law to promote such competition. If competitive markets satisfy the wishes of individuals, and the law corrects potential failures, this mechanism improves consumer welfare in a competition sense. To take the example of consent, if it is freely given, specific, informed, and unambiguous, it can be a tool for stimulating competition for market offers that individuals consciously approve of and support. A number of individual rights enshrined in the GDPR (eg the right to obtain information, the right to data

[74] Elettra Bietti, 'Consent as a Free Pass: Platform Power and the Limits of the Informational Turn' (2020) 40 Pace Law Review 310, 386.

portability, the right to object) may have a similar effect. Insofar as by exercising these rights data subjects effectively express their normative preferences—and as long as their preferences stimulate a market response—data protection and competition work hand in hand. Naturally, not all control-oriented rights and data protection provisions are equally pertinent to make data protection and competition law more coherent. For example, the right to erasure or the right to be forgotten are in that sense less relevant as compared to the right to data portability or the right to an explanation of automatic decision making. What is of essence is that the control tools allow data subjects to express their approval of or dissatisfaction with a product or service.

Despite shaping the data protection legal landscape, the control-oriented approach to data protection and its effectiveness in ensuring individuals' rights continues to be challenged, however.[75] Foreshadowing the challenge of grounding data protection law in the concept of control, van der Sloot asked in his 2014 article: 'How could . . . a model of control be practically effected and applied to information? Is such a model feasible given the developments of Big Data and group profiling? Would an individual right to control provide the individual with any protection in a realistic sense?'[76] Almost a decade later, these questions are as resounding as they were back then. The ideal of control and self-determination on the one hand, and the ability of individuals to understand how their data is processed in complex modern markets and how they can effectively exercise their rights on the other hand, are often in tension.[77] Deep power asymmetries prevalent in the digital economy display the struggle that achieving true individual empowerment certainly entails.

When looked at from a competition perspective—the lens adopted in this section—investing efforts into promoting control under data protection would in theory resonate strongly and positively with competition law as we know it, as already explained. Empowering a vast majority of individuals would help to mitigate the scale-related risk: isolated instances of using data protection control mechanisms or invoking the control-oriented rights by data subjects, while beneficial from a data protection perspective, would probably not be capable of creating enough impetus for the markets to respond.

Upon closer examination of how control in a data protection sense and unrestricted freedom to choose coalesce into an empowerment paradigm that stimulates competition, a conundrum emerges, however, as to what this paradigm might

[75] See eg W Hartzog, 'The Case Against Idealising Control' (2018) 4 European Data Protection Law Review 423.

[76] Bart van der Sloot, 'Do Data Protection Rules Protect the Individual and Should They? An Assessment of the Proposed General Data Protection Regulation' (2014) 4 International Data Privacy Law 307, 324.

[77] Michèle Finck, 'The Limits of the GDPR in the Personalisation Context' (2021) Max Planck Institute for Innovation & Competition Research Paper No 21-11.

mean for the 'type' of competition in digital markets. The question 'How can data protection control be strengthened to facilitate market empowerment?', which has been flagged so far as relevant from a coherence perspective, differs from the more normative question 'Is such enhanced control desired if the objective is to encourage competition "to the top" on data protection?' The latter question deserves further reflection.

2. Beyond individual empowerment: stimulating competition 'to the top'?

If sufficient in scale, and facilitating the process of revealing data subjects' normative preferences, the use of the data protection control-oriented tools can be expected to stimulate market competition, enhancing the well-being of individuals in a way consistent with both data protection and competition law. However, the premise behind individual empowerment does not assume any preference for the type of choices made by data subjects: what matters is that they are in control, not that they select the most data protective options. Similarly, competition law is typically not concerned with how beneficial the choices made by consumers are for them. In this sense, data protection and competition law converge in their approach of not 'judging' how individuals decide to employ control mechanisms and use their freedom to choose. There is thus no guarantee that, if the market responds, competition 'to the top' in a data protection sense will ensue. Indeed, assuming that there is market choice, some consumers might prefer to continue to use a specific provider, even if they discover, for example through relying on their right to data access, that their data is handled in an exploitative manner. The data protection preferences of individuals differ, as does their ability to understand and act upon the consequences of various aspects of data processing.

To further this section's argument, the two following parts reflect more comprehensively on the individualistic dimension of data protection, and how fostering its collective dimension would instead not only benefit data protection, but could also be of value for promoting competition on data protection.

2.1 The weakness of the individualistic dimension of data protection

Individualism that underlies the ideal of empowerment is currently a matter of debate among data protection experts. This debate increasingly reveals the potential flaws of the control paradigm that go beyond the fact that genuine control might not be achievable in the digital environment. Before presenting this critical perspective, the right to an explanation will first be discussed to offer an illustration of how individualism might be reflected in the data subject's use of this right.

2.1.1 The right to explanation as an illustration

The right to an explanation of automated decision making has emerged as a potentially effective mechanism of empowerment and control. It can, at least in theory, stimulate informed decision making by data subjects, as well as improved accountability and transparency of algorithms.

The right to an explanation may stem from four of the GDPR's provisions: the requirement to implement safeguards under Article 22(3), the obligation to provide information under Articles 13(2)(f) and 14(2)(f), and the right of access under Article 15(1)(h). As regards the first legal basis, Article 22(1) GDPR introduces the right of individuals not to be subjected to a decision that is based on automated processing, in case such a decision produces legal, or other significant, effects concerning them. Article 22(3) GDPR lists three exceptions, noting that such automated decision making is permitted if it is necessary to enter into or perform a contract, if it is authorized by EU or Member State law, or when it is explicitly consented to. In the event that one of these exceptions exists, Article 22(3), from which the right to an explanation can be inferred, gives data subjects the right 'to obtain human intervention on the part of the controller, to express his or her point of view and to contest the decision'. Recital 71 which explains Article 22 GDPR explicitly envisages the right 'to obtain an explanation of the decision reached'.

The set of provisions that constitute another possible basis for the right to an explanation are Articles 13(2)(f) and 14(2)(f) GDPR. They require data controllers to provide data subjects with information about 'the existence of automated decision-making, including profiling . . ., meaningful information about the logic involved, as well as the significant and the envisaged consequences of such processing for the data subject'. This information is to be provided at the time when personal data is obtained.

Finally, another provision that can be claimed to form the basis for the right to an explanation is the right of access enshrined in Article 15(1)(h) GDPR, which is formulated in the same way as Articles 13(2)(f) and 14(2)(f) GDPR. The only distinguishing aspect is that the right of access that empowers individuals to obtain from companies information concerning the existence of processing, the logic involved, and the consequences of data processing, needs to be invoked, whereas Articles 13 and 14 impose an obligation on data controllers to provide individuals with that set of information. In *Rijkeboer*, Advocate General Ruiz-Jarabo Colomer, commenting on the right of access, characterized it 'the true *subjective* dimension of the directive which, in short, enables individuals to react in defence of their interests'.[78] Providing individuals with such 'micro-rights', such as a right to access, serves the objective of fostering individual control over personal data.[79]

[78] Case C-553/07 *College van burgemeester en wethouders van Rotterdam v MEE Rijkeboer* [2008] ECLI:EU:C:2008:773, Opinion of AG Ruiz-Jarabo Colomer, para 29 (emphasis added).

[79] Orla Lynskey, *The Foundations of EU Data Protection Law* (OUP 2015) 185.

Given the ambiguous wording of these provisions, it is contestable whether and how they truly empower data subjects. A scholarly disagreement surfaced, for example, as to whether the right to obtain an ex post explanation of the specific decision based on automated processing could be derived from these provisions. Wachter and others expressed scepticism, noting that the GDPR does not mandate a meaningful ex post right to an explanation,[80] thus disagreeing with Goodman and Flaxman, for example, who stated the opposite.[81] Taking sides in this polemic and ascribing to these provisions a specific interpretation—something that will be ultimately done by the Court—is not a requisite for the present analysis. More relevant is to reflect on the ultimate function of this control mechanism and its inherently individualistic underpinnings. This can be explained by reference to the idea of justice: its procedural and substantive dimension.

Justice—together with fairness—is a value frequently invoked in the algorithmic discourse. As regards the right to an explanation, the assertion can be made that equipping individuals with the right to obtain an explanation of algorithmic decision making implies assigning to them the role of 'co-administrators' of justice. At first glance, the right belongs therefore to the sphere of procedural justice: its aim is not to prescribe a specific outcome, but to empower individuals and create an opportunity for them to scrutinize the process of algorithmic decision making and to verify its fairness. The way individuals exercise that right has, however, substantive implications. In contrast to data protection outcome-oriented provisions, entrusting individuals with the administration of justice necessarily implies that they will project their own subjective conceptions of justice on the final judgement. The weight ascribed to different parameters of an algorithmic decision-making process will likely differ depending on personal beliefs. For example, whereas some might consider it fair that the decision is based on information about one's social circle, others might perceive it as unjust. This high level of subjectivity of an assessment of justice also implies that exercising the right to an explanation is likely to foster individual utility understood in terms of subjective preference-satisfaction. It thus provides the means for individuals to express their own vision of substantive justice. As others have observed, '[c]ontrol rights grant citizens the opportunity to choose their own goals to be furthered with their data'.[82] This subjectivity is inherent to other control rights too.

[80] Sandra Wachter, Brent Daniel Mittelstadt, and Luciano Floridi, 'Why a Right to Explanation of Automated Decision-Making Does Not Exist in the General Data Protection Regulation' (2017) 7 International Data Privacy Law 76.

[81] Bryce Goodman and Seth Flaxman, 'European Union Regulations on Algorithmic Decision-Making and a "Right to Explanation"' (ICML Workshop on Human Interpretability in Machine Learning, New York, June 2016).

[82] Inge Graef and Bart van der Sloot, 'Collective Data Harms at the Crossroads of Data Protection and Competition Law: Moving Beyond Individual Empowerment' (2022) 33 European Business Law Review 513, 519–20.

2.1.2 *A critical perspective*

Coming back to the criticism of the individualistic dimension of data protection law's control mechanisms, one of the grounds for it is the fact that the individualistic vision for data protection governance might not always square with the broader collective interest at stake when personal data is gathered and processed. This is particularly so given that there are noteworthy 'data externalities'. As framed by Graef and van der Sloot, 'your choices regarding the collection of your personal data have external effects on others, which you typically do not consider in decisions about the sharing of your own personal data'.[83] As the authors exemplified, sharing genetic data might reveal information about one's family and relatives. In a market and competition sense, such externalities can be described as follows: as individual choices enabled by data protection control tools (eg consent) might shape the market (eg the market responds to the preferences expressed by data subjects), individualistic conduct based on self-interest cannot guarantee that competition on data protection will follow as a result.

Even though our data protection choices have societal repercussions, data protection control-oriented provisions are individualistic in nature as they serve a self-interested individual. Data protection and privacy are as such safeguarded as individual rights, despite the fact that their rationale has a social facet.[84] As Mantelaro noted, data protection is rooted in the model of individual rights, and any collective concerns related to data protection are remedied through individual rights and their enforcement.[85] Even in discussions on group privacy, the traditional approach is grounded in an individualistic ethos, the focus being on individual data subjects as members of the group.[86] Thus, the architecture of data protection 'does not seem to be inspired by the idea of a collective, non-aggregative and super-individual interest',[87] as Mantelero concluded. This persistent reliance on the individualistic rather than the collective dimension of data protection seems ever more difficult to justify.

2.2 The promise of fostering the collective dimension of data protection

To address this criticism, suggestions have been made that a data protection regime that fosters a collective interest should be instigated in lieu of the current one that puts the spotlight on an individual. In her exposition of a relational theory of data governance, Viljoen made the following suggestion:

[83] ibid 514–15.

[84] Alessandro Mantelero, 'Personal Data for Decisional Purposes in the Age of Analytics: From an Individual to a Collective Dimension of Data Protection' (2016) 32 Computer Law & Security Review 238, 241.

[85] Alessandro Mantelero, 'From Group Privacy to Collective Privacy: Towards a New Dimension of Privacy and Data Protection in the Big Data Era' in Linnet Taylor, Luciano Floridi, and Bart van der Sloot (eds), *Group Privacy. New Challenges of Data Technologies* (Springer 2017) 143.

[86] ibid.

[87] ibid.

> The relevant task of data governance is not to reassert individual control over the terms of one's own datafication (even if this were possible) or to maximize personal gain, as leading legal approaches to data governance seek to do. Instead, the task is to develop the institutional responses necessary to represent (and adjudicate among) the relevant population-level interests at stake in data production. In other words, responding adequately to the economic imperatives and social effects of data production will require moving past proposals for individualist data-subject rights and toward theorizing the collective institutional forms required for responsible data governance.[88]

Recent research on group privacy also abandons its more established understanding of groups as the collections of the individuals and champions the collective-oriented framework. Framed differently, it starts focusing on the question how to 'move from "their" to "its" privacy with regard to the group'.[89] The centrality of user control might also not be a fair, effective, and justified policy choice, as argued by others, in particular given that the GDPR is not limited to control-centric legal provisions, but also includes other tools that could remove the burden of control from individuals and result in fairer data governance.[90] A disproportionate focus on control as a guiding notion and ideal to strive for in data governance might therefore have counter-effects, obscuring other—potentially more promising—conceptualizations of data protection.

The proposition to depart from the individualistic premise inherent in the GDPR would necessitate that data controllers and, ultimately, data protection enforcers bear a much greater responsibility for protecting personal data as compared to that which the current protection regime envisages. While both the compliance flaws and the enforcement flaws are well recognized, far more intellectual effort should be invested in reflecting on how a data governance system that does not assign to data subjects the task of control should be set up. Moving forward, Viljoen asserted that data governance 'may plausibly retrieve spheres of life from private governance and begin to develop new alternatives'.[91]

From a competition perspective, assigning a more inconsequential role to the mechanism of control—and creating instead a data protection system that functions effectively without that component—can be expected to create more incentives to compete on data protection, or at least be hoped to transform the digital economy into a more data protection-friendly space. As already indicated, competition law is by and large disinterested in whether or not choices made by

[88] Salomé Viljoen, 'A Relational Theory of Data Governance' (2021) 131 Yale Law Journal 573, 579.

[89] Linnet Taylor, Luciano Floridi, and Bart van der Sloot, 'Introduction: A New Perspective on Privacy' in Linnet Taylor, Luciano Floridi, and Bart van der Sloot (eds), *Group Privacy: New Challenges of Data Technologies* (Springer 2017) 2.

[90] Bietti (n 62) 2.

[91] Viljoen (n 88) 654.

individuals in their consumer roles benefit their own welfare. Their choices are rather assumed to do so. Even though this assumption has profound weaknesses (see Chapter 2 Section B), competition law makes important inferences from individuals' market behaviour about what collectively societies value, and, by extension, about what competition law should protect. Low prices, greater quality, better choice, and more innovation constitute a set of such inferred assumptions about the valued competition parameters. If a data protection governance system is established where these are not individual choices, but rather compliance with data protection principles and obligations is at the core, the prospect of eradicating 'toxic competition' from digital markets is far more likely.

While this section has taken a competition perspective to reflect on the desirable reorientation of data protection, a transition towards the collective dimension can also be a boon for data protection, as already mentioned. The current technological landscape is 'one where risks relating to the use of big data may play out on the collective level'.[92] As individuals are 'incidental' rather than 'central' to certain data processing activities (eg analysing data based on patterns and group profiles), preserving the established individualistic understanding of data protection carries profound risks.[93]

D. Limiting unintended competition repercussions

Data protection law generates both intended and unintended consequences for market competitiveness. Some of the negative repercussions presented by commentators might, in fact, be desirable as long as competition on data protection is stimulated as a result. Consequences such as accelerated market exit or lack of market entry for data-exploitative firms cannot be labelled as unintended data protection effects—even though they might be considered as having adverse impacts on competition for data. At the same time, if data protection law's unintended impacts take the shape of a further consolidation of power for the already large technology companies, or diminish market opportunities for smaller undertakings with innovative business models, urgent steps should be taken to remedy those effects.

A number of examples illustrate how a data protection regime such as the GDPR might entrench the power of large firms. Disproportionately higher compliance costs for small firms are a prominent concern.[94] Noteworthy also are the less evident and entirely unenvisaged impacts of the substantive rules of data protection.

92 Taylor, Floridi, and van der Sloot (n 89) 2.

93 ibid.

94 See eg Martin Brodin, 'A Framework for GDPR Compliance for Small- and Medium-Sized Enterprises' (2019) 4 European Journal for Security Research 243.

Gal and Aviv noted, for example, that consent might be more straightforward to obtain when the business model relies on internal data collection, resulting in favourable circumstances for powerful and diversified undertakings that have various internal units, such as Alphabet or Meta.[95] In addition, the fact that data subjects may be more likely to trust and give consent to companies they know—'brand effect'—might leave smaller and newer market operators at a competitive disadvantage.[96] There are also empirical studies that centre on the GDPR's impact on market structures in specific industries. Johnson and his colleagues, for example, focused on web technology (ie vendors providing support services to websites, eg raising ad revenue or measuring visitor activity), and found that the GDPR 'restricts website use of web technology vendors, while increasing the relative concentration among web technology vendors'.[97] The end result, namely the entrenched power of Google and Facebook in this market, is far from desirable.

The EU is not the only jurisdiction where the potential negative spillover effects of data protection regulation are discussed. Phillips, former FTC Commissioner, noted in his 2018 speech a few questions that the proponents of new privacy rules must ask:

> Are we willing to allow a reduction in competition or innovation? What competitive price are we willing to pay for greater privacy protection? Are we willing, for instance, to allow the biggest technology companies—lately the focal points of discussion about both privacy and competition—to entrench further?[98]

The last question in particular indicates that the potential negative competition repercussion of privacy regulations should also be seen as disturbing from a privacy angle.

Jurisdictions that reflect on or are in the process of creating their own data protection frameworks should certainly engage with such questions. Jurisdictions where data protection rules are already in place need to envisage mechanisms that mitigate certain adverse spillover effects on competition—particularly the entrenchment of incumbents, which harms both data protection and competition. As data protection law is a market-shaping instrument, it cannot be given carte blanche to facilitate certain negative market phenomena that other policies,

[95] Michal S Gal and Oshrit Aviv, 'The Competitive Effects of the GDPR' (2020) 16 Journal of Competition Law & Economics 349, 363.

[96] Noah Joshua Phillips, 'Keep It: Maintaining Competition in the Privacy Debate' (Internet Governance Forum, Washington, 27 July 2018) 8; Samuel G Goldberg, Garrett A Johnson and Scott K Shriver, 'Regulating Privacy Online: An Economic Evaluation of the GDPR' (2022) Law & Economics Center at George Mason University Scalia Law School, Research Paper Series No 22-025.

[97] Garrett A Johnson, Scott K Shriver, and Samuel G Goldberg, 'Privacy & Market Concentration: Intended & Unintended Consequences of the GDPR' (2022) <https://papers.ssrn.com/sol3/papers.cfm?abstract_id=3477686> accessed 5 October 2022.

[98] Phillips (n 96).

including competition law, might then need to rectify. The establishment of positive synergies under sectional coherence demands from data protection law the attachment of much more weight to such negative repercussions, not least because such increased attention can also be expected to yield indirect data protection benefits. Indeed, market contestability is one of the preconditions for data protection-friendly alternatives to emerge.

It is complex to envisage all the ways in which data protection frameworks such as the GDPR might be able to strengthen economic power in digital markets: many impacts are, indeed, unpredictable. A tool that would certainly aid in uncovering some of data protection law's unintended repercussions for the market structure is a sector inquiry, which competition authorities already make regular use of. Joint sector inquiries conducted by data protection and competition authorities could offer a useful way forward if sufficient resources are available. From a data protection perspective, if negative spillover effects consisting in power consolidation can then be clearly associated with specific data protection mechanisms, and can at the same time be reasonably expected to harm the rights and freedoms of individuals, it should be in data protection law's interest to find solutions to remedy such unintended consequences. Any potential solution should not, however, imperil the protection of personal data. From a data protection stance, the relevant question is thus: 'What causes a greater risk to the rights and freedoms of individuals: the spillover competition effects that facilitate market concentration, or a modified way of interpreting or enforcing certain data protection provisions or principles that are the source of such spillover effects?'

E. Conclusions

It will be seen that the ways of achieving sectional coherence outlined in this chapter differ from those presented in Chapter 5 on competition law in one major and conspicuous respect: the substantive adjustments suggested here do not require data protection law to 'bend' for the sake of protecting or promoting competition. Instead, the suggested avenues for reform—or improvement—are expected to foster competitiveness as much as they are expected to benefit the fundamental rights and freedoms of individuals. Thus, no compromise is required. The status of data protection as a fundamental human right in the EU, which normatively prevails over the economic goals of competition law as we know it, is the sole justification for this approach.

Furthermore, and relatedly, the discussion in this chapter might be subject to criticism for not sufficiently engaging with the question how to rectify the negative spillover effects that data protection has on 'competition for data', centring instead on data protection's role in fostering 'competition on data protection'. The selection of this angle is entirely intentional. One can indeed present numerous ideas for data protection principles to be weakened or done away with in order to foster a data economy. Some such ideas that might ultimately yield individual or societal benefits (eg rethinking data protection rules in the context of research) deserve to be thoroughly reflected upon. If, however, the aim of weakening the protection system is to perpetuate the current data exploitation dynamics, where what matters are companies' bottom lines, any such debate has a flawed premise. The time is ripe to redirect attention towards incentivizing a data economy grounded in respect for fundamental rights and freedoms,[99] rather than in exploiting vulnerabilities, biases, and the prevailing economic structures.

Having said that, a broader reflection that data protection law in Europe should undertake as soon as possible is how to approach—and possibly revive—its economic goal of promoting the free flow of data, not least because inattention to this objective can justifiably invite criticism as to the precise role of this explicitly stated goal of the GDPR. The internal coherence of data protection law would also benefit from a clearer exposition of how the free flow of data is presently realized, and where it should be positioned in the hierarchy of data protection law's objectives.

[99] Ezrachi and Stucke suggested creating positive and negative incentives to eradicate 'toxic innovation' in digital markets: Ariel Ezrachi and Maurice E Stucke, *How Big-Tech Barons Smash Innovation—And How to Strike Back* (HarperCollins 2022) 203–04.

7
The Big Picture

A. Introduction

If set in motion, the process of transitioning towards coherence between data protection and competition law can be expected to have several high-level implications. Whereas the granular repercussions of coherently interpreting and enforcing the two fields of law have been explained in the preceding chapters, the present discussion turns to a number of macro-level ramifications and related challenges. With this objective, and in the spirit of offering concluding observations, the chapter sketches out and explains conceptual, practical, constitutional, and institutional implications of sectional coherence, as well as the applicability and relevance of this book's proposals in other jurisdictions.

B. Conceptual implications

Concepts play a vital role in the legal domain. Von der Pfordten noted:

> Nobody can deny that modern law is comprised of norm or rules or principles. But not only in normal but especially in hard cases, concepts like human dignity, life, liberty, art, science, religion, property, contract, fraud, negligence, and murder, as well as their interpretation, play a decisive role. The norms or rules or principles in which these concepts occur are often only the outer costume, that is, the outer means to cause the recipient to fulfil the required action. But the main question of content of adjudication is frequently one of conceptual analysis.[1]

Theorizing sectional coherence and the methods of achieving it bring into the spotlight numerous fundamental concepts that are the bedrocks of a coherence-based legal transformation. Realizing the proposals put forward in this book pivots on a readiness to re-examine well-established legal notions and to reflect on how their meanings can be altered. 'Concepts of and about law have no given meaning that is fixed for all time' as maintained by Frändberg.[2] The concepts of 'dominance', 'abuse',

[1] Dietmar von der Pfordten, 'About Concepts in Law' in Jaap C Hage and Dietmar von der Pfordten (eds), *Concepts in Law* (Springer 2009) 18.
[2] Åke Frändberg, 'An Essay on Legal Concept Formation' in Hage and von der Pfordten, ibid 1.

Coherence between Data Protection and Competition Law in Digital Markets. Klaudia Majcher, Oxford University Press.
 DOI: 10.1093/oso/9780198885610.003.0008

'power', 'harm', 'exploitation', 'efficiencies', 'risk', 'empowerment', 'freedom', and 'effectiveness' are a few illustrations provided in the book of how a legal transformation is contingent upon a new construction of leading concepts. The catalogue of the concepts included in this book's analysis is by no means comprehensive, however. From more operational notions such as 'entry barriers' or 'data minimization' to the aspirational and objective-defining concepts, for example 'welfare' and 'protection of rights', they all hold enormous potential to be the tools via which data protection and competition law can become more synergetic, and create opportunities for future research.

Redefining the concepts, however aligned the end result might be with the normative goal, cannot, however, lead to a legal paralysis caused by prevailing uncertainty. 'Intellectual competition' among academics or practitioners in reconceptualizing key legal notions is certainly of value as it is a vehicle for adapting the law to the changing empirical and normative realities. At the same time, consensus-building within the legal community in the course of redefining pivotal legal concepts, as well as a gradual implementation of new definitions and the establishment of safeguards (ie finding alternatives to fines for violations of provisions that include newly redefined concepts), are key.

C. Practical implications

To discuss the practical dimension of coherence-building interpretations and enforcement activities, a distinction can be made between 'corresponding' and 'complementary' legal approaches that result from sectional coherence, and which are outlined in the following two sections.

1. Corresponding legal approaches

A 'corresponding legal approach' refers to an enforcement activity that ultimately results in the same legal qualification of a specific market practice under data protection and competition law. A concrete example is a twin data protection and competition enforcement action targeting a powerful company that collects large amounts of personal data, and violates both the data minimization principle of the GDPR and Article 102 TFEU. As sectional coherence is a principle that informs a substantive assessment only, it can be realized provided that a given practice satisfies the procedural demands of the two legal areas: above all, such practice needs to fall under the scope of both data protection and competition law.

Once the same practice falls under the scope of the two legal areas and the substantive provisions of these laws are interpreted in a coherent way, at least two relevant scenarios can be envisaged for how such a case might unfold in practice. The first scenario is that the case will be pursued by one authority only (ie a competition or a data protection authority): enforcement priorities differ and some agencies might simply not have enough resources to investigate it. Corresponding legal approaches would thus substantially boost the likelihood of the practice problematic from the viewpoint of both data protection and competition law to be reviewed and, if proved to be illegal, addressed by at least one type of authority. If only competition law intervenes, the advantage is that competition enforcement would indirectly mitigate an important inconsistency in EU law related to the amount of the fine for violating data protection and competition law, hence potentially result in a more effective outcome. If a data protection agency is the intervening one, the benefit might be a more immediate result. Although the GDPR does not impose a strict time frame for investigations, Article 57(1)(f) GDPR indicates that complainants must be informed about the progress and outcome of the investigation within 'a reasonable period'. In practice, the enforcement might therefore be quicker than in competition law, the latter often being criticized as too slow.[3] This is highly relevant, as a fast-changing digital environment requires an equally fast legal response.

The second scenario envisages parallel enforcement actions targeting the same market behaviour. This scenario might materialize when a competition authority sanctions conduct that has been already found to breach data protection law, and vice versa. One might pose a valid question at this stage: what about the risk of redundancy? Framed differently, would it not be redundant to assign oversight of the same or similar practices to two different areas of law? For example, why should competition law intervene in certain instances of data exploitative practices if there are already other authorities that are or ought to be doing exactly that? If one area of the law does not usefully complement but rather merely overlaps with what the other one is able achieve, what is the benefit? While valid, such questions are premised on a conviction that parallel efforts are inherently redundant, hence unnecessary. Yet, it should be borne in mind that parallelism might be a noteworthy 'contingency plan' in the case of ineffective intervention by one legal area, which might be owing to many various factors. Discussing redundancy, scholars have invoked the following example: '[a]lthough the Boeing 777 can fly hours on a single engine, no one thinks that the pilot should turn the second engine off while in flight, or that Boeing should just build 777s with a single engine'.[4] In their view, while 'the costs of redundancy and overlap are visible and attract attention, the benefits of redundancy are less visible and require more in-depth investigation'.[5]

[3] eg it took the Commission seven years to complete its investigation in the *Google Shopping* case: *Google Search (Shopping)* (Case AT.39740) Commission Decision of 27 June 2017. There are, however, legitimate reasons, in particular the protection of companies' rights of defence, that justify the length of antitrust proceedings.

[4] David A Hyman and William E Kovacic, 'Why Who Does What Matters: Governmental Design and Agency Performance' (2014) 82 George Washington Law Review 1446, 1460–61.

[5] ibid 1461.

One should not, therefore, reject redundancy altogether, and ask instead about the level of redundancy that is optimal and the contexts in which it might be necessary.

While dual enforcement might thus be a valid choice for responding to particularly harmful behaviour in digital markets, the *ne bis in idem* principle should be duly observed. The principle *ne bis in idem*, or double jeopardy, is enshrined in Article 50 of the EU Charter and in Article 4 of Protocol No 7 of the European Convention on Human Rights,[6] and it constitutes a fundamental principle of EU law.[7] Its aim is to protect natural and legal persons from being tried twice for the same offence of a criminal nature[8] within the EU.

Two noteworthy recent judgments issued by the CJEU clarify protection against double jeopardy where competition law regulates the conduct already addressed by sectoral rules (*bpost*[9]), or where it is applied simultaneously by various NCAs (*Nordzucker*[10]).[11] The Court confirmed that for the *ne bis in idem* principle to apply, there 'must be a prior final decision' (the *bis* condition), and 'the prior decision and the subsequent proceedings or decisions must concern the same facts' (the *idem* condition).[12] It ruled that the existence of identical material facts—a precondition for applying the *ne bis in idem* principle—'must be understood to mean a set of concrete circumstances stemming from events which are, in essence, the same, in that they involve the same perpetrator and are inextricably linked together in time and space'.[13] Any limitation of the fundamental right guaranteed in Article 50 of the EU Charter might, however, be justified under Article 52(1) if such a limitation is prescribed by law, is necessary, and genuinely meets the objectives of general interest recognized by the EU or the need to protect the rights and freedoms of others.[14] In *bpost*, the CJEU thus concluded that the Charter does not preclude a legal person from being fined under EU competition law where, on the same facts, that person has already been charged under sectoral rules. The Court asserted that 'public

[6] On the interpretation of art 4, see eg ECtHR, *Sergey Zolotukhin v Russia*, Application No 14939/03, judgment of 10 February 2009; ECtHR, *A and B v Norway*, Application Nos 24130/11 and 29758/11, judgment of 15 November 2016.

[7] Joined Cases C-238, 244, 245, 247, 250–52 and 254/99 P *Limburgse Vinyl Maatschappij and Others v Commission* [2002] ECLI:EU:C:2002:582, para 59.

[8] To establish whether the proceedings and penalties are of a criminal nature, three criteria are relevant: (1) legal classification under national law; (2) intrinsic nature of the offence; and (3) degree of severity of the penalty: Case C-117/20 *bpost SA v Autorité belge de la concurrence* [2022] ECLI:EU:C:2022:202, para 25.

[9] *bpost*, ibid.

[10] Case C-151/20 *Bundeswettbewerbsbehörde v Nordzucker AG and Others* [2022] ECLI:EU:C:2022:203.

[11] For an analysis of the two cases, see eg Pieter van Cleynenbreugel, '*BPost* and *Nordzucker*: Searching for the Essence of *Ne Bis in Idem* in European Union Law' (2022) 18 European Constitutional Law Review 357. For a discussion of the *ne bis in idem* principle in the context of EU competition policy in digital markets, see Marco Cappai and Giuseppe Colangelo, 'Applying *ne bis in idem* in the Aftermath of *bpost* and *Nordzucker*: The Case of EU Competition Policy in Digital Markets' (2023) 60 Common Market Law Review 431.

[12] *bpost SA v Autorité belge de la concurrence* (n 8) para 28.

[13] ibid para 37.

[14] ibid paras 40–41.

authorities can legitimately choose complementary legal responses to certain conduct that is harmful to society through different procedures forming a coherent whole so as to address different aspects of the social problem involved', provided that the accumulation of legal responses 'do not represent an excessive burden for the individual concerned'.[15] What can justify the duplication of efforts and render them proportionate is the fact that 'two sets of proceedings are pursuing distinct objectives of general interest which it is legitimate to protect cumulatively'[16]—a requirement that can be rather effortlessly proved in cases of competition and data protection application to identical material facts, even though the two sets of law also share important objectives. As the CJEU further stipulated, a double sanction is justified provided that there are 'clear and precise rules' making it possible for a legal person to predict: (1) which acts or omissions are subject to duplication of proceedings and penalties; (2) that the two competent authorities coordinate with each other; (3) that the two sets of proceedings are conducted 'in a sufficiently co-ordinated manner within [and] approximate timeframe'; and (4) that the imposed penalties 'correspond to the seriousness of the offences committed'.[17] These are thus considerations that data protection and competition authorities should take into account when contemplating enforcement action where identical conduct has already been sanctioned under another set of rules.

Besides the *ne bis in idem* principle, what should also be considered in cases of parallel enforcement is the issue of competence, particularly in instances where an authority responsible for the enforcement of one area of the law directly refers to legal rules that belong to another. The question of competence arose, for example, in the context of the Bundeskartellamt's *Facebook* decision, where the German authority relied on the GDPR's provisions to apply competition law.[18] Responding to claims of a lack of competence to enforce data protection law, the Bundeskartellamt noted that 'it merely applied the European principles as important indications for its assessment under competition law of whether the conduct of a dominant company is appropriate'.[19] It also argued that its competence is not restricted by the GDPR's provisions on cooperation and consistency, as it cannot be concluded from the GDPR that data protection authorities have a monopoly in applying and interpreting data protection law.[20] According to the German authority, the GDPR's cooperation provisions do not intend to limit or restrict enforcement aimed at protecting the fundamental right to data protection. This can be derived from the fact that data protection authorities are not the only ones which can take action to protect data: action can also be taken under the civil law (eg by affected individuals

[15] ibid para 49 (emphasis added).
[16] ibid.
[17] ibid para 58.
[18] Bundeskartellamt, Decision B6-22/16 of 6 February 2019 (*Facebook*).
[19] ibid para 536.
[20] ibid para 539.

under Article 82 GDPR, consumer protection organizations and competitors under the Act against Unfair Competition).[21]

A more nuanced view on the issue was expressed by Advocate General Rantos in response to the preliminary questions submitted in this case. As he opined:

> [T]he examination of an abuse of a dominant position on the market may justify the interpretation, by a competition authority, of rules other than those relating to competition law, such as those of the GDPR, while specifying that such an examination is carried out in an incidental manner and is without prejudice to the application of that regulation by the competent supervisory authorities.[22]

Responding to the question about the principle of sincere cooperation enshrined in Article 4(3) TEU, Advocate General Rantos stressed that a lack of cooperation between a competition authority and the supervisory authorities within the meaning of the GDPR could give rise to differing interpretations of the GDPR.[23] To mitigate this risk, a competition authority has a duty to inform the relevant data protection authority and cooperate.[24] In cases where a data protection authority 'has ruled on the application of certain provisions of the GDRP in respect of the same practice or similar practices', a competition authority cannot deviate from that interpretation.[25]

The reasoning of the Advocate General is sound, and one may expect the CJEU to agree with his Opinion in its upcoming judgment. In the long run, it is indeed precisely enhanced cooperation between different authorities that should be fostered to remedy the problem of potential inconsistencies that may arise in the instances of parallel enforcement, and to ensure more coherent enforcement, as this chapter will discuss in Section D.

2. Complementary legal approaches

Sectional coherence might not only result in corresponding legal approaches (eg dual qualifications of a practice as legal or illegal), but in certain circumstances can manifest itself as a legal complementarity.

One divergence between data protection and competition law that offers an opportunity for data protection and competition law to usefully complement one another is the fact that while data protection endows individuals with rights in

[21] ibid para 540.

[22] Case 252/21 *Meta Platforms and Others v Bundeskartellamt* [2022] ECLI:EU:C:2022:704, Opinion of AG Rantos, para 24.

[23] ibid para 26.

[24] ibid para 31.

[25] ibid para 30.

addition to regulating market conduct on the supply side, competition law regulates the supply market side only. The fact that data protection law addresses directly the demand side can have implications for competition law, as this book has already discussed: if exercised effectively, the individual rights guaranteed in data protection law might shape and 'discipline' the supply market side. The caveat, as Chapter 6 Section C illustrated, is that due to the individualistic dimension of the individual rights enshrined in the GDPR, the market might not as a result be stimulated in a way aligned with broader societal interests. As regards competition law's contribution, this area of law can complement data protection law by creating the right conditions for data protection-friendly services to emerge, as well as indirectly facilitating individual choice.

Both fields of law also have at their disposal mechanisms to pre-empt conduct undesirable from the perspective of the other legal field. Merger control is the most evident tool for achieving this. Likewise, proposals to consider market power in data protection risk assessments, as well as to integrate the power factor in various balancing mechanisms, can prevent the accumulation of data power, having positive spillover effects on competition.

D. Constitutional implications

As things stand, it is unclear whether EU law mandates coherence between its various policies and laws. As illustrated in Chapter 4, the interpretation of the horizontal Article 7 TFEU that explicitly refers to the notions of consistency and coherence, depending on the language version of the Treaty, is inconclusive. More precisely, it remains unsettled whether the coherence principle has a narrow meaning implying solely lack of contradictions between different laws or policies, or whether it should be read as a broader and more demanding principle implying presence of positive connections between different elements of the legal system in pursuing certain objectives. These two interpretations imply markedly different requirements that those tasked with applying them—agencies and courts—need to follow. It is also unclear what constitutional force the principle of coherence has at present.

This book is a call for clarity in that regard. While there is value in the vagueness of the principle of coherence—the notion's ambiguity renders it possible for the CJEU, for example, to instrumentalize and use it as it sees fit—even more value would be derived from its clear definition. Various policy and legal fields within the EU system interconnect on many levels and in multiple respects. Clarifying the constitutional approaches grounded in coherence between the various sets of rules that embrace dissimilar values is, in fact, an embodiment of a broader debate on creating and promoting unity within the EU legal system that recognizes constitutional and value pluralism. As Avbelj and Komárek noted:

> The world pervaded by plurality also requires a minimum degree of coherence and, more importantly, it calls for a meta language through which the actors situated at different (epistemic) sites could reflexively engage with each other by recognizing their differences with a simultaneous commitment to a certain shared framework of co-existence.[26]

Maduro similarly asserted that '[f]or pluralism to be viable in a context of a coherent legal order, there must be a common basis for discourse', namely 'a set of principles shared by all the participants'.[27] A common meta language—something directly related to the issue of building a constitutional narrative in the EU—can, in the view of others, be found in the core values of the Union laid down in Article 2 TEU: 'respect for human dignity, freedom, democracy, equality, the rule of law and respect for human rights, including the rights of persons belonging to minorities'.[28] Building substantive unity, homogeneity, and stability of the EU through the values that span its legal system would then 'indicate that the constitutional legal order is resting on deeper roots than "only" the goals related to successful economic integration, legal approximation or a strong internal market'.[29] Clarifying, formalizing, and enforcing the constitutional principle of coherence have enormous potential to deliver precisely that substantive unity that in many 'sections' of EU law is long-awaited. This constitutional transformation would need to be accompanied by increased openness to see synergies across legal areas, awareness-raising, solid cross-sectional legal expertise, and effective institutional structures.

E. Institutional implications

From the standpoint of institutional design, an optimal bureaucratic structure is contingent on the ends to be achieved.[30] Sectional coherence is thus unlikely to materialize without reforming the institutions responsible for enforcing data protection and competition law and introducing cooperation mechanisms to accompany

[26] Matej Avbelj and Jan Komárek, 'Introduction' in Matej Avbelj and Jan Komárek (eds), *Constitutional Pluralism in the European Union and Beyond* (Hart Publishing 2012) 55–56.

[27] Miguel Poiares Maduro, 'Contrapunctual Law: Europe's Constitutional Pluralism in Action' in Neil Walker (ed), *Sovereignty in Transition* (Hart Publishing 2003) 524.

[28] These values, as art 2 TEU further stipulates, 'are common to the Member States in a society in which pluralism, non-discrimination, tolerance, justice, solidarity and equality between women and men prevail'.

[29] Oliver Mader, 'Enforcement of EU Values as a Political Endeavour: Constitutional Pluralism and Value Homogeneity in Times of Persistent Challenges to the Rule of Law' (2019) 11 Hague Journal on the Rule of Law 133, 137.

[30] Jacob E Gersen, 'Designing Agencies' in Daniel A Farber and Anne Joseph O'Connell (eds), *Research Handbook on Public Choice and Public Law* (Edward Elgar 2010) 334, cited in Kati J Cseres, 'Integrate or Separate: Institutional Design for the Enforcement of Competition Law and Consumer Law' (2013) Amsterdam Law School Research Paper No 2013-03, 11.

substantive decision making. As Chapter 3 showed, even though the enforcement practice in digital markets has over the past years revealed both tensions between these two legal fields and multiple opportunities for them to be in sync, institutional reforms are disturbingly absent in the EU and beyond.

This section reflects on the institutional implications of sectional coherence, and in particular on the need for a more synergetic institutional structure. Its first part presents ideas for introducing 'cooperative enforcement' of data protection and competition law. The second part complements that discussion with a broader view on potential institutional risks of expanding the prerogatives of agencies, and proposes strategies to mitigate these risks.

1. Conceptualizing cooperative enforcement

To create an institutional environment fit for the purpose of realizing the benefits of sectional coherence, data protection and competition law enforcement need to transform into a cooperative effort. The term 'cooperative enforcement' is commonly associated with the type of approach that seeks to induce compliance through flexible means and assistance, and can be contrasted with 'coercive enforcement' that focuses on deterrence through sanctions.[31] The relationship that these two forms of enforcement refer to is one between the enforcer and the addressee of the regulation. This section conceptualizes cooperative enforcement differently in that it centres on the horizontal relationship between the relevant enforcers: for the purpose of this discussion, between data protection and competition authorities. The idea of cooperative enforcement understood in a similar way, as cooperation between enforcers, has recently been put forward by Olivier Guersent, Director-General of the Directorate-General for Competition, in the context of the DMA. Bringing into the spotlight the emerging trend of 'new global and cooperative enforcement', he noted that 'the future will be more made of joint investigations and of collective actions', and that the interplay between the DMA, national competition law, and EU competition law requires various enforcers to be as 'collectively effective as possible'.[32] Guersent limited his observations to the broadly understood area of competition law enforced in a multi-layered setting (ie national and EU level), disregarding, however, the role of other relevant agencies, including the data protection authorities.

[31] See eg Dietrich H Earnhart and Robert L Glicksman, 'Coercive vs. Cooperative Enforcement: Effect of Enforcement Approach on Environmental Management' (2015) 42 International Review of Law and Economics 135, 135–36.

[32] Lewis Crofts, 'EU's Digital Markets Act Ushers in New Era of "Cooperative" Enforcement, Guersent Says' *Mlex* (10 October 2022) <https://content.mlex.com/#/content/1415604> accessed 14 October 2022.

To offer a blueprint for a truly 'cooperative enforcement' that spans divergent but interconnected legal fields, the following paragraphs flag the types of choices available while designing a cooperative enforcement model, namely: (1) intra and/or inter-institutional; (2) formal and/or informal; (3) ad hoc and/or structured; and (4) open and/or closed, and present suggestions for choices to be made moving forward.

Intra- and/or inter-institutional. A transition towards sectional coherence requires a two-pronged strategy consisting in building intra-institutional expertise and introducing a new inter-institutional cooperation paradigm. The former can be realized by competition authorities hiring data protection experts, for example. In February 2023, the EU Directorate-General for Competition announced its intention to hire a Chief Technology Officer, which is a promising first step towards enriching the expertise of its competition team. As substantive coherence requires a thorough reflection on the themes that are already part of the mandate of other authorities, inter-institutional cooperation should complement any intra-institutional reforms. Strengthening inter-institutional links is vital in order to find common approaches on issues such as the nature of analysed legal problems, their gravity, or optimal solutions.

Formal versus informal. While informal exchanges between various authorities should always be encouraged, informal cooperation alone cannot be expected to provide the most effective avenue for bridging data protection and competition law. The formalization of cooperative enforcement should thus take place though introducing formal procedural mechanisms for cooperation. To this effect, the Commission could prepare a notice similar to that on cooperation with the Network of Competition Authorities.[33] Even though Commission's notices are not binding, they provide useful guidance. In the course of preparation of such guidance, or any other initiative aimed at the formalization of cooperation with the data protection authorities, the EDPS and/or the EDPB should be involved.

Structured and/or ad hoc. Depending on the objective to be achieved, the form of cooperation between competition and data protection authorities can be envisaged as ad hoc or structured. All the enforcement activities of competition agencies that include conducting complex legal assessments (eg defining antitrust harm, finding an appropriate remedy, evaluating mergers) require a structured approach based on procedural frameworks. Structuring the enforcement activities would bring the necessary predictability of how cases are reviewed. From a data protection perspective, a structured form of cooperation should be envisaged to support data protection agencies when they investigate data protection violations by large

[33] European Commission 'Notice on cooperation within the Network of Competition Authorities' [2004] OJ C101/03.

technology companies. In such instances, structured cooperation with competition agencies would be of value to appropriately conduct power assessments relevant under a few data protection provisions (eg freedom of consent), for example. Ad hoc cooperation, on the other hand, would be an appropriate method of approaching initiatives such as market inquiries. For example, whenever a competition authority conducts a wide-scale investigation into a sector where personal data plays a prominent part, data protection expertise should be sought on an ad hoc basis.

Open and/or closed. The risks posed by technological innovations and new ways of using existing technologies are diverse in nature and can often be expected to fall under the scope of more than one sets of rules. In addition, in the course of devising the best ways to remedy infringements, competent agencies might need to tap into the pool of knowledge developed by other specialized agencies. Any cooperative model for enforcing data protection and competition law needs therefore to foresee collaborative mechanisms allowing other relevant agencies to come aboard where necessary. Open cooperative structures are expected to become even more pertinent in the future, not least because the interplay between the various regulatory initiatives at the EU level, such as the DMA, the DSA, the AI Act,[34] and the Data Act,[35] to name but a few, are becoming more evident. For example, in instances where algorithms shape the visibility of online content in a way potentially problematic for competition and data protection, valuable cooperation aimed at knowledge-sharing should be established with the European Centre for Algorithmic Transparency (ECAT), which was set up by the EU to provide technical assistance and guidance with respect to the rules on algorithmic accountability and transparency audits enshrined in the DSA. A forward-looking cooperative enforcement model for digital markets should thus have an inherently open format.

Finding an effective cooperation strategy is a challenging but vital step for making sectional coherence operational. Devising the most appropriate cooperation structures is not the only institutional challenge that sectional coherence entails, however. As mentioned, coherence's inevitable repercussion is the expansion of agencies' missions—in particular, the missions of the competition authorities. Thus, the conundrum related to the phenomenon of multifactored missions will now be addressed.

[34] European Commission, 'Proposal for a Regulation of the European Parliament and of the Council laying down harmonised rules on Artificial Intelligence (Artificial Intelligence Act) and amending certain Union legislative acts', COM (2021) 206 final.

[35] European Commission, 'Proposal for a Regulation of the European Parliament and of the Council on harmonised rules on fair access to and use of data (Data Act)', COM (2022) 68 final.

2. Mitigating risks carried by multifactored missions

In a recent essay, Tirole laid out a powerful critique of expanding the prerogatives of competition agencies.[36] His critique was a response to the current calls for broadening competition authorities' missions to various societal considerations such as climate change or inequality. As the sectional coherence advocated in this book might be subject to similar criticism, this section engages with the argument that points to the multifaceted risk carried by broadening the missions of the competition authorities, and offers suggestions on how to mitigate that risk.

1.1 The problem with expanded prerogatives

To illustrate the scenario in which there was a right outcome, but a wrong process, Tirole flagged the Commission's *Car Emissions* decision.[37] In 2021, the Commission found that Daimler, BMW, and the Volkswagen group had colluded on technical developments related to nitrogen oxide cleaning. Specifically, even though these car manufacturers had in their possession the technology to limit harmful emissions beyond that legally mandated under EU emissions standards, they decided not to compete on achieving improved exhaust gas cleaning—a collaboration that violated Article 101 TFEU. Despite its clearly negative environmental repercussions, the collusion also had some welfare-enhancing effects (eg larger space in the boots of cars). This led Tirole to conclude that enforcing EU environmental standards was the task of environmental ministries rather than the competition authorities responsible for protecting the interest of consumers who partially benefited from the cartel. He critically noted that 'the competition authority substituted itself for failing environmental regulation',[38] and compared the *Car Emissions* decision to the Bundeskartellamt's *Facebook* decision, where, arguably, the German competition authority stepped in due to the weak enforcement of the GDPR. As Tirole pointed out, there is a twin market and political failure at the core of such cases.[39] An optimal response to such a twin failure is, in his view, a narrow mission rather than a broad mandate. There are a few reasons for that, which are worthy of a short discussion.

As Wilson postulated in his book *Bureaucracy: What Government Agencies Do and Why They Do It*,[40] to create agency culture and an expert environment, an agency needs to be provided with a sense of mission, clear objectives, and well-defined tasks. New tasks, especially when they compete with the agency's core responsibilities, should generally be avoided. Relatedly, multifactored missions

[36] Jean Tirole, 'Socially Responsible Agencies' (2022).
[37] *Car Emissions* (Case AT.40178) Commission Decision of 8 July 2021.
[38] Tirole (n 36) 6.
[39] ibid.
[40] James Q Wilson, *Bureaucracy: What Government Agencies Do and Why They Do It* (Basic Books 1990), cited in Tirole (n 36) 7.

might fail because if several actors are in charge, then nobody, in fact, takes responsibility. Without proper coordination, there is also a risk of policy incoherence. Besides, multiple missions sometimes imply undefined expectations, which may have deleterious effects on agencies' accountability. Another concern is 'mission substitution': this may occur when additional missions are not matched by additional resources to realize new objectives. One should also not ignore incentive issues. Referring to his earlier article co-authored with Dewatripont and Jewitt,[41] Tirole argued that expanded objectives commonly reduce total agency efforts, creating a 'grasp all, lose all' situation.[42] The incentives are thus stronger when the mandate is construed narrowly.

In the competition law context, one repeatedly stumbles upon the argument that tasking competition authorities with new responsibilities should be avoided as doing so might result in 'mission creep', in particular given that the goals of competition law are already rather imprecise. According to Brennan, if 'antitrust becomes a tool for fixing a wide assortment of social ills, its role as the protector of efficiency through competition will be diluted', and there will be 'nothing left to take its place'.[43] As argued by others, creating an amorphous mandate of a competition agency that goes well beyond welfare and efficiency considerations is likely to deflect the authority from an unambiguous commitment to promoting competitive markets and to imperil its performance-related accountability.[44] Cooper warned that expanding the scope of antitrust law to encompass new values, for example privacy, would inject a substantial degree of subjectivity into competition assessments.[45] He considered subjectivity not only a problem in and of itself; subjectivity is also closely associated with overdeterrence. As the economics of accidents teach us, subjective judgements and related uncertainty make potential violators take too much precaution, which in Cooper's view would in the context of data result in limiting beneficial data collection and processing to avoid antitrust repercussions.[46] While stifled innovation is certainly a negative spillover effect of which to be mindful, it can also be claimed that taking precaution in the context of personal data processing would result in a net benefit for individuals.

[41] Mathias Dewatripont, Ian Jewitt, and Jean Tirole, 'The Economics of Career Concerns, Part I: Comparing Information Structures' (1999) 66 The Review of Economic Studies 183.

[42] Tirole (n 36) 8.

[43] Tim Brennan, 'Antitrust and the Perils of Mission Creep' (*Milken Institute Review*, 25 May 2018) <https://www.milkenreview.org/articles/antitrust-and-the-perils-of-mission-creep> accessed 4 October 2022.

[44] Michael Trebilcock and Edward M Iacobucci, 'Designing Competition Law Institutions: Values, Structure, and Mandate' (2010) 41 Loyola University Chicago Law Journal 455, 465.

[45] James C Cooper, 'Privacy and Antitrust: Underpants Gnomes, the First Amendment, and Subjectivity' (2013) 4 George Mason Law Review 1129, 1143.

[46] ibid 1145. In making the claim about over-precaution, Cooper referred to Steven Shavell, *Foundations of Economic Analysis of Law* (Harvard UP 2004) 224–27.

In view of the critique of expanded prerogatives described earlier, the following section offers a set of 'mitigation strategies' that could be implemented to limit potential risks.

1.2 Mitigation strategies

The argument that a fuzzy mandate assigned to an authority may at best impinge upon its effectiveness and at worst transform it into a dysfunctional organization has considerable merit. In designing a competition authority's mandate to achieve sectional coherence, mitigation measures should thus be put in place to guarantee its long-term effectiveness. Hyman and Kovacic put forward a number of factors that they consider proxies for the long-term success of an agency's mission: (1) policy coherence; (2) branding and credibility; (3) capacity and capability; (4) resilience; (5) cohesion; and (6) collateral effects on the regulatory ecosystem.[47] This framework can serve as a checklist in reflecting on how setting sectional coherence in motion might affect the mandate of competition authorities in particular.

Policy coherence. The first factor on the list, namely policy coherence, goes to the core of the potential risks that might result from expanding the responsibilities of competition authorities to include privacy-related concerns. The risk of frustrating internal policy coherence has been already discussed in Chapter 4 that reflected on how sectional coherence might affect 'local coherence' (ie coherence within one field of law only). As that chapter suggested, any legal solution that strengthens sectional coherence and simultaneously frustrates local coherence is acceptable insofar as it achieves rational acceptability in a given legal community *thanks to* its moral superiority/rightness and *despite* its formal inferiority. Such a normative assessment would thus need to be conducted first in order to establish whether the benefits of sectional coherence outweigh the costs of disturbing internal policy coherence—an assessment in which the value ascribed to data protection should play a prominent role.

Branding and credibility. The next step requires reflecting on whether and how sectional coherence would affect 'the clarity and strength of the agency's brand'.[48] What might 'confuse or dilute the brand' is when the duties of an agency are excessively diversified or stand in conflict with one another.[49] The result of a weak brand might be poor guidance to the agency's officials as well as its weakened external credibility.[50]

47 David A Hyman and William E Kovacic, 'Why Who Does What Matters: Governmental Design and Agency Performance' (2014) 82 George Washington Law Review 1446. 'Political implications', the seventh category listed by the authors, will not be discussed given its limited relevance for the purpose of this section.

48 ibid 1472.

49 ibid.

50 ibid.

When it comes do expanding competition authorities' mandates along the lines described in this book, there is little risk that their reputation and credibility will be reduced as a result—as long as the new objectives to be pursued are formulated clearly and comprehensively. In Europe, where data protection implications of competitive activities are well acknowledged, and the value of data protection is enshrined in EU constitutional law (as opposed to the economic consumer welfare goal, which as such does not appear in the EU Treaties), the reputation of competition agencies can only increase as a result of giving it the prerogative to reflect on one of the Union's fundamental human rights. Explaining how a competition mandate should encompass data protection—a necessary step to ensure the agency's credibility—is also unlikely to pose a hurdle.

Capacity and capability. To design an effective mandate, any mismatch between the responsibilities assigned to an authority and the means it has at its disposal to effectively perform them should be properly addressed. Indeed, '[a]ssigning *N* + *1* functions to an agency with the people, powers, knowledge, and credibility to handle only *N* duties invites failure'.[51] As already discussed, to effectively implement sectional coherence, adequate expertise (either in-house or external) and sufficient resources are requisite. Besides capacity, an agency needs to be capable of performing complex assessments at the interface of competition and data. Having the capability to perform complex analysis means making as few Type I and Type II enforcement errors as possible—the goal that the model of cooperative enforcement outlined in the preceding section is precisely designed to achieve.

Resilience. The adaptability and sustainability of the functions assigned to an agency is another proxy of their long-term effectiveness.[52] As the values of data protection and competitiveness are not ephemeral, and data-based as well as data-supported business models are here to stay, the resilience-related concern is unlikely to materialize in the near future. While external circumstances might incentivize authorities to shift priorities (eg placing more emphasis on 'green competition law'), data protection, given its status as a fundamental human right in the EU, should as a result not be pushed into the background. Thus, a competition policy mandate that would require a competition authority to more thoroughly scrutinize the data protection implications of competitive activities is unlikely to become obsolete, even in the long run.

Cohesion. From an intra-institutional standpoint, expanded prerogatives might have the undesirable effect of creating tensions across departments within a single agency.[53] Thus, if the EU Directorate-General for Competition decided to introduce a 'data protection unit', for example, or internally incorporate data protection expertise in another way, it must strive for achieving a high degree of internal

[51] ibid 1747.
[52] ibid 1501–02.
[53] ibid 1470.

cohesion by properly coordinating the functions of such new unit with the functions of other teams, achieving genuine 'jointness'.

Collateral effects on the regulatory ecosystem. Sectional coherence and the resulting institutional and procedural changes will to a certain extent 'disrupt' the regulatory environment. For example, a new data protection unit within a competition authority might acquire certain functions akin to those performed by a data protection agency, giving rise to potential tensions. Institutional and organizational reforms should therefore be introduced cautiously, in a way that any valuable features of the existing regulatory ecosystem are preserved.

Overall, expanding the mandate of an agency for it to become better aligned with the mission of sectional coherence is not undemanding. Yet, the alternative, namely maintaining the institutional silos and preserving the old organizational structures, would imply turning a blind eye to the existing and emerging concerns in digital markets. The response to such new concerns must not be 'business as usual', but rather an active effort to challenge the established ways of organizing and cooperating. Given that the online space is poised to become an even more perplexing amalgamate of actors, markets, technologies, interactions, and modes of conduct, the future of enforcement should be increasingly cooperative. In the long run, the current institutional and organizational enforcement model could learn from the governance network theory that champions multifaceted interactions between the relevant actors. Already in 1990s, governability theory scholars had indicated the 'responsiveness to the heightened complexity of governing and to the growing consensus needs' as important triggers for the emergence of cooperative policy networks.[54] Given that similar triggers are now conspicuously present in the regulatory and enforcement realms related to digital markets, cooperation rather than isolation should be the way forward.

F. Implications for other jurisdictions

The emerging and established concerns explored in this book are not confined to any one jurisdiction. The activities of the largest technology companies such as Meta, Alphabet, or Apple are global in scope, and so are the repercussions of how they design and operate their services. Wherever their activities do not reach, local counterparts provide alternative products or services that might give rise to corresponding privacy and competition risks. While this book's analysis has included insights into how authorities and courts outside the EU have so far approached the legal issues at the interface of data protection and competition law (see Chapter 4),

[54] Renate Mayntz, 'Modernization and the Logic of Interorganizational Networks' (1993) 6 Knowledge & Policy 3, 5.

the extendibility of the findings and proposals related to sectional coherence in other jurisdictions merits a brief analysis.

It must be emphasized from the outset that in reflecting on the potential convergence of laws and enforcement approaches, one should be cognizant of various domestic idiosyncrasies, which inevitably render some of the recommendations designed for the EU legal system fully or partially irrelevant. Divergences between jurisdictions must, in fact, be the primary lens through which one should approach the applicability of a set of legal proposals to other legal systems. In regard to competition law, Stiglitz noted:

> Just like there should not be a single intellectual property regime for all countries, there should not be a single competition policy for all countries. Just as there should be a development-oriented trade regime and a development-oriented intellectual property regime, there should be a developmentally oriented competition regime and antitrust policy.[55]

As regards data protection, while there is already a global profusion of data protection laws resulting in a high level of convergence of data protection standards and principles,[56] it would be erroneous and naïve to believe that the EU-focused proposals will always resonate equally well in other parts of the world.

The discussion that follows flags three relevant types of divergence between jurisdictions, namely: (1) legal frameworks; (2) enforcement strategies; and (3) institutions, as well as the repercussions that those divergences might have for 'globalizing' sectional coherence between data protection and competition law.

Legal frameworks. The global relevance of sectional coherence hinges strongly on the design of a legal system: whether a particular jurisdiction has data protection and competition frameworks in place and, if so, how their rules are designed. At present, data protection and competition laws are ubiquitous. As at the beginning of 2022, there were a total of 157 countries with data protection/privacy laws, amounting to 67 per cent of the 232 independent jurisdictions having such frameworks, albeit of different quality.[57] The spread of antitrust laws has been also swift. There are currently over 125 jurisdictions that have enacted competition rules, and the vast majority of them have an active enforcement authority.[58]

While the omnipresence of data protection and competition frameworks bodes well for the global expansion of the idea of sectional coherence, the substantive

[55] Joseph E Stiglitz, 'Towards a Broader View of Competition Policy' in Tembinkosi Bonakele, Eleanor M Fox, and Liberty Mncube (eds), *Competition Policy for the New Era. Insights from the BRICS Countries* (OUP 2017) 16.

[56] Graham Greenleaf, 'Now 157 Countries: Twelve Data Privacy Laws in 2021/22' (2022) 176 Privacy Laws & Business International Report 3.

[57] ibid.

[58] OECD, 'OECD Competition Trends 2020' (2020) 15.

divergences between the laws might limit the applicability of some specific proposals. As regards data protection, while the GDPR has been and continues to be a 'global template' for other jurisdictions,[59] important divergences between data protection laws can be identified. Contrary to the GDPR, the California Consumer Privacy Act of 2018, for example, does not require the processing of personal data to be a priori based on a specific legal ground.[60] In China, the Personal Information Protection Law of the People's Republic of China (PIPL) imposes additional data protection obligations (eg regular publication of reports on data protection) on platform providers that process 'large' amounts of data and have 'complicated' business operations, such as Alibaba, Baidu, or Tencent.[61] In Australia, as in some other jurisdictions, there is no right to data portability enshrined in its privacy law. While these are just some examples, similar substantive divergences span the world's data protection laws, making some of the book's proposals obsolete from the perspective of non-EU jurisdictions.

Even though competition laws display a relatively high level of convergence across jurisdictions, they also feature notable dissimilarities. One illustration is a competition law prohibition of unfair or exploitative pricing, which was stressed as relevant in the discussion on sectional coherence in the EU. While such a prohibition is explicitly enshrined in the EU Treaty, jurisdictions such as the US, Australia, Canada, and Mexico are not empowered to challenge exploitative pricing strategies by dominant firms unless such strategies are collusive or also have exclusionary effects.[62] The lack of a unified approach towards justifications, which in the EU was developed through the case law, might be another stumbling block on the path towards globalizing sectional coherence along the lines proposed in this book.

The EU legal system is also unique in that it features in its constitutional treaty the concepts of consistency and coherence, which underpin the guiding principle of sectional coherence. While the anchoring of the book's discussion in one of the EU's constitutional provisions (art 7 TFEU) helped to construe a legal narrative, and coherence's constitutional status can be invoked to justify the need to comply with sectional coherence, nothing prevents other jurisdictions from implementing sectional coherence as a guiding policy notion in designing the relationship between their data protection and competition laws.

Enforcement strategies. In countries with data protection and competition regimes, a number of considerations might influence how the laws are enforced. In the field of competition law, enforcement priorities of competition agencies hinge upon a number of idiosyncratic considerations that vary across jurisdictions. As described in the 2021 report on *ICN Agencies' Case Prioritisation and Initiation*,

[59] Greenleaf (n 56) 8.

[60] DataGuidance and Future of Privacy Forum, 'Comparing privacy laws: GDPR v. CCPA' (2022) 23.

[61] See Daniel Albrecht, 'Chinese First Personal Information Protection Law in Contrast to the European GDPR' (2022) 1 Computer Law Review International, 4–5.

[62] See OECD, 'Exploitative pricing in the time of COVID-19' (2020) 3.

factors that influence competition priorities include the importance of particular sectors to consumers (eg agriculture, education, food, funeral services, and energy), the likely effectiveness of an intervention, the effective and efficient use of resources, current issues of importance (eg sustainability, digital economy, issues arising from the Covid-19 pandemic), as well as national economic or public interests.[63] In jurisdictions where the primary goals are sustained growth and development, for instance, the attention of the governments might be directed towards economic policy instruments other than competition, even though competition law is an important tool for promoting innovation (eg laggard innovation, which is more relevant in developing countries) and productivity growth.[64] The level of market development may thus have a direct bearing on the enforcement priorities of various authorities.

Competition culture is another relevant and related point of divergence. As the enforcement of competition laws is usually highly contextual and pivots on domestic circumstances, it cannot be expected that this book's focus on law enforcement in digital markets is of interest for jurisdictions where the empirical landscape differs in certain fundamental respects. Even if digital markets are elevated to a competition enforcement priority, jurisdictions might have different approaches as regards the desired intensity of enforcement. Inherent in competition policy is the balancing of the risks of under-enforcement and over-enforcement—and how that balance plays out depends on the domestic circumstances of each country.[65] Sectional coherence, which is likely to be more accepting of Type II errors (over-enforcement), might not be the preferred avenue for a number of competition enforcers.

Similar divergences might affect the efforts that various jurisdictions invest into data protection enforcement. Varied cultural norms and visions for a data economy in particular can be expected to have a bearing on how a specific jurisdiction approaches data protection law and, relatedly, its interactions with competition law.

Institutions. Even if in a particular jurisdiction digital markets are elevated to an enforcement priority, and the relevant authority has the mandate to intervene to remedy data-related anti-competitive behaviour, for example, it might experience budgetary constraints and struggle with lack of expertise, preventing it from engaging in the complex investigations and assessments that sectional coherence necessitates. Lack of independence might constitute another obstacle for enforcing the law, whether competition law or data protection law, in a way considered

[63] International Competition Network, 'ICN Agencies' Case Prioritisation and Initiation' (2021) 10–12.

[64] See Thomas Cheng, 'Why Competition Law Is So Important for Developing Countries' (*ProMarket*, 14 July 2020) <https://www.promarket.org/2020/07/14/why-competition-law-is-so-important-for-developing-countries/> accessed 10 October 2022.

[65] Stiglitz (n 55) 16.

adequate (eg embracing sectional coherence) from the standpoint of a competition or a data protection agency.

G. Conclusions

This chapter's discussion has revealed a number of significant conceptual, practical, constitutional, and institutional implications of sectional coherence, as well as whether and when the book's ideas pivoting around sectional coherence could be replicated in other jurisdictions. The multifaceted repercussions make it evident that transitioning towards sectionally coherent competition and data protection law is not straightforward, the envisaged changes deeply affecting the law and the institutional structures as we know them. While an incremental approach towards synergizing data protection and competition law might help to mitigate the risks intrinsic in the wide-ranging legal and institutional shifts required to achieve sectional coherence, incrementalism should not stand in the way of swiftly remedying new data harms that unfold in this day and age and responding to the social demands on the law.

Final Reflections

Data protection and competition law continue to be approached as isolated fields of law, even though data, power, and harm are deeply and conspicuously entangled in modern digital markets. Isolation in a substantive sense and isolation in an institutional sense are evidenced in the modern approaches to these two areas of law not only in Europe, but also in several other jurisdictions. The global phenomenon of data protection and competition law norms and values encountering each other and interacting in a variety of empirical contexts is in and of itself an intriguing area of study. An inquiry into how their interactions should be shaped takes it one step further, and requires an urgent normative reflection on the future trajectories of these laws, in particular as data protection and competition law are powerful tools in the hands of public authorities for shaping digital reality. The urgency is justified by the stakes involved: as we are witnessing a transition from a control to a surveillance society,[1] social, economic, political, and ethical concerns related to digitalization loom large.

This book is underpinned by the premise that purism—that is, confining individual legal areas solely to a narrow set of predetermined goals—becomes increasingly indefensible in an age of unprecedented empirical challenges and risks. Data protection and competition law provide rich grounds for explicating, theorizing, and operationalizing the idea of sectional coherence between two purposely insulated areas of law and reflecting on how they can converge to our collective benefit. Going beyond the narrow notion of consistency and efforts to remedy conflicts, the ideas outlined in this book represent a quest for a more synergetic handling of legal questions at the interface of these two fields. There are a number of methods for fostering sectional coherence: a mutual cross-fertilization of notions, 'borrowing' legal meanings from the other legal area, commonly tackling different aspects of problematic market practices through independent interpretations, or simply adequately enforcing the extant laws.

From a competition perspective, the understanding of power and harm, as well as the approaches to antitrust and merger justifications and remedies, need to evolve to more thoroughly encompass the fundamental right to data protection. As regards data protection law, the focus should lie predominantly in ensuring its effective enforcement, not least because data protection belongs to a toolbox of

[1] Antoinette Rouvroy and Yves Poullet, 'The Right to Informational Self-Determination and the Value of Self-Development: Reassessing the Importance of Privacy for Democracy' in Serge Gutwirth and others (eds), *Reinventing Data Protection?* (Springer 2009) 45.

Coherence between Data Protection and Competition Law in Digital Markets. Klaudia Majcher, Oxford University Press.
 DOI: 10.1093/oso/9780198885610.003.0009

instruments that have the potential to reshape the current model of competition. In addition, a number of substantive readjustments of data protection law can help to stimulate competition on data protection. A few notable examples include approximating the notions of risk and power, rethinking how power should affect balancing between conflicting interests and rights in data protection assessments, moving away from an individualistic towards a collective approach in data protection law, and limiting the unintended repercussions of data protection law on competition.

Overall, the solutions proposed in this book not only purport to address a multidimensional market failure evidently present in digital markets, but also, or rather predominantly, to positively and proactively stimulate the markets towards delivering greater protection of personal data. Coherent, rather than isolated, approaches to digital markets are critical for a new model of competition to emerge: one where personal data exploitation does not pervasively span economic activities in the digital economy. In addition to establishing new synergies and entrusting the discussed legal fields with consciously integrating, or at least more actively reflecting on, the values inherent in the other one, a 'protection loop' that undoubtedly exists in relation to competition and data protection law needs to be acknowledged too. This loop's premise is straightforward: data protection law and competition law are in a two-way, mutually dependent relationship. As they share a common value base, competition law can be assumed to benefit data protection, and data protection law can facilitate competition. Thus, next to reflecting on possible substantive and institutional amendments, any debate about coherence needs to recognize how the actual enforcement of the extant law can be part of the solution.

A relative flexibility of assessment tools and the open-endedness of many of the legal concepts enshrined in data protection and competition law bode well for converting them into a more synergetic whole. Yet, trade-offs and a difficult debate on these fields' outer substantive limits is an inherent component of a study of their sectional coherence. The current fixity on keeping data protection and competition law in siloes brings to the fore some noteworthy concerns. Above all, decreased predictability of the law if its rules and norms are to always respond to new empirical and normative phenomena. As scholars noted:

> The value of predictability is in tension with the obverse value of flexibility where the evolution of economic theory and the idiosyncrasies of particular industries, transactions, or practices may require reevaluation and refinement of preexisting rules, policy positions, or adjudicative decisions.[2]

[2] Michael Trebilcock and Edward M Iacobucci, 'Designing Competition Law Institutions: Values, Structure, and Mandate' (2010) 41 Loyola University Chicago Law Journal 455, 458.

And yet, leaving the law as it is, is far from satisfactory, even though its predictability as well as its internal consistency and coherence might be adversely affected in a short term as a result of integrating into its assessments new concerns and risks. A careful balance between breaking path dependence and respecting precedent is a challenging, but a necessary one to strike if data protection and competition law are to adequately fulfil their functions.

New substantive designs of competition and data protection law must also be complemented by institutional reform. Even though some institutions might be traditionally suspicious of cross-disciplinary hybridization, it must be borne in mind that substantive outcomes are a function of an institutional design. If intra- and inter-institutional structures remain unchanged, efforts invested into synergizing data protection and competition law might prove futile.

The paradigm provided by sectional coherence reflects a more holistic view of two areas of law that have so far operated in silos: a view that supports the incorporation of a wider range of policy objectives within individual legal fields while remaining sensitive to the challenges this inevitably entails. With such a pluralistic ethos, there would seem to be prospects even for further exploring the commonalities across other interlinked fields of the digital economy and approximating their rules and norms. Regulations aimed at governing selected aspects of digital markets abound. In the EU, a panoply of regulatory initiatives—the Digital Markets Act, the Digital Services Act, the Data Act, the Data Governance Act, the AI Act, and the European Chips Act, to name a few prominent examples—create a complex web of instruments that will inevitably interact with one another and with other established fields of law. This book's discussion can serve as a blueprint for creating a system of legal governance for the digital economy where its individual constitutive elements support, rather than frustrate, the objectives and values promoted by other instruments. Most importantly, one where a holistic approach to law is adopted to effectively protect individuals' rights, freedoms, and their well-being in the age of digital transformation.

Bibliography

Aarnio A, 'On Rational Acceptability. Some Remarks on Legal Justification' in Patrick Nerhot (ed), *Law, Interpretation and Reality. Essays in Epistemology, Hermeneutics and Jurisprudence* (Springer 1990)

Access Now, 'Three Years Under the GDPR. An Implementation Progress Report' (2021)

Acquisti A, 'The Economics and Behavioural Economics of Privacy' in Julia Lane and others (eds), *Privacy, Big Data, and the Public Good: Frameworks for Engagement* (CUP 2014)

Acquisti A and Grossklags J, 'Privacy Attitudes and Privacy Behavior' in Jean L Camp and Stephen Lewis (eds), *Economics of Information Security* (Springer 2004)

Acquisti A and Varian HR, 'Conditioning Prices on Purchase History' (2004) 24 Marketing Science 367

Adler MD, 'Future Generations: A Prioritarian View' (2009) 77 George Washington Law Review 1478

Adler MD and Sanchirico CW, 'Inequality and Uncertainty: Theory and Legal Applications' (2006) 155 University of Pennsylvania Law Review 279

Ahlborn C and Padilla J, 'From Fairness to Welfare: Implications for the Assessment of Unilateral Conduct under EC Competition Law' in Claus-Dieter Ehlermann and Mel Marquis (eds), *European Competition Law Annual 2007: A Reformed Approach to Article 82 EC* (Hart Publishing 2008)

Akman P, *The Concept of Abuse in EU Competition Law* (Hart Publishing 2012)

Albors-Llorens A, 'The "Essential Facilities" Doctrine in EC Competition Law' (1999) 58 Cambridge Law Journal 490

Albors-Llorens A, 'The Role of Objective Justification and Efficiencies in the Application of Article 82 EC' (2007) 44 Common Market Law Review 1727

Albrecht D, 'Chinese First Personal Information Protection Law in Contrast to the European GDPR' (2022) 1 Computer Law Review International

Armstrong M, 'Competition in Two-Sided Markets' (2006) 37 RAND Journal of Economics 668

Armstrong M, 'Price Discrimination' (2007) MPRA Paper No 4693

Arrieta A, 'Facebook's Laughable Campaign Against Apple Is Really Against Users and Small Businesses' (*Electronic Frontier Foundation*, 18 December 2020) <https://www.eff.org/deeplinks/2020/12/facebooks-laughable-campaign-against-apple-really-against-users-and-small> accessed 18 June 2022

Article 29 Data Protection Working Party (A29WP), 'Opinion 15/2011 on the Definition of Consent' (2011)

A29WP, 'Advice Paper on Essential Elements of a Definition and a Provision on Profiling within the EU General Data Protection Regulation' (2013)

A29WP, 'Opinion 02/2013 on Apps on Smart Devices' (2013)

A29WP, 'Statement of the Working Party on Current Discussions Regarding the Data Protection Reform Package' (2013)

A29WP, 'Opinion 05/2014 on Anonymisation Techniques' (2014)

A29WP, 'Opinion 06/2014 on the notion of legitimate interests of the data controller under Article 7 of Directive 95/46/EC' (2014)

A29WP, 'Opinion 8/2014 on the on Recent Developments on the Internet of Things' (2014)

A29WP, 'Statement on the Role of a Risk-Based Approach in Data Protection Legal Frameworks' (2014)

A29WP, 'Guidelines on the Right to Data Portability' (2017)

A29WP, 'Guidelines on Automated Individual Decision-Making and Profiling for the Purposes of Regulation 2016/679' (2018)

A29WP, 'Guidelines on consent under Regulation 2016/679' (2018)

A29WP, 'Guidelines on Transparency under Regulation 2016/679' (2018)

A29WP, 'Position paper on the derogations from the obligation to maintain records of processing activities pursuant to Article 30(5) GDPR' (2018)

Athey S and Scott Morton F, 'Platform Annexation' (2022) 2–3 <https://papers.ssrn.com/sol3/papers.cfm?abstract_id=3786434> accessed 5 October 2022

Auer D and Petit N, 'Two-Sided Markets and the Challenge of Turning Economic Theory Into Antitrust Policy' (2015) 60 Antitrust Bulletin 426

Ausloos J, *The Right to Erasure in EU Data Protection Law. From Individual Rights to Effective Protection* (OUP 2020)

Ausloos J, 'Balancing in the GDPR: Legitimate Interests v. Right to Object' (*CiTiP*, 2017) <https://www.law.kuleuven.be/citip/blog/balancing-in-the-gdpr-legitimate-interests-v-right-to-object/> accessed 26 September 2022

Australian Competition & Consumer Commission, 'Regulators cooperate to improve privacy compliance' (12 March 2002) <https://www.accc.gov.au/media-release/regulators-co-operate-to-improve-privacy-compliance> accessed 29 March 2022

Australian Competition & Consumer Commission, 'Digital Platforms Inquiry—Final Report' (2019)

Australian Competition & Consumer Commission, 'ACCC Rejects Google Behavioural Undertakings for Fitbit Acquisition' (22 December 2020) <https://www.accc.gov.au/media-release/accc-rejects-google-behavioural-undertakings-for-fitbit-acquisition> accessed 4 September 2022

Australian Competition & Consumer Commission, 'Consumer Data Right (CDR). Memorandum of Understanding with the Office of the Australian Information Commissioner' (2020)

Australian Competition & Consumer Commission, 'Updating Competition and Consumer Law for Digital Platform Services' (2022) Discussion Paper for Interim Report No 5

Australian Government, 'Digital Platforms: Government Consultation on ACCC's Regulatory Reform Recommendations' (2022)

Autor D and others, 'Concentrating on the Fall of the Labor Share' (2017) 107 American Economic Review 180

Autoridade da Concorrência, 'Digital Ecosystems, Big Data and Algorithms' (2019)

Autorità Garante della Concorrenza e del Mercato, 'Investigation Opened against Google for Abuse of Dominant Position in Data Portability' (14 July 2022) A552 <https://en.agcm.it/en/media/press-releases/2022/7/A552> accessed 18 July 2022

Autoritat Catalana de la Competència, 'The Data-Driven Economy. Challenges for Competition' (2016)

Autorité de la concurrence, 'Opinion No 18-A-03 of 6 March 2018 on Data Processing in the Online Advertising Sector' (2016)

Autorité de la concurrence, 'Targeted Advertising/Apple's Implementation of the ATT Framework. The Autorité Does Not Issue Urgent Interim Measures against Apple but Continues to Investigate into the Merits of the Case' (17 March 2021) <https://www.auto

ritedelaconcurrence.fr/en/press-release/targeted-advertising-apples-implementation-att-framework-autorite-does-not-issue> accessed 18 June 2022

Autorité de la concurrence, 'The Autorité de La Concurrence Starts Proceedings Ex Officio to Analyse Competition Conditions in the Cloud Computing Sector' (27 January 2022) <https://www.autoritedelaconcurrence.fr/en/press-release/autorite-de-la-concurrence-starts-proceedings-ex-officio-analyse-competition> accessed 28 September 2022

Autorité de la concurrence and Bundeskartellamt, 'Competition Law and Data' (2016)

Avbelj M and Komárek J, 'Introduction' in Matej Avbelj and Jan Komárek (eds), *Constitutional Pluralism in the European Union and Beyond* (Hart Publishing 2012)

Averitt NW and Lande RH, 'Consumer Sovereignty: A Unified Theory of Antitrust and Consumer Protection Law' (1997) 65 Antitrust Law Journal 713

Averitt NW and Lande RH, 'Using the "Consumer Choice" Approach to Antitrust Law' in Paul Nihoul, Nicolas Charbit, and Elisa Ramundo (eds), *Choice—A New Standard for Competition Law Analysis?* (Concurrences 2016)

Bach D and Ziermann F, 'Conglomerate Foreclosure in the Metaverse' (*D'Kart*, 22 June 2022) <https://www.d-kart.de/en/blog/2022/06/22/conglomerate-foreclosure-in-the-metaverse/> accessed 2 September 2022

Balboni P and others, 'Legitimate Interest of the Data Controller New Data Protection Paradigm: Legitimacy Grounded on Appropriate Protection' (2013) 3 International Data Privacy Law 244

Balebako R and others, '"Little Brothers Watching You": Raising Awareness of Data Leaks on Smartphones' (9th Symposium on Usable Privacy and Security, Newcastle, July 2013)

Balkin JM, 'Free Speech in the Algorithmic Society: Big Data, Private Governance, and New School Speech Regulation' (2018) 51 UC Davis Law Review 1149

Bandura A, 'Toward a Psychology of Human Agency' (2006) 1 Perspectives on Psychological Science 164

Bania K, 'Fitting the Digital Markets Act in the Existing Legal Framework: The Myth of the "without Prejudice" Clause' [2022] European Competition Journal 1

Barocas S and Selbst AD, 'Big Data's Disparate Impact' (2016) 104 California Law Review 671

Barwise P, 'Nine Reasons Why Tech Markets Are Winner-Take-All' (*London Business School Review*, 10 July 2018) <https://www.london.edu/think/nine-reasons-why-tech-markets-are-winner-take-all> accessed 4 March 2022

Basedow J, 'The Modernization of European Competition Law: A Story of Unfinished Concepts' (2007) 42 Texas International Law Journal 13

Batchelor B and Murray G, 'Internet of Things: Antitrust Concerns in the Pipeline?' (*Kluwer Competition Law blog*, 12 May 2016) <http://competitionlawblog.kluwercompetitionlaw.com/2016/05/12/internet-of-things-antitrust-concerns-in-the-pipeline/> accessed 10 March 2022

Battista Ratti G and Rodríguez JL, 'On Coherence as a Formal Property of Normative Systems' (2015) 27 Journal for Constitutional Theory and Philosophy of Law 131

Behrens P, 'The Consumer Choice Paradigm in German Ordoliberalism and Its Impact on EU Competition Law' in Paul Nihoul, Nicolas Charbit, and Elisa Ramundo (eds), *Choice—A New Standard for Competition Law Analysis?* (Concurrences 2016)

Behringer S and Filistrucchi L, 'Areeda–Turner in Two-Sided Markets' (2015) 46 Review of Industrial Organization 287

Bennett M, Brouwer H, and Claassen R (eds), *Wealth and Power: Philosophical Perspectives* (Routledge 2022)

Bertea S, 'The Argument from Coherence: Analysis and Evaluation' (2005) 25 Oxford Journal of Legal Studies 369

Bietti E, 'Consent as a Free Pass: Platform Power and the Limits of the Informational Turn' (2020) 40 Pace Law Review 310

Bietti E, 'The Discourse of Control and Consent over Data in EU Data Protection Law and Beyond' (2020) Stanford University Aegis Paper Series No 2001

Binns R, 'Data Protection Impact Assessments: A Meta-Regulatory Approach' (2017) 7 International Data Privacy Law 22

Binns R, 'Third Party Tracking in the Mobile Ecosystem' (10th ACM Conference on Web Science, Amsterdam, May 2018)

Binns R, 'Tracking on the Web, Mobile and the Internet-of-Things' (2022) 8 Foundations and Trends in Web Science 1

Bits of Freedom, 'Why the "Legitimate Interest" Test Fails to Protect the Interests of Users and the Regulation Needs to Be Amended' (2011) <https://www.bof.nl/live/wp-content/uploads/20121211_onderzoek_legitimate-interests-def.pdf>

Blockx J, 'The Limits of the "More Economic" Approach to Antitrust' (2019) 42 World Competition 475

Boerman S, Kruikemeier S, and Zuiderveen Borgesius FJ, 'Online Behavioural Advertising: A Literature Review and Research Agenda' (2017) 46 Journal of Advertising 363

Bostoen F, 'Online Platforms and Pricing: Adapting Abuse of Dominance Assessments to the Economic Reality of Free Products' (2019) 35 Computer Law & Security Review 263

Bostoen F and Mândrescu D, 'Assessing Abuse of Dominance in the Platform Economy: A Case Study of App Stores' (2020) 16 European Competition Journal 431

Bourreau M and de Streel A, 'Digital Conglomerates and EU Competition Policy' (2019) CERRE Report

Bourreau M and Perrot A, 'Digital Platforms: Regulate before It's Too Late' (2020) 60 Conseil d'analyse économique 1

Brennan T, 'Antitrust and the Perils of Mission Creep' (*Milken Institute Review*, 25 May 2018) <https://www.milkenreview.org/articles/antitrust-and-the-perils-of-mission-creep> accessed 4 October 2022

BRICS Competition Authorities, 'BRICS in the Digital Economy: Competition Policy in Practice Report' (2019)

BRICS Competition Law and Policy Centre, 'Digital Era Competition: A BRICS View' (2019)

Brkan M, 'The Essence of the Fundamental Rights to Privacy and Data Protection: Finding the Way Through the Maze of the CJEU's Constitutional Reasoning' (2019) 20 German Law Journal 864

Brockhoff J and others, 'Google/DoubleClick: The First Test for the Commission's Nonhorizontal Merger Guidelines' [2008] Competition Policy Newsletter No 2

Brodin M, 'A Framework for GDPR Compliance for Small- and Medium-Sized Enterprises' (2019) 4 European Journal for Security Research 243

Brook O, 'Struggling with Article 101(3): Diverging Approaches of the Commission, EU Courts, and Five Competition Authorities' (2019) 50 Common Market Law Review 121

Bulst FW and De Vinck S, 'Understanding the Metaverse—A Competition Perspective' *European American Chamber of Commerce* (17 October 2022) <https://eaccny.com/news/chapternews/dg-comp-understanding-the-metaverse-a-competition-perspective/> accessed 5 November 2022

Bundeskartellamt, 'Working Paper—Market Power of Platforms and Networks' (2016)

Bundeskartellamt, 'Guidance on Transaction Value Thresholds for Mandatory Pre-Merger Notification (Section 35 (1a) GWB and Section 9 (4) KartG)' (2018)

Bundeskartellamt, 'Proceeding against Apple Based on New Rules for Large Digital Companies (Section 19a(1) GWB)—Bundeskartellamt Examines Apple's Significance for Competition across Markets' (21 June 2021) <https://www.bundeskartellamt.de/SharedDocs/Meldung/EN/Pressemitteilungen/2021/21_06_2021_Apple.html;jsessionid=BB40E379A1063BE8F3AB4360E4182121.1_cid387?nn=3591568> accessed 4 June 2022

Bundeskartellamt, 'Bundeskartellamt Reviews Apple's Tracking Rules for Third-Party Apps' (14 June 2022) <https://www.bundeskartellamt.de/SharedDocs/Meldung/EN/Pressemitteilungen/2022/14_06_2022_Apple.html;jsessionid=A8BB89473F8FEE64A25828B2829E6306.2_cid362?nn=3591568> accessed 4 June 2022

Bundeskartellamt, 'Control of Abusive Practices' (nd) <https://www.bundeskartellamt.de/EN/Abusecontrol/abusecontrol_node.html> accessed 11 June 2022

Bundeswettbewerbsbehörde, 'Considerations on Digitalization Challenges in the Economy and Competition Law Enforcement' (2020)

Burrell J, 'How the Machine "Thinks": Understanding Opacity in Machine Learning Algorithms' (2016) 3 Big Data & Society 1

Butcher M, 'UK Class Action Lodged against Meta Seeks £2.3 Billion in Damages to Facebook U.K. Users' *Techcrunch* (14 January 2022) <https://techcrunch.com/2022/01/13/uk-class-action-lodged-against-meta-seeks-3-1bn-for-breach-of-competition-law/> accessed 14 May 2022

Buttarelli G, 'Keynote Speech' (BEUC DIGIFORUM, Brussels, 20 June 2016)

Buttarelli G, 'This Is Not an Article on Data Protection and Competition Law' [2019] CPI Antitrust Chronicle

Bygrave LA and Tosini L, 'Article 4(11). Consent' in Christopher Kuner, Lee A Bygrave, and Christopher Docksey (eds), *The EU General Data Protection Regulation (GDPR). A Commentary* (OUP 2020)

Caffarra C and Ryan J, 'Ending the "Data Free-For-All": Antitrust vs GDPR Enforcement' *Euractiv* (22 January 2021) <https://www.euractiv.com/section/digital/opinion/ending-the-data-free-for-all-antitrust-vs-gdpr-enforcement/> accessed 3 June 2022

Caffarra C and Valletti T, 'Google/Fitbit Review: Privacy IS a Competition Issue' (*VoxEU*, 4 March 2020) <https://cepr.org/voxeu/blogs-and-reviews/googlefitbit-review-privacy-competition-issue> accessed 11 April 2022

Caffarra C, Crawford G, and Ryan J, 'The Antitrust Orthodoxy Is Blind to Real Data Harms' (*VoxEU*, 22 April 2021) <https://voxeu.org/content/antitrust-orthodoxy-blind-real-data-harms> accessed 14 May 2022

Caillaud B and Jullien B, 'Chicken and Egg: Competition among Intermediation Service Providers' (2003) 34 RAND Journal of Economics 309

Calligaris S, Criscuolo C, and Marcolin L, 'Mark-Ups in the Digital Era' (2018) OECD Science, Technology and Industry Working Papers No 2018/10

Cannon C, 'Antitrust Enforcers Enter the Metaverse' *Lexology* (16 March 2022) <https://www.lexology.com/library/detail.aspx?g=99eb485b-0e45-451b-b2b5-4ba35a5c2971> accessed 19 March 2022

Cappai M and Colangelo G, 'Applying *ne bis in idem* in the Aftermath of *bpost* and *Nordzucker*: The Case of EU Competition Policy in Digital Markets' (2023) 60 Common Market Law Review 431

Cavalleri MC and others, 'Concentration, Market Power and Dynamism in the Euro Area' (2019) European Central Bank, Working Paper Series No 2253

Chen J and Stallaert J, 'An Economic Analysis of Online Advertising Using Behavioral Targeting' (2014) 38 Management Information Systems Quarterly 429

Chen C, Frey CB, and Presidente G, 'Privacy Regulation and Firm Performance: Estimating the GDPR Effect Globally' (2022) The Oxford Martin Working Paper Series on Technological and Economic Change Working No 2022-1

Cheng T, 'Why Competition Law Is So Important for Developing Countries' (*ProMarket*, 14 July 2020) <https://www.promarket.org/2020/07/14/why-competition-law-is-so-important-for-developing-countries/> accessed 10 October 2022

Chiavetta R, 'How a "Technical Expert" Factors into the Google-Fitit Acquisition' *IAAP* (9 June 2021) <https://iapp.org/news/a/how-a-technical-expert-factors-into-the-google-fitbit-acquisition/> accessed 15 April 2022

Chiriţă AD, *The German and Romanian Abuse of Market Dominance in the Light of Article 102 TFEU* (Nomos 2011)

Chiriţă AD, 'A Legal-Historical Review of the EU Competition Rules' (2014) 63 International and Comparative Law Quarterly 281

Citron DK and Solove DJ, 'Privacy Harms' (2022) 102 Boston University Law Review 793

Clarke R, 'An Evaluation of Privacy Impact Assessment Guidance Documents' (2011) 1 International Data Privacy Law 111

Clifford D and Ausloos J, 'Data Protection and the Role of Fairness' (2018) 37 Yearbook of European Law 130

Coates K, *Competition Law and Regulation of Technology Markets* (OUP 2011)

Cole R, 'Privacy, Vulnerability, and Affordance' (2017) 66 DePaul Law Review 591

Comisión Federal de Competencia Económica, 'Rethinking Competition in the Digital Economy' (2018)

Commission Nationale de l'informatique et des Libertés, Délibération de la formation restreinte no SAN-2019-001 du 21 janvier 2019 concernant la société Google LLC

Commission Nationale de l'informatique et des Libertés, Délibération de la formation restreinte no SAN-2022-025 du 29 décembre 2022 concernant la société Apple

Competition and Consumer Commission of Singapore, 'CCCS Revises Competition Guidelines for Greater Clarity and Guidance' (31 December 2021) <https://www.cccs.gov.sg/media-and-consultation/newsroom/media-releases/cccs-revises-competition-guidelines-for-greater-clarity-and-guidance.> accessed 11 February 2022

Competition and Markets Authority, 'Online Platforms and Digital Advertising, Market Study Final Report' (2020)

Competition and Markets Authority, 'Notice of Intention to Accept Modified Commitments Offered by Google in Relation to Its Privacy Sandbox Proposals, Case Number 50972' (26 November 2021)

Competition and Markets Authority, 'Merger Assessment Guidelines' (2021)

Competition and Markets Authority, 'CMA to keep "close eye" on Google as it secures final Privacy Sandbox commitments' (11 February 2022) <https://www.gov.uk/government/news/cma-to-keep-close-eye-on-google-as-it-secures-final-privacy-sandbox-commitments> accessed 29 May 2022

Competition and Markets Authority, 'Completed Acquisition by Facebook, Inc (Now Meta Platforms, Inc) of Giphy, Inc Final Report on the case remitted to the CMA by the Competition Appeal Tribunal' (18 October 2022)

Competition and Markets Authority, 'Mobile Ecosystems—Market Study Final Report' (2022)

Competition and Markets Authority, 'CMA third update report on implementation of the Privacy Sandbox commitments' (January 2023)

Competition and Markets Authority, 'Final Order made by the Competition and Markets Authority pursuant to section 84 of the Enterprise Act 2002, *Meta Platforms, Inc./Giphy, Inc.*' (6 January 2023)

Competition and Markets Authority and Information Commissioner's Office, 'Competition and Data Protection in Digital Markets: A Joint Statement between the CMA and the ICO' (2021)

Competition and Markets Authority, Australian Competition and Consumer Commission, and Bundeskartellamt, 'Joint Statement on Merger Control Enforcement' (2021)

Competition Bureau of Canada, 'Big Data and Innovation: Key Themes for Competition Policy in Canada' (2018)

Competition Commission of India, 'Market Study on the Telecom Sector in India. Key Findings and Observations' (2021)

Competition Commission of India, Suo Moto Case No 91 of 2021, Updated Terms of Service and Privacy Policy for WhatsApp Users

Competition Commission of South Africa, 'Competition Commission Conditionally Approves the Google/Fitbit Merger' (22 December 2022)

Competition Commission Singapore, 'Data: Engine for Growth—Implications for Competition Law, Personal Data Protection, and Intellectual Property Rights' (2017)

Competition Policy International, 'Poland Probes Apple Over App Tracking Transparency Rules' (3 December 2021) <https://www.competitionpolicyinternational.com/poland-probes-apple-over-app-tracking-transparency-rules/> accessed 23 June 2022

Competition Policy International, 'Tech Giants Form Metaverse Standards, Excluding Apple' (22 June 2022) <https://www.competitionpolicyinternational.com/tech-giants-form-metaverse-standards-excluding-apple/> accessed 18 September 2022

Condorelli D and Padilla J, 'Harnessing Platform Envelopment in the Digital World' (2020) 16 Journal of Competition Law & Economics 143

Constine J, 'Facebook Rolls out AI to Detect Suicidal Posts before They're Reported' *Techcrunch* (27 November 2017) <https://techcrunch.com/2017/11/27/facebook-ai-suicide-prevention/?guccounter=1> accessed 13 February 2022

Consumer Policy Research Centre, 'Data and Technology Consumer Survey' (2020)

Cooper JC, 'Privacy and Antitrust: Underpants Gnomes, the First Amendment, and Subjectivity' (2013) 4 George Mason Law Review 1129

Costa-Cabral F and Lynskey O, 'Family Ties: The Intersection between Data Protection and Competition in EU Law' (2017) 54 Common Market Law Review 11

Cowen T, '"Privacy Fixing" After *Texas et al v. Google* and *CMA v. Google (Privacy Sandbox)*: Approaches to Antitrust Considerations of Privacy' (*Competition Policy International*, 26 January 2021) <https://www.competitionpolicyinternational.com/privacy-fixing-after-texas-et-al-v-google-and-cma-v-google-privacy-sandbox-approaches-to-antitrust-considerations-of-privacy/> accessed 11 November 2021

Cozza V and others, 'Experimental Measures of News Personalization in Google News' in Sven Casteleyn, Peter Dolog, and Cesare Pautasso (eds), *Current Trends in Web Engineering: ICWE 2016 International Workshops* (Springer 2016)

Cramer Flood E, 'Global Digital Ad Spending Update Q2 2020' eMarketer (6 July 2020) <https://www.emarketer.com/content/global-digital-ad-spending-update-q2-2020> accessed 17 February 2022

Crane DA, 'Legal Rules for Predatory Innovation' [2013] Concurrences No 4-2013, Art No 58811

Crémer J, de Montjoye Y-A, and Schweitzer H, 'Competition Policy for the Digital Era' (2019) Report for the European Commission

Cremona M, 'Coherence Through Law: What Difference Will the Treaty of Lisbon Make?' (2008) 3 Hamburg Review of Social Sciences 11

Crofts L, 'Vestager's "Fairness" Mantra Rattles through EU Competition Law' *Mlex* (15 November 2016) <https://mlexmarketinsight.com/news-hub/editors-picks/area-of-expertise/antitrust/vestagers-fairness-mantra-rattles-through-eu-competition-law> accessed 4 November 2021

Crofts L, 'EU's Digital Markets Act Ushers in New Era of "Cooperative" Enforcement, Guersent Says' *Mlex* (10 October 2022) <https://content.mlex.com/#/content/1415604> accessed 14 October 2022

Cseres KJ, 'The Impact of Regulation 1/2003 in the New Member States' (2010) 5 Competition Law Review 145

Cseres KJ, 'Towards a European Model of Economic Justice: The Role of Competition Law' in Hans-Wolfgang Micklitz (ed), *The Many Concepts of Social Justice in European Private Law* (Edward Elgar 2011)

Cseres KJ, 'Integrate or Separate: Institutional Design for the Enforcement of Competition Law and Consumer Law' (2013) Amsterdam Law School Research Paper No 2013-03

Cukier K and Mayer-Schönberger V, 'The Rise of Big Data: How It's Changing the Way We Think About the World' (2013) 92 Foreign Affairs 28

Cunningham C, Ederer F, and Ma S, 'Killer Acquisitions' (2021) 129 Journal of Political Economy

Custers B and Malgieri G, 'Priceless Data: Why the EU Fundamental Right to Data Protection Is at Odds with Trade in Personal Data' (2022) 45 Computer Law & Security Review 1

Cyphers B, 'Don't Play in Google's Privacy Sandbox' (*Electronic Frontier Foundation*, 30 August 2019) <https://www.eff.org/deeplinks/2019/08/dont-play-googles-privacy-sandbox-1> accessed 4 June 2022

Cyphers B and Doctorow C, 'Privacy Without Monopoly: Data Protection and Interoperability' (2021) Electronic Frontier Foundation

Czapracka K, 'The Essential Facilities Doctrine and the *Bronner* Judgment Clarified: Case C-165/19 P *Slovak Telekom v Commission*' (2022) 13 Journal of European Competition Law & Practice 278

Dahlgren P, 'Media, Knowledge and Trust: The Deepening Epistemic Crisis of Democracy' (2018) 25 Journal of the European Institute for Communication and Culture 20

Dahlqvist F, Patel M, and Shulman J, 'Growing Opportunities in the Internet of Things' *McKinsey* (22 July 2019) <https://www.mckinsey.com/industries/private-equity-and-principal-investors/our-insights/growing-opportunities-in-the-internet-of-things> accessed 8 March 2022

Data Protection Commission, 'Annual Report 2017' (2018)

DataGuidance and Future of Privacy Forum, 'Comparing privacy laws: GDPR v. CCPA' (2022)

Data Protection Commission, Decision of the Data Protection Commission Made Pursuant to Section 111 of the Data Protection Act 2018 in the matter of Twitter International Company, Case IN-19-1-1 (9 December 2020)

Data Protection Commission, Decision of the Data Protection Commission Made Pursuant to Section 111 of the Data Protection Act, 2018 and Articles 60 and 65 of the General Data Protection Regulation in the matter of WhatsApp Ireland Ltd., Case IN-18-12-2 (20 August 2021)

Davilla M, 'Unravelling the Complexity of Blockchain and EU Competition Law' (2022) 13 Journal of European Competition Law & Practice 387

Dawson M, 'Better Regulation and the Future of EU Regulatory Law and Politics' (2016) 53 Common Market Law Review 1209

De Hert P and others, 'The Right to Data Portability in the GDPR: Towards User-Centric Interoperability of Digital Services' (2018) 34 Computer Law & Security Review 193

de Hingh A, 'Some Reflections on Dignity as an Alternative Legal Concept in Data Protection Regulation' (2018) 19 German Law Journal 1269

De Locker J and Eeckhout J, 'Global Market Power' (2018) NBER Working Paper Series, Working Paper No 24768

De Wachter J and Peeters C, 'Advocate General Rules on the One-Stop Shop Mechanism' (2021) 7 European Data Protection Law Review 129

Dean B, 'DuckDuckGo Usage Stats for 2022' *Backlinko* (5 April 2021) <https://backlinko.com/duckduckgo-stats> accessed 5 July 2022

Demetzou K, 'Risk to the "Rights and Freedoms": A Legal Interpretation of the Scope of Risk under the GDPR' in Dara Hallinan and others (eds), *Data Protection and Privacy*, vol 12 (Bloomsbury Publishing 2021)

Department for Digital, Culture, Media & Sport, 'National Data Strategy' (2020)

Dewatripont M, Jewitt I, and Tirole J, 'The Economics of Career Concerns, Part I: Comparing Information Structures' (1999) 66 The Review of Economic Studies 183

Dias Sant'ana T and others, 'The Structure of an Innovation Ecosystem: Foundations for Future Research' (2020) 58 Management Decision 2725

Díez F and others, 'The Rise of Corporate Market Power and Its Macroeconomic Effects' (2019) IMF World Economic Outlook

Directorate-General for Justice and Consumers, 'Comments of DG Justice and Consumers on a request for information from the European Ombudsman—Complaint by the Irish Council for Civil Liberties (ICCL), ref. 97/2022/PB' (2022)

Dorsey E, Rybnicek J, and Wright JD, 'Hipster Antitrust Meets Public Choice Economics: The Consumer Welfare Standard, Rule of Law, and Rent-Seeking' [2018] CPI Antitrust Chronicle

Ducci F and Trebilcock M, 'Structural vs. Behavioural Remedies in Big Tech Sectors' [2020] CPI Antitrust Chronicle

Dunne N, 'Public Interest and EU Competition Law' (2020) 65 Antitrust Bulletin 256

Dworkin R, *Law's Empire* (Hart Publishing 1998)

Dylko I and others, 'The Dark Side of Technology: An Experimental Investigation of the Influence of Customizability Technology on Online Political Selective Exposure' (2017) 73 Computers in Human Behavior 181

Earnhart DH and Glicksman RL, 'Coercive vs. Cooperative Enforcement: Effect of Enforcement Approach on Environmental Management' (2015) 42 International Review of Law and Economics 135

Eberle EJ, 'Observations on the Development of Human Dignity and Personality in German Constitutional Law: An Overview' (2012) 33 Liverpool Law Review 201

Edmundson WA, 'Comments on Coherence Theory in the Philosophy of Law' (1994) 1 <https://papers.ssrn.com/sol3/papers.cfm?abstract_id=1147392> accessed 4 January 2023

Ehlermann C-D, 'The Contribution of EC Competition Policy to the Single Market' (1992) 29 Common Market Law Review 257

Ehrenberg K, 'Pattern Languages and Institutional Facts: Functions and Coherence in the Law' in Michał Araszkiewicz and Jaromir Šavelka (eds), *Coherence: Insights from Philosophy, Jurisprudence, and Artificial Intelligence* (Springer 2013)

Eisenmann T, Parker G, and Van Alstyne M, 'Platform Envelopment' (2011) 32 Strategic Management Journal 1270

Elhauge E, 'Tying, Bundling, and the Death of the Single Monopoly Profit Theory' (2009) 123 Harvard Law Review 397

Englehardt S and Narayanan A, 'Online Tracking: A 1-Million-Site Measurement and Analysis' (23rd ACM Conference on Computer and Communications Security, Vienna, October 2016)

Esayas SY, 'Data Privacy in European Merger Control: Critical Analysis of Commission Decisions Regarding Privacy as a Non-Price Competition' (2019) 40 European Competition Law Review 166

Esayas SY and Svantesson D, 'Digital Platforms Under Fire: What Australia Can Learn From Recent Developments in Europe (2018) 43 Alternative Law Journal 275

Esteve A, 'The Business of Personal Data: Google, Facebook, and Privacy Issues in the EU and the USA' (2017) 7 International Data Privacy Law 36

European Commission, 'Guidelines on the assessment of horizontal mergers under the Council Regulation on the control of concentrations between undertakings' [2004] OJ C31/03

European Commission, 'Notice on cooperation within the Network of Competition Authorities' [2004] OJ C101/03

European Commission, 'Guidelines on the method of setting fines imposed pursuant to Article 23(2)(a) of Regulation No 1/2003' [2006] L C210/2

European Commission, 'Antitrust: Guidance on Commission Enforcement Priorities in Applying Article 82 to Exclusionary Conduct by Dominant Firms—Frequently Asked Questions' (3 December 2008) MEMO/08/761 <https://ec.europa.eu/commission/presscorner/detail/en/MEMO_08_761> accessed 21 November 2021

European Commission, 'Commission Notice on Remedies Acceptable under Council Regulation (EC) No 139/2004 and under Commission Regulation (EC) No 802/2004' [2008] OJ C267/01

European Commission, 'Guidelines on the assessment of non-horizontal mergers under the Council Regulation on the control of concentrations between undertakings' [2008] OJ C265/6

European Commission, 'Antitrust: Commission accepts Microsoft commitments to give users browser choice' (16 December 2009) IP/09/1941 <https://ec.europa.eu/commission/presscorner/detail/en/IP_09_194> accessed 6 September 2022

European Commission, 'Guidance on the Commission's enforcement priorities in applying Article 82 of the EC Treaty to abusive exclusionary conduct by dominant undertakings' [2009] OJ C45/1

European Commission, 'Impact Assessment Accompanying Regulation (EU) 2016/679 and Directive (EU) 2016/680' (Staff Working Paper), SEC (2012) 72 final

European Commission, 'Antitrust: Commission Fines Microsoft for Non-Compliance with Browser Choice Commitments' (6 March 2013) IP/13/196 <https://ec.europa.eu/commission/presscorner/detail/en/IP_13_196> accessed 12 July 2022

European Commission, 'Mergers: Commission fines Facebook €110 million for providing misleading information about WhatsApp takeover' (18 May 2017) IP/17/1369 <https://ec.europa.eu/commission/presscorner/detail/en/IP_17_1369> accessed 11 June 2022

European Commission, 'Data Protection Regulation One Year on: 73% of Europeans Have Heard of at Least One of Their Rights' (13 June 2019) IP/19/2956 <https://ec.europa.eu/commission/presscorner/detail/en/IP_19_2956> accessed 1 February 2022

European Commission, 'Data Protection as a Pillar of Citizens' Empowerment and the EU's Approach to the Digital Transition—Two Years of Application of the General Data Protection Regulation' (Staff Working Document), SWD (2020) 115 final

European Commission, 'Final Report—Sector Inquiry into Consumer Internet of Things', COM (2020) 19 final

European Commission, 'Impact Assessment Report Accompanying Proposal for a Regulation of the European Parliament and of the Council on contestable and fair markets in the digital sector (Digital Markets Act)' (Staff Working Document), SWD (2020) 363 final

European Commission, 'Joint Statement Ahead of the 2nd Year Anniversary of the General Data Protection Regulation' (20 May 2020) Statement/20/913 <https://ec.europa.eu/commission/presscorner/detail/en/statement_20_913> accessed 24 March 2022

European Commission, 'Antitrust: Commission Opens Investigation into Possible Anticompetitive Conduct by Google in the Online Advertising Technology Sector' (22 June 2021) IP/21/3143 <https://ec.europa.eu/commission/presscorner/detail/en/ip_21_3143> accessed 25 March 2022

European Commission, 'Commission Guidance on the Application of the Referral Mechanism Set out in Article 22 of the Merger Regulation to Certain Categories of Cases' (Communication) COM (2021) 1959 final

European Commission, 'Evaluation of Procedural and Jurisdictional Aspects of EU Merger Control' (Staff Working Document), SWD (2021) 66 final

European Commission, 'Industry Concentration and Competition Policy' (2021) Competition Policy Brief, Issue 2021-02

European Commission, 'Approval of the content of a draft for a Communication from the Commission 'Guidelines on the applicability of Article 101 of the Treaty on the Functioning of the European Union to horizontal co-operation agreements' (Communication), COM (2022) 1159 final

European Commission,'Commission Notice on the definition of the relevant market for the purposes of Union competition law', Draft (2022)

European Commission, 'Commission Staff Working Document Accompanying Report from the Commission to the Council and the European Parliament "Final Report—Sector Inquiry into Consumer Internet of Things"' COM (2022) 19 final

European Commission, 'Amendments to the Communication from the Commission Guidance on the Commission's enforcement priorities in applying Article 82 of the EC Treaty to abusive exclusionary conduct by dominant undertakings' (Communication), COM (2023) 1923 final

European Commission, 'Antitrust: Commission announces Guidelines on exclusionary abuses and amends Guidance on enforcement priorities' (27 March 2023) IP/23/1911 <https://ec.europa.eu/commission/presscorner/detail/eN/ip_23_1911> accessed 28 March 2023

European Commission, 'Further specifying procedural rules relating to the enforcement of the General Data Protection Regulation' (2023) <https://ec.europa.eu/info/law/better-regulation/have-your-say/initiatives/13745-Further-specifying-procedural-rules-relating-to-the-enforcement-of-the-General-Data-Protection-Regulation_en> accessed 27 February 2023

European Consumer Organisation, 'Google's Fitbit Takeover: EU Merger Control Proves Unable to Protect Consumers in the Digital Economy' (17 December 2020) <https://www.beuc.eu/press-releases/googles-fitbit-takeover-eu-merger-control-proves-unable-protect-consumers-digital> accessed 14 June 2022

European Consumer Organisation, 'Consumer Groups File Complaint against WhatsApp for Unfairly Pressuring Users to Accept Its New Policies' (9 July 2021) <https://www.beuc.

eu/press-releases/consumer-groups-file-complaint-against-whatsapp-unfairly-pressuring-users-accept-its> accessed 19 June 2022

European Data Protection Board, 'Safeguarding Privacy in a Connected World A European Data Protection Framework for the 21st Century' (Communication), COM (2012) 9 final

European Data Protection Board, 'Guidelines 3/2018 on the Territorial Scope of the GDPR (Article 3)' (2018)

European Data Protection Board, 'Statement of the EDPB on the Data Protection Impacts of Economic Concentration' (2018)

European Data Protection Board, Decision 01/2020 on the Dispute Arisen on the Draft Decision of the Irish Supervisory Authority Regarding Twitter International Company under Article 65(1)(a) GDPR (9 November 2020)

European Data Protection Board, 'Statement on Privacy Implications of Mergers' (2020)

European Data Protection Board, Urgent Binding Decision 01/2021 on the Request under Article 66(2) GDPR from the Hamburg (German) Supervisory Authority for Ordering the Adoption of Final Measures Regarding Facebook Ireland Limited (12 July 2021)

European Data Protection Board, Binding Decision 3/2022 on the Dispute Submitted by the Irish SA on Meta Platforms Ireland Limited and its Facebook Service (Art. 65 GDPR) (5 December 2022)

European Data Protection Supervisor, 'Opinion on the Commission's Communication on "Unleashing the potential of Cloud Computing in Europe"' (2012)

European Data Protection Supervisor, 'Privacy and Competitiveness in the Age of Big Data: The Interplay Between Data Protection, Competition Law and Consumer Protection in the Digital Economy' (2014)

European Data Protection Supervisor, 'Opinion 8/2016 on Coherent Enforcement of Fundamental Rights in the Age of Big Data' (2016)

European Data Protection Supervisor, 'Opinion 2/2021 on the Proposal for a Digital Markets Act' (2021)

European Data Protection Supervisor, 'Opinion 1/2023 on the Proposal for an Interoperable Europe Act' (2023)

European Ombudsman, 'Decision on whether the European Commission collects sufficient information to monitor Ireland's implementation of the EU's General Data Protection Regulation (GDPR)' (Case 97/2022/PB)

European Parliament, 'Resolution on the Protection of the Rights of the Individual in the Face of Developing Technical Progress in the Field of Automatic Data Processing' [1975] OJ C60/48.

European Parliament, 'Report on the proposal for a regulation of the European Parliament and of the Council on the protection of individual with regard to the processing of personal data and on the free movement of such data (General Data Protection Regulation)' (2013)

European Parliament, 'Fundamental Rights Implications of Big Data: Data Protection, Non-Discrimination, Security and Law Enforcement (2016/2225(INI))' [2018] OJ C263/82

European Parliament, 'Resolution on the Commission Evaluation Report on the Implementation of the General Data Protection Regulation Two Years after Its Application (2020/2717(RSP))' [2021] OJ C494/129

Evans DS, 'The Antitrust Economics of Multi-Sided Platform Markets' (2003) 20 Yale Journal on Regulation 325

Evans DS, 'Why Different Jurisdictions Do Not (and Should Not) Adopt the Same Antitrust Rules' (2009) 10 Chicago Journal of International Law 161

Evans DS and Schmalensee R, 'The Industrial Organization of Markets with Two-Sided Platforms' (2007) 3 Competition Policy International 151

Ezrachi A, 'Sponge' (2016) 5 Journal of Antitrust Enforcement 49

Ezrachi A, *Virtual Competition: The Promise and Perils of the Algorithm-Driven Economy* (Harvard UP 2016)

Ezrachi A, *EU Competition Law: An Analytical Guide to the Leading Cases* (7th edn, Hart Publishing 2021)

Ezrachi A and Robertson VHSE, 'Competition, Market Power and Third-Party Tracking' (2019) 42 World Competition 5

Ezrachi A and Stucke ME, *How Big-Tech Barons Smash Innovation—And How to Strike Back* (HarperCollins 2022)

Falque-Pierrotin I, Chairwoman of A29WP, Letter to Jan Koum, Co-Founder of WhatsApp (24 October 2017)

Faull J and Nikpay A, *The EU Law of Competition* (3rd edn, OUP 2014)

Federal Trade Commission, *Google/DoubleClick*, Statement of the Federal Trade Commission, FTC File No 071-0170 (20 December 2007)

Federal Trade Commission, 'Mobile Privacy Disclosures: Building Trust Through Transparency' (2013) Staff Report

Federal Trade Commission, 'Internet of Things: Privacy & Security in a Connected World' (2015) Staff Report

Federle A, 'The Interplay of Data Protection and Competition Law—Issues Beyond the *Facebook* Case' *(Bird & Bird,* 19 March 2019) <https://www.twobirds.com/insights/2019/global/the-interplay-of-data-protection-and-competition-law-issues-beyond-the-facebook-case> accessed 2 September 2022

Ferretti F, 'Data Protection and the Legitimate Interest of Data Controllers: Much Ado about Nothing or the Winter of Rights?' (2014) 51 Common Market Law Review 843

Filistrucchi L, Geradin D, and van Damme E, 'Identifying Two-Sided Markets' (2013) 36 World Competition 33

Finck M, 'Blockchains and Data Protection in the European Union' (2018) 4 European Data Protection Law Review 17

Finck M, 'Blockchain and the General Data Protection Regulation: Can Distributed Ledgers Be Squared with European Data Protection Law?' (2019) Study for the European Parliament

Finck M, The Limits of the GDPR in the Personalisation Context' (2021) Max Planck Institute for Innovation & Competition Research Paper No 21-11

Fletcher A, 'Predatory Pricing in Two-Sided Markets: A Brief Comment' (2007) 3 Competition Policy International 221

Fletcher A, 'Digital Competition Policy: Are Ecosystems Different?' (2020) Background Paper, 134th Meeting of the OECD Competition Committee

Fletcher A and Hansen D, 'The Role of Demand Side Remedies in Resolving Competition Concerns' in Damien Gerard and Assimakis Komninos (eds), *Remedies in EU Competition Law* (Wolters Kluwer 2020)

Floridi L, 'On Human Dignity as a Foundation for the Right to Privacy' (2016) 29 Philosophy & Technology 307

Folger J, 'What Does Metaverse Mean and How Does This Virtual World Work?' *Investopedia* (5 August 2022) <https://www.investopedia.com/metaverse-definition-5206578> accessed 12 March 2022

Fortes F and Swift M, 'Data Protection Issues to Get Closer Look in US Merger Analyses from FTC Commissioner Bedoya' *Mlex* (9 November 2022) <https://content.mlex.com/#/content/1423773> accessed 3 April 2022

Fourberg, N and others, 'Online Advertising: The Impact of Targeted Advertising on Advertisers, Market Access and Consumer Choice' (2021) Study requested by the European Parliament Committee on the Internal Market and Consumer Protection

Fox EM, 'US and EU Competition Law: A Comparison' in Edward M Graham and David J Richardson (eds), *Global Competition Policy* (Institute for International Economics 1997)

Fox EM, 'Platforms, Power, and the Antitrust Challenge: A Modest Proposal to Narrow the U.S.–Europe Divide' (2019) 98 Nebraska Law Review 23

Fox EM and Baschenhof P, 'History of (In)Equality in Competition Law and Its Guide to the Future' in Jan Broulik and Kati Cseres (eds), *Competition Law and Economic Inequality* (Hart Publishing 2022)

Frändberg Å, 'An Essay on Legal Concept Formation' in Jaap C Hage and Dietmar von der Pfordten (eds), *Concepts in Law* (Springer 2009)

Franklin C, 'The Burgeoning Principle of Consistency in EU Law' (2011) 30 Yearbook of European Law 42

Frischmann BM and Selinger E, *Re-Engineering Humanity* (CUP 2018)

Fuller LL, 'Positivism and Fidelity to Law: A Reply to Professor Hart' (1958) 71 Harvard Law Review 630

Furman J, 'Unlocking Digital Competition. Report of the Digital Competition Expert Panel' (2019)

Gal MS and Aviv O, 'The Competitive Effects of the GDPR' (2020) 16 Journal of Competition Law & Economics 349

Gartenberg C, 'Why Apple's New Privacy Feature Is Such a Big Deal' *The Verge* (27 April 2021) <https://www.theverge.com/2021/4/27/22405474/apple-app-tracking-transparency-ios-14-5-privacy-update-facebook-data> accessed 4 June 2022

Gaudin G and Mantzari D, '*Google Shopping* and the As-Efficient-Competitor Test: Taking Stock and Looking Ahead' (2022) 13 Journal of European Competition Law & Practice 125

Gebicka A and Heinemann A, 'Social Media & Competition Law' (2014) 37 World Competition 149

Gellert R, 'Why the GDPR Risk-Based Approach Is about Compliance Risk, and Why It's Not a Bad Thing' in Erich Schweighofer, Franz Kummer, and Christoph Sorge (eds), *Trends and Communities of legal informatics, Proceedings of the 20th International Legal Informatics Symposium* (Austrian Computer Society 2017)

Gellert R, *The Risk-Based Approach to Data Protection* (OUP 2020)

Gellert R, 'Personal Data's Ever-Expanding Scope in Smart Environments and Possible Path(s) for Regulating Emerging Digital Technologies' (2021) 11 International Data Privacy Law 196

Gellman R, 'Fair Information Practices: A Basic History—Version 2.21' (2021) 9 <https://papers.ssrn.com/abstract=2415020> accessed 25 January 2022

Geradin D and Petit N, 'Price Discrimination under EU Competition Law: The Need for a Case-by-Case Approach' (2005) GCLC Working Paper No 07/05

Geradin D, Katsifis D, and Karanikioti T, 'Google as a de Facto Privacy Regulator: Analysing the Privacy Sandbox from an Antitrust Perspective' (2021) 17 European Competition Journal 617

Gerard D, 'Fairness in EU Competition Policy: Significance and Implications' (2018) 9 Journal of European Competition Law & Practice 211

Gerard D, Komninos A, and Waelbroeck D (eds), *Fairness in EU Competition Policy: Significance and Implications. An Inquiry Into the Soul and Spirit of Competition Enforcement in Europe* (Bruylant 2020)

Gerber DJ, 'Fairness in Competition Law: European and U.S. Experience' (Conference on Fairness and Asian Competition Laws, Kyoto, March 2004)

Gerber DJ, 'Two Forms of Modernisation in European Competition Law' (2007) 31 Fordham International Law Journal 1235

German Federal Ministry of Economic Affairs, 'A New Competition Framework for the Digital Economy' (2019)

Gersen JE, 'Designing Agencies' in Daniel A Farber and Anne Joseph O'Connell (eds), *Research Handbook on Public Choice and Public Law* (Edward Elgar 2010)

Gilbert P and Pepper R, 'Privacy Considerations in European Merger Control: A Square Peg for a Round Hole' [2015] CPI Antitrust Chronicle

GlobalDate Thematic Intelligence, 'Epic Games Is Strengthening Its Metaverse Ambition' *Verdict* (20 April 2022) <https://www.verdict.co.uk/epic-games-metaverse/> accessed 12 March 2022

Goldberg SG, Johnson GA, and Shriver SK, 'Regulating Privacy Online: An Economic Evaluation of the GDPR' (2022) Law & Economics Center at George Mason University Scalia Law School, Research Paper Series No 22-025

González Fuster G, *The Emergence of Personal Data Protection as a Fundamental Right* (Springer 2014)

González Fuster G and others, 'The Right to Lodge a Data Protection Complaint: OK, But Then What? An Empirical Study of Current Practices under the GDPR' (Access Now 2022)

Goodman B and Flaxman S, 'European Union Regulations on Algorithmic Decision-Making and a "Right to Explanation"' (ICML Workshop on Human Interpretability in Machine Learning, New York, June 2016)

Graef I, *EU Competition Law, Data Protection and Online Platforms: Data as Essential Facility* (Wolters Kluwer 2016)

Graef I, 'Rethinking the Essential Facilities Doctrine for the EU Digital Economy' (2019) 53 Revue juridique Thémis de l'Université de Montréal 33

Graef I and Van Berlo S, 'Towards Smarter Regulation in the Areas of Competition, Data Protection and Consumer Law: Why Greater Power Should Come with Greater Responsibility' (2021) 12 European Journal of Risk Regulation 674

Graef I and van der Sloot B, 'Collective Data Harms at the Crossroads of Data Protection and Competition Law: Moving Beyond Individual Empowerment' (2022) 33 European Business Law Review 513

Graef I, Clifford D, and Valcke P, 'Fairness and Enforcement: Bridging Competition, Data Protection, and Consumer Law' (2018) 8 International Data Privacy Law 200

Graef I, Tombal T, and de Streel A, 'Limits and Enablers of Data Sharing. An Analytical Framework for EU Competition, Data Protection and Consumer Law' (2019) TILEC Discussion Paper No DP 2019-024

Graying C, UK Lord Chancellor, Letter to Viviane Reding, European Commission Vice-President in charge of Justice, Fundamental Rights and Citizenship (4 June 2013)

Greenleaf G, 'Global Data Privacy Laws 2021: Despite COVID Delays, 145 Laws Show GDPR Dominance' (2021) 169 Privacy Laws & Business International Report 3

Greenleaf G, 'Now 157 Countries: Twelve Data Privacy Laws in 2021/22' (2022) 176 Privacy Laws & Business International Report 3

Guggenberger N, 'The Essential Facilities Doctrine in the Digital Economy: Dispelling Persistent Myths' (2021) 23 Yale Journal of Law & Technology 301

Gugler P, 'Transparency and Competition Policy in an Imperfectly Competitive World' in Jens Forssbæck and Lars Oxelheim (eds), *The Oxford Handbook of Economic and Institutional Transparency* (OUP 2015)

Gundlach GT, 'Predatory Practices in Competitive Interaction: Legal Limits and Antitrust Considerations' (1990) 9 Journal of Public Policy & Marketing 129

Gutwirth S, 'Short Statement about the Role of Consent in the European Data Protection Directive' (2012) <http://works.bepress.com/serge_gutwirth/80/> accessed 1 October 2022

Hamburg Commissioner for and Data Protection and Freedom of Information, Anordnung des HmbBfDI gegen Facebook (11 May 2021)

Hannak A and others, 'Measuring Price Discrimination and Steering on E-Commerce Web Sites' (ACM Internet Measurement Conference, Vancouver, November 2014)

Hartzog W, 'The Case Against Idealising Control' (2018) 4 European Data Protection Law Review 423

Haslehner W, '"Consistency" and Fundamental Freedoms: The Case of Direct Taxation' (2013) 50 Common Market Law Review 737

Haucap J, 'Competition and Competition Policy in a Data-Driven Economy' (2019) 54 Intereconomics 201

Hausman DM, *Preference, Value, Choice, and Welfare* (CUP 2012)

Hawk BE, 'System Failure: Vertical Restraints and EC Competition Law' (1995) 32 Common Market Law Review 973

Hawk BE, 'About "Competition on the Merits": A Comparative View of Article 82 EC and s. 2 Sherman Act' [2005] Concurrences No 3-2005, Art No 232

Hazlett TW, 'The Nirvana Fallacy in "Hipster Antitrust"' (2021) 28 George Mason Law Review 1253

Healey D, 'Abuse of Dominance' in *Dictionary of Competition Law*, Concurrences, Art No 20101

Helberger N, 'Facebook Is a New Breed of Editor: Social Editor' (*LSE Media Policy Project*, 15 September 2016) <https://blogs.lse.ac.uk/mediapolicyproject/2016/09/15/facebook-is-a-new-breed-of-editor-a-social-editor/> accessed 3 May 2022

Helberger N, 'On the Democratic Role of News Recommenders' (2019) 7 Digital Journalism 993

Helberger N, 'The Political Power of Platforms: How Current Attempts to Regulate Misinformation Amplify Opinion Power' (2020) 8 Digital Journalism 842

Hellenic Competition Commission, 'Press Release—the HCC approves Delivery Hero's acquisition of four companies subject to commitments' (20 April 2022) <https://www.epant.gr/en/enimerosi/press-releases/item/2189-press-release-the-hellenic-competition-commission-approves-delivery-hero-s-acquisition-of-four-companies-subject-to-commitments.html> accessed 30 August 2022

Hern A, 'Facebook Lets Advertisers Target Users Based on Sensitive Interests' *The Guardian* (16 May 2018) <https://www.theguardian.com/technology/2018/may/16/facebook-lets-advertisers-target-users-based-on-sensitive-interests> accessed 16 February 2022

Hijmans H, *The European Union as Guardian of Internet Privacy: The Story of Art 16 TFEU* (Springer 2018)

Hijmans H, 'Article 1. Subject-Matter and Objectives' in Christopher Kuner, Lee A Bygrave, and Christopher Docksey (eds), *The EU General Data Protection Regulation (GDPR). A Commentary* (OUP 2020)

Hildebrandt M, 'Defining Profiling: A New Type of Knowledge?' in Mireille Hildebrandt and Serge Gutwirth (eds), *Profiling of the European Citizen: Cross-Disciplinary Perspectives* (Springer 2008)

Hildebrandt M, 'Law as Information in the Era of Data-Driven Agency' (2016) 79 Modern Law Review 1

Hodges C, 'Comments on GDPR Enforcement: EDPB Decision 01/2020' (2021) 9 <https://papers.ssrn.com/sol3/papers.cfm?abstract_id=3765602> accessed 2 July 2022

Hoehn T, 'Challenges in Designing and Implementing Remedies in Innovation Intensive Industries and the Digital Economy' in Damien Gerard and Assimakis Komninos (eds), *Remedies in EU Competition Law* (Wolters Kluwer 2020)

Hoffman J and Gonzalez Otero B, 'Demystifying The Role of Data Interoperability in the Access and Sharing Debate' (2020) 11 Journal of Intellectual Property, Information Technology and E-Commerce Law 252

Holzweber S, 'Tying and Bundling in the Digital Era' (2018) 14 European Competition Journal 342

Hon K, Hörnle J, and Millard C, 'Data Protection Jurisdiction and Cloud Computing—When Are Cloudusers and Providers Subject to EU Data Protection Law? The Cloud of Unknowing' (2012) 26 International Review of Law, Computers & Technology 129

Hong H, 'What Are Digital Ecosystems and What Are Their Characteristics?' (*OECD On the Level*, 9 January 2021) <https://oecdonthelevel.com/2021/01/09/digital-ecosystems-a-new-economic-paradigm/> accessed 4 March 2022

Hoofnagle CJ, van der Sloot B, and Borgesius FZ, 'The European Union General Data Protection Regulation: What It Is and What It Means' (2019) 28 Information & Communications Technology Law 65

House of Commons, Digital, Culture, Media and Sport Committee, 'Disinformation and "Fake News": Final Report' (2019)

Houses of the Oireachtas, Joint Committee on Justice, 'Report on Meeting on 27 April 2021 on the Topic of GDPR' (2021)

Hustinx P, 'EU Data Protection Law: The Review of Directive 95/46/EC and the Proposed General Data Protection Regulation', *Collected Courses of the European University Institute's Academy of European Law*, 1–12 July 2013

Hutt WH, *Economists and the Public: A Study of Competition and Opinion* (Alden Press 1936)

Hyman DA and Kovacic WE, 'Why Who Does What Matters: Governmental Design and Agency Performance' (2014) 82 George Washington Law Review 1446

Ibáñez Colomo P, 'Article 101 TFEU and Market Integration' (2016) 12 Journal of Competition Law & Economics 749

Ibáñez Colomo P, 'Beyond the "More Economics-Based Approach": A Legal Perspective on Article 102 TFEU Case Law' (2016) 53 Common Market Law Review 709

Ibáñez Colomo P, 'Self-Preferencing: Yet Another Epithet in Need of Limiting Principles' (2020) 43 World Competition 417

Ibáñez Colomo P, 'The Notion of Abuse after the Android Judgment (Case T-604/18): What Is Clearer and What Remains to Be Clarified (I)' (*Chillin'Competition*, 28 September 2022) <https://chillingcompetition.com/2022/09/28/the-notion-of-abuse-after-the-android-judgment-case-t%e2%80%91604-18-what-is-clearer-and-what-remains-to-be-clarified-i/> accessed 11 October 2022

Ibáñez Colomo P and Kalintiri A, 'The Evolution of EU Antitrust Policy: 1966–2017' (2020) 83 Modern Law Review 321

Ibitoye V, 'Competition Regulators "Picking up Pieces" of Patchy GDPR Enforcement, Coscelli Says' *Mlex* (21 April 2021) <https://mlexmarketinsight.com/news/insight/comp

etition-regulators-picking-up-pieces-of-patchy-gdpr-enforcement-coscelli-says> accessed 18 June 2022

Information Commissioner's Office, 'Data Protection Act 1998, Undertaking: WhatsApp Inc' (12 March 2018)

International Competition Network, 'ICN Agencies' Case Prioritisation and Initiation' (2021)

Jacobides MG, 'How to Compete When Industries Digitize and Collide: An Ecosystem Development Framework' (2022) 64 California Management Review 99

Jacobides MG and Lianos I, 'Ecosystems and Competition Law in Theory and Practice' (2021) CLES Research Paper Series UCL No 1/2021

Janßen R and others, 'GDPR and the Lost Generation of Innovative Apps' (2022) NBER Working Paper No 30028

Japan Fair Trade Commission, 'Guidelines Concerning Abuse of a Superior Bargaining Position in Transactions between Digital Platform Operators and Consumers that Provide Personal Information' (2019)

Japan Fair Trade Commission, 'Report Regarding the Trade Practices of Digital Platforms' (2019)

Japan Fair Trade Commission, 'Report of the Study Group on Data and Competition Policy' (2021)

Japan Fair Trade Commission, 'Summary of Report Regarding Cloud Services' (2022)

Jaquet-Chiffelle D-O, 'Direct and Indirect Profiling in the Light of Virtual Persons' in Mireille Hildebrandt and Serge Gutwirth (eds), *Profiling the European Citizen: Cross-Disciplinary Perspectives* (Springer 2008)

Johnson GA, Shriver SK, and Goldberg SG, 'Privacy & Market Concentration: Intended & Unintended Consequences of the GDPR' (2022) <https://papers.ssrn.com/sol3/papers.cfm?abstract_id=3477686> accessed 5 October 2022

Jones A and Sufrin B, *EU Competition Law: Text, Cases, and Materials* (4th edn, OUP 2011)

Jones A and Sufrin B, *EU Competition Law: Text, Cases, and Materials* (6th edn, OUP 2016)

Jones A, Surfin B, and Dunne N, *EU Competition Law: Text, Cases, and Materials* (7th edn, OUP 2019)

Jones Harbour P, 'Dissenting Statement of Commissioner Pamela Jones Harbour, Google/Double Click, FTC File No 071-0170' (20 December 2007)

Kalimo H and Majcher K, 'The Concept of Fairness: Linking EU Competition and Data Protection Law in the Digital Marketplace' (2017) 42 European Law Review 210

Kaltheuner F and Bietti E, 'Data Is Power: Towards Additional Guidance on Profiling and Automated Decision-Making in the GDPR' (2018) 2 Journal of Information Rights, Policy and Practice

Kamara I and De Hert P, 'Understanding the Balancing Act Behind the Legitimate Interest of the Controller Ground: A Pragmatic Approach, Working Paper' (2018) 4 Brussels Privacy Hub 5

Kaminski ME, 'The Case for Data Privacy Rights (Or "Please, a Little Optimism")' (2022) 97 Notre Dame Law Review Reflection 385

Kant T, 'A History of the Data-Tracked User' (*The MIT Press Reader*, 8 October 2021) <https://thereader.mitpress.mit.edu/a-history-of-the-data-tracked-user/> accessed 16 February 2022

Kaspersky, 'What are Cookies?' (nd) <https://www.kaspersky.com/resource-center/definitions/cookies> accessed 4 May 2022

Kaplow L, 'On the Choice of Welfare Standards in Competition Law' (2011) Harvard Law and Economics Discussion Paper No 693

Kemp K, 'Concealed Data Practices and Competition Law: Why Privacy Matters' (2020) 16 European Competition Journal 628

Kerber W, 'Data Sharing in IoT Ecosystems and Competition Law: The Example of Connected Cars' (2019) 15 Journal of Competition Law & Economics 381

Kerber W and Specht-Riemenschneider L, 'Synergies between Data Protection Law and Competition Law' (2021) <https://papers.ssrn.com/sol3/papers.cfm?abstract_id=3977039> accessed 24 June 2022

Khan LM, 'Remarks of Chair Lina M. Khan' (CRA Conference, Brussels, 31 March 2022) <https://www.ftc.gov/news-events/news/speeches/remarks-chair-lina-m-khan-charles-river-associates-conference-competition-regulation-disrupted-times> accessed 20 July 2022

Khan LM, 'Amazon's Antitrust Paradox' (2017) 126 Yale Law Journal 710

Khan LM, 'The New Brandeis Movement: America's Antimonopoly Debate' (2018) 9 Journal of European Competition Law & Practice 131

Khan LM and Vaheesan S, 'Market Power and Inequality: The Antitrust Counterrevolution and its Discontent' (2017) 11 Harvard Law and Policy Review 234

Klonick K, 'The New Governors: The People, Rules, and Processes Governing Online Speech' (2018) 131 Harvard Law Review 1598

Köcher S and others, 'New Hidden Persuaders: An Investigation of Attribute-Level Anchoring Effects of Product Recommendations' (2019) 95 Journal of Retailing 24

Kokott J and Sobotta C, 'The Distinction between Privacy and Data Protection in the Jurisprudence of the CJEU and the ECtHR' (2013) 3 International Data Privacy Law 222

Koksal I, 'The Benefits of Applying Blockchain Technology in Any Industry' *Forbes* (23 October 2019) <https://www.forbes.com/sites/ilkerkoksal/2019/10/23/the-benefits-of-applying-blockchain-technology-in-any-industry/> accessed 10 March 2022

Kolasinski MK, 'Interpretation of the Remedy in the *Google Shopping* Decision and Its Consequences' (2020) 4 European Competition and Regulatory Law Review 4

Koops B-J, 'The Trouble with European Data Protection Law' (2014) 4 International Data Privacy Law 250

Kosta E, 'The Future of Data Protection: Collapse or Revival?' (2014) 28 International Review of Law, Computers & Technology 115

Kosta E, 'Conditions for Consent' in Christopher Kuner, Lee A Bygrave, and Christopher Docksey (eds), *The EU General Data Protection Regulation (GDPR): A Commentary* (OUP 2020)

Kotschy W, 'The Proposal for a New General Data Protection Regulation—Problems Solved?' (2014) 4 International Data Privacy Law 274

Kotschy W, 'Article 6. Lawfulness of Processing' in Christopher Kuner, Lee A Bygrave, and Christopher Docksey (eds), *The EU General Data Protection Regulation (GDPR): A Commentary* (OUP 2020)

Kotzur M, 'Article 7 [Principle of Coherence]' in Rudolf Geiger, Daniel Erasmus-Khan, and Markus Kotzur (eds), *European Union Treaties. A Commentary* (Hart Publishing 2015)

Kozyreva A and others, 'Public Attitudes towards Algorithmic Personalization and Use of Personal Data Online: Evidence from Germany, Great Britain, and the United States' (2021) 8 Humanities and Social Sciences Communications 3

Krafft TD, Gamer M, and Zweig KA, 'What Did You See? A Study to Measure Personalization in Google's Search Engine' (2019) 8 EPJ Data Science 38

Krämer J, Senellart P, and de Streel A, 'Making Data Portability More Effective for the Digital Economy' (2021) <https://papers.ssrn.com/sol3/papers.cfm?abstract_id=3866495 18> accessed 3 July March 2022

Kramer S, 'Metaverse Privacy Concerns: Are We Thinking About Our Data?' *Forbes* (1 June 2022) <https://www.forbes.com/sites/forbestechcouncil/2022/06/01/metaverse-privacy-concerns-are-we-thinking-about-our-data/> accessed 5 June 2022

Kranenborg H, 'Commentary on Article 8' in Steve Peers and others (eds), *The EU Charter of Fundamental Rights: A Commentary* (Hart Publishing 2014)

Kress K, 'Coherence' in Dennis Patterson (ed), *A Companion to Philosophy of Law and Legal Theory* (Blackwell 1999)

Kuebler-Wachendorff S and others, 'The Right to Data Portability: Conception, Status Quo, and Future Directions' (2021) 44 Informatik Spektrum 264

Kuhn T and others, 'EU General Court Confirms European Commission's Article 22 EUMR Referral Policy' (*Kluwer Competition Law Blog*, 18 July 2022) <http://competitionlawblog.kluwercompetitionlaw.com/2022/07/18/eu-general-court-confirms-european-commissions-article-22-eumr-referral-policy/> accessed 23 July 2022

Kuner C, 'The European Commission's Proposed Data Protection Regulation: A Copernican Revolution in European Data Protection Law' (2012) Bloomberg BNA Privacy and Security Law Report 1

Kuner C, 'Territorial Scope and Data Transfer Rules in the GDPR: Realising the EU's Ambition of Borderless Data Protection' (2021) Cambridge Legal Studies Research Series, Paper No 20/2021

Kuner C, Bygrave LA, and Docksey C, 'Background and Evolution of the EU General Data Protection Regulation (GDPR)' in Christopher Kuner, Lee A Bygrave, and Christopher Docksey (eds), *The EU General Data Protection Regulation (GDPR): A Commentary* (OUP 2020)

Laidler J, 'High Tech Is Watching You' *The Harvard Gazette* (4 March 2019) <https://news.harvard.edu/gazette/story/2019/03/harvard-professor-says-surveillance-capitalism-is-undermining-democracy/> accessed 15 February 2022

Lambrecht A and Tucker CE, 'Can Big Data Protect a Firm from Competition?' (2015) <https://papers.ssrn.com/sol3/papers.cfm?abstract_id=2705530> accessed 10 July 2022

Lancieri F, 'Narrowing Data Protection's Enforcement Gap' (2022) 74 Maine Law Review 15

Lancieri F and Pereira Neto CMS, 'Designing Remedies for Digital Markets: The Interplay Between Antitrust and Regulation' (2021) 18 Journal of Competition Law & Economics 613

Lande RH, 'Consumer Choice as the Best Way to Re-Center the Mission of Competition Law' in Paul Nihoul, Nicolas Charbit, and Elisa Ramundo (eds), *Choice—A New Standard for Competition Law Analysis?* (Concurrences 2016)

Langlois G, 'Participatory Culture and the New Governance of Communication: The Paradox of Participatory Media' (2013) 14 Television and New Media 91

Langus G and Lipatov V, 'Does Envelopment through Data Advantage Call for New Regulation?' (2021) CESifo Working Papers No 8932

Leibowitz J, 'Concurring Statement of Commissioner Jon Leibowitz, Google/Double Click, FTC File No 071-0170' (20 December 2007)

Leitenberger J, 'Keynote Speech' (14th Annual Conference of the GCLC on Remedies in EU Competition Law, Brussels, 31 January 2019)

LePan N, 'Visualizing the Length of the Fine Print, for 14 Popular Apps' *Visual Capitalist* (18 April 2020) <https://www.visualcapitalist.com/terms-of-service-visualizing-the-length-of-internet-agreements/> accessed 18 February 2022

Letter from Chris Grayling, UK Lord Chancellor, to Viviane Reding, European Commission Vice-President in charge of Justice, Fundamental Rights and Citizenship (4 June 2013)

Letter from Isabelle Falque-Pierrotin, Chairwoman of A29WP, to Jan Koum, Co-Founder of WhatsApp (24 October 2017)

Letter from Jessica L Rich, Director of the Federal Trade Commission Bureau of Consumer Protection, to Erin Egan, Chief Privacy Officer, Facebook, and to Anne Hoge, General Counsel, WhatsApp Inc (10 April 2014)

Letter from Viviane Reding, European Commission Vice-President in charge of Justice, Fundamental Rights and Citizenship, to Chris Grayling, UK Lord Chancellor (6 June 2013)

Levenbook BB, 'The Role of Coherence in Legal Reasoning' (1983) 3 Law and Philosophy 355

Levy D (Facebook), 'Speaking Up for Small Businesses' (2020) <https://www.facebook.com/business/news/ios-14-apple-privacy-update-impacts-small-business-ads> accessed 18 June 2022

Lianos I, 'Some Reflections on the Question of the Goals of EU Competition Law' (2013) CLES Working Paper Series No 3/2013

Lianos I, 'Polycentric Competition Law' (2018) 71 Current Legal Problems 161

Lianos I, 'Reorienting Competition Law' (2022) Journal of Antitrust Enforcement 1

Lianos I and Carballa-Smichowski B, 'A Coat of Many Colours—New Concepts and Metrics of Economic Power in Competition Law and Economics' (2022) Journal of Competition Law & Economics 1

Lipsky AB Jr, 'The Global Antitrust Explosion: Safeguarding Trade and Commerce or Runaway Regulation' (2002) 26 Fletcher Forum of World Affairs 59

Liza Lovdahl Gormsen v Meta Platforms, Inc. and Others, Notice of Application to Commence Collective Proceedings Under Section 47B of the Competition Act 1998, Case No 1433/7/7/22

Lowe P, 'DG Competition Review of the Policy on Abuse of Dominance' in Barry E Hawk (ed), *International Law & Policy: Annual Proceedings of the Fordham Corporate Law Institute 2003* (Juris Publishing 2004)

Lu S, 'Data Privacy, Human Rights, and Algorithmic Opacity' (2022) 110 California Law Review 101

Lynskey O, 'Deconstructing Data Protection: The "Added-Value" of a Right to Data Protection in the EU Legal Order' (2014) 63 International and Comparative Law Quarterly 569

Lynskey O, *The Foundations of EU Data Protection Law* (OUP 2015)

Lynskey O, 'Aligning Data Protection Rights with Competition Law Remedies? The GDPR Right to Data Portability' (2017) 42 European Law Review 28

Lynskey O, 'Regulating "Platform Power"' (2017) LSE Law, Society and Economy Working Papers No 1/2017 <https://papers.ssrn.com/sol3/papers.cfm?abstract_id=2921021> accessed 14 July 2022

Lynskey O, 'A Legal Response to Data-Driven Mergers' in Emre Bayamlioğlu and others (eds), *Being Profiled: Cogitas Ergo Sum. 10 Years of Profiling the European Citizen* (Amsterdam UP 2018)

Lynskey O, 'Grappling with "Data Power": Normative Nudges from Data Protection and Privacy' (2019) 20 Theoretical Inquiries in Law 189

Lynskey O, 'Towards a Holistic Approach to Effective Data Protection' (*LSE Business Review*, 7 June 2022) <https://blogs.lse.ac.uk/businessreview/2022/06/07/towards-a-holistic-approach-to-effective-data-protection/> accessed 22 August 2022

MacCormick N, *Legal Reasoning and Legal Theory* (Clarendon Press 1978)

MacCormick N, 'Coherence in Legal Justification' in Aleksander Peczenik, Lars Lindahl, and Bert van Roermond (eds), *Theory of Legal Science* (D Reidel Publishing 1984)

MacCormick N, *Rhetoric and the Rule of Law* (OUP 2005)

Mader O, 'Enforcement of EU Values as a Political Endeavour: Constitutional Pluralism and Value Homogeneity in Times of Persistent Challenges to the Rule of Law' (2019) 11 Hague Journal on the Rule of Law 133

Maduro MP, 'Contrapunctual Law: Europe's Constitutional Pluralism in Action' in Neil Walker (ed), *Sovereignty in Transition* (Hart Publishing 2003)

Maier-Rigaud FP, 'Behavioural versus Structural Remedies in EU Competition Law' in Philip Lowe, Mel Marquis, and Giorgio Monti (eds), *European Competition Law Annual 2013: Effective and Legitimate Enforcement of Competition Law* (Hart Publishing 2016)

Majcher K, 'Coherence between EU Data Protection and Competition Law in the Digital Market' (PhD in Law, Vrije Universiteit Brussel 2020)

Majcher K and Robertson VHSE, 'Protecting Personal Data and the Environment: Doctrinal Challenges for EU Competition Law in Our Day and Age' (2022) 47 European Law Review 622

Makris S, 'EU Competition Law as Responsive Law' (2021) 23 Cambridge Yearbook of European Legal Studies 228

Malgieri G and Niklas J, 'Vulnerable Data Subjects' (2020) 37 Computer Law & Security Review

Mancini J, 'Making Online Markets More Competitive: The Benefits and Challenges of Conglomerate Merger Review' (2021)

Mandrescu D, 'Tying and Bundling by Online Platforms—Distinguishing between Lawful Expansion Strategies and Anti-Competitive Practices' (2021) 40 Computer Law & Security Review 1

Mangabeira Unger R, *What Should Legal Analysis Become* (Verso Books 1996)

Mangalindan J, 'Amazon's Recommendation Secret' *Fortune* (30 July 2012) <http://fortune.com/2012/07/30/amazons-recommendation-secret/> accessed 17 March 2022

Manne G and Sperry B, 'The Problems and Perils of Bootstrapping Privacy and Data into an Antitrust Framework' [2015] CPI Antitrust Chronicle

Mansell R, 'Platforms of Power' (2015) 43 Intermedia 20

Mantelero A, 'Competitive Value of Data Protection' (2013) 3 International Data Privacy Law 229

Mantelero A, 'From Group Privacy to Collective Privacy: Towards a New Dimension of Mantelero A, 'Personal Data for Decisional Purposes in the Age of Analytics: From an Individual to a Collective Dimension of Data Protection' (2016) 32 Computer Law & Security Review 238

Privacy and Data Protection in the Big Data Era' in Linnet Taylor, Luciano Floridi, and Bart van der Sloot (eds), *Group Privacy. New Challenges of Data Technologies* (Springer 2017)

Mantelero A, 'Fundamental Rights Impact Assessment in the DSA' in Joris von Hoboken and others (eds), *Putting the Digital Services Act into Practice: Enforcement, Access to Justice, and Global Implications* (Varfassungsbooks 2023)

Mardsen P, 'Google Shopping for the Empress's New Clothes—When a Remedy Isn't a Remedy (and How to Fix It)' (2020) 11 Journal of European Competition Law & Practice 553

Marr B, 'The 5 Biggest Internet Of Things (IoT) Trends in 2022' *Forbes* (13 December 2021) <https://www.forbes.com/sites/bernardmarr/2021/12/13/the-5-biggest-internet-of-things-iot-trends-in-2022/> accessed 12 April 2022

Martin-Bariteau F, 'Blockchain and the European Union General Data Protection Regulation: The CNIL's Perspective' (2018) Blckchn.ca Working Paper Series No 2018-01

Mathisen G, 'Consistency and Coherence as Conditions for Justification of Member State Measures Restricting Free Movement' (2010) 47 Common Market Law Review 1021

Mayntz R, 'Modernization and the Logic of Interorganizational Networks' (1993) 6 Knowledge & Policy 3

McDermott Y, 'Conceptualising the Right to Data Protection in an Era of Big Data' (2017) 4 Big Data & Society 1

McFadden DL, 'Revealed Stochastic Preference: A Synthesis' (2005) 26 Economic Theory 245

McGarry J, 'The Possibility and Value of Coherence' (2013) 34 Liverpool Law Review 17

McGee P, 'Snap, Facebook, Twitter and YouTube Lose Nearly $10bn after iPhone Privacy Changes' *Financial Times* (31 October 2021) <https://www.ft.com/content/4c19e387-ee1a-41d8-8dd2-bc6c302ee58e> accessed 18 June 2022

Meagher M, *Competition Is Killing Us: How Big Business Is Harming Our Society and Planet—and What to Do About It?* (Penguin Business 2020)

Medich J, 'Edge Computing is about to Solve the IoT's Biggest Problems' *Wired* (25 January 2021) <https://www.wired.co.uk/article/edge-computing-iot> accessed 8 March 2022

Merrill Corporation, 'GDPR Burdens Hinder M&A Transactions in the EMEA Region, According to Merrill Corporation Survey' (13 November 2018) <https://www.datasite.com/us/en/company/news/press-releases/gdpr-burdens-hinder-m-a-transactions-in-the-emea-region.html> accessed 10 October 2022

Meta, 'Founder's Letter' (28 October 2021) <https://about.fb.com/news/2021/10/founders-letter/> accessed 12 March 2022

Ministry of Corporate Affairs, Government of India, 'Report of Competition Law Review Committee' (2019)

Ministry of Economy, Trade and Industry (Japan), 'Key Points on the Act of Improving Transparency and Fairness of Digital Platforms' (2021)

Mittelstadt BD and others, 'The Ethics of Algorithms: Mapping the Debate' (2016) 3 Big Data & Society 1

Mohan M, 'Platform Mergers: Tips for Getting the Deal Through' (*Kluwer Competition Law Blog*, 16 May 2019) <http://competitionlawblog.kluwercompetitionlaw.com/2019/05/16/platform-mergers-tips-for-getting-the-deal-through/#_ftn1> accessed 14 July 2022

Monti G, *EC Competition Law* (CUP 2007)

Monti G, 'Taming Digital Monopolies: A Comparative Account of the Evolution of Antitrust and Regulation in the European Union and the United States' (2022) 67 Antitrust Bulletin 40

Monti G and Feases AR, 'The Case Against Google: Has the U.S. Department of Justice Become European?' (2021) 35 Antitrust Magazine 26

Moral Soriano L, 'A Modest Notion of Coherence in Legal Reasoning. A Model for the European Court of Justice' (2003) 16 Ratio Juris 296

Motta M, *Competition Policy: Theory and Practice* (CUP 2004)

Motta M and de Streel A, 'Excessive Pricing in Competition Law: Never Say Never?' (Conference organized by the Swedish Competition Authority, Stockholm, 9 November 2007)

Muchmore M, 'What Is Microsoft's Metaverse Strategy?' *PC Magazine* (25 May 2022) <https://uk.pcmag.com/business-1/140569/what-is-microsofts-metaverse-strategy> accessed 27 May 2022

Mundt A, Interview by Richard Whish and Amelia Fletcher in anticipation of the 4th Innovation Economics Conference for Antitrust Lawyers [2020] Concurrences

Nair V, Munilla Garrido G, and Song D, 'Exploring the Unprecedented Privacy Risks of the Metaverse' (2022) ArXiv

Nazzini R, *Normative Theory of Competition Law* (OUP 2011)

Nazzini R, *The Foundations of European Union Competition Law: The Objectives and Principles of Article 102* (OUP 2011)

Nemeth J, 'Blockchain, Behavioural Remedies, and Merger Control: How Can Access Remedies Do Better?' (2022) 13 Journal of European Competition Law & Practice 167

Newman JM, 'Antitrust in Zero-Price Markets: Foundations' (2015) 164 University of Pennsylvania Law Review 149

Nguyen D and Paczos M, 'Measuring the Economic Value of Data and Cross-Border Data Flows: A Business Perspective' (2020) OECD Digital Economy Papers No 297, 10–12

Ni Loideain N, 'A Port in the Data-Sharing Storm: The GDPR and the Internet of Things' (2019) 4 Journal of Cyber Policy 178

Nihoul P, '"Freedom of Choice": The Emergence of a Powerful Concept in European Competition Law' in Paul Nihoul, Nicolas Charbit, and Elisa Ramundo (eds), *Choice—A New Standard for Competition Law Analysis?* (Concurrences 2016)

Nonet P and Selznick P, *Law and Society in Transition: Toward Responsive Law* (Harper and Row 1978)

O'Donoghue R, 'The Death of the Theory of Everything Under Article 102?' (Global Competition Law Centre Conference, Brussels, February 2016)

O'Donoghue R and Padilla J, *The Law and Economics of Article 102 TFEU* (3rd edn, Hart Publishing 2020)

O'Donoghue R and Padilla J, *The Law and Economics of Article 102 TFEU* (2nd edn, Hart Publishing 2013)

Ofcom, 'Data, Digital Markets and Refusal to Supply' (2022) Economic Discussion Paper Series No 6

OECD, 'Policy Roundtable: Competition on the Merits' (2005) DAF/COMP(2005)27

OECD, 'Policy Roundtable: Excessive Prices' (2011) DAF/COMP(2011)18

OECD, 'Exploring the Economics of Personal Data: A Survey of Methodologies for Measuring Monetary Value' (2013) OECD Digital Economy Papers No 220

OECD, 'Cloud Computing: The Concept, Impacts and the Role of Government Policy' (2014) OECD Digital Economy Papers No 240

OECD, 'Blockchain Technology and Competition Policy' (2018) Issues Paper by the Secretariat, DAF/COMP/WD(2018)47

OECD, 'Considering Non-Price Effects in Merger Control' (2018) Background Note by the Secretariat, DAF/COMP(2018)2

OECD, 'Market Concentration' (2018) Issue Paper by the Secretariat, DAF/COMP/WD(2018)46

OECD, 'OECD Blockchain Primer' (2018)

OECD, 'Rethinking Antitrust Tools for Multi-Sided Platforms' (2018)

OECD, 'Abuse of Dominance in Digital Markets' (2020) Background Note by the Secretariat (DAF/COMP/GF(2020)4)

OECD, 'Conglomerate Effects of Mergers—Note by the European Union' (2020) DAF/COMP/WD(2020)8

OECD, 'Exploitative pricing in the time of COVID-19' (2020)

OECD, 'OECD Competition Trends 2020' (2020)

OECD, 'Ex Ante Regulation of Digital Markets' (2021) OECD Competition Committee Discussion Paper

OECD, 'OECD Competition Trends 2021, Volume II, Global Merger Control' (2021)

OECD, 'The Evolving Concept of Market Power in the Digital Economy' (2022) OECD Competition Policy Roundtable Background Note

Office of Fair Trading, 'The Economics of Online Personalised Pricing' (2013)

Ohlhausen MK and Okuliar A, 'Competition, Consumer Protection and the Right (Approach) to Privacy' (2015) 80 Antitrust Law Journal 121

O'Loughlin K and others, 'Reviewing the Data Security and Privacy Policies of Mobile Apps for Depression' (2019) 15 Internet Interventions 110

Ordover JA and Willig RD, 'An Economic Definition of Predatory Product Innovation' (1987) 17 Journal of Reprints for Antitrust Law and Economics 301

Oremus W, 'How Much Is Your Privacy Really Worth?' *OneZero* (19 September 2019) <https://onezero.medium.com/how-much-is-your-privacy-really-worth-421796dd9220> accessed 28 February 2022

Oremus W, 'Why Facebook Won't Let You Control Your Own News Feed' *The Washington Post* (15 November 2021) <https://www.washingtonpost.com/technology/2021/11/13/facebook-news-feed-algorithm-how-to-turn-it-off/> accessed 17 February 2022

Pace LF and Seidel K, 'The Drafting and the Role of Regulation 17: A Hard-Fought Compromise' in Kiran Klaus Patel and Heike Schweitzer (eds), *The Historical Foundations of EU Competition Law* (OUP 2013)

Parker G and Van Alstyne M, 'Two-Sided Network Effects: A Theory of Information Product Design' (2005) 51 Management Science 1494

Parker G, Petropoulos G, and Van Alstyne M, 'Digital Platforms and Antitrust' (2020) Bruegel Working Paper No 06/2020

Parker G, Petropoulos G, and Van Alstyne M, 'Platform Mergers and Antitrust' (2021) 30 Industrial and Corporate Change 1307

Parret L, 'The Multiple Personalities of EU Competition Law: Time for a Comprehensive Debate on Its Objectives' in Daniel Zimmer (ed), *The Goals of Competition Law* (Edward Elgar 2012)

Pasquale F, *The Black Box Society: The Secret Algorithms That Control Money and Information* (Harvard UP 2016)

Pasquale F and Bracha O, 'Federal Search Commission? Access, Fairness, and Accountability in the Law of Search' (2008) 93 Cornell Law Review 1150

Patel KK and Schweitzer H, 'Introduction' in Kiran Klaus Patel and Heike Schweitzer (eds), *The Historical Foundations of EU Competition Law* (OUP 2013)

Patterson MR, *Antitrust Law in the New Economy: Google, Yelp, LIBOR, and the Control of Information* (Harvard UP 2017)

Peczenik A, 'Coherence, Truth and Rightness in the Law' in Patrick Nerhot (ed), *Law, Interpretation and Reality. Essays in Epistemology, Hermeneutics and Jurisprudence* (Springer 1990)

Peczenik A, *Scientia Juris: Legal Doctrine as Knowledge of Law and as a Source of Law* (Springer 2005)

Peczenik A, *On Law and Reason* (Springer 2009)

Peppet SR, 'Regulating the Internet of Things: First Steps Toward Managing Discrimination, Privacy, Security, and Consent' (2014) 93 Texas Law Review 85

Pera A and Todino M, 'Enforcement of EC Competition Rules: Need for a Reform?' in Barry E Hawk (ed), *Annual Proceedings of the Fordham Corporate Law Institute* (Fordham Corporate Law Institute 1997)

Personal Data Protection Commission Singapore and Competition and Consumer Commission of Singapore, 'Data Portability' (2019)

Petit N, 'Technology Giants, the "Moligopoly" Hypothesis and Holistic Competition: A Primer' (2016) <https://papers.ssrn.com/sol3/papers.cfm?abstract_id=2856502> accessed 4 March 2022

Phillips NJ, 'Keep It: Maintaining Competition in the Privacy Debate' (Internet Governance Forum, Washington, 27 July 2018) 8

Posner R, *Economic Analysis of Law* (9th edn, Wolters Kluwer 2014)

Posner E and Weyl GE, *Radical Markets: Uprooting Capitalism and Democracy for a Just Society* (Princeton UP 2018)

President Joseph R Biden Jr, 'Executive Order on Promoting Competition in the American Economy' (2021) <https://www.whitehouse.gov/briefing-room/presidential-actions/2021/07/09/executive-order-on-promoting-competition-in-the-american-economy/> accessed 13 September 2022

Purtova N, 'The Law of Everything. Broad Concept of Personal Data and Future of EU Data Protection Law' (2018) 10 Law, Innovation and Technology 40

Quelle C, 'Enhancing Compliance under the General Data Protection Regulation: The Risky Upshot of the Accountability- and Risk-Based Approach' (2018) 9 European Journal of Risk Regulation 502

Quinn P and Malgieri G, 'The Difficulty of Defining Sensitive Data—The Concept of Sensitive Data in the EU Data Protection Framework' (2022) 22 German Law Journal 1538

Ramírez Pérez SM, 'The Evolution of the Law on Articles 85 and 86 EEC [Articles 101 and 102 TFEU]' in Kiran Klaus Patel and Heike Schweitzer (eds), *The Historical Foundations of EU Competition Law* (OUP 2013)

Rato M and Petit N, 'Abuse of Dominance in Technology-Enabled Markets: Established Standards Reconsidered?' (2013) 9 European Competition Journal 1

Raz J, *Ethics in the Public Domain: Essays in the Morality of Law and Politics* (Clarendon Press 1994)

Reims R, 'The Problem of Requiring Firms to Develop an Alternative Monetisation Strategy through Competition Law' (*LSE Business Review*, 30 March 2022) <https://blogs.lse.ac.uk/businessreview/2022/03/30/the-problem-of-requiring-firms-to-develop-an-alternative-monetisation-strategy/> accessed 20 July 2022

Reuters Institute, 'Digital News Report' (2022)

Reuters Staff, 'Google Closes Fitbit Deal as U.S., Australia Probes Continue' *Reuters* (14 January 2021) <https://www.reuters.com/article/us-fitbit-m-a-alphabet-idUSKBN29J1WR> accessed 14 April 2022

Richards M, 'Canada Hires Chief Digital Enforcement Officer' *Global Competition Review* (3 July 2019) <https://globalcompetitionreview.com/article/canada-hires-chief-digital-enforcement-officer> accessed 30 March 2022

Ristaniemi M and Majcher K, 'Blockchains in Competition Law—Friend or Foe?' (*Kluwer Competition Law Blog*, 21 July 2018) <http://competitionlawblog.kluwercompetitionlaw.com/2018/07/21/blockchains-competition-law-friend-foe/> accessed 10 March 2022

Ritter C, 'Refusal to Deal and "Essential Facilities": Does Intellectual Property Require Special Deference Compared to Tangible Property?' (2005) 28 World Competition 281

Robertson VHSE, *Competition Law's Innovation Factor: The Relevant Market in Dynamic Contexts in the EU and the US* (Hart Publishing 2020)

Robertson VHSE, 'Merger Review in Digital and Technology Markets: Insights from National Case Law' (2022) Report for Directorate-General for Competition

Rochet J-C and Tirole J, 'Platform Competition in Two-Sided Markets' (2003) 1 Journal of the European Economic Association 990

Rousseva E, 'The Concept of "Objective Justification" of an Abuse of a Dominant Position: Can It Help to Modernise the Analysis under Article 82 EC?' (2006) 2 Competition Law Review 27

Rouvroy A and Poullet Y, 'The Right to Informational Self-Determination and the Value of Self-Development: Reassessing the Importance of Privacy for Democracy' in Serge Gutwirth and others (eds), *Reinventing Data Protection?* (Springer 2009)

Rubinfeld DL and Gal MS, 'Access Barriers to Big Data' (2017) 59 Arizona Law Review 229

Rule CF and Howley DJ, 'Structural Remedies' (2021) Global Competition Review <https://globalcompetitionreview.com/guide/the-guide-merger-remedies/fourth-edition/article/structural-remedies> accessed 5 December 2022

Ruohonen J and Hjerppe K, 'The GDPR Enforcement Fines at Glance' (2022) 106 Information Systems 101876

Russo B and others, 'Cloud Computing and the New EU General Data Protection Regulation' (2018) 5 IEEE Cloud Computing 58

Ryan J, 'Formal GDPR Complaint against Google's Internal Data Free-for-All' (16 March 2020) <https://brave.com/google-internal-data-free-for-all/> accessed 20 July 2022

Samuelson PA, 'A Note on the Pure Theory of Consumer's Behaviour' (1938) 5 Economica 61

Schaub F and others, 'A Design Space for Effective Privacy Notices' (11th Symposium on Usable Privacy and Security, Ottawa, July 2015)

Schermer B, 'Risks of Profiling and the Limits of Data Protection Law' in Bart Custers and others (eds), *Discrimination and Privacy in the Information Society. Data Mining and Profiling in Large Databases* (Springer 2013)

Schiavello A, 'On "Coherence" and "Law": An Analysis of Different Models' (2001) 14 Ratio Juris 233

Schrepel T, 'Predatory Innovation: The Definite Need for Legal Recognition' (2018) 21 Science and Technology Law Review 19

Schrepel T, *Blockchain + Antitrust. The Decentralization Formula* (Edward Elgar 2021)

Schreurs W and others, '*Cogitas, Ergo Sum*. The Role of Data Protection Law and Non-Discrimination Law in Group Profiling in the Private Sector' in Mireille Hildebrandt and Serge Gutwirth (eds), *Profiling of the European Citizen: Cross-Disciplinary Perspectives* (Springer 2008)

Schwartz PM, 'Property, Privacy, and Personal Data' (2004) 117 Harvard Law Review 2056

Schwartz PM and Peifer KN, 'Transatlantic Data Privacy Law' (2017) 106 Georgetown Law Journal 115

Schweitzer H and others, 'Modernising the law on abuse of market power' (2018) Report for the German Federal Ministry for Economic Affairs and Energy

Schweitzer H and others, 'Data Access and Sharing in Germany and in the EU: Towards a Coherent Legal Framework for the Emerging Data Economy. A Legal, Economic and Competition Policy Angle' (2022)

Seaver N, 'Captivating Algorithms: Recommender Systems as Traps' (2018) 24 Journal of Material Culture 421

Seelinger D, 'The Facebook Decision: Is Everything Clear Now?' (*D'Kart*, 27 June 2020) <https://www.d-kart.de/en/blog/2020/06/27/die-facebook-entscheidung-ist-jetzt-alles-klar/> accessed 14 May 2022

Sekiguchi T, 'Google-Fitbit Deal Wins Approval from Japan with Its Global Remedies' *Mlex* (14 January 2021) <https://content.mlex.com/#/content/1256622> accessed 14 April 2022

Sen A, 'Behaviour and the Concept of Preference' (1973) 40 Economica 241

Sen A, 'Rational Fools: A Critique of the Behavioural Foundations of Economic Theory' (1977) 6 Philosophy & Public Affairs 317

Sen A, 'Internal Consistency and Choice' (1993) 61 Econometrica 495

Shavell S, *Foundations of Economic Analysis of Law* (Harvard UP 2004)

Sherman A and Feiner L, 'Amazon, Microsoft and Alphabet Went on a Buying Spree in 2021 despite D.C.'s Vow to Take on Big Tech' *CNBC* (22 January 2022) <https://www.cnbc.com/2022/01/22/amazon-microsoft-alphabet-set-more-deals-in-2021-than-last-10-years.html> accessed 3 April 2022

Siragusa M, 'The Millenium Approaches: Rethinking Article 85 and the Problems and Challenges in the Design and Enforcement of the EC Competition Rules' (1997) 21 Fordham International Law Journal 650

Smeulders B, Crama Y, and Spieksma FCR, 'Revealed Preference Theory: An Algorithmic Outlook' (2019) 272 European Journal of Operational Research 803

Snoep M, 'Speech' (CRA Conference, Brussels, 10 December 2019)

Sokol D and Comerford R, 'Antitrust and Regulating Big Data' (2016) 23 George Mason Law Review 1129

Sokol D and Ma J, 'Understanding Online Markets and Antitrust Analysis' (2017) 15 Northwestern Journal of Technology and Intellectual Property 43

Sokol D and Zhu F, 'Harming Competition and Consumers Under the Guise of Protecting Privacy: An Analysis of Apple's IOS 14 Policy Updates' (*Competition Policy International*, 27 May 2021) <https://www.competitionpolicyinternational.com/harming-competition-and-consumers-under-the-guise-of-protecting-privacy-an-analysis-of-apples-ios-14-policy-updates/> accessed 18 June 2022

Solove DJ, *Understanding Privacy* (Harvard UP 2008)

Solove DJ, 'The Myth of the Privacy Paradox' (2021) 89 George Washington Law Review 1

Southerton C, 'Datafication' in Laurie A Schintler and Connie L McNeely (eds), *Encyclopedia of Big Data* (Springer 2020)

Stakheyeva H, 'Test SIEC' in *Global Dictionary of Competition Law*, Concurrences Art No 89155

Stanford Encyclopaedia of Philosophy, 'Epistemology' <https://plato.stanford.edu/entries/epistemology/> accessed 6 July 2022

Stanford Encyclopedia of Philosophy, 'Free Will' <https://plato.stanford.edu/entries/freewill/> accessed 2 October 2022

Steffel M, Williams EF, and Pogacar R, 'Ethically Deployed Defaults: Transparency and Consumer Protection Through Disclosure and Preference Articulation' (2016) LIII Journal of Marketing Research 865

Stigler Committee on Digital Platforms, 'Final Report' (2019)

Stigler GJ, 'The Origin of the Sherman Act' (1985) 14 Journal of Legal Studies 1

Stiglitz JE, 'Towards a Broader View of Competition Policy' in Tembinkosi Bonakele, Eleanor M Fox, and Liberty Mncube (eds), *Competition Policy for the New Era. Insights from the BRICS Countries* (OUP 2017)

Stolton S, 'Vestager: Metaverse Poses New Competition Challenges' *Politico* (18 January 2022) <https://www.politico.eu/article/metaverse-new-competition-challenges-margrethe-vestager/> accessed 14 March 2022

Stucke ME, 'When More Is Better and When Less Is More: Behavioural Antitrust and Choice' in Paul Nihoul, Nicolas Charbit, and Elisa Ramundo (eds), *Choice—A New Standard for Competition Law Analysis?* (Concurrences 2016)

Stucke ME, 'Addressing Personal Data Collection as Unfair Methods of Competition' (2022) University of Tennessee Legal Studies Research Paper No 439, 31 <https://papers.ssrn.com/sol3/papers.cfm?abstract_id=4186226> accessed 14 October 2022

Swift M, 'Facebook's History with Onavo Resonates for Privacy Experts Worried about Giphy Purchase' *Mlex* (23 June 2020) <https://mlexmarketinsight.com/news-hub/editors-picks/area-of-expertise/data-privacy-and-security/facebooks-history-with-onavo-resonates-for-privacy-experts-worried-about-giphy-purchase> accessed 13 May 2022

Tajana A, 'If I Had a Hammer ... Structural Remedies and Abuse of Dominant Position' (2006) 1 Competition and Regulation in Network Industries 3

Tambini D, 'How advertising fuels fake news' (*LSE Media Policy Project blog*, 24 February 2017) <https://blogs.lse.ac.uk/medialse/2017/02/24/how-advertising-fuels-fake-news/> accessed 17 February 2022

Tau B and McMillan R, 'Google Bans Apps With Hidden Data-Harvesting Software' *The Wall Street Journal* (6 April 2022) <https://www.wsj.com/articles/apps-with-hidden-data-harvesting-software-are-banned-by-google-11649261181> accessed 11 July 2022

Taylor C, 'DPC Rejects Criticism of Its Regulation of Big Tech Companies' *The Irish Times* (27 April 2021) <https://www.irishtimes.com/business/technology/dpc-rejects-criticism-of-its-regulation-of-big-tech-companies-1.4549370> accessed 19 June 2022

Taylor L, Floridi L, and van der Sloot B, 'Introduction: A New Perspective on Privacy' in Linnet Taylor, Luciano Floridi, and Bart van der Sloot (eds), *Group Privacy. New Challenges of Data Technologies* (Springer 2017)

Temple Lang J, 'Monopolisation and the Definition of "Abuse" of a Dominant Position under Article 86 EEC Treaty' (1979) 16 Common Market Law Review 345

Tene O, '*LinkedIn v. HiQ* and the Trans-Atlantic Privacy Divide' (*IAPP*, 22 April 2022) <https://iapp.org/news/a/linkedin-v-hiq-and-the-transatlantic-privacy-divide/> accessed 20 July 2022

Tene O and Polonetsky J, 'Big Data for All: Privacy and User Control in the Age of Analytics' (2013) 11 Northwestern Journal of Technology and Intellectual Property 293

The Economist, 'Too Much of a Good Thing' (26 March 2016) <https://www.economist.com/briefing/2016/03/26/too-much-of-a-good-thing> accessed 1 March 2022

Thibodeau P, 'Rotenberg Fears Internet "Privacy Meltdown" from Google-DoubleClick Combo' *Computer World* (20 December 2007) <https://www.computerworld.com/article/2538270/q-a--rotenberg-fears-internet--privacy-meltdown--from-google-doubleclick-combo.html> accessed 2 April 2022

Tirole J, 'Socially Responsible Agencies' (2022)

Tombal T, 'The GDPR: A Shield to a Competition Authority's Data Sharing Remedy?' in Jean Herveg (ed), *Deep Diving into Data Protection: 1979–2019 : Celebrating 40 Years of Research on Privacy and Data Protection at the CRIDS* (Larcier 2021)

Trebilcock M and Iacobucci EM, 'Designing Competition Law Institutions: Values, Structure, and Mandate' (2010) 41 Loyola University Chicago Law Journal 455

Trotta D, 'Wall Street Critic Warren Vows to Break up Amazon, Facebook, Google' *Reuters* (8 March 2019) <https://www.reuters.com/article/us-elizabethwarren-technology-idUSKCN1QP1M0> accessed 14 July 2022

Tucker DS and Wellford HB, 'Big Mistakes Regarding Big Data' (2014) The Antitrust Source <https://papers.ssrn.com/sol3/papers.cfm?abstract_id=2549044> accessed 10 July 2022

Tretyakov SV, 'Between Efficiency and Effectiveness' (2015) Basic Research Program, Working Papers Series, WP BRP 21/LAW/2014

Turner S and others, 'The Exercisability of the Right to Data Portability in the Emerging Internet of Things (IoT) Environment' (2020) 23 New Media & Society 2861

Uberti D, 'Come the Metaverse, Can Privacy Exist?' *The Wall Street Journal* (4 January 2022) <https://www.wsj.com/articles/come-the-metaverse-can-privacy-exist-11641292206?page=1> accessed 13 March 2022

US Department of Justice, 'Justice Department and Federal Trade Commission Seek to Strengthen Enforcement Against Illegal Mergers' (18 January 2022) <https://www.ftc.gov/news-events/news/press-releases/2022/01/federal-trade-commission-justice-department-seek-strengthen-enforcement-against-illegal-mergers> accessed 11 February 2022

Van Bael & Bellis, *Competition Law of the European Union* (6th edn, Wolters Kluwer 2021)

van Cleynenbreugel P, '*BPost* and *Nordzucker*: Searching for the Essence of *Ne Bis in Idem* in European Union Law' (2022) 18 European Constitutional Law Review 357

van de Waerdt PJ, "Everything the Data Touches Is Our Kingdom': Market Power of 'Data Ecosystems" (2023) 46 World Competition 65

van der Aalst W, Hinz O and Weinhardt C, 'Big Digital Platforms' (2019) 61 Business & Information Systems Engineering 645

van der Sloot B, 'Do Data Protection Rules Protect the Individual and Should They? An Assessment of the Proposed General Data Protection Regulation' (2014) 4 International Data Privacy Law 307

van der Vijver T, 'Objective Justification and Article 102 TFEU' (2012) 351 World Competition 55

Van Gerven G and others, 'Data and Privacy in EU Merger Control' (2022) Global Competition Review <https://globalcompetitionreview.com/guide/digital-markets-guide/second-edition/article/data-and-privacy-in-eu-merger-control#footnote-014> accessed 5 December 2022

Varian HR, 'Price Discrimination' in Richard Schmalensee and Robert D Willig (eds), *Handbook of Industrial Organization*, vol 1 (Elsevier 1989)

Varian HR, Farrell J, and Shapiro C, *The Economics of Information Technology: An Introduction* (CUP 2014)

Veale M and Zuiderveen Borgesius FJ, 'Adtech and Real-Time Bidding under European Data Protection Law' (2022) 23 German Law Journal 226

Vestager M, 'The Values of Competition Policy' (CEPS Corporate Breakfast, Brussels, 13 October 2015)

Vestager M, 'Protecting Consumers from Exploitation' (Chillin' Competition Law Conference, Brussels, 21 November 2016)

Vestager M, 'What Competition Can Do—and What It Can't' (Chillin' Competition Law Conference, Brussels, 25 October 2017)

Vestager M, 'Fairness and Competition' (GCLC Annual Conference, Brussels, 25 January 2018)

Vestager M, 'Privacy and Competition in an Age of Data' (IAPP Europe Data Protection
Vestager M, 'When Technology Serves People' (Brain Bar event, Budapest, 1 June 2018)
Congress, Brussels, 21 November 2019)

Vestager M, 'Defending Competition in a Digital Age' (Florence Competition Summer Conference, Florence, 24 June 2021)

Vezzoso S, 'Competition Policy in Transition: Exploring Data Portability's Roles' (2021) 12 Journal of European Competition Law & Practice 357

Viljoen S, 'A Relational Theory of Data Governance' (2021) 131 Yale Law Journal 573

von der Pfordten D, 'About Concepts in Law' in Jaap C Hage and Dietmar von der Pfordten (eds), *Concepts in Law* (Springer 2009)

Voss A, 'How to Bring GDPR into the Digital Age' *Politico* (25 March 2021) <https://www.politico.eu/article/gdpr-reform-digital-innovation/> accessed 24 June 2022

Vrabec HU, *Data Subject Rights under the GDPR* (OUP 2021)

W3C Working Group, 'Tracking Compliance and Scope' (2019) <https://www.w3.org/TR/tracking-compliance/> accessed 15 February 2022

W3C Working Group, 'Tracking Preference Expression (DNT)' (2019) <https://www.w3.org/TR/tracking-dnt/> accessed 15 February 2022

Wachter S, 'The GDPR and the Internet of Things: A Three-Step Transparency Model' (2018) 10 Law, Innovation and Technology 266

Wachter S and Mittelstadt BD, 'A Right to Reasonable Inferences: Re-Thinking Data Protection in the Age of Big Data and AI' (2019) 2019 Columbia Business Law Review 494

Wachter S, Mittelstadt BD, and Floridi L, 'Why a Right to Explanation of Automated Decision-Making Does Not Exist in the General Data Protection Regulation' (2017) 7 International Data Privacy Law 76

Wahl N, 'Recent Trends at the Court of Justice of the European Union' [2018] Concurrences No 4-2018, Art No 88071

Wahl N, 'Exploitative High Prices and European Competition Law: A Personal Reflection' (Conference organized by the Swedish Competition Authority, 9 November 2007)

Wang W, 'Structural Remedies in EU Antitrust and Merger Control' (2011) 34 World Competition 571

Warren E, 'Here's How We Can Break up Big Tech' *Medium* (8 March 2019) <https://medium.com/@teamwarren/heres-how-we-can-break-up-big-tech-9ad9e0da324c> accessed 14 July 2022

Wasastjerna MC, 'The Role of Big Data and Digital Privacy in Merger Review' (2018) 14 European Competition Journal 417

Watzinger M and Schnitzer M, 'The Breakup of the Bell System and Its Impact on US Innovation' (2023) Center for Economic Policy Research, Discussion Paper No 17635

Weitzenboeck EM and others, 'The GDPR and Unstructured Data: Is Anonymization Possible?' (2022) 12 International Data Privacy Law 184

Westin AF, *Privacy and Freedom* (Athenum 1967)

Whish R and Bailey D, *Competition Law* (7th edn, OUP 2012)

White A and Ali H, 'Google-Fitbit Probe Isn't for Data Watchdogs, Vestager Says' *Bloomberg* (25 February 2020) <https://www.bloomberg.com/news/articles/2020-02-25/google-fitbit-probe-is-for-me-not-data-watchdogs-vestager-says> accessed 5 May 2022

Wiedemann K, 'Data Protection and Competition Law Enforcement in the Digital Economy: Why a Coherent and Consistent Approach Is Necessary' (2021) 52 International Review of Intellectual Property and Competition Law 915

Wiedemann K, 'A Matter of Choice: The German Federal Supreme Court's Interim Decision in the Abuse-of-Dominance Proceedings *Bundeskartellamt v. Facebook* (Case KVR 69/19)' (2020) 51 International Review of Intellectual Property and Competition Law 1168

Wilford E, '10 IoT Technology Trends to Watch in 2022' *IoT Analytics* (26 January 2022) <https://iot-analytics.com/iot-technology-trends/> accessed 10 March 2022

Wils WPJ, 'Ten Years of Regulation 1/2003-A Retrospective' (2013) 4 Journal of European Competition Law & Practice 293

Wils WPJ, 'The Obligation for the Competition Authorities of the EU Member States to Apply EU Antitrust Law and the Facebook Decision of the Bundeskartellamt' [2019] Concurrences No 3-2019, Art No 91034 58

Wilson JQ, *Bureaucracy: What Government Agencies Do and Why They Do It* (Basic Books 1990)

Wilson T, 'Merger Remedies—Is It Time to Go More Behavioural?' (*Kluwer Competition Law Blog*, 21 February 2021) <https://competitionlawblog.kluwercompetitionlaw.com/

2020/02/21/merger-remedies-is-it-time-to-go-more-behavioural/#_ftn25> accessed 5 December 2022

Witt AC, *The More Economic Approach to EU Antitrust Law* (Hart Publishing 2016)

Witt AC, 'The European Court of Justice and the More Economic Approach to EU Competition Law—Is the Tide Turning?' (2019) 64 Antitrust Bulletin 172

Witt AC, 'Who's Afraid of Conglomerate Mergers?' (2022) 67 Antitrust Bulletin 208

Witti M and Konstantas D, 'IoT and Security-Privacy Concerns: A Systemic Mapping Study' (2018) 10 International Journal of Network Security & Its Applications 25

Woods L, 'Facebook Ireland and the One Stop Shop under the GDPR' (2021) 45 European Law Review 685

Wright D and De Hert P, *Privacy Impact Assessment* (Springer 2012)

Wu T, *The Curse of Bigness: Antitrust in the New Gilded Age* (Columbia Global Reports 2018)

Yeung K and Bygrave LA, 'Demystifying the Modernized European Data Protection Regime: Cross-Disciplinary Insights from Legal and Regulatory Governance Scholarship' (2021) 16 Regulation & Governance 137

Zanfir-Fortuna G and Ianc S, 'Data Protection and Competition Law: the Dawn of 'Uberprotection' (2018) <https://papers.ssrn.com/sol3/papers.cfm?abstract_id=3290824> accessed 30 March 2022

Zingales N, 'Data Protection Considerations in EU Competition Law: Funnel or Straightjacket for Innovation'? (2018) 41 <https://papers.ssrn.com/sol3/papers.cfm?abstract_id=3158008> accessed 4 June 2022

Zuboff S, *The Age of Surveillance Capitalism: The Fight for a Human Future at the New Frontier of Power* (PublicAffairs 2019)

Zuiderveen Borgesius FJ and others, 'Tracking Walls, Take-It-Or-Leave-It Choices, the GDPR, and the EPrivacy Regulation' (2018) 3 European Data Protection Law Review 353

Index

For the benefit of digital users, indexed terms that span two pages (e.g., 52–53) may, on occasion, appear on only one of those pages.